ENGLISH GRAMMAR AND COMPOSITION

JOHN E. WARRINER

Head of the English Department
Garden City High School
Garden City, New York

MARY EVELYN WHITTEN

Assistant Professor of English
North Texas State College
Denton, Texas

CHAPTERS ON SPEECH BY

FRANCIS GRIFFITH

Principal, Richmond Hill High School
Richmond Hill, New York

HARCOURT, BRACE & WORLD, INC.

New York • *Chicago* • *Atlanta* • *Dallas* • *Burlingame*

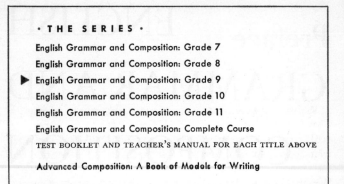

THE AUTHORS: **JOHN E. WARRINER** has taught English for 32 years, in junior and senior high schools and in college. He is the author of *Warriner's Handbook of English: I* and *II* and a coauthor of the *English Workshop* series. **MARY EVELYN WHITTEN,** in addition to teaching English in teachers' colleges, has had several years of experience teaching and supervising the English program in grades 8–12 in Texas and Oklahoma schools. **FRANCIS GRIFFITH,** who has done graduate work at Columbia University and includes in his experience advanced courses at the National University of Ireland, was for many years Chairman of English and Speech in a Brooklyn, New York, high school.

The photograph on the cover of this book shows part of a type case containing the printing type Perpetua, a face designed in 1932 by the English artist Eric Gill. The chapter headings throughout the book are set in this type. Cover photo by Lew Merrim from Monkmeyer.

Preface

Written especially for students in the ninth grade, *English Grammar and Composition: Grade 9* emphasizes the language skills that will not only meet the student's present needs in writing and speaking but will also provide a foundation for the more advanced language courses which lie ahead. Whether the student is completing his last year of junior high school or is beginning his first year in a four-year high school, he should learn the fundamentals of English grammar and usage. He should also put his knowledge into action as he writes and speaks. This textbook, therefore, stresses the important *basic* grammar, usage, and composition skills.

Like the other books in the *English Grammar and Composition* series, this textbook presents the facts about language in a simple and direct manner. Short, clear explanations are given, and are immediately supplemented with exercises. The abundance of these practice exercises is a distinctive feature of the book. Ranging from the simple to the challenging, their scope enables the teacher to choose activities that are best suited to his particular students, however diverse their abilities. The absence of digressions in subject matter makes the book easy to teach and easy to study, and allows the teacher to present the material in his own way.

ARRANGEMENT. The arrangement of the book is flexible. In general, the sections are not rigidly sequential. Just as the content of the book will fit any ninth-grade course of study, the chapters may be taught in any order which a specific course calls for. Many teachers will find it efficient to teach the opening grammar chapters early in the course, while others may prefer to begin with some aspect of writing, or another topic. The book is organized to make such variations in sequence entirely workable. Within parts and chapters, the work follows a logical order.

CONTENT. Part I presents the essentials of traditional grammar, giving the student the terminology necessary for language study and introducing only those terms and facts which are *functional*. As the student progresses, he not only clinches the knowledge that he has acquired in earlier grades but also takes up new grammatical concepts. These essentials of grammar are given thorough treatment, with pages of exercises to help the student master both the familiar and unfamiliar principles. Advanced grammatical concepts—such as voice, mood, parallelism, fine distinctions of usage—are excluded here; these he can learn in the upper grades. Diagrams of sentences are included for those teachers who use this tool as a means of clarifying grammatical relationships, but they are not essential; concepts may be fully learned without them.

Part II deals with acceptable usage. Once again, only the most important facts are presented. The fundamentals of usage, however, are not confined to this section. Throughout the book, at the end of some chapters, the authors have included "Good Usage" features which will attract the student's attention. Their brevity will encourage quick mastery.

In Part III the student will find carefully organized materials to guide him as he plans and writes paragraphs and longer compositions. Chapter 11 stresses the techniques of expository writing. Chapter 12 gives suggestions for writing clear, correct, and original letters. Chapter 13, which was written by Miss Blanche Jennings Thompson, gives instruction in writing various kinds of narrative, ranging from jokes and anecdotes to short stories. The final chapter in this section presents rules on note-taking and report-writing, two skills that foster good study habits and help the student to understand and communicate.

Depending upon the needs of a class, Chapter 15, "The Library," and Chapter 16, "The Dictionary," may be used for reference or as regular units of study. The unabridged dictionary is introduced for the first time in this series, and the content and arrangement of several student dictionaries are explained in detail. Chapter 17, which was written by

Dr. Paul Schweitzer of the Bronx High School of Science, is an important part of the carefully graded vocabulary program running through the series. Here the student not only learns how to add new words to his active vocabulary but also finds a list of vocabulary words especially selected for ninth graders.

The chapters of Part V are the ninth-year portion of the six-year program of speaking and listening in this series. They were written by Mr. Francis Griffith. In this section, the student learns how to speak before groups and in groups and how to use the telephone. Good manners as well as good speech habits are emphasized.

Finally, Part VI deals with the mechanics of written English—with capitalization, punctuation, and spelling. The student reviews capitalization and punctuation rules studied previously and takes up new ones. A summary style sheet of capitalization is included. The spelling chapter presents lists of commonly misspelled words for class assignment, simple spelling rules, and lists of homonyms frequently confused. Exercises accompany the teaching throughout the chapter.

SPECIAL FEATURES. The use of red for printing the rules makes them easy to identify and visually memorable. The colored reference tabs save time in locating rules; the complete index and the abbreviated table of contents on the end papers also make the book an easy-to-use reference tool.

For teachers who desire a means of evaluation separate from the textbook, a booklet of *Teaching Tests* is available from the publisher at a small cost. These tests measure the student's achievement by covering thoroughly the main rules in each "testable" chapter. Comprehensive, objective, and easy to grade, these examination booklets are useful timesavers for teachers. Moreover, by writing his answers upon printed pages, the student avoids needless and time-consuming copywork that frequently is required for other types of testing.

ACKNOWLEDGMENTS. The authors and publishers are especially indebted to Mrs. Arlene Molina, Miami Senior High School, Miami, Florida, and Dr. Paul Schweitzer, of the Bronx High School of Science, New York, New York, who read and criticized the manuscript. Other readers of the series, who have given valuable criticism, are: Mrs. Elizabeth White, Board of Public Instruction, Miami, Florida; Miss Martha Davis, Winn Seale Junior High School, Corpus Christi, Texas; Miss Anna Fort, Deal Junior High School, Washington, D.C.; Brother Charles A. Conefrey, Power Memorial Academy, New York, New York; Miss Olga Achtenhagen, Plainfield High School, Plainfield, New Jersey; Mr. A. T. Krider, John Adams High School, South Bend, Indiana; Miss Margaret B. Dietrich, Westfield Senior High School, Westfield, New Jersey; Mrs. Gladys Kronsagen, Glenbard Township High School, Glen Ellyn, Illinois; Sister Mary David, O.P., Junipero Memorial High School, Monterey, California.

Contents

vii

PART TWO

USAGE

PART THREE

COMPOSITION

PART FIVE

SPEAKING AND LISTENING

PART SIX

MECHANICS

PART ONE

GRAMMAR

CHAPTER 1

The Parts of Speech

THE WORK THAT WORDS DO

When you express your ideas to others, you group words into sentences to make statements, give orders, or ask questions. Each of the words that you choose has a definite function in your sentences, for each one is used as a "part of speech."

Have you ever stopped to think of how fortunate we are to have names for the parts of speech? By using such simple terms as *noun, pronoun, adjective, verb, adverb, preposition, conjunction,* and *interjection,* we can not only talk intelligently about our language but can also classify a half million different words.

As you study this chapter, learn to recognize the eight ways that words work for you in the communication of your ideas.

The Noun

1a. A *noun* is a word used to name a person, place, thing, or an idea.

PERSONS	George, Mary, Bill, Tom Scott
PLACES	New York City, Midwest, Mexico
THINGS	book, chair, sun, cloud, bicycle
IDEAS	justice, courage, hope, love

● EXERCISE 1.   Copy onto your paper each of the following words. After each noun, tell whether it names a person, place, thing, or an idea. If a word does not name, then write *not a noun*.

1. Nell Jones	8. patriotism	15. Detroit
2. England	9. rocket	16. and
3. across	10. bring	17. bad
4. hatred	11. conscience	18. actress
5. King James I	12. gusty	19. rapidly
6. money	13. equality	20. Santa Claus
7. Southwest	14. seaweed	

COMMON AND PROPER NOUNS

Nouns may be classified as either *common* or *proper*. Since in your writing you need to capitalize all proper nouns, you ought to be able to distinguish them from common nouns, which are not capitalized. Can you tell the difference between the two kinds of nouns in the lists below?

COMMON NOUNS	PROPER NOUNS
city	Phoenix, New Orleans, Waco
state	Maine, Ohio, Georgia, Florida
school	Jefferson High School, West Point
mountains	Teton Range, Allegheny Mountains
saint	Saint Valentine, Saint Patrick
month	April, May, August, December
writer	Edgar Allan Poe, Mark Twain

● EXERCISE 2.   There are 50 nouns in the following paragraph. As you list the nouns on your paper, circle all the proper nouns.

1. In our living language, proper nouns occasionally change to common nouns.   2. Losing significance as names of particular people, these words become names for a general class of things.   3. For example, during the nineteenth century, Samuel A. Maverick was unique among ranchers in Texas.   4. Maverick did not regularly brand his calves.

1a

5. Therefore, his neighbors called any unbranded, stray calf "Maverick's yearling." 6. For these cattlemen, a *maverick* soon became a common name for a certain kind of calf, and now *maverick* is standard English for any unbranded animal or motherless calf. 7. Many other words have similar origins. 8. The term *pasteurization* is derived from *Louis Pasteur*, and *mesmerism* comes from *F. A. Mesmer*. 9. "Jock," at one time a nickname in Scotland for a horseman, has changed to *jockey*. 10. Once used exclusively as names of particular people, *silhouette, quisling, mackintosh,* and *watt* have undergone similar changes and no longer begin with capital letters.

● EXERCISE 3. Study the nouns listed below. In class, be prepared to: (1) identify each noun as a common or a proper noun, and (2) if the noun is a common noun, name a corresponding proper noun; if the noun is proper, name a corresponding common noun. Remember that capitalization is one of the signals of a proper noun.

1. woman	6. junior high school	11. theater
2. governor	7. Elizabeth II	12. ocean
3. France	8. Pennsylvania	13. Indians
4. sister	9. Lake Michigan	14. street
5. doctor	10. Harvard University	15. song

The Pronoun

1b. A *pronoun* is a word used in place of a noun.

The prefix *pro–* means "for," and *noun* means "name." A pronoun, then, is a word used for a name. Notice below how pronouns are used to take the place of nouns.

> 1. After arguing with Joe for a while, Joe admitted, "Joe will have to ask Joe's father to help Joe finish the job."

2. After arguing with **himself** for a while, Joe admitted, "**I** will have to ask **my** father to help **me** finish the job." [Notice that the one Joe is kept as a definite person to whom the pronouns refer.]

In the following sentences the pronouns in heavy print take the place of the italicized nouns.

1. How is *Jane?* Is **she** still sick?
2. Harry looked into the *billfold* and found **it** empty.
3. Take the *seeds* out of the warm water, and plant **them** so that **they** will be in the sunlight.

Learn to recognize these pronouns: [1]

I, my, mine, me, myself
you, your, yours, yourself, yourselves
he, his, him, himself
it, its, itself
we, our, ours, us, ourselves
they, their, theirs, them, themselves
who, whose, whom, whoever, whomever
everybody, anybody, somebody
everyone, anyone, someone
none, nobody

As you study these pronouns, make sure that you can correctly spell *their, its, whose, himself,* and *themselves.*

When used to take the place of a noun, each word below is also a pronoun:

this	one, each	some, any, all
that	either, neither	many, more, much, most
these	other, another	what, which
those	both, several, few	whatever, whichever

[1] Words like *their* and *his* (possessive forms of the pronouns *they* and *he*) are called pronouns throughout this book. Some teachers, however, prefer to think of *their, his,* and other possessive pronouns as adjectives because they limit the meaning of nouns: *his* sister, *your* book, *our* team, *their* tents. Follow your teacher's direction in labeling these words.

1b

EXAMPLES   **Is *Ruth* or *Bob* going? Both** are.   [*Both* is a pronoun taking the place of the nouns *Ruth* and
Bob.]

A *few* of the *boys* quit.   [The pronoun *few* is
used for the noun *boys*.]

● EXERCISE 4.   Number from 1 to 20 on your
paper. List the 20 pronouns in the following sentences.
After each pronoun, write the noun to which it refers.

1. Nancy keeps an interesting notebook; in this, she writes
   down the favorite sayings of her teachers.
2. One of the first entries is a quotation of Mr. Adams, her
   speech teacher: "Speech is a mirror of the mind."
3. Another quotes Miss Dugan, who once said, "A person
   should never use a word he can't pronounce or spell.
   The word is not his to use, for it does not belong to
   him."
4. Some of the best advice, however, comes from Coach
   Morris: "Suppose the opposing players are too strong
   for the home team. Since they are four touchdowns
   ahead of us, we can't hope to beat them. My advice is
   to fight even harder than before. Each boy should say
   to himself, 'If we must fall, I will fall forward.' "

● EXERCISE 5.   Copy the following paragraph, and
fill in the 20 blanks with appropriate pronouns. Do
not write in this book.

—— main objection to mystery stories is the effect that
—— have on —— peace of mind. When reading —— of
——, —— imagine that —— is in the closet or just outside the window. Whether the author chooses to have a
victim poisoned or to have —— strangled, —— always
has —— murdered. In a story that —— read recently,
a murderer overpowers a millionaire, twisting and bruising
—— body and casting —— into the cage of a gorilla.
Unlike ——, Helen, —— likes mystery stories as a means
for escape, particularly enjoys reading —— just before
—— goes to sleep. —— favorite stories include —— ——
cause terrible nightmares.

The Adjective

1c. An *adjective* is a word used to modify a noun or a pronoun.

Modify means "to change." To modify a word means to change the meaning of the word by making the meaning more definite.

An adjective modifies or changes the meaning of a noun or a pronoun by answering one of these questions: *What kind? Which one? How many?* Notice how the italicized adjectives below answer these questions about the nouns or pronouns modified.

WHAT KIND?	WHICH ONE?	HOW MANY?
a *blue* dress	*that* flower	*four* times
a *false* note	*third* base	*several* girls
a *rich* lawyer	the *broken* bone	*each* player
a *short* one	the *other* one	*some* others

The adjectives most frequently used in English are *a*, *an*, and *the*. These little words are sometimes called articles.

The position of an adjective in a sentence varies. Usually the adjective precedes the noun or pronoun modified.

He looked at **each** one of the **old** pictures.

Sometimes, however, adjectives follow the word they modify.

The baby, **tired** and **sleepy**, began to whimper.

Other words may separate an adjective from the noun or pronoun modified.

She became very **nervous**.   Charles was **hungry**.

Angry with his sister, Tom began to argue.

1c

● EXERCISE 6. Copy the following sentences onto your paper, and fill in the blanks with adjectives. Answer the questions: *What kind? Which one? How many?* Draw an arrow from each adjective to the noun or pronoun modified.

1. The —— car had —— accessories.
2. —— cats seem ——.
3. At —— o'clock, the —— travelers fretted beneath the —— sun.
4. —— of games, Irene suggested that we sing —— songs.
5. Did you buy a —— coat or a —— one?
6. Pine trees, —— and ——, dotted the horizon.
7. Since the package was ——, he became ——.
8. Anybody, —— or ——, can help us raise money for the —— children.
9. Not —— of high places, she climbed the mountain to watch the sunset, which was very ——.
10. As they saw the —— lightning and heard the —— thunder, the boys, though —— and ——, pretended to be ——.

● EXERCISE 7. Except for *a, an,* and *the,* the sentences below contain no adjectives. Using a separate sheet of paper, revise the sentences by supplying interesting adjectives to modify the nouns or pronouns.

1. I like to read stories about heroes.
2. When he entered the cellar, he heard a noise.
3. At the dance I met the hostess, who was once an actress.
4. I bought a knife, a locket, a lantern, and a book.
5. Hobbes caught the pass, picked up blockers, and raced yards for the touchdown.

● EXERCISE 8. Look for adjectives as you read a newspaper or a magazine. Find a section containing at least 20 adjectives. Clip it out, and paste it onto your paper. Underline the adjectives, and be able to tell in class the words they modify.

● REVIEW EXERCISE A.   Make three columns on your paper.   Label the first column *nouns;* the second, *pronouns;* and the third, *adjectives.* Find the nouns, pronouns, and adjectives below, and list them in the proper column.   Place before each listed word the number of the sentence in which it is found. Do not list *a, an,* or *the.*

1. Strange incidents happen during football games.
2. I remember a particularly funny play in a game between the Tigers and the Lions.
3. The Tigers led by five touchdowns; their opponents had not scored.
4. One of the Tigers received a kick and ran down the field for a touchdown.
5. He had plowed through the Lions so easily! For the fun of it, he kept the ball, ran it back to his end of the field, and tried the play again.
6. This time, however, he met two angry tacklers, who made him bite the dust on the fifty-yard line.
7. I remember another funny incident in a different game.
8. The home team was five yards from pay dirt.
9. On an option play, Mickey Burns, one of our star players, took the ball, wiggled through the line, and barely edged the ball over for a score.
10. At that moment Jim Griggs, our quarterback, made a fantastic mistake.
11. He thought, "With this score, they'll win the game!"
12. Angry and unhappy, Jim then grabbed his own teammate by the heels and tried to drag him back down the field.

The Verb

1d. A *verb* is a word which expresses action or helps to make a statement.

THE ACTION VERB

Words such as *do, come, go,* and *write* are verbs because they express action.   A verb may express an

1d

action that cannot be seen; examples are *believe*, *know*, *fear*, and *think*.

● EXERCISE 9. Make a list of 20 action verbs. Choose at least 5 verbs that express an unseen action.

THE VERB *TO BE*

You should become thoroughly familiar with the various forms of the verb *to be:*

be	shall be
being	will be
am	has been
are	have been
is	had been
was	shall have been
were	will have been

These parts of the verb *to be* have two main uses. They may be used as a helping verb in a verb phrase: *was making, will be helped, are leaving, had been seen.* (See "The Verb Phrase" on page 12.) Or, when standing alone, parts of the verb *to be* may be used as a linking verb.

THE LINKING VERB

Some verbs help to make a statement by serving as a link between two words. These verbs are called linking verbs; they do not express action.[2]

In addition to the verb *to be*, the following verbs are commonly used as linking verbs:

> become, grow
> seem, appear, look
> remain, stay
> feel, smell, taste, sound

In the following sentences each verb in heavy print, which shows a condition rather than action, is a link

---

[2] Linking verbs are also called *state-of-being* verbs.

between the words on either side of it. The word that follows the linking verb is a noun or an adjective that fills out or completes the meaning of the verb.

1. Maggie **is** his sister.   [sister = Maggie]
2. She **became** a housewife.   [housewife = she]
3. The ring **looked** small.   [small ring]
4. The fudge **tastes** good.   [good fudge]
5. He **remained** calm.   [calm he]

● EXERCISE 10. Copy the following sentences, and fill in the blanks with linking verbs. Use a different verb for each blank.

1. The field —— muddy.
2. He —— angry.
3. The alarm —— very loud.
4. Chester —— strong.
5. A lemon —— sour.
6. The water —— deep.
7. She —— a bore.
8. The puppy —— innocent.
9. What —— the score?
10. Did he —— a lawyer?

● EXERCISE 11. Plan to pantomime 10 action verbs before the class. The class will make a list of what the verbs seem to be, and you can check them for accuracy.

● EXERCISE 12. Plan to pantomime 5 sentences using linking verbs before the class, who will write the conditions that seem to be evident. You can check them for accuracy.

● EXERCISE 13. Using the following nouns, write a sentence in which each noun performs an action. Write another sentence in which you show the condition of the noun.

EXAMPLE   1. Mother
          1. Mother bakes wonderful biscuits.   [action verb]
          Mother is a good cook.   [linking verb]

1. aircraft carrier
2. Dr. Smithers
3. Texas ranger
4. photographer
5. football
6. acrobat

THE VERB PHRASE

Verbs often have more than one word: *is leaving, shall be going, was tackled, shall move, has jumped, has been done, may become, was helping.* As these examples show, the verb (like *leaving, going, tackled,* etc.) and its helpers (like *is, shall be, was,* etc.) work together as a unit, which is called a verb phrase.[3]

Learn to recognize these helping verbs: *be* (in all of its forms), *has, have, had, shall, will, can, may, should, would, could, might, must, do, did, does.*

● EXERCISE 14. By adding various helpers, change the verbs listed below into verb phrases.

1. kicked	6. gain	11. sit	16. running
2. make	7. turn	12. worn	17. tried
3. given	8. seen	13. sink	18. falling
4. sorted	9. pull	14. win	19. telling
5. taking	10. gone	15. led	20. broken

● EXERCISE 15. Find and list on your paper the verbs and verb phrases in the following paragraph. Be sure to include all helping verbs, especially when the parts of the verb phrase are separated by other words. (CAUTION: The word *not* is never a verb.)

EXAMPLE   1. We had not yet noticed that the boat was leaking.
    1. **had noticed**
       was leaking

1. Although Frank does not understand many things in his general science class, he grows excited about what he does learn.   2. He is always asking his friends such questions as: "Do you know why a whale is not like other fish?"   3. Then he will proudly give his own answer: "Since the whale must breathe air, he cannot stay under the water for

[3] For further treatment of verb phrases, see page 32.

more than twenty minutes at a time." 4. Frank has learned that whales live a hundred years, that a horse is old at thirty, and that a dog usually dies before it reaches twenty. 5. Frank was amazed when he found out about the deafness of insects. 6. Although many experiments have been made, there is no evidence that wasps, bees, or flies can hear. 7. Different from insects, bats are blind; they must depend upon their ears and their voices. 8. Bats squeak in such a high pitch that the human ear cannot hear the sound. 9. Each squeak makes an echo, which tells the blind bat where it may safely fly. 10. If obstacles should be in its way, it can detect and dodge them because, as Frank has learned, nature has equipped the bat with a kind of radar.

● EXERCISE 16. Although linking verbs are useful, action verbs give life to sentences. Rewrite the following sentences, using vivid, carefully chosen action verbs for the weak linking verbs. The statements below merely *summarize* action; your revisions should *give* the action.

EXAMPLE 1. **That bully is unpopular.** [linking verb]

1. **That bully scowls at strangers, tramples upon his friends, and browbeats his enemies.** [action verbs]

1. Newton grew angry because his girl seemed uninterested.
2. She remained cheerful all evening.
3. The dinner tasted good, for he was hungry.
4. The dog was friendly.
5. Hank had been a great fighter.
6. The small boy seemed afraid of the crowd; he looked pale and sick.
7. Around strangers John is a very shy person.
8. The players were discouraged.
9. She became rich overnight.
10. My sister is very active at school.

The Adverb

1e. An *adverb* is a word used to modify a verb, an adjective, or another adverb.

ADVERBS MODIFYING VERBS

A word that changes the meaning of a verb is an adverb. Study the adverbs in heavy print below, observing that they modify verbs by answering one of these questions: Where? When? How? To what extent (how long or how much)?

WHERE?
1. Play **here.**
2. He drove **there.**
3. I fell **down.**

WHEN?
1. Play **now.**
2. He drives **daily.**
3. I **often** fall.

HOW?
1. Play **well.**
2. He drives **carefully.**
3. I fell **clumsily.**

TO WHAT EXTENT?
1. Do **not** play.
2. He drove **far.**
3. I **almost** fell.

● EXERCISE 17. Fill in the following blanks with adverbs that tell *where* the action was done, *when* the action was done, *how* it was done, or *to what extent* it was done. Use a separate sheet of paper; do not write in this book.

1. She arrived ——.
2. Dan laughed ——.
3. Rhoda screamed ——.
4. He talked —— and ——.
5. Did they win ——?
6. They did —— win ——.
7. While in Montana, I —— wrote letters, but I —— did enjoy receiving them.
8. Could he sing ——?
9. The dog jumped —— and barked ——.
10. Lawrence sighed —— as he —— waited for the telephone to ring.

● EXERCISE 18. Write about 100 words telling about some interesting event — an incident at a ball game, in the classroom, or at a party. Use at least 10 adverbs modifying verbs. Underline the adverbs, and draw arrows from them to the verbs they modify.

ADVERBS MODIFYING ADJECTIVES

A word that modifies an adjective is an *adverb*.

EXAMPLES **An unusually good batter, Bill knocked another home run.** [The adjective *good* modifies the noun *batter*. The adverb *unusually*, telling how good, modifies the adjective *good*.]
The room is spotlessly clean [The adverb *spotlessly* modifies the adjective *clean*, which describes the noun *room*.]

● EXERCISE 19. Find and list the 10 adverbs that modify adjectives in the following paragraph. After each adverb, give the adjective modified.

1. As we traveled down the extremely narrow highway, we noticed that the shoulders were somewhat muddy. 2. After dark a freezing drizzle made the pavement very slippery. 3. Although Paul is an especially good driver, the car skidded around the dangerously sharp curves and over the unusually slick bridges. 4. We were too afraid for words. 5. After a while, however, when familiar landmarks came into view, we became quite confident that we would reach our destination. 6. All the way, Paul had been exceptionally calm. 7. When we stopped in our driveway, though, he admitted, "I am rather tired of driving this wheezing, snorting jalopy."

● EXERCISE 20. Give one adverb modifier for each of the following adjectives. Do not use *too* or *very*.

1. short	6. honest
2. gay	7. sour
3. eager	8. qualified
4. ill	9. great
5. strong	10. dressed

ADVERBS MODIFYING OTHER ADVERBS

Some adverbs modify other adverbs. For example, in the following sentence *late* is an adverb because it tells when: *Eric arrived late.* If you add a word to modify *late*, an adverb, the word you add must also be an adverb.

Eric arrived **too** late.   [The adverb *too* tells how late.]
Eric arrived **very** late.   [The adverb *very* tells how late.]

There are two adverbs in the following sentence. Which adverb modifies another adverb? How do you know?

Bernice nearly always makes a perfect score.

THE FORMS OF ADVERBS

You have probably noticed that many adverbs end in *–ly*. You should also learn, however, that many adjectives also end in *–ly*: the *daily* newspaper, an *early* train, an *only* child, his *untimely* death, a *friendly* person. Moreover, words like *now, then, far, wide, fast, high, already, somewhat, not,* and *right* are often used as adverbs; they do not end in *–ly*. In order to identify a word as an adverb, do not depend upon the form of the ending. Instead, ask yourself: Does this word modify a verb, an adjective, or another adverb? Does it tell when, where, how, or to what extent?

● EXERCISE 21. Number from 1 to 40 and list in order the 40 adverbs in these sentences. After each adverb, write the word it modifies. Be able to tell whether the word modified is a verb, an adjective, or another adverb.

1. Cindy, my toy terrier, has four very tiny puppies.
2. They can hardly take six steps without falling.
3. These young puppies usually lie in their bed and sleep quietly.

4. Nearly always hungry, they often awake and whimper for food.
5. Snickie, an unusually smart runt, frequently gets into mischief.
6. She will probably be a very fat dog.
7. Already somewhat greedy, Snickie bolts her food hurriedly.
8. The diet of the puppies now consists wholly of hamburger meat and milk.
9. Since I always whistle before I give them food, they come quickly at a whistle.
10. When they hear the sound, the puppies promptly stumble forward and soon eat their meat from the bowl.
11. While she grudgingly shares the food with her brothers, Snickie surely does eat fast.
12. The other night I found Snickie howling as if her heart were hopelessly broken.
13. Never before had I heard her cry so pitifully.
14. I could not imagine the cause of her misery.
15. Evidently she was not in any physical pain.
16. Finally I discovered the cause of her alarmingly loud yelps.
17. She had heard a man on television who was gaily whistling a hit song.
18. Awakened by the whistling, Snickie had eagerly left the bed and had dived greedily into an empty bowl.
19. When she did not find any food, she was indeed disappointed.
20. She then gave voice to her distress with long, loud howls.

The Preposition

1f. A word used to show the relationship of a noun or a pronoun to some other word in the sentence is a *preposition*.

A preposition shows an important relationship of a **noun** or a **pronoun** to another word in the sen-

1f

tence. In the examples below, the prepositions, in heavy print, make a great difference in meaning as they relate *house* to *walked* and *him* to *book*.

I walked **to** the house.   The book **by** him is new.
I walked **around** the house.   The book **about** him is new.
I walked **through** the house.   The book **for** him is new.

Learn to recognize the following words, which are commonly used as prepositions:

aboard	between	on
about	beyond	over
above	but (meaning *except*)	since
across	by	through
after	concerning	throughout
against	down	to
along	during	toward
among	except	under
around	for	underneath
at	from	until
before	in	up
behind	into	upon
below	like	with
beneath	of	within
beside, besides	off	without

Some prepositions consist of more than one word: *instead of, in spite of, on account of, according to*.

● EXERCISE 22. In every sentence below, there are at least two prepositions, sometimes more. Number from 1 to 10 on your paper. After each number write the prepositions in the corresponding sentence.

EXAMPLE 1. **At** midnight he started reading a novel **by** Pearl Buck.
          1. **At, by.**

1. Mike Jenkins has fallen in love with Mary Haynes.
2. He constantly talks about her to everyone.
3. During history class he does not listen to his teacher.

4. He is too busy gazing at Mary, who sits across the aisle from him.
5. When she smiles, he grins like the Cheshire cat in *Alice in Wonderland*.
6. He often walks down the hall with her and carries her books for her.
7. Sometimes he looks into her eyes and mumbles to her.
8. One day I heard him mumble something about "the windows of the soul."
9. When we tease Mary, she often says, "After all, I am puzzled by Mike's strange behavior."
10. On account of his shyness, Mike never asks Mary for a date.

1g. A *prepositional phrase* is a group of words beginning with a preposition and ending with a noun or a pronoun.

Below is a list of prepositional phrases:

like *John*	**beside** the *water*
with *him*	**of** the *street*
for *us*	**over** the *fence*
without a *word*	**upon** the *top shelf*

▶ CAUTION: Do not confuse prepositions with adverbs. Prepositions, which begin phrases, are always followed by a noun or a pronoun.

ADVERB   I looked **around.**

PREPOSITIONAL PHRASE   I looked **around** the room.

In both sentences, the words in heavy print tell where I looked, but in the second sentence, "around," since it is followed by a noun, is a *preposition* and introduces a *prepositional phrase*.

● EXERCISE 23. Write the first and last words of the 24 prepositional phrases in the next paragraph. Number your list by sentences, keeping the phrases from each sentence together.

1g

EXAMPLE   1. The peach tree on the hill is in full bloom.
            1. **on — hill**
               in — bloom

1. Vitamins are necessary for good health.   2. Vitamin A promotes the growth of young animals and is essential to the proper development of their eyes.   3. If you cannot see in the dark, perhaps you should drink more milk, which is rich in vitamins.   4. Yellow vegetables like carrots also contain vitamin A.   5. If you have trouble with digestion or if your appetite is below normal, you may need vitamin B.   6. Among the foods containing this vitamin are eggs, green vegetables, and meats.   7. According to my druggist, liver, which contains vitamin B, is a safeguard against anemia.   8. For an adequate supply of this vitamin, eat plenty of tomatoes.   9. If you are susceptible to colds, vitamin C may help you resist them.   10. In the spring or during the summer, you can get vitamin D by a trip to a sunny beach.   11. Vitamin D, derived from sunshine and found in fish-liver oils, prevents rickets.   12. When you look at a menu, decide upon a well-balanced meal fortified with vitamins.

The Conjunction

1h.   A word which joins words or groups of words is a *conjunction*.

Conjunctions may join single words:

    Bill **or** Kate   tall **and** handsome
    Bill **and** Kate   short **but** handsome

Conjunctions may also join groups of words:

    on the desk **or** in the drawer
    singing songs **and** playing games

The joined groups of words may be complete ideas:

    The crowd cheered noisily, **for** Jones had scored.
    I dialed her number, **but** she did not answer.

There are three kinds of conjunctions: *co-ordinating* conjunctions, *correlative* conjunctions, and *subordinating* conjunctions.

Co-ordinating conjunctions connect words, phrases, and clauses of the same kind:

baseball **and** tennis   [two nouns]
at home **or** in the library   [prepositional phrases]
I talked with Thelma at the party, **but** she did not tell me about the accident.   [two main clauses]

Correlative conjunctions are used in pairs, with other words dividing them.

1. **Both** Sue **and** Jack entertained the class.
2. The freshmen asked **not only** for a big celebration **but also** for a special holiday.
3. **Either** you must wash the dishes, **or** you will have to clean the bedroom.
4. **Neither** his aunt **nor** his uncle could guess the answer to the riddle.

Since you will study subordinating conjunctions in connection with subordinate clauses (see page 77), at present you need to learn to identify only two kinds:

CO-ORDINATING CONJUNCTIONS	CORRELATIVE CONJUNCTIONS
and	both . . . and
but	not only . . . but also
or	either . . . or
nor	neither . . . nor
for	whether . . . or

● EXERCISE 24.   Using a separate sheet of paper, fill in the blanks with *correlative* conjunctions. Be able to tell whether they join words, phrases, or complete ideas.

1. ——— Judy ——— Gus will be nominated.
2. He is ——— ——— bored ——— ——— grumpy.

1h

3. I am going to buy Christmas gifts for —— Miss Hughes —— her mother.
4. My boss gave me an ultimatum: "—— you get to work on time, —— you can start looking for another Saturday job."
5. —— Sammy —— Clarence could remember her last name.
6. Ralph is —— in the swimming pool —— at the bowling alley.
7. —— —— did he ask her to the prom, —— he —— made a date for the game next Friday.
8. I painted —— the kitchen —— the hall a bright green.
9. I am cold, —— in the water —— out of it.
10. You can go there —— by train —— by bus.

● EXERCISE 25. How many co-ordinating and correlative conjunctions are in the following sentences? Number on your paper from 1 to 10. Write all the conjunctions from the same sentence after the corresponding number on your paper. (Separate the conjunctions by commas.) Be prepared to tell whether they are correlative or co-ordinating conjunctions.

1. I have fished in the Colorado River many times, but I never catch any fish.
2. Not only have I tried live bait, but I have also used artificial lures.
3. Whether I go early in the morning or late in the afternoon, the fish either aren't hungry or won't eat.
4. Using both worms and minnows, I have fished for perch and bass, but I catch only turtles or eels.
5. The postman told me last winter that my poor luck was caused neither by my lack of skill nor by the wrong bait.
6. He advised me to fish at either Lake Travis or Marshall Ford, for there, he said, the fish are more plentiful.
7. He also suggested that I buy a spinning reel and a special kind of lure.

8. I saved my money and bought both the reel and the lure, for I was determined to make a big catch.
9. Last Saturday was very cold, but I decided to try my luck at Lake Travis; I caught nothing.
10. An old man and his companion told me that my new lure was made only for white bass when they spawn in the spring; the man started to tell me a different way to catch fish, but I didn't stay to listen.

The Interjection

1i. Words expressing emotion and having no grammatical relation to other words in the sentence are *interjections*.

Words which show strong feeling — like *Ouch! Whew! Ahem!* and *Well!* — are interjections. Since these words show anger, surprise, or excitement, they are usually followed by an exclamation point. Sometimes, when the exclamation is mild, the interjection is followed by a comma.

EXAMPLES **Oh!** Don't hit me so hard.
Bah! He's no actor.
Well, do it yourself then.

Determining Parts of Speech

1j. What part of speech a word is depends upon how the word is used.

In different contexts the same word may be used as different parts of speech.

1. A quarterback sneak gained a first **down.** [noun]
2. He made a small **down** payment. [adjective]
3. She glanced **down.** [adverb]
4. She glanced **down** the hall. [preposition]
5. Marty did **down** the champion in the fifth round. [verb]

1i-j

Before you do any of the following exercises, care
fully study this summary:

RULE	PART OF SPEECH	USE	EXAMPLES
1a	**noun**	names	*Dick, sea*
1b	**pronoun**	takes the place of a noun	*he, it* *someone*
1c	**adjective**	modifies a noun or a pronoun	*lazy, free* *good, sick*
1d	**verb**	shows action or helps to make a statement	*run, play* *was, seem*
1e	**adverb**	modifies a verb or another modifier	*usually* *very, too*
1f	**preposition**	relates a noun or a pronoun to another word, begins a phrase	*by* (Sue) *beside* (him) *for* (her)
1h	**conjunction**	joins words	*and, but, or*
1i	**interjection**	shows strong feeling	*Wow! Yipe!*

● EXERCISE 26. Number from 1 to 10 on your
paper. Study the use of each italicized word in the
following sentences. Place beside the proper number
the part of speech of the italicized word. Be able to
justify your answer by giving the *use* of the word in
the sentence. Use the following abbreviations:

n.	noun	*adv.*	adverb
pro.	pronoun	*prep.*	preposition
v.	verb	*conj.*	conjunction
adj.	adjective	*interj.*	interjection

1. Our team had four *runs.*
2. He *runs* faster than a rabbit.
3. I broke the fragile *glass.*
4. The *glass* top protects the finish.
5. Gusts of wind blew through the *open* window.
6. Please *open* this jar of pickles.

7. Let's eat the watermelon out in the *open*.
8. The coffee boiled *over*.
9. Jet jumped *over* the rope.
10. The show is *over* by now.

● REVIEW EXERCISE B. Number from 1 to 25 on your paper. After copying each italicized word in the paragraph below, give its part of speech. Use abbreviations.

1. *After* school Jim and *I* studied for our geography test together. 2. In a *little* while, I commented to Jim, "I have *always* dreamed of a trip to England. *My!* I wish I *could* go *sometime*." 3. Jim and I then decided, for fun, that we would make *plans* for an *imaginary* tour. 4. Soon *we* forgot all about our *test*. 5. In our mind's eye, we *viewed* the many sights of London. 6. We visited Westminster Abbey, *which* has the Poets' Corner, and saw Buckingham Palace, in which the royal family lives. 7. Jim *and* I then went to St. Paul's *Cathedral* and *admired* the *beauty* of its Renaissance architecture. 8. Next we *visited* Stratford on Avon, the place *of* Shakespeare's birth. 9. We traveled to Wales and saw interesting sights *along* the coast, which was *beautiful indeed*. 10. Of course, we returned to *America*, conveniently enough, at bedtime; but *tomorrow* we may not pass our test on American *geography*.

● REVIEW EXERCISE C. Number from 1 to 33. Copy the following italicized words in a column on your paper. After each one, give its part of speech. Use abbreviations. Be able to explain its use in the sentence.

I *thought* that it *was* my *turn* to shoot. *With* girls hovering over *me like* buzzards *over* a *dead rabbit*, I *tried* to break for the *basket*, *but* just as I *pushed* the ball up *toward* the basket, the *blast* of the referee's *whistle reached* my ears. The *action* stopped *short*, *and* the players crashed *into* one *another*. All of *us pivoted* to face the *man in* the *black* and white *shirt*. *Harshly* he *roared* at me: "*Hey!* No. 34, since when have *guards* been *permitted* to shoot?"

GOOD USAGE ———————————————

them, those:	*Them* is a pronoun, never an adjective. *Those* may be used as an adjective.
	WRONG **Them** roses are beautiful.
	RIGHT **Those** roses are beautiful.

of, have: Do not use *of* for *have*. *Of* is a preposition. *Have* is a verb or verb helper.

        WRONG   I could **of** done better.

        RIGHT   I could **have** done better.

beside, besides: *Beside* means "by the side of." *Besides* means "in addition to."

        RIGHT   They sat down **beside** us.

                  Besides food we'll need heavy blankets.

in, into: Careful speakers use *in* to mean "within" and *into* to mean "movement from the outside to the inside."

        RIGHT   He is **in** the next room.

                  I dived **into** the water.

anywheres, everywheres, nowheres: Use these words and others like them without the *s*.

        RIGHT   We did not go **anywhere**.

irregardless: The correct word is *regardless*.

        RIGHT   **Regardless** of the outcome, I will try my best to win.

had ought: Never use *ought* with *had*.

        RIGHT   She **ought** to be there by now.

                  He **ought** not to lose his temper.

CHAPTER 2

The Parts of a Sentence

SUBJECT, PREDICATE, COMPLEMENT

In Chapter 1 you identified separate words as parts of speech. In this chapter you will learn how these words are grouped to express your thoughts in sentences. Understanding the structure of a sentence will help you to speak and write clear and correct sentences.

In your everyday conversations, you often express your thoughts by using only pieces of sentences. Between classes, for example, you may hurriedly remark to a friend, "A history test. Tomorrow morning, first period. No skating tonight." Among friends in a familiar situation, this conversation is both clear and natural. In *written* English, however, you should always complete your ideas. Whether you are writing an examination paper or an important business letter, you should always express your thoughts in clear and complete sentences.

The Sentence

2a. A *sentence* is a group of words containing a verb and its subject and expressing a completed thought.

As the basic unit of written expression, a sentence must have a completed thought. The nucleus of a completed thought is the subject and the verb.

2a

SENTENCES   **The party** | soon **ended.**
              We | **left** at nine o'clock.

The noun or pronoun upon which the thought centers is the *subject* of the sentence. In the first sentence above, the noun *party* is the subject of the verb *ended*. In the second sentence, the pronoun *We* is the subject of the verb *left*.

A sentence *fragment*, however, is a group of words *not* expressing a completed thought. Since a fragment is only a part of a sentence, it should not stand by itself.

FRAGMENTS   1. in a minute
             2. helped Edith all morning
             3. an interesting city
             4. a boy in my class
             5. hoping to hear from you soon

These groups of words can become sentences only when other words are added to make the thoughts complete:

SENTENCES   1. I'll be ready in a minute.
             2. Ruth helped Edith all morning.
             3. New Orleans is an interesting city.
             4. A boy in my class has his own shop.
             5. I am hoping to hear from you soon.

● EXERCISE 1.   Listed below are groups of words that are only pieces of sentences, fragments of thoughts. After numbering from 1 to 20 on your paper, revise each of these fragments by adding words to make the thought complete. (As you make revisions, remember to capitalize the first word of each sentence and to end the sentence with a period.)

1. for a day or two
2. wanted to surprise her
3. smiling his way into the room

4. about five miles north of here
5. catching the fast ball
6. from daylight until dark
7. five hundred miles an hour
8. three horses, two cows, and a pig
9. watched the fight on television
10. a dash of salt
11. talking in his sleep
12. got your message last night
13. without saying a word
14. a gallon of strawberry ice cream
15. trying to find out her address
16. a motel with a swimming pool
17. wishing you luck
18. some money for school supplies
19. feel like chocolate pie
20. see you later

In written English, even one fragment is usually a serious error. If you did not make a perfect score on Exercise 1, then you probably do not understand the structure of a sentence. To write complete sentences with ease, learn the parts of a sentence that are explained in this chapter.

Subject and Predicate

2b. A sentence consists of two parts: the *subject* and the *predicate.*

(1) The *subject* of the sentence is that part about which something is said.

The subjects of the following sentences are in heavy print.

My father owns a hardware store.
The leader of the gang admitted defeat.
A scream in the night is frightening.

2b

The subject may come at the end of the sentence rather than at the beginning.

> Across the street is **a golf course.**
> In the middle of the road stands **a detour sign.**
> Flying around the pier were **hungry seagulls.**

● EXERCISE 2.   Using a separate sheet of paper, fill in each of the following blanks with a subject that will logically complete the thought.

1. —— is my English teacher.
2. —— growled a warning.
3. —— scooted over to the curb.
4. —— glittered in the moonlight.
5. —— flippantly tossed a coin to the beggar.
6. —— suddenly leaped to her feet.
7. —— arrived by railway express.
8. In the center of the town is ——.
9. Lying on the desk was ——.
10. Among those old letters is ——.

(2) The *predicate* of a sentence says something about the subject.

The predicates below are in heavy print.

> The club members **planned a hen party.**
> Congested traffic **caused us to be late.**

The predicate may come before the subject.

> **In their back yard are** two vicious dogs.
> **Behind Elizabeth stood** the principal.

● EXERCISE 3.   Write 10 sentences using the following subjects. Add predicates, words that say something about the subjects.

1. my sore thumb
2. plastic dishes
3. the road to the lake
4. my uncle in Iowa
5. acres and acres of cotton
6. the famous clown
7. a bed of zinnias
8. my best friend
9. the front of the theater
10. all kinds of fireworks

● EXERCISE 4.   Number in a column from 1 to 10. After the corresponding number on your paper, write the subject of each sentence.

1. Every student in our school should know that any fire must have heat, fuel, and oxygen.
2. He can with this knowledge prevent or combat destructive fires.
3. Among the most common fire extinguishers is water.
4. Water reduces the heat.
5. It also excludes oxygen.
6. The firemen in our town sometimes use chemicals instead of water.
7. The vapor of carbon tetrachloride can often smother the flames of liquids like paint or oil.
8. In many indoor extinguishers is a mixture of soda and acid.
9. Some public buildings in large cities have built-in sprinkling systems.
10. These systems automatically turn themselves on during a fire.

● EXERCISE 5.   Remembering that a sentence must have a subject *and* a predicate, revise the following fragments to make the thoughts complete.

1. the restless passengers
2. discovered the Pacific Ocean
3. flashing neon signs
4. rolled down the mountainside
5. dropped thirty degrees during the night
6. a capsized canoe
7. completely destroyed the old building
8. soared high above the dark clouds
9. the kites overhead
10. the spectators near the ring

2c. The *simple predicate* or the *verb* is the principal word or group of words in the complete predicate.

2c

So far, you have learned to recognize the *complete predicate* as the part of a sentence that says something about a subject. The backbone or main word of the complete predicate is always a verb or a verb phrase, which is sometimes called the *simple predicate*.

THE VERB PHRASE

A verb having more than one word is a verb phrase. The following are examples of verb phrases:

is typing	could have gone	has sat
will write	can be expected	was broken

As you learn to distinguish the simple predicate from the complete predicate, keep in mind the various verb helpers that are commonly used as parts of verb phrases: *shall, will, has, have, had, do, does, did, may, might, can, could, should, would, am, is, are, was, were, be,* and *been.*

Study the following examples, noticing the difference between the complete predicate and the simple predicate or the verb.

The puppy barked furiously at every strange noise.

COMPLETE PREDICATE   barked furiously at every strange
noise

VERB   barked

My brother will leave for camp tomorrow.

COMPLETE PREDICATE   will leave for camp tomorrow
VERB   will leave

● EXERCISE 6.   Number in a column from 1 to 10. Find the verb in each of the sentences below, and write it after the proper number on your paper. If you find a verb phrase, be sure to include all helpers.

1. In speech class we have been learning parliamentary procedure.

2. Miss Perkins, our teacher, has organized the class as a kind of legislative assembly.
3. We are learning the rules fast and easily.
4. Each member of the class is a "senator" from some state.
5. For example, I am recognized as "Senator Davis from Delaware."
6. Yesterday Ralph Beane was elected chairman of the group.
7. In the Future Farmers of America, he has already learned a great deal about parliamentary procedure.
8. Each senator may introduce any original "bill" for discussion.
9. Today my original resolution called for a six-day school week and four months off in the summer.
10. The motion died for the lack of a second!

2d. The *simple subject* is a word naming the person, place, thing, or idea about which something is said.

In isolating the simple subject from the complete subject, you select the most important word in the subject, the word naming the person, place, thing, or idea being talked about.

My brown and white shirt is missing.

COMPLETE SUBJECT   **My brown and white shirt**
SUBJECT   **shirt**

The time for the meeting has been changed.

COMPLETE SUBJECT   **The time for the meeting**
SUBJECT   **time**

▶ NOTE: Throughout the rest of this book, the word *subject* will be used to mean *simple subject*.

FINDING THE SUBJECT

The best way to find the subject of a sentence is to find the verb first. After you have found the verb, ask "Who?" or "What?" in front of the verb.

2d

My sister needs a haircut.   [The verb is *needs*. Who needs? The answer is *sister*, the subject.]

Around the bend came a freight train.   [The verb is *came*. What came? The *train* came; therefore, *train* is the subject.]

One of his listeners was noisy.   [The verb is *was*. Who was? *One* was. *One*, then, is the subject.]

The subject of a sentence is usually a noun or a pronoun. Not all nouns, however, are subjects. For example, there are four nouns in the following sentence, but only one of them, *man*, is the subject.

Every man in the office left his money in the safe.

● EXERCISE 7.   Find the subject of each of the following sentences first by finding the verb and then by asking "Who?" or "What?" in front of the verb. After numbering from 1 to 10, list on your paper each verb and its subject. Be sure to include all parts of a verb phrase. (CAUTION: Remember that the word *not* is an adverb.)

1. The study of English grammar is like a ladder.
2. An important rule is a step toward good usage.
3. Everyone should take each step safely and surely before going on to the next step.
4. Sometimes, however, a student may not understand an important grammatical principle.
5. For instance, someone in your class may not learn about verbs.
6. The steps on the ladder run from the verb to its subject.
7. After the subject come complements.
8. The student's lack of knowledge of verbs may cause him serious difficulty.
9. Actually, he has missed a step on the ladder.
10. The next step may be too high for him to reach.

THE SUBJECT IN AN UNUSUAL POSITION

Sentences which ask questions and sentences which begin with *here* or *there* have a word order that places the subject in an unusual position.

1. *Sentences Which Ask Questions*

Questions often begin with a verb or with a verb helper. They also frequently begin with words like *what, when, where, how,* or *why.* Either way, the subject ordinarily *follows* the verb or verb helper. For instance:

Has **Paul** finished his homework yet?
Where Is he now?

Of course, you can find the subject first by finding the verb and then by asking "Who?" or "What?" in front of the verb. You can also turn the question into a statement.

Is the **building** very old? The **building** is very old.
Didn't **Tom** go? **Tom** didn't go.
What is **that? That** is what.

By making a statement out of a question, you place the subject in its usual position, where it is easier to identify.

2. *Sentences Which Begin with* **There** *or* **Here**

There or *here* is never the subject unless spoken of as a word (as in this very sentence). When *there* or *here* comes at the beginning of a sentence, drop the first word, and move the verb to where it is needed to make sense.

1. **There** is a log cabin on the other side of the lake.
   A log **cabin is** on the other side of the lake.

2. **Here** are your tennis shoes in the closet.
   Your tennis **shoes are** in the closet.

When you are looking for the subjects of sentences beginning with *here* or *there*, you can also cross out the *here* or *there* and then ask "Who?" or "What?" in front of the verb.

Here comes Joan.   [*Here* is not the subject. Who comes? *Joan* comes; *Joan* is the subject.]

There were two dimes on the table.   [*There* is not the subject. What were? *Dimes* is the subject.]

● EXERCISE 8.   After numbering from 1 to 20, find and list the subjects and verbs in the following sentences. (Consider proper nouns as one word.)

1. What is a clay pigeon?
2. When was the Hall of Fame established?
3. Why does the needle of a compass always point north?
4. In what city is the Kentucky Derby held?
5. Why does a falling barometer indicate the approach of a storm?
6. Here is a sharp pencil.
7. Has there been any rainfall here?
8. Here are two postcards.
9. There were no strangers among us.
10. There goes Fritz Lane with his rifle.
11. Is your locker open?
12. Who was Aaron Burr?
13. Where is Deadwood Gulch?
14. Are there any apples in the kitchen?
15. What does your name mean?
16. There was a camera in the car pocket.
17. Here is a free pass to the wrestling match.
18. Is there a banana in my lunch box?
19. There is a "monkey island" in San Antonio.
20. When did America discover baseball?

THE UNDERSTOOD SUBJECT

In a sentence that makes a request or gives a command, the subject is usually not stated. It is called an *understood subject*.

EXAMPLES   **Now listen to me.**
                Please hand me the sports section.

In the first sentence, *who* is to listen? *You* are. In the second, *who* is to hand me the sports section? Again, *you* are. In each sentence, then, *you* is the understood subject.

Compound Subjects and Verbs

2e. When the subject consists of two or more connected words, it is called a *compound* subject.

The conjunctions most commonly used to connect the words of a compound subject are: *and, or*. Study the following sentences.

   Elaine is going with me. [The verb phrase is *is going.* Who is going? *Elaine* is the simple subject.]
   Elaine and Nancy are going with me. [Who are going? Both Elaine and Nancy. *Elaine* and *Nancy*, then, form the compound subject.]
   Is Elaine or Nancy going? [Who is going? Either Elaine or Nancy. The compound subject is *Elaine, Nancy.*]

● EXERCISE 9.   Find and list the compound subjects as well as the verbs in the following sentences.

EXAMPLE   **1. My cat and your dog are natural enemies.**
              1. cat, dog — are

1. History and arithmetic are my favorite courses.
2. Either James or Fred will help you.
3. The mountains and the lakes in Idaho are beautiful.
4. Last night both Hazel and Harry seemed happy about our plans.
5. In the refrigerator are cookies and ice cream.

● EXERCISE 10.   Write answers to the following questions with original sentences using compound subjects.

2e

1. Who are your teachers?
2. What are some of the sights of New York City?
3. What makes a Christmas tree beautiful?
4. Who are the officers of your class?
5. Who are your favorite movie stars?

2f. A *compound verb* consists of two or more verbs joined by a connecting word.

Verbs can also be compound, as the following sentences indicate.

Roy **played** his guitar and **sang** cowboy songs.
You **should visit** Ann or **write** her a letter.

● EXERCISE 11. After numbering from 1 to 10, make a list of the compound verbs in these sentences. Be sure to include verb helpers.

1. Stop, look, and whistle.
2. During class Jack stretched, yawned, and sighed.
3. At the rodeo Vaughan leaped upon the wild steer and stayed on him for four full minutes.
4. Must you always worry or complain?
5. My hound can bark, sit up, or lie down.
6. Pauline can neither sing nor dance.
7. Between two and three o'clock I will either be studying in Room 17 or reading in the library.
8. Can you type a letter or take shorthand?
9. Many men from Tennessee fought and died at the Alamo.
10. The ball lingered for a few seconds on the edge of the basket and then fell through for a score.

● EXERCISE 12. Write about 100 words describing someone in action — a football player making a score, your father shaving, a neighbor repairing his house or barn, a cheerleader yelling for victory, a woman driving down Main Street. If you wish, describe yourself in action. Use at least 10 compound verbs.

2g. The subject of a verb is never in a preposi-
tional phrase.

You will remember that a prepositional phrase begins with a preposition and ends with a noun or a pronoun: *to the bank, by the door, in the picture, of a book, on the floor, after class, at intermission, for them, except him.* Since the prepositional phrase contains a noun or a pronoun, and since it often comes before the verb, you may make the mistake of thinking that the noun following a preposition is the subject. Avoid this mistake by crossing out prepositional phrases. In that way, you can often isolate the subject. For example:

One ~~of the boys~~ helped us.

When you ask "Who helped?" you may be tempted to answer "boys helped." But *boys* cannot be the subject because it is part of a prepositional phrase. *One* must be the subject of the sentence. Crossing out prepositional phrases is especially helpful when the subject follows the verb.

~~In the middle of the lake~~ is a small island.

Neither *middle* nor *lake* can be the subject because each word is a part of a prepositional phrase. The subject of *is* has to be *island*.

● EXERCISE 13. Copy the following sentences onto your paper. After crossing out all prepositional phrases, underline each verb twice and its subject once.

1. That house by the railroad tracks is my home.
2. Mr. Ayres of the Federal Investment Company sold it to us last month.
3. Everything about the house except its location is very satisfactory.
4. Every hour or so trains of all shapes and sizes roar through our back yard.

2f-g

5. The vibrations of the heavy freight trains cause the most damage.
6. Sometimes a picture on the living room wall crashes to the floor.
7. The oven door of the gas range habitually snaps open.
8. Yesterday at breakfast a piece of plaster from the ceiling fell into Dad's coffee.
9. The thunderous clanking of the trains completely absorbs and overpowers the sound of our television.
10. The various advertisers on our television remind me of the patent medicine men of silent movies.

● REVIEW EXERCISE A. Try to make a perfect score on this exercise, which is a mastery test on subjects and verbs. After you have copied, double space, the following sentences, your job is this:

1. Cross out all prepositional phrases so that you can isolate the verb and the subject.
2. Cross out a *here* or *there* at the beginning of a sentence, thus eliminating these words as possible subjects.
3. Underscore all verbs twice; be sure to include all helpers and all parts of a compound verb.
4. Underscore all subjects once; be sure to underscore all parts of a compound subject.

EXAMPLES   Between the houses are two large trees and a high hedge.

There is a spider on your left shoulder.

1. Why have paperback books become so popular during the last few years?
2. There is a variety of subject matter in these cheap editions.
3. Some of these books give you the batting average of every professional baseball player in the national leagues since 1876.
4. Here is another reason for the popularity of paperback books.

5. Within the reach of everyone is the low price.
6. Along with the low price is the small size.
7. A businessman on a subway, a taxicab driver in a spare moment, or a student in a drugstore can read and enjoy these small, cheap books.
8. Before the five o'clock rush, clerks in grocery stores hover over a mystery story or thumb through a book of cartoons.
9. Park strollers sit quietly in the sun and read poetry or short stories.
10. The subject matter, economy, and size of the paperback books account for their tremendous popularity.

Classification of Sentences by Type

2h. Sentences may be classified as *declarative, imperative, interrogative,* or *exclamatory.*

(1) A *declarative sentence* makes a statement.

Since you usually make statements that *declare* something, most of your sentences are declarative. All declarative sentences are followed by periods.

EXAMPLES   The Dodgers won the first inning.
               The tallest animal in the world is a giraffe.

(2) An *imperative sentence* gives a command or makes a request.

A command or a request usually has the understood subject *you*. Like the declarative sentence, the imperative sentence is followed by a period.

EXAMPLES   Turn right at the next corner.
               Please send me your free catalogue.

(3) An *interrogative sentence* asks a question.

To *interrogate* means to *ask*. An interrogative sentence is followed by a question mark.

2h

EXAMPLES   **Where is Roy going now?**
Why can't we ever see the other side of the moon?

(4) An *exclamatory sentence* expresses strong feeling.

A sentence expressing strong feeling is always followed by an exclamation point.

EXAMPLES   **What a race!**
How lucky you are!

If you show strong feeling when making a statement, asking a question, or giving a command, then your sentence is exclamatory.

EXAMPLES   **I won the booby prize!**
Wasn't he funny!
Help! Call the police!

● EXERCISE 14.   Classify each of the following sentences according to its purpose. After numbering from 1 to 10, write *declarative*, *imperative*, *interrogative*, or *exclamatory* after the corresponding number on your paper.

1. Wasn't that an exciting ending to our ball game?
2. The bases were loaded, and Raymond was next at bat.
3. What a tense moment!
4. Would he strike out as usual, or would he make a miraculous hit?
5. After rubbing his hands in the sand, Raymond took a firm grip on the bat.
6. "I'm going to knock this one," he thought, "to the west side of Kalamazoo!"
7. He spoke to the catcher. "Stand back out of my way."
8. The ball was low, fast, tricky.
9. Crack! The ball whizzed past the fielders and then crashed into a window a half block away!
10. When an angry fist shook itself through the broken window, all the players quickly scampered out of sight — all except Raymond, who took plenty of time to

enjoy his walk to home plate before going over to make friends with the fist.

● EXERCISE 15.   Copy the last word of each of the following sentences, and then give the correct mark of punctuation. Classify each sentence as imperative, declarative, interrogative, or exclamatory.

EXAMPLE   1. **What is Joe's middle name**
          1. **name?   interrogative**

1. Do you know what causes a rainbow
2. Why is it that no one has ever found the pot of gold at the end of it
3. What hope a rainbow brings after a storm
4. Look to the east
5. Two rainbows are in the sky now
6. How beautiful they are together
7. One appears to be the shadow of the other
8. How many different colors are there
9. Notice the shades of red and violet
10. Why must a rainbow suddenly vanish into the air when the sun disappears in the west

● EXERCISE 16.   Write 10 sentences: 3 declarative, 2 imperative, 2 interrogative, and 3 exclamatory.

Diagraming Sentences

In order to write good sentences, you should have in your mind a clear picture of the ways in which sentences are built. Many students find that they can understand a sentence better when they use a diagram. The diagram is a quick picture of how the various parts of a sentence fit together and how the words are related.

1. *Diagraming the Subject and the Verb*

A diagram begins with a straight horizontal line on your paper. This line is for the main parts of the sentence or the "sentence base." Approximately in the center of the horizontal line is a short vertical one, which crosses the horizontal line. The vertical line divides the subject from the verb. To the left of the line is the subject; to the right is the verb.

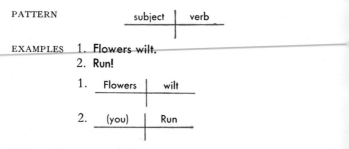

PATTERN

EXAMPLES   1. Flowers wilt.
          2. Run!

When the sentence has a compound subject, diagram it as in the following example. Notice the position of the joining word on the dotted line.

Parents and **teachers** were invited.

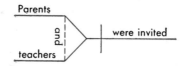

If the verb is compound, it is diagramed in this way:

Babies **wiggle** and **whimper**.

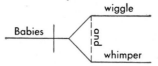

● EXERCISE 17.   Diagram the following sentences.

1. Charles snores.
2. Stop!
3. Men and women voted.
4. Bill sang and danced.
5. He and I talked and laughed.

2. *Diagraming Adjectives and Adverbs*

Adjectives modify nouns or pronouns, and adverbs modify verbs, adjectives, or other adverbs. Both adjectives and adverbs are written on slanted lines connected to the words they modify.

PATTERN

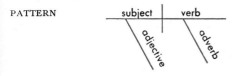

EXAMPLE   **The gun has not been fired.**

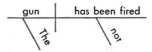

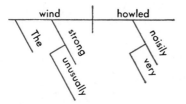

An adverb that modifies an adjective or an adverb is placed on a line connected to the adjective or adverb modified, as follows:

The unusually strong wind howled **very noisily.**

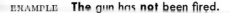

● EXERCISE 18.   Diagrams for the following sentences are given for you. Copy these on your paper, and fill them in correctly.

1. Each boy listened attentively.

2. Do not gossip.

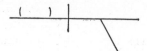

3. The scouts arose very early.

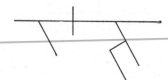

4. The big airliner landed safely.

5. An extremely interesting book nearly always **sells.**

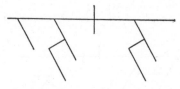

3. *Diagraming the Word* There

You have already learned that the word *there* may be used to begin a sentence. *There* is not the subject. In such a sentence, the subject follows the verb, and *there* does not modify anything. It is diagramed in this way:

There are several problems here.

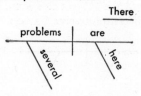

Often, however, *there* is an adverb telling where. Then it is diagramed as an adverb, on a line connected to the verb.

EXAMPLE **Move there.**

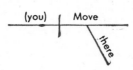

● EXERCISE 19. After you have decided how *there* is used in each of the following sentences, diagram the sentences.

1. There were a few complaints.
2. There it is!
3. There is nothing here.
4. My kitten lay there quietly.
5. Will you sit there?

● REVIEW EXERCISE B. Diagram each of the following sentences.

1. Blue jays and squirrels often quarrel.
2. There is only one pencil here.
3. Rosalie graciously smiled and bowed.
4. There was much hubbub.
5. The fire flickered weakly and then died.

● REVIEW EXERCISE C. Answer each of the following questions by using complete sentences.

1. What is the definition of a sentence?
2. How do you find the subject of a sentence?
3. What is the difference between a complete subject and a simple subject?
4. What is an interrogative sentence? Give an example, correctly punctuated.
5. How is an adverb diagramed? Illustrate your answer.

● REVIEW EXERCISE D. In separate sentences, use an example of each of the following and underline it.

EXAMPLE 1. a prepositional phrase
1. We danced <u>until ten o'clock</u>.

1. a verb phrase
2. a compound verb
3. a compound subject
4. an understood subject
5. an adverb modifying an adjective

The Sentence Base

Every sentence has a base. This base may be compared to the main framework of a building. It is that part of the sentence on which are suspended all other parts. A sentence base may consist of only two parts: the subject and the verb.

EXAMPLE   A **bird** in the yard **is diving** at the cat.

Frequently, however, a sentence base has three parts: subject, verb, and complement.

EXAMPLE   **Mr. Hodges** then **made** a long **assignment.**

Complements

2i A *complement* is a word that completes the meaning begun by the subject and verb.

A group of words can have a subject and a verb and still not have a completed thought. Notice how these sentences need other words to make the meaning complete.

John is taking	[What?]
My brother seems	[What?]
The Giants defeated	[Whom?]
I met	[Whom?]

If you add words to complete the meaning, then the sentences will make sense.

> John is taking **vitamins.**
> My brother seems **happy.**
> The Giants defeated **the Dodgers.**
> I met **Paul's sister.**

The words *vitamins*, *happy*, *Dodgers*, and *sister* are complements; they complete the thought of the sentence. The complement may be a noun, a pronoun, or an adjective.

Study the structure of these sentences. The base of each sentence — subject, verb, complement — is in heavy print.

1. A **stranger approached me.**
2. **I brought** along a **box** of matches.
3. The **man** in the moon **looks friendly.**
4. At that time **labor was** very **cheap.**
5. A tape **recorder provided** background **music.**

● EXERCISE 20.   Complete the meaning of the following sentences by adding a complement to each.

1. I caught
2. That book looks
3. Her telephone manners are
4. My mother has been
5. A boy in the back row raised
6. Yesterday in history class I answered
7. Shall we punish
8. A stitch in time saves
9. At the end of the act, Kenneth lowered
10. The word *integrity* means

● EXERCISE 21.   Write 5 sentences using the following sentence bases. Do not be satisfied with adding only one or two words. Make *interesting* sentences.

2i

	SUBJECT	VERB	COMPLEMENT
1.	clown	amused	crowd
2.	pilot	felt	confident
3.	Wanda	runs	errands
4.	men	used	machines
5.	explorers	had	courage

● EXERCISE 22.   Using each word below as a complement, write 10 sentences. Underline each sentence base.

EXAMPLE   1. tornado
     1. **Everyone** in the small village anxiously **watched** the approaching **tornado.**

1. touchdown	6. fickle
2. monkey	7. puzzle
3. shark	8. prediction
4. comic	9. tomboy
5. irresistible	10. thunderstruck

● EXERCISE 23.   Make three columns on your paper. Label the first *subject*, the second *verb*, and the third *complement*. Find the base of each sentence and enter the parts in the appropriate column.

1. The history of the English stage is very interesting.
2. In the beginning the Church gave plays for instruction.
3. The stories of early English drama were usually Biblical ones.
4. Frolicsome actors, however, eventually grew too irreverent for religious purposes.
5. Clergymen then recommended the abolition of acting inside the Church.
6. At the same time, they encouraged the development of moral themes in drama outside the Church.
7. The actors presented their plays on wagons in the open air.
8. The top of the wagon soon became a convenient place for "heaven."

9. There the "angels" in the play could address the sinners on earth below.
10. In Shakespeare's time, the upper stage was an important part of the theater.
11. It was especially useful for eavesdroppers.
12. Shakespeare used the upper stage for the famous balcony scene in *Romeo and Juliet*.

THE SUBJECT COMPLEMENT

2j. Complements that describe or explain the simple subject are called *subject complements*.

Some complements refer to the subject:

My name is **Andrew.**

Bluebonnets in bloom are **beautiful.**

In the first sentence, the complement *Andrew* explains the subject *name*. In the second, the complement *beautiful* describes the subject *bluebonnets*.

A subject complement is linked to the subject by linking verbs only: *feel, taste, smell, look, grow, become, seem, appear, remain, stay, sound,* and *be.*[1]

The subject complement may be an adjective, or it may be a noun or a pronoun.

(1) If the subject complement is an adjective, it is called a *predicate adjective*.

EXAMPLES   This pie tastes **good.**
            Luke looks **strong.**

(2) If the subject complement is a noun or a pronoun, it is called a *predicate nominative*.

EXAMPLES   James will be my **partner.**
            This is **she.**

2j

[1] For other forms of *be,* see page 10.

● EXERCISE 24.   In the sentences of Exercise 23 there are 6 subject complements. Make a list of them. After each adjective, write *predicate adjective;* after each noun or pronoun, *predicate nominative.*

● EXERCISE 25.   Orally complete the following sentences by using adjectives, nouns, or pronouns as subject complements. Tell whether the complement is a predicate adjective or a predicate nominative.

1. Roses are
2. This is
3. I feel
4. This perfume smells
5. The nurse seemed

6. Henry became
7. The girl was
8. That stranger may be
9. The gun looked
10. Is he

DIAGRAMING THE SUBJECT COMPLEMENT

As a part of the sentence base, the subject complement is placed on the horizontal line with the subject and verb. It comes after the verb. A line *slanting toward the subject* drawn upward from the horizontal line separates the subject complement from the verb.

PATTERN   subject | verb \ subject complement

PREDICATE NOMINATIVE   **Hilda is a popular girl.**

Hilda | is \ girl

PREDICATE ADJECTIVE   **Hilda is popular.**

Hilda | is \ popular

● EXERCISE 26.   Diagram the following sentences.

1. Superstitions are illogical beliefs.
2. A black cat or a torn picture is bad luck.

3. A four-leaf clover has traditionally remained a symbol of good fortune.
4. Some superstitious people grow very fearful.
5. Broken mirrors and tortured effigies seem terrible omens.

THE OBJECT COMPLEMENT

The object complement does not refer to the subject.

EXAMPLE   **Vivian opened the door.**

In this sentence, the object complement *door* does not explain or describe the subject *Vivian*, and *opened* is an action verb rather than a linking verb. *Object complements receive the action of the verb* or *name the result of the action.* Study the following sentences:

SUBJECT	VERB	OBJECT COMPLEMENT
1. Ruth	drank	milk.
2. Father	makes	money.
3. Praise	encourages	us.

Object complements are usually called simply *objects*. There are two kinds of objects: the *direct* and the *indirect*.

2k. **The *direct object* receives the action expressed by the verb or names the result of the action.**

The direct object receives from the subject an action stated by the verb.

EXAMPLE   **Hefty Harry hit Mortimer on the jaw.**

Here the direct object is *Mortimer*, who received the action expressed by the verb *hit*. A direct object always answers the question "What?" or "Whom?" *after* an *action* verb. For example, Hefty Harry hit whom? He hit Mortimer; so *Mortimer* is the direct object.

2k

The direct object may also name the result of the action expressed by the verb.

EXAMPLE   **Her collection of water colors won a prize.**

● EXERCISE 27.   Find and list the direct objects in these sentences. (CAUTION: Like the subject, the direct object is never a part of a prepositional phrase.)

1. Proverbs often contradict each other.
2. A faint heart never won a fair lady.
3. A fool's boldness frightens an angel.
4. Love conquers all things.
5. Love runs a headlong course to desperate madness.
6. Experience teaches the best lessons.
7. Learning teaches more truths in one year than experience in twenty.
8. Curiosity characterizes a vigorous intellect.
9. Curiosity killed the cat.
10. Do proverbs always tell the truth?

21. An *indirect object* tells *to whom* or *for whom* the action of the verb is done.

The indirect object is a noun or a pronoun that normally comes before the direct object.

DIRECT OBJECT   **Miss Smith teaches history.**
INDIRECT OBJECT   **Miss Smith teaches us history.**

In these sentences, *what* does Miss Smith teach? She teaches *history*, which is the direct object of both sentences. *To whom?* To *us*. *Us*, then, is the indirect object.

The indirect objects in the sentences below are in heavy print. Each one tells *to whom* or *for whom* something is done.

1. He showed **her** the lantern.
2. The doctor gave **Mother** good advice.
3. I bought **him** a new ball.
4. My cousin left **Jim** a message.

If the words *to* and *for* are used, the words following them are parts of prepositional phrases and not indirect objects.

PREPOSITIONAL PHRASES **I sold tickets to the girls.**
Nancy saved some cake for me.

INDIRECT OBJECTS **I sold the girls tickets.**
Nancy saved me some cake.

● EXERCISE 28.   Using a separate sheet of paper, fill in these blanks with indirect objects.

1. George built —— a dog house.
2. I gave —— another chance.
3. She lent —— her binoculars.
4. James offered —— a ride.
5. He sent —— a pet alligator.

● EXERCISE 29.   List on your paper the direct and the indirect objects in the following sentences. You will not find an indirect object in every sentence.

EXAMPLE   1. **Please lend me your handkerchief.**
         1. **me, handkerchief**

1. My first airplane ride gave me a real thrill.
2. The stewardess told us about the safety belts.
3. After we had fastened them, the plane roared up into the night.
4. Then my sister Sally suddenly informed me about our excellent chances for a crash.
5. Terrifying flames from the motors were leaving their fiery tracks across the black sky.
6. The stewardess smiled and offered Sally a peppermint.
7. She quickly consoled us with a single remark.
8. "The excess fuel catches fire, a normal occurrence on an airplane."
9. After a while the stewardess showed my family a bright city below us.
10. We marveled at the beauty of the flashing neon lights; they reminded me of a fabulous living jewel against a background of black velvet.

21

COMPOUND COMPLEMENTS

As the following sentences indicate, complements may be compound.

COMPOUND SUBJECT COMPLEMENTS   **An educated man is courteous** and **intelligent.**
My best friends are Donald and **Sam.**

COMPOUND OBJECT COMPLEMENTS   **My little sister is always eating popcorn** or **candy.**
~~We sent **Ted** and **Walter** an invitation.~~

● EXERCISE 30.   Write 5 sentences using compound subject complements and 5 sentences using compound object complements.

DIAGRAMING DIRECT AND INDIRECT OBJECTS

The *direct object* is diagramed in almost the same way as the predicate nominative. The only difference is that the line separating the direct object from the verb is *vertical* (not slanting).

PATTERN

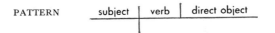

EXAMPLE   **Everyone played games.**

Everyone | played | games

The compound direct object is diagramed in this way:

They sell bicycles and sleds.

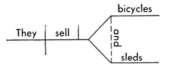

The *indirect object* is diagramed on a horizontal line beneath the verb.

EXAMPLE   **He paid me two dollars.**

● EXERCISE 31.   Diagram the following sentences.

1. A mugwump is a fence sitter.
2. The material feels thick and stiff.
3. The clown threw me a kiss.
4. My uncle brought us watermelons and cantaloupes.
5. Will you hand me a needle and thread?

● REVIEW EXERCISE E.   Number from 1 to 50. Then make a list of the italicized words in the passage below. After each word, write the correct one of the following identifications, using these abbreviations:

> s.   subject
> v.   verb
> p.a. predicate adjective
> p.n. predicate nominative
> d.o. direct object
> i.o. indirect object

(1) *Many* of Edgar Allan Poe's stories do not deal with horror or terror. Not (2) *all* of his main characters are ghosts or (3) *devils*. Poe has written many comic (4) *tales*. For instance, "The Business Man" or "Loss of Breath" (5) *gives* the (6) *reader* a (7) *chance* for hearty laughter.

In "The Business Man" is a particularly funny (8) *character*. He (9) *is* extremely (10) *shrewd* and makes money by outwitting the other fellow. This "Peter Profit" (11) *entered* the "Organ-Grinding" business. First, however, he opened his organ and (12) *gave* (13) *it* several hard (14) *licks* with a hammer. Then the (15) *noise* of the organ (16) *sounded* (17) *terrible*. Under the windows of his victims, the little (18) *man* with an eye for business played his (19) *organ* until the annoyed listeners paid him to hush. This (20) *business*, however, gave the hero a (21) *headache*. He (22) *changed*

(23) *jobs*. He (24) *became* more (25) *ambitious*. His next venture (26) *was* cat growing. Soon (27) *cats* of all kinds (28) *were running* all over the neighborhood. Finally, the (29) *citizens* in the community (30) *made* an (31) *agreement*. They (32) *would pay* the (33) *owner* of the cats to shut down his business. (34) *This*, of course, (35) *was* exactly the (36) *idea!* The (37) *hero* of this tale (38) *thinks* of many other schemes for getting rich in a hurry.

In "Loss of Breath" is another amusing (39) *character*. The (40) *author* saw the (41) *humor* of the expression, "I've lost my breath." He (42) *based* a (43) *story* on it. The main (44) *character* in "Loss of Breath" (45) *is* (46) *Mr. Lacko-breath*. Angry with his wife, he (47) *argues* furiously and loses his breath. Then the unhappy husband begins a long (48) *search* for his lost breath. Finally he finds it. On the very day of the argument, a (49) *man* by the name of Mr. Windenough had "caught his breath." The end of the story is a happy (50) *one*.

GOOD USAGE

Avoid the following common errors:

and etc.: Since *etc.* is an abbreviation of the Latin *et cetera*, which means "and other things," you are using *and* twice when you write *and etc.* The *etc.* is enough.

all the farther, all the faster: These phrases are poor English when used to mean "as far as," "as fast as."

WRONG   This is **all the farther** the trail goes.
RIGHT   This is **as far as** the trail goes.

CHAPTER 3

Phrases and Clauses

PREPOSITIONAL AND VERBAL PHRASES, MAIN AND SUBORDINATE CLAUSES

Now that you can identify the parts of a sentence base, you are ready to study more advanced grammar. Your next job is to learn the function of groups of words in a sentence. This chapter begins with prepositional phrases, which you already have learned to identify, and proceeds gradually to unfamiliar and more complicated sentence structure. If you will carefully study each definition as you go along, however, you will find that advanced grammar is easy to master and that the knowledge of it will help you write better sentences.

The Phrase

You have already learned that a group of words used as a verb is a *verb phrase: am leaving, has won, will do, had been worrying*. Groups of words may be used not only as verbs but also as adjectives, adverbs, and nouns.

3a. A *phrase* is a group of words used as a single part of speech and not containing a verb and its subject.

If a group of words has a subject *and* a verb, then the group of words is *not* a phrase.

PHRASES   **during the afternoon**   [no subject or verb]
            has been working   [a verb without a subject]

NOT A PHRASE   **after he had left**   [a subject *and* a verb:
               he is the subject of *had left*]

● EXERCISE 1. Study the following groups of words and decide whether or not each group is a phrase. After numbering from 1 to 10, write *p.* for *phrase* or *n.p.* for *not a phrase* after the appropriate number.

1. was running
2. when she finally arrived
3. between you and me
4. will be competing
5. of the story
6. because Sue won
7. after you go
8. has been ironed
9. in the deep water
10. if the bell rings

PREPOSITIONAL PHRASES

3b. A *prepositional phrase* is a group of words beginning with a preposition and ending with a noun or pronoun.

Examples of prepositional phrases are:

PREPOSITION	NOUN OR PRONOUN
at	the **store**
for	**them**
among	those **books**

3c. The noun or pronoun which ends the prepositional phrase is the object of the preposition which begins the phrase.

The prepositional phrases in the following sentence are in heavy print.

During the night, cold gusts **of wind** blew **across the prairie.**

Here *night* is the object of the preposition *during*. *Wind* is the object of the preposition *of*. How is the noun *prairie* used? What preposition does it follow?

● EXERCISE 2.   List in order the 20 prepositions in these sentences. After each preposition, write its object. Keep together the words from each sentence.

EXAMPLE   1. **In the morning we will go to the fair.**
         1. **In — morning**
           to — fair

1. Your eyelid is like the shutter of a camera.
2. When you open your eyelids, the retina in your eye reacts to rays of light and takes a picture.
3. The retina is located behind the pupil, which adjusts itself to the prevailing light.
4. In the darkness, the pupils of your eyes expand so that they can admit as much light as possible.
5. In bright light, however, the pupils become small, shutting out light that you do not need for clear vision.
6. When you step out of a dark theater into the sunlight, your eyes adjust themselves within a few seconds.
7. Do you know that pictures of things around you enter the eye upside down?
8. Your brain reverses the images for you.
9. Some people are troubled by nearsightedness.
10. Farsightedness is caused by short eyeballs, which do not let the eye focus on nearby objects.

THE PREPOSITIONAL PHRASE USED AS AN ADJECTIVE

The prepositional phrases in this sentence are used as adjectives because each describes a noun or a pronoun.

A man from Chicago bought six crates of citrus fruit.

The prepositional phrase *from Chicago,* telling *which* man, is used as an adjective modifying the noun *man.* *Of citrus fruit* is also used as an adjective because it

3b-c

modifies the noun *crates*. When a prepositional phrase is used as an adjective it is called an adjective phrase.

3d. An *adjective phrase* modifies a noun or a pronoun.

Study the following pairs of sentences, and notice how the phrases are used as adjectives.

ADJECTIVES	ADJECTIVE PHRASES
The **Dallas** team won.	The team **from Dallas** won.
I lost the **show** tickets.	I lost the tickets **to the show**.
We need a **hunting** knife.	We need a knife **for hunting**.

● EXERCISE 3. Revise the following sentences by using adjective phrases in place of the italicized adjectives.

1. The paper prints *school* news.
2. I have bought some *cat* food.
3. We admired his *rose* garden.
4. The *hall* lamp is broken.
5. The *spring* rains helped the farmers.

THE PREPOSITIONAL PHRASE USED AS AN ADVERB

When a prepositional phrase tells *when*, *where*, *how*, *how much*, or *how far* the action of the verb takes place, then it is used as an adverb and is called an adverb phrase.

EXAMPLES **I dived into the water.** [The adverb phrase *into the water* tells *where* I dived.]
The train arrived at two o'clock. [The adverb phrase *at two o'clock* tells *when* the train arrived.]
He missed the target by a foot. [*By a foot* is an adverb phrase telling *to what extent*.]
By chance he met her yesterday. [*By chance* is an adverb phrase telling *how*.]

3e. An *adverb phrase* modifies a verb, an adjective, or an adverb.

Notice how a prepositional phrase can take the place of an adverb:

ADVERBS	ADVERB PHRASES
She spoke **hastily.**	She spoke **in haste.**
Bruce drives **carefully.**	Bruce drives **with care.**
Sometimes I oversleep.	**At times** I oversleep.

The adverb phrases in the right column above modify verbs. The phrase *in haste* tells how she spoke; *with care* tells how Bruce drives; *at times* tells when I oversleep.

An adverb phrase may also modify an adjective or an adverb.

EXAMPLES   These shoes are too small **for comfort.** [The adverb phrase *for comfort* modifies the adjective *small.*]

Never **in a million years** will he admit defeat! [The adverb phrase *in a million years* modifies the adverb *never.*]

● EXERCISE 4. Make a list of the prepositional phrases used as adverbs in these sentences. After each adverb phrase write the word it modifies. Number your list by sentences, keeping the words from each sentence together.

1. Last Sunday in Chicago it was too hot for words.
2. My friends and I drove to Lincoln Park for a cool outing.
3. At first we ate our big picnic lunch with gusto.
4. Later in the day, however, we walked around the park.
5. A most unusual monument stands near the picnic grounds.
6. This monument shows humanity as it marches forward toward death.

3d-e

7. In Rockefeller Center I once saw another artist's concept of time.
8. Three men are painted on the ceiling; they represent the Past, Present, and Future.
9. No matter where you stand in that room, the Past's eyes are turned away from you.
10. The eyes of the Present, however, look straight at you.

DIAGRAMING ADJECTIVE AND ADVERB PHRASES

The preposition which begins a phrase is placed on a slanting line leading down from the word the phrase modifies. The noun or pronoun which ends the phrase is placed on a horizontal line connected to the slanting line.

Our laboratory at school is furnished with modern equipment.

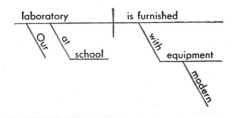

● EXERCISE 5.   Diagram the following sentences.

1. The members of our class went to the art gallery.
2. One painting on the wall commanded our attention.
3. In the picture a group of old women are huddled together.
4. Their mouths sneer at the passers-by.
5. Their tongues obviously speak of evil things.
6. We looked at the painting more closely.
7. The group of women actually forms the face of Satan!
8. Beneath the picture is an explanation.
9. It consists of a single word.
10. The word of explanation is "Gossip."

Verbals and Verbal Phrases

A verbal is a word formed from a verb but used as another part of speech. There are three kinds of verbals: *participles*, *gerunds*, and *infinitives*.

THE PARTICIPLE

3f. A *participle* is a word formed from a verb and used as an adjective.

The participle acts as both a verb and an adjective. It is half verb and half adjective; it is a "verbal adjective."

EXAMPLES **The speeding** jet broke through the sound barrier.
Encouraged, we worked even harder than before.

In the first sentence, *speeding* is part verb because it carries the action of the verb *speed*. It is also part adjective because it modifies the noun *jet*. In the second sentence, *encouraged*, formed from the verb *encourage*, modifies the pronoun *we*. Both *speeding* and *encouraged*, then, are participles.

(1) Participles which show action in the present are called *present participles*. They end in –ing.

Present participles are used as adjectives; they modify a noun or a pronoun.

PRESENT PARTICIPLES **Waiting** patiently, we played **guessing** games.
The screaming siren startled us.

Waiting is a present participle because it modifies the pronoun *we*. The participle *screaming* modifies the noun *siren*. Both *waiting* and *screaming*, then, are used as adjectives. In the first example, how is *guessing* used?

▶ NOTE: Not all words ending in –*ing* are participles. When used as part of a verb phrase, a word ending in –*ing* is not a participle.

3f

VERB PHRASES   Henry **was waiting** for the signal.

She **has been studying** for an hour.

Here *waiting* and *studying* are parts of action verbs; they do not modify anything.

(2) Participles which show action in the past are called *past participles.*

Past participles regularly end in *–d, –ed, –t, –n,* or *–en.*

EXAMPLES   The **embarrassed** actor missed his cue. [The past participle *embarrassed* modifies the noun *actor*.]

Visibly **shaken,** he was unable to speak. [*Shaken* is a past participle modifying the pronoun *he*.]

● EXERCISE 6. Number from 1 to 10 on your paper. Make a list of the participles in the following sentences. After the participle write the noun or pronoun modified. Be prepared to tell whether each is a present or a past participle.

1. The radio announcer spoke sadly to the listening audience.
2. His trained voice held them in its spell.
3. "I have distressing news to relate," he told them.
4. "Mudville has lost the game; the defeated team is in deep disgrace."
5. Pausing briefly, he went on.
6. "Overconfident and swaggering, our proud players made one mistake after another.
7. "They swung their bats so recklessly that the opposing pitcher easily struck them out.
8. "Angered, the few men who tried to reach base never succeeded.
9. "Therefore, our planned victory celebration will not take place.
10. "And now," he concluded, "an exciting word from our sponsor,"

THE PARTICIPIAL PHRASE

3g. **When a participle introduces a group of related words, all of which act together as an adjective, this word group is called a *participial phrase*.**

The participial phrase in each of the following sentences is in heavy print. An arrow points to the noun or pronoun which the phrase modifies.

1. **Running up the tree,** the squirrel outwitted the dog.

2. **Annoyed by our noise,** he complained to our parents.

3. I noticed a pipe **leaking in the basement.**

4. Frank, **tackled hard on the fifty-yard line,** was seriously injured.

● EXERCISE 7. Use the following participial phrases in sentences of your own. Be sure to place each phrase very close to the noun or pronoun it modifies. If you use a participial phrase to begin a sentence, put a comma after the phrase, and write the word modified after the comma.

EXAMPLE   1. balancing a book on his head
          1. Balancing a book on his head, Larry walked the tightrope.

1. expressing his approval
2. blaming me for the accident
3. buried beside the edge of the river
4. pointing to the referee
5. acting like a bashful chipmunk
6. left alone in the dark
7. swallowing the sandwich in large chunks
8. puzzled by his sarcastic remarks
9. trained to respect authority
10. holding the medicine in one hand and the squirming kitten in the other

3g

THE GERUND

3h. The *gerund* is a word formed from a verb and used as a noun.

A gerund is part noun and part verb. It is formed from a verb. Like nouns, gerunds are used as subjects, complements, or objects.

GERUNDS USED AS SUBJECTS   **Learning** can be fun.
Studying will certainly keep low grades away.

GERUNDS USED AS COMPLEMENTS OR OBJECTS   His favorite pastime is **swimming.** [predicate nominative]
Jack enjoys **hunting.** [direct object]
That tool is used for **drilling.** [object of the preposition]

Gerunds always end in *–ing,* but not all words ending in *–ing* are gerunds; they may be present participles or part of a verb phrase. For instance, there are three words ending in *–ing* in the following sentence, but only one of them, *singing,* is a gerund.

Watching the judges in the balcony, Gwen was *trying* to win the contest with her loud **singing.**

Watching is a present participle modifying *Gwen,* and *trying* is part of a verb phrase. Only *singing,* used as object of the preposition *with,* is a gerund.

● EXERCISE 8.   After you have listed each gerund in the sentences below, write how each is used: *subject, predicate nominative, direct object,* or *object of the preposition.*

1. Many students enjoy playing basketball.
2. The first requirement of the game is fast thinking.
3. Rhythm is needed for skillful dribbling.
4. Smooth jumping often helps in scoring.
5. Precise timing is one of the most important abilities of a good basketball player.

THE GERUND PHRASE

3i. **A** *gerund phrase* **is a phrase containing a gerund.**

The gerund phrases in these sentences are in heavy print. Notice that each one is used as a noun.

1. **The loud knocking at the gate** frightened Macbeth. [subject]
2. My pet peeve is **going to bed at nine o'clock.** [predicate nominative]
3. I also dislike **getting up early in the morning.** [direct object]
4. He makes money by **selling newspapers.** [object of the preposition]

● EXERCISE 9. Write 4 sentences, each containing one or more gerund phrases. Be prepared to tell how each one is used in the sentence.

THE INFINITIVE

3j. **An** *infinitive* **is a verbal consisting of** *to* **followed by a verb.**

To buy, to carry, to say, to be seen, to have done are examples of infinitives. Infinitives may be used as nouns, adjectives, or adverbs.

INFINITIVES USED AS NOUNS **To question** is **to learn.** [*To question* is the subject, and *to learn* is the predicate nominative.]
  We soon agreed to follow. [*To follow* is direct object of the verb *agreed.*]
  Betty was about to faint. [*To faint* is object of the preposition *about.*]

INFINITIVES USED AS ADJECTIVES **We needed a guide to lead.** [*To lead* modifies the noun *guide.*]
  That is one way to go. [*To go* describes the noun *way.*]

3h-j

INFINITIVES USED AS ADVERBS   **She put the cake in the oven to bake.** [*To bake* modifies the verb *put.*]
My dog is too old to learn. [*To learn* modifies the adjective *old.*]

THE INFINITIVE PHRASE

3k. A phrase which contains an infinitive is an *infinitive phrase.*

Infinitive phrases may be used in the same ways as infinitives. Study these examples of infinitive phrases.

1. **To interrupt a speaker** is impolite. [noun]
2. Sara has gone **to visit her aunt in Arizona.** [adverb]
3. I was afraid **to jump into the deep water.** [adverb]

▶ CAUTION: *To* plus a noun or a pronoun — *to him, to the store* — is a prepositional phrase, not an infinitive. An infinitive consists of *to* plus a *verb.*

● EXERCISE 10.   Make a list of the infinitives and infinitive phrases in the following sentences. After each one give its use: *noun, adjective,* or *adverb.* Be able to give reasons for your answers.

1. To give advice is easy.
2. We wanted to solve the problems.
3. Ned plans to go.
4. I went to the gymnasium to find him.
5. One way to keep a secret is to forget it.
6. That is an interesting book to read.
7. According to an old proverb, two women may be able to keep a secret if one of them is dead.
8. She decided to wait for her.
9. The best way to have a friend is to be one.
10. The door is not easy to open.

● EXERCISE 11.   Write 10 original sentences using at least one infinitive phrase in each sentence. Underline each phrase, and be able to tell how it is used in the sentence.

● REVIEW EXERCISE A. There are 20 verbals in the following paragraphs. Make a list of them. In class be able to tell how each one is used. Number the verbals according to sentences.

EXAMPLE   1. **Turning to Channel 8, I started to watch the wrestling matches.**
    1. **Turning**
       to watch
       ~~**wrestling**~~

1. Having Hephzibah Schleirbeck for a name, I have gone through life as a kind of handicapped person. 2. Knowing that my name is unusual, I am patient with strangers. 3. After all, pronouncing or spelling Hephzibah Schleirbeck is not easy.

4. One day a friend, excited about a new family car, tried to tell me about it by making a long-distance telephone call. 5. Not remembering my number, she spelled my name over and over again for the operator. 6. Exhausted by efforts to understand, the operator remarked, "It seems to me the number would be easier to remember than the name."

7. When I am calling the dentist, I sometimes get a quick appointment by changing my name to Mary Smith or Jane Jones. 8. Occasionally, however, I forget to answer to Mary or Jane. 9. When this happens, the embarrassed dentist looks at me strangely. 10. He seems to think I'm a criminal using an alias. 11. I must find another way to change my name. 12. My one desire is to marry a man named John Henry.

The Clause

31. A group of words that contains a verb and its subject and is used as a part of a sentence is called a *clause*. **3k-1**

The difference between a clause and a phrase is that a clause has a verb *and* a subject; whereas a phrase does not.

PHRASES   **with the wild stallion** [no subject or verb]
          has been snoring [a verb without a subject]
CLAUSES   **when the wild stallion swam the river** [a subject *and* a verb: *stallion swam*]
          who has been snoring [subject: *who;* verb: *has been snoring*]

DISTINGUISHING BETWEEN MAIN AND SUBORDINATE CLAUSES

3m. **A *main* (or *independent*) *clause* expresses a completed thought and can stand by itself as a sentence.**

A main (independent) clause standing by itself is called a sentence, but when written as a part of a sentence, it is called a main clause.

SENTENCES   **My neighbors have sold their home.**
            They will move to Denver next week.

Each of these sentences has a verb and a subject and expresses a completed thought. When these completed thoughts are combined into one long sentence, they become main clauses, *parts* of a sentence.

MAIN CLAUSES   **My neighbors have sold their home,** and **they will move to Denver next week.**

Main clauses are frequently joined by co-ordinating conjunctions: *and, but, or, nor, for.*

3n. **A *subordinate* (or *dependent*) *clause* does not express a completed thought and cannot stand alone.**

A subordinate clause depends upon a main clause to make the meaning complete

SUBORDINATE CLAUSE   If she bakes a cake ...   [What then?]

 Subordinate Clause   Main Clause
SENTENCE   If she bakes a cake, we can have a party.

● EXERCISE 12.   Some of the following groups of words are subordinate clauses incorrectly written as sentences. Some are complete sentences. After numbering from 1 to 10, identify each group of words by writing either *sentence* or *subordinate clause* after the corresponding number on your paper.

1. As we were traveling in the Pacific Northwest.
2. We left Portland behind and drove through a beautiful valley.
3. Which is located near the Willamette River.
4. In the valley were farms and orchards, but farther south were towering mountains and forests.
5. After we had stopped and taken pictures of Crater Lake.
6. Father yelled, "All aboard! Eureka! We're going to find it!"
7. When we reached Eureka.
8. Which is on the coast of California.
9. We spent a long time at a huge lumber mill.
10. If you ever stop overnight in Eureka.

RELATIVE PRONOUNS IN SUBORDINATE CLAUSES

3o. **A relative pronoun is a pronoun which introduces a subordinate clause and relates to another word or idea in the sentence.**

The relative pronouns are *who*, *whom*, *whose*, *which*, and *that*. They are called *relative* because they *relate* to other words or ideas in the sentence. In the examples

3m-o

below, the relative pronouns are the subjects of the subordinate clauses which they introduce.

Bananas that ripen on the tree are often ruined by insects. [The relative pronoun *that* introduces the subordinate clause and relates to the word *bananas*.]

A highway which has six lanes is usually heavily traveled [*Which* relates to *highway*.]

Who, *whom*, and *whose* relate to people only; *which* relates to things only; *that* relates to people or things.

● EXERCISE 13. List on your paper each relative pronoun in the following sentences. After each pronoun, give the word to which it relates.

1. Terriers are dogs that can jump very high.
2. Shirley, who is my best friend, once visited a kennel.
3. The kennel, which is only five miles south of town, was filled with lively terriers.
4. Every dog bounced up and down like a springboard that has loose hinges.
5. The man who owns the dogs said, "I really don't feed them Mexican jumping beans."

Relative pronouns may also be used as objects and predicate nominatives, as you will learn in the following paragraph.

COMPLEMENTS AND MODIFIERS IN SUBORDINATE CLAUSES

The verb in a subordinate clause may have a direct object, a predicate nominative, or a predicate adjective. A subordinate clause may also contain modifiers.

Study the make-up of these subordinate clauses:

Buy a sled that can take rough treatment. [*Treatment* is the direct object of the verb *can take*. *Rough*, of course, modifies *treatment*.]

We didn't know who she was. [The relative pronoun *who* is the predicate nominative.]

If the hero of the play is sick, will John take the part?
[*Sick* is the predicate adjective, and *of the play* is an adjective
phrase modifying *hero*.]

This is the doctor whom you called. [The relative pronoun *whom* is the direct object of the verb *called*.]

● EXERCISE 14. Find and list on your paper the
subordinate clauses in these sentences. Underline
each verb twice and each subject once. If the verb
in the subordinate clause has a complement, identify
the complement by writing above it *d.o.* for *direct
object*, *p.n.* for *predicate nominative*, or *p.a.* for *predicate
adjective*. Be able to explain the use of any modifier in
each subordinate clause.

1. When humid air becomes cool, a fog often forms.
2. Fog looks like a cloud that has lost its way.
3. Often the warm sun, which evaporates the moisture in
   the air, causes a fog to disappear.
4. Mr. Randolph, who is our weatherman, forecasts smog
   for tomorrow.
5. Since smog is a mixture of fog and smoke, it usually
   outlasts simple fog.

The Adjective Clause

**3p. An *adjective clause* is a subordinate clause
used as an adjective to modify a noun or a
pronoun.**

An adjective clause is usually introduced by a
relative pronoun that is placed very close to the word
that the clause modifies. The adjective clauses in the
following sentences are in heavy print, and the arrow
points to the noun or pronoun that each clause
modifies.

I need a coat **that is light and warm.**

The answers **which I gave** were wrong.

3p

● EXERCISE 15.   Write 10 sentences using subordinate clauses as adjectives. Draw an arrow from each adjective clause to the noun or pronoun it modifies.

● EXERCISE 16.   The groups of sentences below are choppy and babyish. Revise them by using adjective clauses to make each pair of sentences one long sentence. Remember that the clause must come as near as possible to the word it modifies. (Be sure to use a main clause for the more important idea.)

EXAMPLES   1. The horse has a broken leg. The animal is standing near the gate.
　　　　　　1. The horse that is standing near the gate has a broken leg.
　　　　　　2. The car was a new red convertible. It plunged into the heavy moving van.
　　　　　　2. The car, which was a new red convertible, plunged into the heavy moving van.

1. I fell madly in love with the artist. He lives next door.
2. I stumbled over a scooter. It was on the doorstep.
3. My father paid over a hundred dollars for the chair. The chair is in the bedroom.
4. A monkey lost its temper. It began throwing rocks at us.
5. The tall man coaches our football team. He is wearing a green tie.

The Adverb Clause

3q. An *adverb clause* is a subordinate clause used as an adverb.

An adverb clause tells *how, when, where, why, how much,* or *under what conditions* the action of the main verb takes place.

EXAMPLES   **After he had thought it over,** he apologized. [The adverb clause *After he had thought it over* tells *when* he apologized.]

Because she felt dizzy, Pauline sat down for a while. [*Because she felt dizzy* tells *why* Pauline sat down.]

If it rains tomorrow, we will postpone the picnic. [*If it rains tomorrow* tells *under what conditions* we will postpone the picnic.]

SUBORDINATING CONJUNCTIONS

To *subordinate* means to reduce something to a position of less importance, to a *sub order*. A *subordinating conjunction* introduces a subordinate clause, which is of less emphasis than a main clause.

Become thoroughly familiar with this list of subordinating conjunctions.[1]

after	before	unless
although	if	until
as	in order that	when
as if	since	whenever
as long as	so that	where
as soon as	than	wherever
because	though	while

These conjunctions usually introduce adverb clauses.

● EXERCISE 17.   After numbering from 1 to 10, write the subordinating conjunction and the last word of each adverb clause in the following sentences; then write what the clause tells: when, where, how, why, how much, under what conditions?

EXAMPLES   1. When the telephone rang, I answered it.
  1. When — rang   when
  2. I will leave so that you can study.
  2. so that — study   why

1. If you wish to be a conversational bore at a party, do these things.

[1] As you know, *after, before, since, until,* and *as* may also be used as prepositions.

2. When another person is speaking, interrupt him.
3. As soon as he starts telling a joke, you can steal his thunder by giving away the punch line.
4. You can then tell better jokes after he stops trying to be funny.
5. Later you can change the subject so that you can brag about yourself.
6. While you are talking about your heroic deeds or keen intelligence, bring in as many uninteresting details as possible.
7. Before you tell about saving a child's life, you might spend a half hour talking about your strong muscles.
8. Whenever the occasion arises, you should complain to your hostess and criticize her guests.
9. Unless you monopolize every conversation, you won't be a professional "party pooper."
10. Enjoy yourself as you crowd others off the floor, because you will probably never be invited again.

● EXERCISE 18. Write 10 sentences of your own using the following subordinate clauses as adverbs. (When it begins a sentence, an adverb clause is usually followed by a comma.)

EXAMPLE   1. as soon as we had finished eating
           1. As soon as we had finished eating, the cab driver honked impatiently.

1. although it has not quit snowing
2. if he should make a home run now
3. unless my father changes his mind
4. so that it will be a complete surprise
5. if the concrete has too much water in it
6. as if he had just seen a monster from Mars
7. after you add the eggs to the mixture
8. when he was leaving the theater
9. while the electricity was off
10. since the house was supposed to be haunted

The Noun Clause

3r. A *noun clause* is a subordinate clause used as a noun.

Like any noun, a noun clause may be used as a subject, a complement, or an object.

Study the structure of the following sentences.

Nouns	*Noun Clauses*
SUBJECT His **decisions** are important.	**What he decides** is important.
PREDICATE NOMINATIVE The champion will be the best **fighter**.	The champion will be **whoever fights best**.
DIRECT OBJECT She knows our **secret**.	She knows **what our secret is**.
INDIRECT OBJECT They give each **arrival** a name tag.	They give **whoever comes** a name tag.
OBJECT OF A PREPOSITION I will vote for the **sophomores**.	I will vote for **whoever is a sophomore**.

Noun clauses are usually introduced by *that, what, whatever, who, whoever, whom,* and *whomever.*

● EXERCISE 19. List on your paper the first and the last word of each noun clause in these sentences. Then tell how the noun clause is used: *subject, predicate nominative, direct object, indirect object,* or *object of a preposition.* (You will not find noun clauses in every sentence.)

EXAMPLE   1. She said that she likes to play tennis.
　　　　　 1. that — tennis   direct object

3r

1. What I like best about a rodeo is the excitement.

2. My cousin Lynn often talks about what he used to do as a rodeo rider.
3. He will give whoever is interested an exciting account of his adventures.
4. One time in Iowa the other cowboys knew that "Five Minutes till Midnight" was too dangerous a horse for anyone to ride.
5. That he had the courage to ride the wild horse was what Lynn wanted to prove to everyone.
6. The tense crowd watched Lynn as he jumped upon the back of the horse that no cowboy had ever ridden before.
7. He won the prize money for what he did; he stayed on the bucking horse until the whistle blew.
8. Upon hearing the whistle, Lynn knew that he had won.
9. The second that Lynn relaxed, however, the angry stallion tossed him high into the air.
10. Whoever saw Lynn sail through space that day will never forget how he turned a flip in mid-air and then landed safely on his feet.

● REVIEW EXERCISE B.   After numbering from 1 to 20, classify the italicized subordinate clauses in the following paragraphs by writing *adjective*, *adverb*, or *noun* after the proper number on your paper. Be able to give reasons for your answers.

All around you there are millions of things (1) *that you cannot see*, (2) *although you may have an excellent pair of eyes.* (3) *As we try to pry into the nature of the invisible world around us*, we make use of telescopes and microscopes. (4) *What these inventions can reveal* is astonishing. (5) *If you are not convinced*, then you should do (6) *what we did in the laboratory last week:* look at the leg of a fly under a microscope. Hundreds of germs, (7) *which it is impossible to see with the naked eye*, infest the fly's leg. Under the microscope, (8) *what you least expect* suddenly becomes visible. The smallest particle of living matter has cells (9) *that are made of protoplasm.* In the center of a cell is a nucleus. Certainly the microscope is a kind of "open sesame" to another world.

According to scientists (10) *who know*, the nucleus of an atom, (11) *which no human eye has ever seen*, is almost too small to imagine. Some say, however, (12) *that we can estimate the size of atoms*. (13) *If we could place 250,000,000 hydrogen atoms in a row*, they would be about an inch long. Of course, (14) *when a hydrogen bomb explodes*, the destruction (15) *which follows* shows (16) *what man can do by splitting those invisible atoms*.

(17) *As time passes*, men will probably find out more and more about the unseen. New inventions may show us (18) *what the inside of an atom really looks like*. (19) *As we continue to explore the invisible world around us*, we should always be concerned about (20) *how we can use the new knowledge for the benefit of mankind*.

Sentences Classified According to Structure [2]

3s. Classified according to structure, there are four kinds of sentences: *simple, compound, complex,* and *compound-complex*.

(1) A *simple sentence* has one main clause and no subordinate clauses.

EXAMPLE   At the end of the day, we gathered around the campfire to tell ghost stories.

(2) A *compound sentence* has two or more main clauses but no subordinate clauses.

EXAMPLE   Clyde wants to become a lawyer, and Lucy is studying to be a welfare worker.

(3) A *complex sentence* has one main clause and one or more subordinate clauses.

EXAMPLE   If you wash the sweater, it will stretch.

[2] For classification of sentences according to purpose, see pages 41–42.

3s

(4) A *compound-complex sentence* contains two or more main clauses and one or more subordinate clauses.

EXAMPLE   Since I had seen him the day before, I knew that he was unhappy, but I did not guess that he would give up his plans.

● EXERCISE 20.   After numbering from 1 to 10, classify the following sentences according to structure.

1. One day last week while I was riding a bus in Chicago, I noticed two career girls.
2. Not far from me, they were standing in the crowded aisle.
3. Fortunately I was comfortably seated, and I enjoyed listening to their conversation.
4. One of the girls looked as though she were about sixteen years old.
5. Her companion, about two years older, quietly fretted as she tried to keep her balance on the swaying bus, and she was obviously bored with the long speeches of her younger friend, who chattered enthusiastically about "making good in the big city."
6. This ambitious girl talked about her job at a shoe factory, and she discussed the personality of her boss.
7. Clinging to a narrow strap with one hand and clutching the back of my seat with the other, the older girl remained silent.
8. "I'm going to work hard," the first girl continued, "so that I can deserve a promotion, for all that I want in life is to get ahead."
9. Her weary companion finally spoke.
10. "All that I want is to get a seat."

● REVIEW EXERCISE C.   Number from 1 to 10, and then copy the first word and the last word of each italicized phrase or clause in the paragraphs below. After each, write the correct one of the following identifications: *participial phrase*, *gerund phrase*, *infinitive phrase*, *adjective clause*, *adverb clause*, *noun clause*.

(1) *Watching the river yesterday,* I started (2) *thinking about the moods of streams and oceans.* I believe (3) *that each body of water has its own personality.*

(4) *Pushed forward by high winds,* ocean waves often crash angrily against the shore, (5) *as though they are jealous of the earth's stability.* Unlike turbulent oceans, the gay streams (6) *which frolic through the ravines of the Rockies* are content (7) *to use the earth as a playground.*

(8) *Because oceans and streams really aren't like people,* I am imagining things. Men like Matthew Arnold, however, have written poems about (9) *the churning of muddy waters* and about the melancholy sea's "eternal note of sadness." (10) *To look upon an ocean or a stream as a personality* is not so fantastic after all.

GOOD USAGE ━━━━━━━━━━━━━

being as, being that: Use *since* or *because.*

WRONG   **Being as** it's getting late, the catfish should start biting.

RIGHT   **Since** it's getting late, the catfish should start biting.

WRONG   **Being that** we're tired, let's go to bed now and take a fresh start in the morning.

RIGHT   **Because** we're tired, let's go to bed now and take a fresh start in the morning.

when, where: Do not use *when* or *where* incorrectly in writing a definition.

WRONG   An intermission is **when** the actors and the audience take a short break.

RIGHT   An intermission is a short break for the actors and the audience.

WRONG   An aquarium is **where** fish are kept.

RIGHT   An aquarium is a place in which fish are kept.

PART TWO

USAGE

CHAPTER 4

Writing Complete Sentences

SENTENCE FRAGMENTS AND RUN–ON SENTENCES

The Sentence Fragment

After studying Chapter 3, you should be able to tell the difference between a sentence and an incomplete thought. You ought to know that a *part* of a sentence (such as an isolated phrase or a subordinate clause by itself) should never be written as though it were a sentence, with a capital at the beginning and a period at the end. If your compositions still contain fragments, however, then you need to study this chapter carefully.

The sentence fragment is a separated piece of a sentence that does not express a completed idea. It is often written as a kind of afterthought and follows a complete sentence.

1. The teacher said that the test was too hard. **That he had graded it leniently.**
2. Clara and Betty learned to like each other. **Working together for a common goal.**

In the first example above, the subordinate clause that is incorrectly punctuated as a complete sentence is a fragment, only a piece of an idea. *That he had graded it leniently* does not make sense *by itself;* the meaning is not clear. *Working together for a common goal,* in the second example, is also a fragment; it has no subject and no verb, and it does not express a complete thought. These fragments should be joined to the sentences preceding them.

1. The teacher said that the test was too hard **and that he had graded it leniently.**
2. **Working together for a common goal,** Clara and Betty learned to like each other.

As these examples show, a fragment may be joined to the end of the sentence preceding it or may be placed at the beginning of the sentence.

● EXERCISE 1.   The sentence fragments below are italicized. Eliminate each fragment by attaching it to the sentence which precedes it. Write your sentences after the proper numbers on your paper.

1. We like to do things. *When we can do them well.*
2. Carol counts her calories. *Hoping to lose weight.*
3. I live in Chicago. *A very windy city.*
4. On a stormy day Benjamin Franklin experimented with a kite. *Because he wanted to show the identity of electricity and lightning.*
5. I waited for a long silver bass to strike my bait. *After I had thrown my chugger plug about twenty yards.*
6. We did an especially good job of mowing and trimming the grass. *Trying to deserve a generous tip.*
7. Before my history class I usually take time to gulp down a coke. *Which certainly tastes good on a hot afternoon.*
8. As the drill came closer, I wanted to shove it away. *To tell the dentist that I had changed my mind.*
9. In Wyoming we traveled through Cody. *A city named for W. F. Cody. Better known as "Buffalo Bill."*
10. A legendary American figure is P. T. Barnum. *A show-man who believed that a sucker is born every minute.*

● EXERCISE 2.   How good is your "sentence sense"? Find out by deciding whether or not each group of words below is a sentence. Number from 1 to 10 on your paper. After the proper number, write *F* for *fragment* or *S* for *sentence*.

1. Asking for permission to leave class early.
2. To tell you all about my experiences in Canada last summer.
3. On the other side of the mountain is a beautiful valley.
4. But can you prove it?
5. After rehearsal we got together and memorized our lines.
6. Lawrence, playing as defensive linebacker for the Indians.
7. Playing the piano is her hobby.
8. An old two-story house with spacious rooms designed to accommodate a large family of a dozen or more.
9. In the spring, when the warm sun shines upon the fresh green beauty of the earth and when red tulips wave in the March winds.
10. When Mother said, "Now I am going to take the bull by the horns and show you how the cow ate the cabbage."

COMMON TYPES OF SENTENCE FRAGMENTS

4a. The subordinate clause must not be written as a sentence.

A subordinate clause always depends upon a main clause to complete its meaning. Notice that these subordinate clauses do not express complete thoughts.

After you comb your hair   [Then what?]
If she arrives by nine o'clock   [What will happen?]

Main clauses must be added to complete the meaning.

Subordinate Clause   Main Clause
After you comb your hair, straighten your tie.

Main Clause   Subordinate Clause
We'll take Sue with us if she arrives by nine o'clock.

Remember that relative pronouns (*which, that, who, whom, whose*) and subordinating conjunctions (see the list on page 77) introduce subordinate clauses. These little words are very important; they can change a complete thought to a fragment.

SENTENCE   **Claude told the truth.**
FRAGMENTS   **Unless** Claude told the truth
                Although Claude told the truth
                Since Claude told the truth

● EXERCISE 3.   Using a separate sheet of paper, fill in the following blanks with 10 main clauses that will logically complete the meaning of these subordinate clauses.

1. If you stay under water too long, ——.
2. When the bell rings, ——.
3. While it is raining, ——.
4. Before you join any organization, ——.
5. —— who is now in Europe.
6. —— that he had gone to the library.
7. —— since we will see him Tuesday.
8. —— which won the game for us.
9. —— because he had forgotten his keys.
10. As soon as he had apologized, ——.

● EXERCISE 4.   Find the 10 fragments in these paragraphs. Each one is a subordinate clause incorrectly written as a sentence. Copy the paragraphs, attaching these fragments to the related main clauses.

Theodore Roosevelt probably knew that a weasel has sly habits. That it can suck out the inside of an egg and do practically no damage to the shell. A person looking at the empty shell can never guess that it has been robbed. Because the weasel evades punishment by shrewd maneuvering. Teddy Roosevelt associated weasels with words. Which are sometimes evasive. Since they can be understood in two ways.

4a

My girl friend uses "weasel words." Whenever I ask her an important question. As we were leaving the show the other night, for example. I asked her a simple question. Which was, "Did you enjoy the movie?"

She answered hesitantly, "Well, yes — and no." What was I to think? I do wish that she would say what she means. And that she would mean what she says.

Another time, I asked her if she would like to go steady with me. Until we graduate from high school. Again she replied without answering, "Well, more — or less." Every time that she weasels out of one of my questions, she smiles at me charmingly. As if she is thinking, "No boy can ever understand the mind of a girl."

4b. Participial phrases and gerund phrases must not be written as sentences.

Since a phrase does not have a subject and a verb, it cannot express a completed thought. A sentence has a subject *and* a verb. Phrases are fragments, *parts* of a sentence.

Do not write participial and gerund phrases as sentences. As you learned in Chapter 3, present participles and gerunds are verbals ending in *–ing*. Past participles usually end in *–d*, *–ed*, *–t*, *–n*, *–en*. By themselves, these verbals are fragments. Like subordinate clauses, they depend upon main clauses to make their meaning complete.

FRAGMENTS   1. **Turning the corner on two wheels**
              2. **Chosen by the people**

SENTENCES

Participial Phrase
1. **Turning the corner on two wheels,**

                    Main Clause
                    the jalopy roared down Main Street.

Main Clause   Participial Phrase
2. **The rebels wanted a leader chosen by the people.**

● EXERCISE 5. Revise the 10 fragments in the following paragraph by attaching them logically to main clauses. Copy the paragraph, changing the punctuation so that there will be no verbal phrases standing by themselves.

Blown about like a reed in the wind. Bobby could never make a decision. His family and friends pointed out this fault. By criticizing him constantly. One day last week, however, Bobby did think, decide, and act quickly. Proving himself to everyone. One of his friends, Tim Ellis, was standing in the middle of the street. Flying a kite. Not seeing an approaching car. Tim didn't get out of its way. Having no time to warn Tim. Bobby dashed forward. He saved Tim's life. By pushing his friend out of the path of the speeding car. The car, however, did hit Bobby. Breaking his leg. And bruising his face. Bobby is now a hero. Praised and honored by all.

● EXERCISE 6. Below are verbal phrases standing alone, incorrectly written as sentences. Write 10 complete sentences by adding a main clause to each of the verbal phrases.

1. Getting there early.
2. Before going to bed.
3. Like riding a stubborn donkey.
4. Listening attentively in class.
5. Grabbing a fly swatter.
6. Parched by the hot sun.
7. Determined to win his approval.
8. After paying the check.
9. Without even saying good-by.
10. Hobnobbing over a chocolate soda.

● REVIEW EXERCISE A. Some of the following groups of words are sentences; others are subordinate clauses or verbal phrases incorrectly written as sentences. Number on your paper from 1 to 25. Place *S* after the corresponding number of each complete sen-

4b

tence. Write *F* after the corresponding number of each fragment. Be prepared to tell how you would correct each fragment by making it a part of a related sentence.

1. In 1628 William Harvey published his new theory.
2. Which explained the circulation of the blood by the motion of the heart.
3. Stated twelve years earlier.
4. This theory set forth the idea that the heart is a kind of pump.
5. Forcing the blood through the veins.
6. Medical men began studying the circulation of the blood.
7. Since Harvey's discovery, they have learned that the blood gives life to cells in the body.
8. These cells die without the supplies.
9. Furnished by the blood.
10. Blood also cleans out cells.
11. By carrying away waste products.
12. That are poisonous.
13. In the blood stream are red blood cells.
14. Which are carriers of oxygen.
15. Provided by the lungs.
16. Every day new red blood cells are born.
17. Because old ones wear out.
18. There are also white cells in the blood stream.
19. The white cells destroy harmful germs.
20. By encircling them.
21. Some cells die as they fight the germs.
22. Too many white cells in the blood stream may indicate a serious infection.
23. This could be a bad appendix.
24. When they are needed to fight hordes of germs.
25. The body manufactures a great number of white cells.

THE APPOSITIVE

An *appositive* is a word (or group of words) which means the same thing as the noun it follows. Usually it identifies or explains the noun.

EXAMPLES   **Have you met my cousin, Alfred Morris?**   [*Alfred Morris*, an appositive, identifies the noun *cousin*.]

The Story of My Life, **an autobiography by Helen Keller,** tells about the education of a blind and deaf girl.   [*An autobiography by Helen Keller* is an appositive explaining the name of the book.]

4c. An appositive must not be written as a sentence.

An appositive cannot stand by itself as a completed thought. It should always be attached to the noun it explains or identifies. Notice that the appositives above are set off by commas.

FRAGMENT   After the speech, we had an interview with Mr. Barnes. **The mayor of our town.**

SENTENCE   After the speech, we had an interview with Mr. Barnes, **the mayor of our town.**

● EXERCISE 7.   The appositives below are incorrectly written as sentences. After numbering on your paper from 1 to 5, show how you would punctuate the groups of words. Do not rewrite the sentences. After the proper number, write the word before each inserted mark of punctuation as well as the word following it.

EXAMPLES   1. We ate lunch at a downtown café. A little hole in the wall on Fourth Street.

1. **café, a**

2. Mr. Melton gave us a map of Oak Ridge. An engineer at the plant.

2. **Melton, an — plant, gave**

1. You should know Ralph Simons. The custodian at our school.

2. We all like Mr. Warren. Our new history teacher.

3. After school we hiked over to Mr. Downing's ranch. A place that is a boy's paradise.
4. There we enjoyed riding his horses. Beautiful and well-trained animals.
5. Stubby eagerly pecked at the corn in Paul's hand. My little pet rooster.

4d. Avoid other sentence fragments.

Below is a list of other common types of fragments, ranging from isolated infinitive phrases to unattached items in a series. Although you do not need to learn the names of these, you should be able to recognize them as incomplete ideas so that you can avoid using sentence fragments in your compositions.

1. I am determined to become a better student. **To study harder than ever before.**
2. Acorns are eaten not only by squirrels. **But also by birds and pigs.**
3. He forgot where he was. **Lost his temper.**
4. The people of Grand Rapids, a city in Michigan, manufacture many products. **Such as chemicals, furniture, metal products, and equipment for railroads.**

Each fragment above should be joined to the preceding main clause. Number 2, for example, should be rewritten in this way: *Acorns are eaten not only by squirrels but also by birds and pigs.* How would you revise the other fragments?

● EXERCISE 8.   Rewrite each item below so that there will be no fragment in it. Place the fragments with related main clauses.

1. My best friend is Fred Thompson. A boy who likes other people.
2. I need some school supplies. Such as a notebook, a package of typing paper, and a ruler.
3. Miss Brown asked us to write a composition. To suggest ways of improving our school.

4. I like all kinds of sports. Especially tennis and baseball.
5. We'll need refreshments. Like brownies and hot chocolate.
6. This all-purpose cleanser brightens pots and pans. For instance, copper-bottomed skillets.
7. I don't know how to cook good vegetables. To keep them from tasting flat.
8. On Saturdays I not only help Mom around the house. But also work with Dad in the yard.
9. Charles outgrew his childish temper tantrums. Became a country preacher.
10. I learned many things at camp. Like how to put up a tent.

The Run-on Sentence

When you punctuate a fragment as a sentence, you apparently do not know what a sentence is. You use unnecessary capitals and periods. When you write run-on sentences, you do not know when a sentence ends. You use commas (or no mark of punctuation) instead of periods.

IMPORTANT END PUNCTUATION

4e. A sentence should be followed by an end mark: the period, question mark, or exclamation point.

Sentences should never be run together without punctuation.

WRONG **Where are Riff and Raff those cats won't come when I call them.**

RIGHT **Where are Riff and Raff? Those cats won't come when I call them.**

The comma should never take the place of an important end mark like the period, question mark, or exclamation point.

4d-e

WRONG   In the early spring the people in town are annoyed
         by a new kind of grass that spoils the beauty of their
         lawns, ranchers are glad to see this "rescue" grass
         cover their pastures.

RIGHT   In the early spring the people in town are annoyed
         by a new kind of grass that spoils the beauty of their
         lawns. Ranchers are glad to see this "rescue" grass
         cover their pastures.

● EXERCISE 9.   You will find the following passages
hard to read because run-on sentences always interfere with the clear expression of ideas. After you have
decided where each sentence should end, write the
last word of each completed idea on your paper.
Place a period after the word, and then write the
first word of the next sentence, beginning it with a
capital letter.

EXAMPLE   1. We had planned an all-day picnic in a pasture
              near the river, just after we arrived there, how-
              ever, the girls built a fire to roast marshmallows
              the strong wind carried sparks to the tall, dry
              grass, we spent the day fighting fire.
           1. **river. Just**
              marshmallows. The
              grass. We

1. Today is a lazy Friday, in English class I find it hard
   to keep my mind on punctuation and grammar outside
   the sun is shining it is a wonderful time for being outdoors, for my teacher, however, the spring sunshine
   seems to be a signal for hard work this is her medicine
   for curing spring fever.
2. It is fun to grow ornamental peppers, if you have one
   plant, you can start a forest of them because each pod
   has scores of seeds, each one is a potential plant in the
   spring tiny white and purple blossoms appear.
3. These blossoms slowly transform themselves into green
   pods later the green turns to purple then it changes to
   yellow and orange finally it becomes a bright red, since

each pod is at a different stage of growth, the plant looks like a Christmas tree in August.

4. At the age of nineteen, my mother taught arithmetic in a little town in Missouri since she loved her students and her work Mother was happy as a single girl.

5. She had two boy friends — Frank, my father, and Percival, a neighbor neither one could win Mother's hand in marriage for five years Percival proposed to her in vain.

6. To get her to marry him, Frank told her that unless she said yes, he would run away to New York and never see her again she didn't know that this was a trick since she didn't want him to leave, she married him, when Percival heard the news, he fainted.

● REVIEW EXERCISE B.   Write a composition about 200 words in length, introducing either a good friend or a member of your family to the class. Point out three or four characteristics. Use short true stories and interesting examples to explain your main ideas regarding his or her habits, interests, and activities. After you have written the composition, read each sentence orally, one by one. Use end marks of punctuation where they are needed, and be very sure to eliminate all sentence fragments and run-on sentences.

CHAPTER 5

Agreement

SUBJECT AND VERB, PRONOUN AND ANTECEDENT

When two words "agree" with each other grammatically, they have the same number. Both words
are plural, or both are singular.

Singular and Plural Number

**5a. When a word refers to one person or thing, it
is singular in number. When a word refers to
more than one, it is plural in number.**

These nouns and pronouns are singular because
they name only one person or thing: *man, student,
someone, I, it, box*. These are plural because they refer
to more than one: *men, students, several, we, they, boxes*.[1]

●EXERCISE 1. Number in a column from 1 to 20
on your paper. After copying each of the words below,
write *singular* after each singular word and *plural* after
each plural word.

1. men	3. rulers	5. mile	7. either
2. one	4. gallon	6. parents	8. neither

---

[1] For rules regarding the formation of the plural of nouns, see
page 512.

9. both	12. tennis	15. foot	18. woman
10. few	13. each	16. teeth	19. lakes
11. these	14. mountains	17. everyone	20. year

Unlike nouns, most verbs ending in a single *s* are singular: *this seems, one does, she hopes*. Most verbs not ending in *s* are plural except when used with the singular *I* and *you*.

SINGULAR	PLURAL
one thinks	many think
he sees	both see
it stops	they stop
this looks	these look
she tries	we try

Is, was, and *has* are singular: *he is, I was, one has. Are, were,* and *have* are plural, except when used with the singular pronouns *I* and *you: they are, several were, many have* — but *I have, you are, you were.*

Agreement of Subject and Verb

5b. A verb agrees with its subject in number.

In order to speak and write correctly, you must be able to make the verbs you use agree with their subjects. Study the number of the subjects and verbs in the following sentences.

1. Many **students** in high school **are planning** to go to college. [The helping verb *are* agrees with *students;* both the subject and the verb are plural.]
2. Not every **student** in high school **is planning** to go to college. [The singular helping verb *is* agrees with the singular subject *student.*]
3. Some **girls** in my class **bring** their lunches. [The plural verb *bring* agrees with the plural subject *girls.*]
4. A **girl** in my class **brings** her lunch. [The verb *brings* agrees with the subject *girl;* both are singular.]

5a-b

● EXERCISE 2.   Which one of the words in parentheses agrees with the given subject?

1. one (swims, swim)
2. many (swims, swim)
3. he (goes, go)
4. several (goes, go)
5. everyone (hopes, hope)
6. they (hopes, hope)
7. this (takes, take)
8. these (takes, take)
9. you (is, are)
10. you (was, were)

5c. The number of the subject is not changed by a prepositional phrase following the subject.[2]

Remember that a verb agrees in number with its subject, not with a part of a prepositional phrase. *The subject is never in a prepositional phrase.*

EXAMPLE   **A lawn** with many trees **is** beautiful.

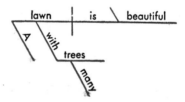

● EXERCISE 3.   *Oral Drill.* Repeat each of the following sentences *aloud* three times, stressing the italicized words.

1. Many *facts* in this textbook *are* important.
2. A *knowledge* of rules *helps* you use English correctly.
3. *Errors* in verb usage *are* particularly noticeable.
4. Correct *spelling*, in addition to usage of verbs, *is* also essential to good writing.
5. *Men* in the business world *look* for correct English in a letter of application.
6. A *letter* with many mistakes *does* not make a good impression.

[2] For exceptions to the rule, see Rule 5e.

7. My *father*, along with two other officials, often *hires* applicants.
8. *One* of my friends *hopes* to work for Father's company.
9. Not *one* of the employers, however, *was* pleased with my friend's letter of application.
10. "Every *man* in my office *says* '*you were*,'" commented my father.

● EXERCISE 4. After numbering from 1 to 10, write on your paper the correct form of the verb in parentheses. After the verb, write its subject.

1. Some students in my class (was, were) very interested in the new club.
2. Our boys, in position at the line of scrimmage, (was, were) awaiting the snap of the pigskin.
3. The first sight of Broadway, with its flashing lights and bright colors, (impresses, impress) a visitor.
4. A change in the rules often (confuses, confuse) the spectators.
5. The silence inside the Carlsbad Caverns (is, are) awe-inspiring.
6. The colors in the room (seems, seem) to flow into one another.
7. The cars on this expressway (travels, travel) at a high rate of speed.
8. The stack of papers (was, were) on his desk.
9. That album of records now (costs, cost) almost five dollars.
10. Tiny pieces of colored icing (makes, make) the cake attractive.

5d. The following common words are singular: *each, either, neither, one, everyone, everybody, no one, nobody, anyone, anybody, someone, somebody.*

These words are often followed by phrases that contain a plural word. Even so, since a verb always

5c-d

agrees with its *subject* (not with a word in a phrase), singular subjects such as *each, either, neither, one, everyone* always take singular verbs.

Read the following sentences aloud, stressing the subjects and verbs in heavy print.

1. **Each** of the boys **is** willing to help. [*each one is*]
2. **Neither** of the books **has** the answer. [*neither one has*]
3. **Either** of those **is** satisfactory. [*either one is*]
4. **Everyone** who belongs to the Boy Scouts **tries** to do a good deed every day.
5. **Everybody** in the stands **was** standing up.

5e. The following common words are plural: *several, few, both, many.* *Some, any, none, all,* and *most* may be either singular or plural.

Study the use of subjects and verbs in these sentences. Read the sentences aloud.

1. **Several** of the boys **are** going to the track meet.
2. **Both** of my parents **were** at the meeting.
3. **A few** of the girls **seem** pleased.
4. **All** of the tickets **have** been sold. [*all tickets have*]
5. **All** of the paint **is** gone. [*all paint is*]
6. **Some** of the books **need** to be mended. [*some books need*]
7. **Some** of the food **needs** to be cooked. [*some food needs*]

● EXERCISE 5.   Try to make a perfect score on this exercise, which covers both Rules 5d and 5e. Number on your paper from 1 to 20. Select from the pair of verbs in each sentence the correct one to agree with the subject. Write this verb after the proper number on your paper. After the verb, write the subject.

1. Each of the speakers (have, has) good voice control.
2. Somebody in the crowd (were, was) whistling softly.
3. Not one of the doors (are, is) locked.

4. Several of the girls (know, knows) the answer.
5. A few of the children (were, was) playing marbles.
6. Either of these (are, is) a real bargain.
7. Neither of the problems (looks, look) hard.
8. Some of my friends (enjoy, enjoys) reading science fiction.
9. Both of those Western movies (are, is) exciting.
10. All of the newsboys (get, gets) up before six o'clock.
11. Many of the freshmen (were, was) unusually alert.
12. (Have, Has) any of the new members arrived yet?
13. Everyone in the office (start, starts) to work at eight.
14. (Do, Does) either of you want a glass of lemonade?
15. Nobody in my family (have, has) ever ridden in a cub plane.
16. A few of her suggestions (were, was) helpful.
17. Neither of the stores (are, is) open on Sunday.
18. Everybody on the school grounds (have, has) been talking about the game.
19. Each of us (make, makes) money by baby-sitting.
20. Many of the students (type, types) forty words a minute.

● REVIEW EXERCISE A. Number in a column on your paper from 1 to 20. Read each sentence aloud. If the verb agrees with the subject, write a plus sign (+) on your paper after the proper number. If the verb does not agree with the subject, write a zero (0).

1. One of the stories end happily.
2. In late October the leaves on that tree turns dark red.
3. Each of his sons practice medicine.
4. Sometimes a leak in gas pipes is hard to find.
5. The bridges on Highway 34 are extremely narrow.
6. The numbers on the license plate was covered with mud.
7. Yesterday you was asking me about camp.
8. Every one of the clerks have to punch the time clock.
9. One of his assistants answer the telephone.
10. Our assignment for the next two days cover events during the American Revolution.

5e

11. Some of these pictures in the family album show how hair styles change.
12. A set of golf clubs stand in the corner.
13. Most of us now agree to these plans.
14. Each of the farmers use modern machines.
15. Some of the salt in these shakers is damp.
16. A carton of cold drinks was in the refrigerator.
17. Neither of the hurdles look easy.
18. Some of the players was really trying.
19. Does each of the girls play the piano?
20. Both of the hedges looks scrubby.

5f. *Don't* and *doesn't* must agree with their subjects.

With the subjects *I* and *you* and with plural subjects, use *don't* (*do not*).

EXAMPLES   *I* **don't** know him.
You **don't** mean that.
They **don't** have definite plans.
These **don't** fit.

With other subjects, use the singular *doesn't* (*does not*).

EXAMPLES   *He* **doesn't** play a banjo.
She **doesn't** eat fried foods.
It **doesn't** really matter.
One **doesn't** fit.
This **doesn't** make sense.

The errors in the use of *don't* and *doesn't* are usually made when *don't* is incorrectly used with *it*, *he*, or *she*. Remember always to use *doesn't* with these singular subjects: *it doesn't, he doesn't, she doesn't, one doesn't.*

● EXERCISE 6.   *Oral Drill*. Get your ears accustomed to correct usage by reading these sentences *aloud* five times.

1. It doesn't look good.
2. She doesn't talk much around boys.
3. Doesn't he seem shy?
4. This doesn't bother him.
5. One doesn't lie if he is honest.

● EXERCISE 7. After numbering from 1 to 10, write in a column on your paper the correct form (*don't* or *doesn't*) for each sentence below.

1. This —— influence me.
2. —— he like sour pickles?
3. No, he ——.
4. These —— suit me.
5. It —— look much like rain.
6. Each one —— expect to win.
7. They —— intend to go.
8. —— Mervyn have a birthday soon?
9. —— either of you want a piece of pie?
10. She —— ever wear fancy hats.

● REVIEW EXERCISE B. Number in a column on your paper from 1 to 20. Read each of the following sentences *aloud*. If the verb and the subject are in agreement, write a plus sign (+) after the proper number. If the sentence is incorrect (if the subject and verb do not agree), then write a zero (0) after the proper number.

1. Has any one of you ever been to Canada?
2. A few of my relatives live in Quebec.
3. Each of them know both French and English.
4. Either of these languages are understood in the places of business.
5. Some of the people in Quebec still use spinning wheels and hand looms.
6. One of my uncles there uses a horse and buggy as well as an oxcart.
7. Several of the old forts in Quebec is open to tourists.
8. Everyone in my family like to vacation near Round Inn Lake.

5f

9. All of us also enjoy watching the sleds as they race down steep hills.
10. Both of my cousins in Canada prefers curling to any other sport.
11. Neither of them, however, is a particularly good player.
12. Don't Shirley know what curling is?
13. Each of the boys here knows.
14. Curling is much like bowling, but not one of the players use a ball.
15. The contestants in the game slides a stone along an alley of ice toward a goal.
16. Some of the other Canadian sports are hockey, skiing, and skating.
17. The Husky races in Canada also provide a thrill for everyone.
18. Next year my father don't plan to visit Quebec.
19. Both of my parents are planning to go to Alberta.
20. Lake Louise, near many snow-capped mountains, is one of the most beautiful lakes in North America.

The Compound Subject

5g. Most compound subjects joined by *and* are plural and take a plural verb.

The following compound subjects, joined by *and*, name more than one person or thing and must take plural verbs:

1. **Ned** and **Paul** *are* good friends. [Two are.]
2. **My notebook** and **my pencil** *were* in his locker. [Two things were.]
3. **The man** and **his sons** *work* for us. [Several persons work.]

If a compound subject names only one person or thing, then the verb must be singular:

1. **The secretary and treasurer** *plans* to resign. [One person plans.]

2. **Ham and eggs** *is* a good breakfast dish. [The one combination is.]

In the sentences above, the compound subjects are thought of as units (*one person*, *one dish*) and are naturally singular.

5h. Singular subjects joined by *or* or *nor* are singular and take a singular verb.

EXAMPLES   Henry *or* Carl **is** going to Denver. [Either Henry is going, or Carl is going — not both.]
Neither the living room *nor* the bedroom **was** redecorated. [Neither one was redecorated.]

● EXERCISE 8.   Answer the following questions by using compound subjects joined by *and*, *nor*, and *or*. Make your answers complete sentences, and be sure that every verb agrees with its subject.

1. Is Boston or Brooklyn the capital of New York State?
2. What kinds of storms cause great damage?
3. Is an orange or a lemon considered "citrus" fruit?
4. What are some of the changes on new cars?
5. What gifts please a four-year-old child?

● EXERCISE 9.   From the parentheses in the following sentences, choose the correct verb. Write it in a column on your paper after the appropriate number.

1. James and Ralph (are, is) paying the bill.
2. James or Ralph (are, is) paying the bill.
3. Neither the cap nor the shirt (belong, belongs) to me.
4. During traffic jams, both courtesy and caution (help, helps) a driver to avoid accidents.
5. My father and mother often (tease, teases) my sister about being a tomboy.
6. Bananas and peanut butter (make, makes) a good sandwich.

5g-h

7. (Was, Were) you and I supposed to go there?
8. Either Joan or her sister (do, does) the supper dishes.
9. Neither Jack nor Martha (think, thinks) that we can win.
10. A mule or a donkey (is, are) not half so stubborn as my Siamese cat.

5i. When two subjects, one of which is singular and the other is plural, are joined by *or* or *nor,* the verb agrees with the nearer word.

In the following sentence, the verb cannot agree with both subjects because one is plural and the other is singular. A choice must be made; so the verb agrees with the nearer word.

ACCEPTABLE   **Either Kate or her brothers were to entertain the guests.**

Because of awkwardness, these constructions should be avoided.

BETTER   **The guests expected entertainment from Kate or her brothers.**

● REVIEW EXERCISE C.   *Oral Drill.* Repeat each of the following sentences *aloud* three times.

1. Every *one* of the members *has* voted for Paul.
2. *It* really *doesn't* sound too bad.
3. *Doesn't* he *or* Ned want the job?
4. A *few* of the windows *were* locked.
5. *Each* of the boys *is* dependable.
6. Donald *and* Richard *work* hard.
7. Neither Mr. Jones *nor* his secretary *answers* the telephone.
8. *Nobody* in the group *has* sold many tickets.
9. *Were you* absent Friday?
10. The beautiful *leaves* in the late autumn *make* me want to stay outdoors.

Other Problems in Agreement

5j. The verb agrees with the subject, *not* with the predicate nominative.

When the subject and the predicate nominative are of different numbers, you should always remember that *the verb agrees with the subject.*

RIGHT   These **taxes are** one problem of the senators.
RIGHT   One **problem is** these taxes.
BETTER   The senators must cope with the problem of these taxes.

5k. When the subject comes after the verb as in sentences beginning with *here is, there is,* and *where is,* be especially careful to determine the subject and make sure that it agrees with the verb.

In the following sentences each subject agrees with its verb.

Here **is** my **suggestion.**
There **is** a **café** near by.
Where **is Louise** now?
Here **are** my **suggestions.**
There **are** several **cafés** near by.
Where **are John** and **Louise?**

In our daily conversations we increase the likelihood of error by using contractions such as *here's, there's,* and *where's.*

WRONG   Where's those books?
RIGHT   Where **are** those **books?**
WRONG   There's Bruce and Tom.
RIGHT   There **are Bruce** and **Tom.**

5i-k

5l. Together with, in addition to, including, as well as, and similar constructions following the subject do not affect the number of the subject.

A singular subject has a singular verb. Do not be misled by phrases beginning with *together with, including, as well as,* and *in addition to* that come between the subject and the verb.

EXAMPLES   My **father,** *as well as* my mother, **is** eager to see our play.
The beautiful **design,** *together with* its performance, **makes** this car a best seller.

● REVIEW EXERCISE D.   *Oral Drill.* Repeat each of the following sentences *aloud* three times, stressing the italicized words.

1. Every *one* of the students *tries* to please Mr. Wilson.
2. There *are* four *keys* to the building.
3. Ernest *or* Wanda *has* already been here.
4. There *are* a *piece* of chalk and several *erasers* in the other room.
5. My *brother*, along with his best friends, never *meets* a stranger.
6. Where *are* those *letters?*
7. *Does each* of you write for the school paper?
8. *Neither* of the jokes *was* amusing.
9. *It doesn't* interfere with my schoolwork.
10. The *cat*, together with her kittens, *was* hungry.

5m. Collective nouns may be either singular or plural.

Collective nouns are singular in form, but they name a *group* of persons or things. Examples are:

group	committee	club	family
flock	herd	swarm	public
jury	army	audience	assembly
class	team	faculty	fleet

Collective nouns may be used with plural verbs when the speaker is thinking of the individual parts of the group; they may be used with singular verbs when the speaker is thinking of the group as a unit.

EXAMPLES   **The class was too large for the room.** [*Class* is thought of as a unit.]

The class were arguing about the plans. [*Class* is thought of as individuals.]

● EXERCISE 10. Select 5 collective nouns and write 5 pairs of sentences showing clearly how the nouns you choose may be either singular or plural.

● REVIEW EXERCISE E. Number on your paper from 1 to 20. Choose the correct verb in parentheses, and write it after the appropriate number.

1. During the intermission, a poor selection of records (was, were) played.
2. It is hard to keep your eyes on a tennis ball when there (is, are) pretty girls watching you.
3. The driver and his wife (was, were) unhurt.
4. In every detective story, there (is, are) usually a murder, a motive, suspects, clues, and discovery and punishment.
5. The use of radar, as well as the two-way radio, (makes, make) it possible for the state patrol to operate efficiently.
6. The actor's jovial manner and his ability to ad-lib (adds, add) to the merriment.
7. Because of heavy rains there (is, are) more grass and flowers than usual at this time of year.
8. Where (is, are) the small nails?
9. An airplane with four engines (has, have) arrived at Gate 4.
10. The mechanics at the inspection station (checks, check) lights and brakes.
11. Nobody in the group (wants, want) to go home now.
12. He certainly (doesn't, don't) like to make speeches.
13. Neither of the compositions (was, were) interesting.

51-m

14. Not one of the girls (knows, know) the answer.
15. Both of us (was, were) disappointed.
16. Neither Janet nor Bess (has, have) agreed to do the job.
17. Charles Darwin, along with A. R. Wallace, (is, are) remembered for his theory regarding evolution.
18. Here (is, are) a list of the causes of the War of 1812.
19. Oliver, as well as Homer and Alfred, (believes, believe) that she is telling the truth about being tardy.
20. Each of the roosters (starts, start) crowing about five o'clock every morning.

Agreement of Pronoun and Antecedent

5n. A pronoun agrees with its antecedent.

An *antecedent* is a word *going before* a pronoun; it is a word to which the pronoun refers. Carefully study the italicized antecedents of the pronouns (in heavy print) in these sentences.

1. Each *girl* brought **her** own lunch.
2. *Both* of the boys brought **their** lunches.
3. *One* of my friends forgot **his** lunch.

A pronoun and its antecedent agree in number. If an antecedent is plural, the pronoun is plural. If an antecedent is singular, the pronoun is singular.

SINGULAR   Nobody raised **his** hand.

PLURAL   Several *pupils* raised **their** hands.

(1) Use a singular pronoun to refer to *each, either, neither, one, everyone, everybody, no one, nobody, anyone, anybody, someone,* or *somebody*.

EXAMPLES   Each of the men took off **his** hat.

           One of the puppies lost **its** collar.

Notice in the sentences above that a prepositional phrase does not alter the number of the subject. The antecedent is singular in each sentence, and a singular pronoun (*he, she, him, her, it,* or *its*) must be used for agreement.

(2) Two antecedents joined by *and* should be referred to by a plural pronoun.

EXAMPLE   **Helen and Sue** have **their** homework.

(3) Two or more singular antecedents joined by *or* or *nor* should be referred to by a singular pronoun.

EXAMPLE   Neither **Bob nor Tom** has finished **his** homework.

● EXERCISE 11.   Number on your paper from 1 to 10. First, copy the antecedents in the following sentences; then, for each blank below, write a pronoun that will agree with its antecedent.

1. Each of the players looked unhappy because —— had failed the coach.
2. When Susan sees someone that she knows, she always stops and talks to ——.
3. An American should be proud of —— country.
4. Ben or Jeff will lend us —— boat.
5. Several of the convicts refused to eat —— food.
6. Steve and Richard talked about —— stamp collections.
7. Each of the girls displayed —— handiwork.
8. Both of the boys forgot —— promises.
9. Everyone needs —— own fountain pen.
10. Neither apologized for —— blunders.

● EXERCISE 12.   Many of the following sentences contain errors in agreement of pronoun and antecedent. Some sentences are correct as they stand; some contain more than one error. Number on your paper from 1 to 10. If the sentence is correct, write C (for correct) after the proper number. If there is an

5n

error in agreement, write the correct form of the pronoun so that it will agree with its antecedent.

1. One of my aunts takes a great deal of pride in her furniture.
2. Knowing this, nobody in our family puts their feet on chairs or sits on beds at Aunt Mary's house.
3. To tease Aunt Mary, however, Uncle Charlie, her brother, deliberately pretends that he is going to abuse her furniture; he used to do more than pretend.
4. In fact, he used to come home late at night, undress in the darkness, and then dive into his bed, nearly knocking every slat out of their place.
5. Each of these plunges left their mark on the rickety bed.
6. At first, both Aunt Mary and my mother offered their advice to Uncle Charlie and asked him to take better care of the furniture.
7. Anybody else in my family would have mended their ways, but not Uncle Charlie; he needed discipline, not advice.
8. Late one night everyone in the house, frightened by the loud noise, suddenly jumped out of their beds, turned on the lights, and ran to Uncle Charlie's room.
9. Not one of us could believe our eyes! Lying in the middle of the floor was Uncle Charlie, groaning loudly.
10. If anyone ever asks you why Uncle Charlie has stopped teasing Aunt Mary, just tell them that one day she merely rearranged her furniture.

(4) When the meaning of the antecedent is clearly plural, the plural pronoun is acceptable, even though grammatically the singular may be preferable.

Sometimes making a pronoun agree with its antecedent is illogical. If the idea of the speaker is definitely plural, then a singular pronoun is unnatural. Here usage differs somewhat from grammar.

AWKWARD   Since every **one** of the students **was** interested in sports, I discussed baseball with **him.**

NATURAL   Since every **one** of the students **was** interested in sports, I discussed baseball with **them.**

BETTER   Since **all** of the students **were** interested in sports, I discussed baseball with **them.**

● EXERCISE 13. Number from 1 to 10. Choose the correct pronoun in parentheses, and write it after the proper number on your paper.

1. Neither of the children grew tired of (his, their) toys.
2. A few of the women did (her, their) shopping early.
3. A banker or a beggar should not waste (his, their) money.
4. If you see somebody on the beach, ask (him, them) what time it is.
5. Nancy and Irene do (her, their) own hair.
6. Each of the teachers expressed (his, their) own views.
7. Watching the quiz program, several in the group recognized (his, their) friends in the audience.
8. Is everyone responsible for (his, their) own equipment?
9. Some of the boys brought (his, their) pets along.
10. If someone drops by while I'm gone, tell (him, them) that I'll be back within an hour.

● REVIEW EXERCISE F. In some of the following sentences, the verbs agree with their subjects, and the pronouns agree with their antecedents. Number in a column from 1 to 25. If the words agree in a sentence, write *C* (for *correct*) after the appropriate number. If the verb does not agree with its subject, or if a pronoun does not agree with its antecedent, write the correct form of the verb or the pronoun after the proper number.

1. Nearly everybody in our crowd collect things. 2. Some of my friends collect stamps, and a few keep old coins. 3. One of the girls keeps locks of hair that are clipped from the heads of various friends. 4. Every lock

in the collection are put in a small envelope and pasted in a book.   5. Bill Reeves, as well as his two brothers, have a collection of old pictures, made as long ago as the 1920's.   6. It seems that almost all of my classmates are always adding to a collection of one kind or another.   7. Each of these friends is proud of his varied assortment.

8. Jack Thompson, however, don't collect anything.   9. One of his favorite pastimes is just watching things — like lizards or birds.   10. If someone goes with Jack on a Saturday walk through the woods, Jack doesn't say much to them.   11. He is too busy watching a bird build their nest or teasing an ant as it plods along with a heavy crumb.

12. Not one of my friends, however, like to read about things as much as I do.   13. Instead of collecting old bottles or watching a robin, I learn about things in other lands.   14. Everybody in my class, as they brag about what they are doing, say I read too much.   15. Each book, as well as every magazine, teaches me far more than some of my friends are willing to admit.   16. For me, the habits of elephants in Africa or of kangaroos in Australia makes interesting reading.

17. In Australia there's many kinds of birds.   18. One of the most interesting birds is the kookaburra.   19. Neither Jack nor Bill knows about the kookaburra, which doesn't live in America.   20. Every one of these birds laugh.   21. It don't chirp, sing, or call as other birds do.   22. Several of them often get together on a fence, and then one of them starts cackling.   23. Quickly the others on the fence add their voices to the chorus.   24. Each bird seems to be enjoying a joke all their own.   25. Anybody passing by will notice the noise, and they will soon burst out laughing too.

GOOD USAGE ─────────────────

fewer, less: Use *fewer* with plural words.
Use *less* with singular words.

RIGHT   **There are fewer days in February than in any other month.**

RIGHT   **Now that I'm in school, I have less time than I did last summer.**

ways, way: Use *way* (not *ways*) in referring to a distance.

RIGHT   **Texarkana is a long way from El Paso.**

you were: Always say *you were*. Never say *you was*.

RIGHT   **You were my only girl friend.**

RIGHT   **You two were asleep.**

where at: Don't use *at* after *where*.

WRONG   **Where is she at?**

RIGHT   **Where is she?**

kind of a, sort of a: The *a* is unnecessary. Leave it out.

WRONG   **What kind of a dog is that?**

RIGHT   **What kind of dog is that?**

CHAPTER 6

The Correct Use of Verbs

PRINCIPAL PARTS, REGULAR AND IRREGULAR VERBS

If you are making serious errors in verb usage (such as *I seen, she begun, he drownded,* or *it busted*), then you should learn the principal parts of troublesome verbs.

The Principal Parts of Verbs

6a. The four basic forms of a verb are the *present*, the *present participle*, the *past*, and the *past participle*.

The forms of a verb express time or "tense." The four principal parts of the verb *eat,* for example, are *eat* (present), *eating* (present participle), *ate* (past), and *eaten* (past participle). Notice in the following sentences how each form is used to express time.

I **have** already **eaten** breakfast.
I **am eating** my dessert now.
I often **eat** my lunch at the school cafeteria.
Yesterday I **ate** a sandwich at the drugstore.
I **will eat** a piece of pie later.

118

Study the following list of the six tense (time) forms of a verb. Giving all the forms of a verb in this way is called "conjugating" the verb.

CONJUGATION OF *TO BE*

PRESENT	PRESENT PARTICIPLE	PAST	PAST PARTICIPLE
am	being	was	been

PRESENT TENSE

Singular	*Plural*
I am	we are
you are	you are
he is	they are

PAST TENSE

Singular	*Plural*
I was	we were
you were	you were
he was	they were

FUTURE TENSE

Singular	*Plural*
I will be	we will be
you will be	you will be
he will be	they will be

PRESENT PERFECT TENSE

Singular	*Plural*
I have been	we have been
you have been	you have been
he has been	they have been

PAST PERFECT TENSE

Singular	*Plural*
I had been	we had been
you had been	you had been
he had been	they had been

6a

FUTURE PERFECT TENSE

Singular	*Plural*
I will have been	we will have been
you will have been	you will have been
he will have been	they will have been

Regular Verbs

6b. A regular verb is one which forms its past and past participle forms by merely adding *–ed* or *–d* to the present forms.

The present forms of regular verbs present no usage problems. Errors do occur, however, in the choice of the past and the past participle forms of regular verbs. You can avoid many errors by remembering that the *–ed* or *–d* form of a regular verb is used for every tense except the present and the future. Do not carelessly omit the *–d* or *–ed* of the past or the past participle of regular verbs like those listed below. You can avoid other mistakes by correcting faulty pronunciation of words like *attacked* and *drowned*.

PRESENT	PAST	PAST PARTICIPLE
ask	asked	(have) asked
experience	experienced	(have) experienced
risk	risked	(have) risked
suppose	supposed	(have) supposed
use	used	(have) used

WRONG	We were suppose to clean the room.
RIGHT	We were **supposed** to clean the room.

WRONG	This has happen before.
RIGHT	This has **happened** before.

WRONG	Yesterday he ask me a question.
RIGHT	Yesterday he **asked** me a question.

WRONG	The child had drownded.
RIGHT	The child had **drowned**.

● EXERCISE 1. *Oral Drill.* Read *aloud* every sentence below five times, stressing the correct pronunciation of each italicized verb.

1. He *asked* her yesterday.
2. The applicant was *experienced*.
3. What has *happened* to Bill?
4. How many were *drowned*?
5. We *attacked* another problem.
6. George *risked* his life.
7. He was *supposed* to wash the car.

Irregular Verbs

6c. An irregular verb is one that does *not* form its past and past participle forms by adding –ed or –d to the present form.

Irregular verbs form their past and past participle forms in various ways: by changing the vowel, by changing consonants, or by making no change at all.

PRESENT	PAST	PAST PARTICIPLE
begin	began	(have) begun
fall	fell	(have) fallen
know	knew	(have) known
catch	caught	(have) caught
put	put	(have) put

Since all six tenses are made from the principal parts, it is very important that you learn the principal parts of the verbs you use. The conjugation of the irregular verb *to be* on page 119 shows how the forms of that verb change to express different tenses.

The principal parts of common irregular verbs are on pages 122 and 123. Failure to know the principal parts of these verbs can cause you to make serious errors.

WRONG **I give him a dollar yesterday.** [Since the action took place in the past, the past tense should have been used.]

RIGHT **I gave him a dollar yesterday.**

6b-c

WRONG   **He had drank all of the punch.** [The past has been used, but the helping verb *had* indicates the past perfect tense and the past participle should have been used.]

RIGHT   **He had drunk** all of the punch.

When you memorize the principal parts of a verb, you will help yourself if you will always include *have* with the past participle. As you repeat them to yourself, say *give, gave, have given* or *drink, drank, have drunk*.

The past participle of a verb which takes an object is also used in expressions in which the verb acts upon its subject rather than on an object. Such a verb is said to be in the *passive voice*. Verbs which act upon their object are said to be in the *active voice*.

PASSIVE VOICE   The letter **was written.**
He **has been chosen.**
My scissors **have been moved.**
Two cups **were broken.**

ACTIVE VOICE   Amy **wrote** the letters.
The judges **have chosen** Mike.
Mother **has moved** my scissors.
We **broke** two cups.

While you may wish to be familiar with these terms, you will have little need for using the concept of *voice* in analyzing or writing sentences.

IRREGULAR VERBS FREQUENTLY MISUSED

PRESENT	PAST	PAST PARTICIPLE
begin	began	(have) begun
blow	blew	(have) blown
break	broke	(have) broken
bring	brought	(have) brought
burst	burst	(have) burst
choose	chose	(have) chosen
come	came	(have) come

do	did	(have) done
drink	drank	(have) drunk
drive	drove	(have) driven
fall	fell	(have) fallen
freeze	froze	(have) frozen
give	gave	(have) given
go	went	(have) gone
know	knew	(have) known
ride	rode	(have) ridden
ring	rang	(have) rung
run	ran	(have) run
see	saw	(have) seen
shrink	shrank	(have) shrunk
speak	spoke	(have) spoken
steal	stole	(have) stolen
swim	swam	(have) swum
take	took	(have) taken
throw	threw	(have) thrown
write	wrote	(have) written

▶ CAUTION: Do not confuse irregular verbs with regular ones. Never say *throwed, knowed, bursted,* or *blowed.*

● EXERCISE 2. Your teacher may dictate to you the present tense of these 25 irregular verbs. Study the list so that you can write from memory the past and the past participle forms for each verb. Place *have* before the past participle.

● EXERCISE 3. Number from 1 to 20. Choose the correct one of the two verbs in parentheses, and write it after the corresponding number on your paper. If there are two verbs in a sentence, write them on the same line. When your paper has been corrected, read each sentence *aloud* several times, stressing the correct verb.

1. Has your sister Ann (drove, driven) much?
2. I know that your father (give, gave) her a car for graduation.

3. Yesterday I (saw, seen) her driving it.
4. The rain had (froze, frozen) on the pavement.
5. Her car (began, begun) to skid.
6. As she (came, come) around the corner, she hit the curb hard.
7. She (run, ran) into a fire hydrant.
8. It (busted, burst, bursted) open, and the water (began, begun) gushing into the street.
9. The firemen soon arrived; they (brung, brought) equipment to repair the damage.
10. After they had (gone, went) away, I replaced the hubcap that had (fallen, fell) off Ann's car wheel.
11. I (did, done) all that I could to help.
12. I (saw, seen) that a tire had (blew, blown, blowed) out.
13. After I had (spoke, spoken) to Ann about that, I noticed that a headlight was (broke, broken).
14. Then I (taken, took) the keys to unlock the trunk.
15. "Hey!" I yelled to Ann. "Your spare tire has been (stole, stolen)."
16. "Oh," she explained, "to make room for packages yesterday, I (throwed, threw) that tire out of the trunk."
17. It was then that I (give, gave) up and called a mechanic to help her.
18. After I had stopped at a café and had (drank, drunk) a cup of hot chocolate, I went on to school.
19. The tardy bell had already (rang, rung).
20. Have you ever (rode, ridden) with a driver like Ann?

● EXERCISE 4. Write 2 original sentences using correctly each verb that you missed in Exercise 3. After your sentences have been checked for accuracy, read the sentences aloud until you feel that you have mastered the troublesome verbs.

● EXERCISE 5. Write in a column on your paper the correct form of the verb given at the beginning of each sentence.

1. *write*   I had —— him a note.
2. *give*   Yesterday he —— me a ticket.
3. *freeze*   The pond was —— over.
4. *blow*   Last night a loud whistle ——.
5. *drive*   I have never —— a car in town.
6. *break*   His little finger is ——.
7. *do*   Have you —— your homework?
8. *come*   Yesterday June —— to the party.
9. *drink*   I have —— two glasses of milk.
10. *burst*   The package suddenly —— open.
11. *swim*   Yesterday I —— to the other side of the lake.
12. *fall*   Many leaves have ——.
13. *shrink*   When I washed the sweater, it ——,
14. *go*   Have they —— swimming?
15. *swim*   I have —— in the ocean only once.
16. *ride*   We had —— about five miles.
17. *catch*   Harvey had not —— the ball.
18. *know*   I have —— him a long time.
19. *begin*   Has it —— to rain?
20. *bring*   We —— our lunches all last week.

● REVIEW EXERCISE A. *Oral Drill.* Read each of the following sentences *aloud* three times, stressing the correct verbs.

1. He *asked* us to go with him.
2. How long *have* you *known* her?
3. They *have broken* the lock.
4. One balloon *burst*.
5. My uncle *came* to see us yesterday.
6. I *had begun* to worry.
7. *Is* the applicant *experienced*?
8. Then the bell *rang*.
9. She *has written* the invitations.
10. He *brought* his first-aid kit.

● REVIEW EXERCISE B. Number in a column on your paper from 1 to 25. Read each of the following sentences *aloud*. If a sentence is correct, write *C* after the proper number. If the form of the verb is wrong, write the correct verb form after the appropriate number.

1. He has already went to meet her.
2. Have you wrote the letter yet?
3. She had drunk her coke.
4. Have you and she took the test?
5. Not a word was spoke.
6. I swam for more than an hour.
7. They come to see us last summer.
8. The lost dog has not been seen here.
9. I knowed I done wrong.
10. The telephone rang insistently.
11. Has either one of you saw that movie?
12. Had he already gone when you came?
13. I use to play marbles.
14. When the pirates attacked the ship, several were drowned.
15. Has the bell rung?
16. Yesterday he give a talk in assembly.
17. A low ball was thrown.
18. He seen that I was angry.
19. Two wild stallions were ridden that day.
20. Not much money was stole.
21. I have swum there several times.
22. Has the skirt shrunk?
23. The prisoner was took to the death house.
24. Had he ran in track meets before?
25. I saw him when he done it.

LIE AND LAY

The verb *lie* means "to rest" or "recline," "to remain in a lying position." Its principal parts are *lie*, *lying*, *lay*, (*have*) *lain*. These forms never take objects.

The verb *lay* means "to put" or "to place (something)." Its principal parts are *lay*, *laying*, *laid*, (*have*) *laid*. These forms may have objects (receivers of the action).

Memorize the following:

PRESENT	PRESENT PARTICIPLE	PAST	PAST PARTICIPLE
lie (to rest)	lying	lay	(have) lain
lay (to put)	laying	laid	(have) laid

Study these examples of the use of the verb *lie*, meaning "to rest" or "to recline."

1. **Lie** down for a while. [no object]
2. A glove **is lying** on the chair. [no object]
3. Yesterday he **lay** down for a nap. [no object]
4. **Has** he **lain** there long? [no object]

Notice how the following examples of the use of the verb *lay* differ from those above. In the sentences below, each verb means "to put" or "to place (something)."

1. **Lay** the *keys* on the table. [*Put* what? The object is *keys.*]
2. **The boys were laying** down their *marbles.* [The boys were *placing* or *putting* what? *Marbles* is the object.]
3. **She laid** her *work* aside. [*Put* what aside? *Work* is the object.]
4. **The hen had laid** three *eggs.* [The object is *eggs.*]

● EXERCISE 6. Read each of the following sentences *aloud* several times. In the light of the information just given, be able to explain why the verb is correct.

1. Where *have* you *laid* the hammer?
2. From now on, *lay* it on this shelf.
3. We *were laying* plans for Saturday night.
4. His skates *were lying* in the closet.
5. I *laid* them there last week.
6. He often *lies* in the sun.
7. He *lay* on the beach for an hour.
8. That book *has lain* there for years.
9. Caroline *laid* the book on the floor.
10. She *laid* it there yesterday, and it *has been lying* there ever since.

● EXERCISE 7. Write 10 original sentences using correctly all of the various forms of the verbs *lie* and *lay*. Think carefully of the *meaning* of each verb.

● EXERCISE 8. After numbering from 1 to 10, write the correct form of the proper verb (*lie* — *lay*) for each of these sentences. Make a perfect score by referring to the forms on page 127 if necessary.

1. An old mine now —— at the foot of the mountain.
2. He —— his glasses aside and frowned.
3. I shall —— down for a few minutes.
4. She had —— on the divan before.
5. The baby was still —— quietly in his cradle.
6. The woman —— the baby in his cradle an hour ago.
7. Is the newspaper —— in the rain?
8. No, I have —— the paper near the fire to dry.
9. Last summer my dog often —— in his doghouse.
10. —— down, Fido.

● EXERCISE 9. Clearly explain the correct usage of *lie* and *lay* by filling in the blanks below with the right form of each verb. Use a separate sheet of paper, and number your answers correctly.

The verb *to* (1) —— means "to put" or "to place (something)." The present participle of *lay* is (2) ——. The past and the past participle have the same form, which is (3) ——. The present form is (4) ——.

The verb *to* (5) —— means "to rest" or "recline." The present participle of *lie* is (6) ——. The past form of *lie* is (7) ——, and the past participle is (8) ——.

The verb *to* (9) ——, with all of its forms, never has an object; however, the forms of (10) —— may have objects.

● EXERCISE 10. Study and read aloud the following groups of sentences, and be prepared to explain why each verb is correct.

1. I *shall lay* the pattern on the material. Now it *is lying* in place. I *laid* it there carefully, and it *will lie* there until

I find out where I *have laid* my scissors. Oh, they *are lying* on the machine.

2. I *have lain* in the cool shade since noon. I have been watching the men who *are laying* some concrete. They *have* already *laid* the framework, which *is* now *lying* in the ground. The concrete *lies* drying within the boards of the frame.

SIT AND SET

The verb *sit* means "to rest in an upright, sitting position." The principal parts of *sit* are *sit, sitting, sat, (have) sat.*

The verb *set* means "to put, to place (something)." The principal parts of *set* are *set, setting, set, (have) set*

Memorize the principal parts of *sit* and *set* so that you can give them readily from memory.

PRESENT	PRESENT PARTICIPLE	PAST	PAST PARTICIPLE
sit (to rest)	sitting	sat	(have) sat
set (to put)	setting	set	(have) set

Study the following examples:

1. **Let's sit** on the porch for a while.
2. **Set** the suitcase on the platform.

You will have little difficulty using these verbs correctly, if you will remember two facts about them: (1) Like *lie*, the verb *sit* means "to be in a certain position." It never has an object. (2) Like *lay*, the verb *set* means "to put (something) down." *Set* does not change to form the past or the past participle. Whenever you mean "to place" or "to put," use *set*.[1]

As you learn the principal parts of these verbs and as you do the oral drills below, be sure that you *pronounce the words correctly*. *Set* ("to put") rhymes with *met*. *Sit* ("to rest") rhymes with *fit*.

---

[1] A use of the verb *set* which does not mean "to put" or "to place" is. The sun color

● EXERCISE 11. *Oral Drill*. Read the sentences below *aloud* several times. Think of the *meaning* of the verbs, and do not go on to other exercises until you feel that you know the right use of *sit* and *set*.

1. Please *sit* here.
2. He *was sitting* near the door.
3. Please *set* the package here.
4. He *was setting* the package there when I entered.
5. She *sat* there and watched me *set* the clock.
6. Where *are* they *sitting*?
7. I often *sit* in that old rocker.
8. I *have sat* there many times.
9. *Set* the flowers near the window.
10. Can your dog *sit* up?

● EXERCISE 12.   Correctly use each of the following in 10 sentences of your own.

1. is sitting	6. has been setting
2. is setting	7. sat
3. has sat	8. set
4. has set	9. will sit
5. has been sitting	10. will set

● EXERCISE 13. Number from 1 to 10 on your paper. Fill the blanks in the following sentences with a correct form of *sit* or *set*, whichever is required by the meaning.

1. Did you —— the hatrack in the hall?
2. You may —— on that footstool.
3. I will —— here in the sun for a while.
4. —— the gun in the closet.
5. Yesterday I —— the lamp on his desk.
6. Now —— still until I tell you this.
7. An hour ago I —— the baby on a pallet.
8. He is still —— there.
9. She had —— near the hostess.
10. Does the guest of honor —— at the head of the table?

● EXERCISE 14. Orally answer the following questions by using the correct forms of *sit* or *set*.

1. Do you sit or set the table?
2. Do you sit or set at the table?
3. Do you ask friends to sit or to set down?
4. Do you sit or set a heavy load down?
5. Are you sitting or setting at your desk?

RISE AND RAISE

The verb *rise* means "to go in an upward direction." Its principal parts are *rise, rising, rose, (have) risen*. Like *lie* and *sit*, the verb *rise* never has an object.

The verb *raise* means "to force something to move in an upward direction." Its principal parts are *raise, raising, raised, (have) raised*. Like *lay* and *set*, *raise* may take an object.

	PRESENT		PAST
PRESENT	PARTICIPLE	PAST	PARTICIPLE
rise (to go up)	rising	rose	(have) risen
raise (to force up)	raising	raised	(have) raised

Study the following examples:

1. The old man **rose** up in protest.
2. The old man **raised** his head quickly.

● EXERCISE 15. *Oral Drill.* Repeat each of the following sentences *aloud* three times, stressing the italicized verbs and thinking of the *meaning* of the sentence.

1. The sun *has* already *risen*.
2. I *raised* my hand.
3. The river *rises* in the spring.
4. My family *rises* early.
5. We *raise* our voices.
6. The man *rose* from his chair.
7. The man *raised* his eyebrow

● EXERCISE 16. Write 10 original sentences correctly using the various forms of *rise* and *raise*.

● EXERCISE 17. After numbering from 1 to 10, write the correct form of *rise* or *raise* for each of the following blanks.

1. Please do not —— your voice.
2. A gentleman —— to his feet when a lady stands.
3. The legislature has —— taxes again.
4. My aunt —— an objection a little while ago.
5. The biscuits have ——.
6. The curtain will —— at nine o'clock.
7. Joe will —— the curtain.
8. The price of coffee has —— steadily.
9. Our grocer has —— the price of coffee.
10. Last night about midnight I —— in order to —— my bedroom window.

● REVIEW EXERCISE C. Number on your paper from 1 to 20. Choose the correct verb in parentheses, and write it after the proper number.

1. (Lay, Lie) the book on the desk.
2. The book is (lying, laying) on the desk.
3. The desk (sets, sits) in the hall.
4. (Set, Sit) the lamp over here.
5. He (rose, raised) from his chair and turned off the newscast.
6. The kite was swiftly (raising, rising) skyward.
7. Yesterday I (lay, laid) in the sun for an hour.
8. Has Mother (lain, laid) down yet?
9. The paper is (lying, laying) on the sidewalk.
10. The river is (raising, rising) steadily.
11. We were (sitting, setting) on a large rock.
12. A hand-painted vase (sits, sets) on the mantelpiece.
13. They had already (lain, laid) their plans.
14. (Sit, Set) down and talk for a while.
15. I (lay, laid) the keys there a few minutes ago.
16. The main pipes (laid, lay) under the floor.
17. A rope was (lying, laying) near the saddle.

18. The sun is (raising, rising) now.
19. Had you (set, sat) on his hat?
20. (Lying, Laying) in the top drawer was the necklace.

Other Common Errors with Verbs

Although you can correct most errors in verb usage by studying principal parts and tense forms, you must know the meanings of some verbs in order to avoid other mistakes in usage.

Learn to distinguish the difference between the verbs listed in pairs below.

accept, except. *Accept* means "to receive." *Except* means "to leave out."

> EXAMPLES　I shall **accept** the gift.
> We did **except** Milton's poem from the list.

affect, effect. *Affect* means "to influence." *Effect* means "to accomplish."

> EXAMPLES　The weather can **affect** a child's behavior.
> The new remedy **effected** astonishing cures.

learn, teach. *Learn* means "to acquire knowledge." *Teach* means "to give out knowledge."

> EXAMPLES　Mr. Hall **teaches** history.
> His students **learn** many important facts.

leave, let. *Leave* means "to go away." *Let* means "to allow" or "to permit."

> EXAMPLES　**Let** the boy sleep. **Let** me explain.
> **Leave** the room immediately.

● EXERCISE 18. Number on your paper from 1 to 10. Choose the correct one of the two words in parentheses, and write it after the proper number.

1. Mr. Tucker (taught, learned) him how to dive from the high board.
2. (Leave, Let) him do as he pleases.

3. I'm willing to (accept, except) his apology.
4. Oh, I can't (learn, teach) you anything!
5. These sandstorms (effect, affect) my sinuses.
6. The sad movie (effected, affected) all of us.
7. Please (leave, let) me do this by myself.
8. Will you (accept, except) this small token of appreciation?
9. The legislature (effected, affected) several changes in the housing laws.
10. He said that he'd (teach, learn) my dog to retrieve.

● EXERCISE 19.   Use each one of the 8 verbs listed on page 133 in sentences of your own.

Consistency of Tense

6d. Do not change needlessly from one tense to another.

When you are writing about events in the past, you should choose verbs in the past tense. Do not suddenly shift, without reason, to the present tense.

WRONG **The bully walked up to me and shakes his fist in my face.** [The verb *walked* indicates past action; whereas *shakes* is present tense.]

RIGHT **The bully walked up to me and shook his fist in my face.** [Both *walked* and *shook* are in the past tense.]

WRONG **Mike figured out the play and quickly tackles Smith behind the line of scrimmage.** [*Figured* is past tense, and *tackles* is present.]

RIGHT **Mike figures out the play and quickly tackles Smith behind the line of scrimmage.** [The verbs are both in the present tense.]

● EXERCISE 20.   Prepare to read aloud the following paragraph in order to eliminate the needless changes of tense. First decide whether the paragraph should be told in the present or past tense throughout.

Then you will need to change the tense of many of the
verbs to achieve consistency.

1 It all started as soon as I got home from school.
2 Here I am in my room, and I am getting ready to
3 study my history lesson. It was about five o'clock.
4 To my surprise, Ned Palmer decided to drop by. He
5 comes dashing into the house, slams the door behind
6 him, and starts yelling for me. What he wanted was a
7 hunting companion. I'm it. He had seen a flock of
8 ducks, which were settling down for the night, on a
9 pond at Dawson's place. Reaching for my gun, I get
10 all excited about racing out to the pond. Imagine our
11 dismay when we arrived and find that Mr. Dawson
12 had just set out a dozen decoys, hoping to lure some
13 real ducks within shooting range.

● EXERCISE 21.   After numbering from 1 to 20,
write either *present* or *past* to indicate the tense of each
verb below.

1. ask	6. chose	11. gasp	16. run
2. give	7. used	12. began	17. reads
3. swam	8. ran	13. choose	18. says
4. suppose	9. come	14. came	19. swim
5. begin	10. use	15. asked	20. gave

● REVIEW EXERCISE D.   Number in a column on
your paper from 1 to 25. Select from each sentence the
correct one of the verb forms in parentheses, and
write it after the corresponding number on your
paper.

1. Does the kitten often (lie, lay) on the rug near the fire?
2. We (use, used) to prowl through the empty warehouse.
3. Yesterday afternoon the county agent (gave, give) us
   a leaflet on soil erosion.
4. He (taught, learned) us all about flood control.
5. They (set, sat) in the back row.
6. I (knowed, knew) the answer.
7. Inez should have (knowed, know, known) better.

6d

8. Ernest (throwed, threw) a fast curve.

9. Last night Paul (came, come) to my party.

10. Dad has (spoke, spoken) to us about this several times.

11. She almost (drownded, drowned).

12. Will you (accept, except) his offer?

13. He walked up to the box office and (bought, buys) two tickets.

14. Please (let, leave) them go to the skating rink.

15. The waters are (rising, raising) dangerously fast.

16. Have you (drunk, drank) all the lemonade?

17. The puppy whimpered and then (lay, laid) still.

18. Snoopy (brung, brought) us the newspaper.

19. Has he ever (written, wrote) a composition?

20. The main spring (bust, burst, busted, bursted).

21. Were any of the dishes (broke, broken)?

22. The testimony of the accused deeply (effected, affected) the jury.

23. I had (set, sat) there a long time.

24. I (seen, saw) a truck stop in front of the gymnasium.

25. We (clumb, climbed) the high mountain.

● REVIEW EXERCISE E. Number in a column on your paper from 1 to 25. Read each of the following sentences *aloud*, and determine whether the verbs are correct or incorrect. If the sentence is correct, write a plus sign (+) after the corresponding number. If a verb in a sentence is wrong, write a zero (0) after the proper number. Be prepared to give the correct verb form for each sentence that you label 0.

1. I use to want a pet monkey all my own.   2. About a year ago, I would sit in the park for hours and watch the antics of the caged monkeys.   3. Since I taken care of Corky, though, I haven't had the slightest desire to have a monkey.

4. Alex, my friend who owns the monkey, ask me to keep Corky for six hours.   5. Since I was very pleased about keeping a real monkey all afternoon, Alex brung Corky over early one Saturday.   6. About one o'clock,

after Alex had went on his way, I made friends with the monkey.   7. For a while we chose to play in the yard.

8. The trouble began when I went into the house to lie down for a nap.   9. As soon as Corky saw me laying on the bed, he started thinking of mischief.   10. I seen that he was not ready to settle down.   11. Suddenly he jumped upon a chair, raised his arms, grabbed the pictures on the wall, and began throwing them at me.   12. I sat up and warned Corky to behave.   13. After rising from my bed, I tied the scoundrel to the leg of the bed.

14. After I had lain down again, I busted out laughing at his angry chattering.   15. No harm had been done; none of tho picture frames were broken.   16. Soon, however, Corky thought of a new way to annoy me; his chain give him enough freedom to climb upon the high bedstead. 17. After sitting there quietly for an instant, he dived hard, right into the middle of my stomach.   18. I howled, "You've went too far, Corky!"   19. Defiantly putting his hands over his deaf ears, Corky begun to bounce up and down on the bed as though celebrating a major victory.

20. After he had attackted me, I no longer wanted him around.   21. Picking him up, I set him in a chair on the back porch.   22. Then I gave him some peanuts and went back to lie down.   23. I had to bribe him because I knowed that I couldn't learn him any manners.

24. When Alex finally come after Corky, I was never so happy to get rid of a guest.   25. After what he done, I won't ever invite that monkey — or any monkey — to my house again.

● REVIEW EXERCISE F. Number from 1 to 50. Write the correct form of the verb given at the beginning of each sentence.

1. *eat*   Have you —— dinner?
2. *attack*   Indians had —— the fort.
3. *catch*   Tom —— the low pass and made a touchdown.
4. *break*   The compass has been —— for weeks.
5. *swim*   We watched the penguins as they —— in the water.

6. *write*   Have you —— to your grandmother?

7. *bring*   Ann —— a raincoat.

8. *give*   Has he been —— another chance?

9. *come*   Last night a bear —— into our tent and got our candy.

10. *burst*   The airplane —— into flames.

11. *drink*   Has Hazel —— her tea?

12. *use*   When I was a child, I —— to dig tunnels.

13. *do*   She —— her best yesterday.

14. *give*   Father has —— us some suggestions.

15. *go*   The well has —— dry.

16. *risk*   The policeman —— his life last night.

17. *ring*   The bell —— an hour ago.

18. *run*   Last year Evans —— for mayor.

19. *break*   The champion has —— the record.

20. *lie*   They had —— down on the grass.

21. *drive*   Have you —— one of the new cars?

22. *choose*   Let's —— a leader.

23. *fall*   I slipped on the ice and ——.

24. *go*   He has —— after groceries.

25. *speak*   The principal has —— to me about it.

26. *ride*   That dude has never —— a horse.

27. *begin*   It has —— to clear in the north.

28. *come*   I noticed that he —— in late.

29. *ring*   Has the bell ——?

30. *happen*   Has this —— before?

31. *see*   Last night I —— him at the drugstore.

32. *take*   Since I had —— my rifle along, we looked for doves as we hiked through the woods.

33. *fall*   A child has —— from the ledge.

34. *climb*   Has he —— the ladder of fame?

35. *go*   Has he already —— to the game?

36. *freeze*   Many of the peach trees were —— by this late cold front.

37. *lie*   Harriet is —— on the couch.

38. *freeze*   Has the lake ——?

39. *speak*   I have —— in public once.

40. *sit*   Carl had just —— down on the newly painted bench.

41. *see*   I have —— him in person.
42. *ask*   Miss Clemons has —— us to help her.
43. *swim*   Have you ever —— here before?
44. *swim*   I —— here last summer.
45. *shrink*   Has the material ——?
46. *choose* Our leader has been ——.
47. *blow*   Yesterday the wind —— with gale force.
48. *take*   I haven't —— the test yet.
49. *run*   Had the clock —— down?
50. *lay*   They have already —— the foundation.

THE OLD–FASHIONED DOUBLE NEGATIVE ——

When you use a double negative like "does*n't* make *no*" or "is*n't no*," you are using old-fashioned English that is no longer acceptable modern grammar.

Before the eighteenth century, the double negative — or triple or quadruple negative — was both useful and popular. The more negatives a person used in a sentence, the more he meant an emphatic "No!" For example, take this sentence:

Girls do not never like no mice nowhere.

At one time, this sentence would have meant that girls do not like mice at any time, at any place.

This piling up of negatives, however, is no longer good English usage. We can express the same idea with only *one* negative:

Girls do not like mice.

Keep your grammar up to date by avoiding such double negatives as "doesn't make no," "isn't no," "hasn't done nothing," "can't help but," "can't hardly," "wasn't none." Instead, say "doesn't make any," "is no," "has done nothing," "can't help," "can hardly," "wasn't any."

CHAPTER 7

The Correct Use
of Pronouns

NOMINATIVE AND OBJECTIVE USES

Nouns and pronouns have *case*. In English there are three cases: *nominative*, *objective*, and *possessive*. The case or form of a noun or a pronoun depends upon its use in the sentence.

Choosing the correct case form for a noun is comparatively simple. The form of a noun remains the same in the nominative and objective cases.

The girl [nominative] **blamed another girl.** [objective]

When a noun shows ownership or relationship, the form changes to the possessive case; usually an apostrophe and an *s* are added.

One girl's dog chased the other girl's cat.

Unlike nouns, however, pronouns have various case forms. To avoid making mistakes with pronouns, you must not only master the various case forms but also learn how to use them.

The Case Forms of Pronouns

Study the following list of pronouns, noticing the changes in form.

NOMINATIVE CASE	OBJECTIVE CASE	POSSESSIVE CASE
Singular		
I	me	my, mine
you	you	your, yours
he, she, it	him, her, it	his, her, its
Plural		
we	us	our, ours,
you	you	your, yours
they	them	their, theirs
Singular or *Plural*		
who	whom	whose
whoever	whomever	whosever

Since the pronouns *you* and *it* do not undergo any changes, they do not present any usage problem. Omitting them from consideration, you will have the following list of pronouns whose nominative case form is different from their objective case form.

NOMINATIVE CASE		OBJECTIVE CASE	
I	they	me	them
he	who	him	whom
she	whoever	her	whomever
we		us	

● EXERCISE 1. Study the above list so that you can write it from memory.

● EXERCISE 2. Your teacher may read to you a mixed-up list of pronouns. Be prepared to write the case of each pronoun.

The Nominative Case

Before studying the following rules, be sure that you have thoroughly memorized these pronouns, which are in the nominative case: *I, he, she, we, they, who, whoever*.

7a. The subject of a verb is in the nominative case.

Notice that each pronoun in heavy print below is in the nominative case.

She and **I** often study together.
We boys try to win every game.
Who said that?

In the sentences above, *She* and *I* are the subjects of the verb *study*, the pronoun *We* is the subject of *try*, and *Who* is the subject of *said*.

● EXERCISE 3.   *Oral Drill*. Recite each of the following sentences *aloud* twice, stressing the correct italicized pronouns.

1. *She* and her brother are twins.
2. *We* girls will furnish refreshments.
3. *They* and *we* were interested in the program.
4. Roger and *I* are partners.
5. Joe and *he* joined the scouts.
6. Why do you and *she* quarrel?
7. My friends and *I* went to the circus.
8. Where are Ted and *he*?
9. *He* knew that *we* students wanted to rest.
10. *They* decided that Jim and *I* had tied.

● EXERCISE 4.   Number from 1 to 10 on your paper. List the pronouns (in the nominative case) that are used as subjects in the following sentences. After each pronoun, write its verb.

1. In that game we boys showed that we could run, and our quarterback passed for long gains.
2. In the first half, Al and he bucked over the goal line for two touchdowns.
3. In the second half, our fullback and I scampered for more than seventy yards.
4. Don, the captain of our team, and I talked with Coach Davis during the half.
5. He and his assistant said that we boys should tighten our defense.
6. While we boys were resting, Don and he planned several plays for the second half.
7. Neither they nor we, warned Coach Davis, had won the game yet.
8. In the last half, providing thrills for all, Don and I marched seventy-five yards for two more touchdowns.
9. Who won? Well, I guess that they had the higher score.
10. What really matters, though, is that we and they played a hard, fast, clean game.

● EXERCISE 5.   Correctly use the following pronouns in sentences of your own.

1. you and I	6. she and they
2. they and Jane	7. Eleanor and he
3. we freshmen	8. he and Joe
4. she and I	9. my sister and I
5. you and he	10. who

7b. A predicate nominative is in the nominative case.

As you will remember, a predicate nominative is a word which completes the meaning of a linking verb and means the same thing as the subject. (See pages 51–52.)

A pronoun used as a predicate nominative follows

7a-b

a form of the linking verb *to be: am, is, are, was, were,* and verb phrases ending in *be* or *been.*

EXAMPLES **This *is* he.**

It may *be* she.

Listening to conversations, you will often hear educated people say, "*It's me.*" Usage has changed the *I* to *me,* and *me* is correct. Of course, *It's I* is also correct. Expressions such as *That's him* or *Had it been her* may be classified as acceptable *oral* English but should probably be avoided in *written* English. As you do the following exercises, follow the rule for written English: *A predicate nominative is in the nominative case.*

● EXERCISE 6. Number from 1 to 10 on your paper. Complete the following sentences by adding pronouns in the nominative case used as predicate nominatives. Write each pronoun after the corresponding number on your paper. Don't use *you* or *it;* use a variety of pronouns.

1. This is ——.
2. Are you ——?
3. That was ——.
4. Those are ——.
5. Can it be ——?
6. It can't be ——.
7. It is ——.
8. It might be ——.
9. Was that ——?
10. I knew it was ——.

The Objective Case

As you will remember, *me, him, her, us, them, whom, whomever* are in the objective case. These pronouns are used as objects: direct objects, indirect objects, or objects of prepositions. (Review pages 53–55.)

7c. The object of a verb is in the objective case.

The object of a verb receives the action of the verb.

EXAMPLES **The sudden noise startled us.** [Here *startled* is
the verb, and *noise* is the subject. The noise
startled *whom*? The answer is *us*, which is the
object of the verb *startled*.]

We elected Kate and him. [*Kate* and *him* form
the compound object of the verb *elected*.]

Failure to use the objective pronouns (*us, me, him,
her, them, whom, whomever*) as objects of the verb leads
to rather serious errors in usage.

Most errors in the use of pronouns are made when
the subject or object is compound (when it has two
parts). This sentence has a compound subject: *He
and I must study for this test.* You can often arrive at the
correct form by simply trying each pronoun separately
with the verb: *He must study; I must study.* You would
never say *Him must study* or *Me must study.* Similarly
you can determine the correct form when an object
is compound: *Paul liked her and me. Paul liked her* (not
she); *Paul liked me* (not *I*).

● EXERCISE 7. *Oral Drill.* Recite each of the following sentences *aloud* three times, stressing the correct, italicized pronouns. After you become familiar
with the right sound of pronouns, your ear can tell
you what pronoun is correct.

1. I saw Jake and *him* downtown.
2. Did you invite Dan and *her*?
3. Tell *him* and *me* about your plans.
4. Has he met Mr. Nevins and *them*?
5. Miss Blair sent *them* and *me* on an errand.
6. Don't leave *them* or *us* off that list.
7. He asked *us* girls to join the club.
8. Can you believe Dick and *him*?
9. Are they expecting *her* and *me*?
10. She gave *us* boys a bushel of apples.

7c

● EXERCISE 8. Number from 1 to 10 on your paper. Supply correct pronouns for the blanks in these sentences. (After you have checked the exercise, read each sentence *aloud* twice.)

1. James knew that he had lost —— and ——.
2. He warned —— (*we* or *us*) students about being absent.
3. I know —— and —— well.
4. The judges named Clara and ——.
5. Leave Ted and —— alone.
6. I found Nancy and —— hard at work.
7. We watched Henry and ——.
8. Mike grabbed Ellen and —— by our hands.
9. Now he needs you and —— more than ever.
10. That dress fits both Sally and ——.

7d. Like the direct object, the indirect object of the verb is in the objective case.

DIRECT OBJECTS   I wrote **Ted** and **him**.
INDIRECT OBJECTS   I wrote **Ted** and **him** a letter.

As you have already learned, an indirect object tells *to whom* or *for whom* something is done. (See pages 54–55.) Pronouns used as indirect objects are in the objective case: *me, us, him, her, them.*

● EXERCISE 9. Number from 1 to 5 on your paper. Supply correct pronouns for the blanks below.

1. Mr. Smith offered Luke and —— a job.
2. Lend —— (*we* or *us*) boys a dollar.
3. Please bring the baby and —— some candy.
4. He taught —— and —— a good lesson.
5. Will you tell —— and —— your plans?

● REVIEW EXERCISE A. Number from 1 to 25. Select the correct one of the two pronouns in parentheses, and write it after the corresponding number on your paper. Be prepared to explain your choice by giving the *use* of each pronoun in the sentence.

1. Where have you and (she, her) been?
2. (He, Him) and (I, me) have been to the fair.
3. (We, Us) boys spent hours looking at free displays.
4. One of the guides showed (us, we) boys the telephone room.
5. He told Arthur and (I, me) about the unusual telephones.
6. You and (she, her) can't guess what happened.
7. After (we, us) boys had said a few words into a telephone, our own voices came back over the wire.
8. This really surprised (he, him) and (I, me).
9. I heard my own voice say, "Joe Jones? Oh, this is (he, him)."
10. Arthur heard his voice boomerang, "(She, Her) and (they, them) aren't here just now. Will you leave (they, them) and (she, her) a message?"
11. Arthur and (I, me) then found another free display.
12. A girl named Sara showed Arthur and (I, me) all kinds of candies.
13. (She, Her) and her sister were advertising powdered sugar.
14. We asked Sara and (she, her) for a sample of their candy.
15. Then they gave (we, us) boys two large sacks full of fudge.
16. (They, Them) and the other people at the fair seemed to enjoy their work.
17. Have you and (she, her) ever seen their "House of Magic"?
18. When the crowd and (we, us) saw the severed head of Charles I there, we asked in horror, "Can this really be (he, him)?"
19. Of course, (they, them) and (we, us) knew that it was only a piece of wax.
20. After all, as we have told you and (she, her), we were in the "House of Magic."
21. A clown and his dwarf singled out (we, us) boys to tease.
22. Seeing my snowy white sweater, the clown and (he, him) scooted over to me.

7d

23. (He, Him) and his dwarf kept waving very big fountain pens in the air.
24. When they squirted black ink all over my white sweater, you can imagine how angry Arthur and (I, me) were.
25. In a matter of seconds, however, (we, us) boys watched the magic ink disappear before our very eyes.

7e. The object of a preposition is in the objective case.

A prepositional phrase begins with a preposition (see the list on page 18) and ends with a noun or a pronoun. The final word in a prepositional phrase is the *object of the preposition* which begins the phrase. When the object of a preposition is a pronoun, you must be careful to use the objective case. The words in heavy print below are objects of prepositions.

for **me**	by **her**	except **them**
near **him**	between **us**	to **whom**

Errors in usage often occur when the object of a preposition is compound. Examine the following prepositional phrases, noting that the pronouns are in the objective case.

with **Jack** and **me**	like **Fran** and **us**
about **you** and **him**	from **you** and **them**
behind **Ted** and **her**	for **him** and **me**

● EXERCISE 10.   Make a list of the prepositional phrases in these sentences.

1. She bought some costume jewelry for her and me.
2. Just between you and me, I don't believe it.
3. To whom is the letter addressed?
4. Marilyn wrote her theme about Barbara and him.
5. In addition to you and us, Aline has the mumps.
6. He said that he couldn't do without you and me.
7. Everybody except Tom and me went to the party.
8. Then we bumped into you and them.

9. Did she ask about Ed and her?
10. We haven't heard a word from them or him.

● EXERCISE 11. *Oral Drill.* Recite each of the following sentences *aloud* twice, stressing the correct, italicized pronouns.

1. Everyone except *her* was looking at Alice and *me.*
2. As for *her* and *me,* we like to play with you and *them.*
3. The man was walking toward Fred and *me.*
4. With the help of Jim and *him,* we can soon finish.
5. He gave the tickets to *us* girls.
6. She was with *whom*?
7. Are you interested in Sylvia or *him*?
8. I have suggestions for Mary and *them.*
9. Behind *us* boys was an angry rattlesnake.
10. Are you talking about Larry or *him*?

● EXERCISE 12. Write 10 sentences of your own, using a variety of pronouns as compound objects of prepositions.

● EXERCISE 13. Number from 1 to 10 on your paper. Supply correct pronouns for each blank below.

1. Is this gift for —— or ——?
2. Please sit by —— and ——.
3. Between you and ——, this is useless.
4. Father explained the motor to —— boys.
5. We were with —— and ——.
6. I am looking at Hazel and ——.
7. Begin the recommendation with "To —— it may concern."
8. We have asked everyone except you and ——.
9. May we go with Lucy and ——?
10. Instead of —— or ——, I was elected as our representative.

● REVIEW EXERCISE B. As you read the following sentences, carefully check the case form of each pronoun. Number from 1 to 20 on your paper. If all of the

7e

pronouns in a sentence are right, write a plus sign (+) after the proper number on your paper. If a pronoun is wrong, write the correct case form of the pronoun.

1. Betty and me know how to keep a secret.
2. Everyone knows that we girls are especially good cooks and gardeners.
3. In fact, she and I have a reputation for making the best date muffins in town.
4. Her grandmother gave her and I the secret recipe years ago.
5. We girls have never let anyone else see this recipe.
6. When our friends beg Betty and I for it, we always list the ingredients for them.
7. Sally and they can never bake muffins the way Betty and I can, though, and with good reason.
8. You see, Betty and I don't mention the most important ingredient when we so graciously share our recipe.
9. Us girls also grow the prettiest flowers in the neighborhood.
10. Like us girls, Bill and Joe, our neighbors, also grow flowers.
11. As Bill and him admit, though, their zinnias and daffodils look as though they need a hospitalization policy.
12. The other day someone in the front yard was yelling for Betty and I.
13. It was them — Bill and Joe.
14. Bill and him had been admiring our healthy zinnias.
15. "Could it be Betty and her?" Joe asked Bill as we joined them.
16. Betty and me assured Joe and him that we were the gardeners.
17. "Gee!" commented Bill. "Do you and her have magic green thumbs?"
18. With her usual charm, Betty said, "We girls will give you and he some of our seeds."
19. He and Joe were delighted, thinking that they could soon raise beautiful flowers.
20. We girls knew better; after all, we had not told Bill and him about our "Grow-Fast Magic Plant Food."

● REVIEW EXERCISE C. Write 20 original sentences correctly using the following.

1. my brother and I	11. she and we
2. my brother and me	12. we students
3. her friend and she	13. us students
4. her friend and her	14. he and she
5. you and I	15. him and her
6. you and me	16. Jean and him
7. they and we	17. Jean and they
8. them and us	18. us girls
9. who	19. Julia and us
10. whom	20. Sam and we

WHO AND WHOM

In spoken English the use of *whom* is gradually disappearing. In fact, when you are speaking, you may correctly begin any question with *Who*, regardless of the grammar of the sentence.

In written English, however, you should distinguish between *who* and *whom*. *Who* is used as a subject or predicate nominative, and *whom* is used as an object.

7f. The case of a relative pronoun is determined by its use in the clause it introduces.

When *who* and *whom* introduce a subordinate clause, they are called relative pronouns. (See page 73.) When you are deciding whether a clause calls for *who* or *whom*, isolate the subordinate clause from the rest of the sentence. Then ask yourself, "How is the pronoun used in its own clause?" If it is used as a subject or a predicate nominative, choose *who*. If it is used as an object of the verb or as the object of a preposition, choose *whom*. Carefully study the make-up of the following subordinate clauses in heavy print.

1. **Tom is a boy who can make a good speech.** [In its own clause, *who* is the subject of *can make*.]

7f

2. **I know who he is.** [In the subordinate clause, *he* is the subject of *is*, and *who* is the predicate nominative.]
3. **Mr. Evans, whom I just met,** is our new coach. [*I* is the subject of *met*. I met *whom*. *Whom* is the direct object in its own clause.]
4. **Mr. Evans, whom I just spoke to,** is our new coach. [In the subordinate clause, *whom* is object of the preposition *to*: *to whom I just spoke*.]

● EXERCISE 14.   Copy on your paper each subordinate clause beginning with *who* or *whom* in the sentences below. Then tell how the relative pronoun (*who* or *whom*) is used in its own clause — as *subject, predicate nominative, object of the verb*, or *object of a preposition*.

1. Mrs. Graves is a hostess who is very gracious.
2. She is a person whom we can trust.
3. Miss Cabot, who teaches history, will soon marry.
4. Bill Smith, whom she teaches, is my brother.
5. I like anyone who has a sense of humor.
6. A man who can laugh at himself usually succeeds.
7. Tell us who she is.
8. He is a man whom I admire.
9. She is the girl whom I was telling you about.
10. Charles, whom I nominated, won the election.

● EXERCISE 15.   Write 10 sentences using subordinate clauses introduced by *who* or *whom*, as follows:

4 using *who* as a subject
1 using *who* as a predicate nominative
3 using *whom* as a direct object
2 using *whom* as the object of a preposition

● EXERCISE 16.   Number on your paper from 1 to 10. After the proper number, give the use of the pronoun in parentheses. Then write the correct pronoun.

1. I admire anyone (who, whom) has patience.
2. The person (who, whom) I admire has patience.

3. I enjoy the company of a child (who, whom) behaves.
4. Miss Brown, (who, whom) sells magazines, is at the door.
5. Is there anyone (who, whom) plans to leave early?
6. He is a teacher (who, whom) I respect.
7. There is the man about (who, whom) you were asking.
8. Can you tell me (who, whom) she is?
9. They asked Margaret, (who, whom) knows the rules.
10. Mr. Teague, (who, whom) I work for, is out of town.

● REVIEW EXERCISE D. Some of the sentences below contain errors in case, and some sentences do not. Number from 1 to 20. If the pronouns in a sentence are correct, write a plus sign (+) after the appropriate number. If a pronoun is incorrect, write the correct form of the pronoun.

1. About nine o'clock us girls left the theater. 2. Out front, waiting to take us home, were Nancy and her sister, who live in our neighborhood. 3. Before Nancy and us had reached the car, however, we noticed a crowd of noisy people who were gathering near a store window. 4. They and I went over there to see what was happening. 5. When we girls had wedged our way through the crowd, we saw flames beating on the glass and crackling up the drapes to the ceiling.

6. At each new burst of fire, my friends and I heard an excited hiss run through the crowd. 7. Soon Nancy and me found ourselves watching the crowd instead of the fire. 8. I could see the yellow and red reflection in the eyes of a man who was standing near my friends and I.   9. While Bernice and them complained about the heat from the blaze, something inside me felt cold as I saw the changing lights show the faces of the crowd, whose expressions revealed complete and fascinated absorption.   10. As I told Nancy and them later, the red glow seemed to come from within each person rather than from the flames.

11. Soon us girls heard the noisy sirens of the firemen, who quickly arrived at the scene.   12. We girls stood back out of the way. 13. Knowing that the fire was about over,

Bernice asked Nancy and I about leaving. 14. We two, however, told Bernice and them "Not yet." 15. In a few minutes her and me heard the firemen boarding their truck. 16. One of the firemen shouted to the crowd and we, "Break it up! The fire is dead!"

17. After they had left, the crowd and I had only the black ashes to watch. 18. Even so, Nancy and I stayed to see the reaction of the men who we had been observing. 19. As the others shuffled away, one man lingered in the semidarkness; it was him, the man who had been standing near me. 20. As he stood silently in front of the store, we girls could see the heavy disappointment in the face that no longer smiled.

The Pronoun in an Incomplete Construction

Notice the difference in meaning that the choice of pronouns can make in sentences with incomplete constructions.

> She gave Mary more than **I**.
> She gave Mary more than **me**.

In the first sentence, the choice of the pronoun *I* indicates that it is the subject of an understood verb: *She gave Mary more than I gave Mary*. In the second sentence, the pronoun *me* is in the objective case; so the meaning is: *She gave Mary more than she gave me*. The case of the pronoun depends upon how the omitted part of the sentence would be completed.

7g. After *than* and *as* introducing an incomplete construction, use the form of the pronoun you would use if the construction were completed.

The following sentences are correct because they clearly express the meaning of the writer. The words inside the brackets show how each sentence could be completed.

EXAMPLES   John told me more than **she** [told me].
John told me more than [he told] **her.**
I am as eager to begin as **he** [is].
Are you as tall as **she** [is]?

● EXERCISE 17. Number from 1 to 10 on your paper. Beginning with the *than* or *as*, complete each sentence below, using the correct form of the pronoun. After the sentence, write the use of the pronoun in its clause, telling whether it is a subject or an object.

EXAMPLE   1. Jane is as brave as (her, she)
        1. **as she is, subject**

1. Vera is as strong as (her, she).
2. I often eat more than (him, he).
3. She can spell much better than (me, I).
4. Did he pay you as much as (me, I)?
5. Ralph is heavier than (him, he).
6. Do you like her better than (me, I)?
7. Father does not drive as fast as (him, he).
8. He is much younger than (her, she).
9. We are as energetic as (them, they).
10. They were as frightened as (us, we).

● REVIEW EXERCISE E. Number on your paper from 1 to 25. After each number, write the correct form of the pronoun in parentheses. Be able to give reasons for your answers.

1. Is Ted going with you and (I, me)?
2. I have a friend (who, whom) likes to work puzzles.
3. The friend (who, whom) I like best is president of our class.
4. All of (we, us) students studied hard for the test.
5. Are you as pleased as (I, me)?
6. After a while Gary and (I, me) started typing the exercises.
7. The customer (who, whom) is pleased is a good advertiser.

7g

8. Is it really (they, them)?
9. Please give that picture to Wanda and (I, me).
10. He can't swim as fast as (I, me).
11. Behind us stood Eric and (he, him).
12. My mother taught Wanda and (I, me) how to use a pressure cooker.
13. Do you need someone (who, whom) is dependable?
14. It may be (she, her).
15. Father told Fred and (I, me) the answer.
16. Some of (we, us) girls preferred to skate.
17. Everyone except (she, her) has joined the club.
18. Surely you can do as well as (he, him).
19. Her brother and (she, her) will help us.
20. Mary Ann, (who, whom) you have met, will be at the party.
21. At the end of the story, who marries (who, whom)?
22. Do tell (we, us) boys what you know.
23. Charles and (we, us) fished far into the night.
24. The man stopped Charles and (we, us) at the gate.
25. Are you and (they, them) going to the banquet?

● REVIEW EXERCISE F. Number on your paper from 1 to 25. If a sentence below has no errors in usage of pronouns, write a plus sign (+) after the corresponding number on your paper. If a pronoun is incorrect, give the right form of the pronoun.

1. Him and his wife are interested in the interpretation of dreams.
2. Last night George and I went over to talk with them.
3. After he had asked us boys to sit down, his wife, who we liked a lot, gave us cokes and cookies.
4. Mr. Snodgrass, who has read many books on psychology, explained one of my dreams.
5. He was particularly interested in the one about my brother and me.
6. In the dream, my brother and me were shivering in the bowling alley.
7. It seemed that us boys had to keep playing, even though both the balls and the pins were solid ice.

8. Suddenly, however, a big surprise came for Teddy and I.

9. When hot winds started blowing through the room, he was as dumfounded as me.

10. Soon steam began to engulf us boys.

11. Everybody except us and the cashier left when the balls and pins melted.

12. The dream ended when the cashier called the police because Teddy and me couldn't pay him for the game; our ice quarters melted as fast as we could take them out of our pockets.

13. Both of us boys wanted Mrs. Snodgrass and him to tell us the meaning of this dream.

14. According to Mr. Snodgrass, I had dreamed of ice because my brother and me had been cold that night in January.

15. Since my mother had brought us boys an extra blanket, we grew warm, and the "steam melted the ice."

16. After he and his wife questioned me further, he and her concluded that the money melted because we boys had not saved enough from our allowances to go bowling.

17. This explanation sounded very logical to George and I.

18. After a while, Mr. Snodgrass asked George, "Are you David Holt's oldest boy? My wife and I were wondering about that the other day."

19. "I am him," answered George, "and I also have a dream for you to unravel."

20. George told Mr. Snodgrass and us about a terrific nightmare.

21. At first his family and him were suffocated by a tornado.

22. Next there was an earthquake that buried his family and he alive.

23. Finally a hurricane washed him and his family out to sea.

24. Poor Mr. Snodgrass, whom we looked to for an interpretation, was completely bewildered; he could not begin to explain the dream to George and I.

25. Mrs. Snodgrass, who kept smiling at us boys, however, was not at all puzzled about the dream; she and I both knew that George had made it all up as he had gone along.

GOOD USAGE

Four don't's regarding pronoun usage:

1. Don't use unnecessary pronouns in a "double subject."

    WRONG   My mother **she** is a good cook.
    RIGHT   My mother is a good cook.

2. Don't use unacceptable forms of pronouns.

    WRONG   hisself, theirselves
    RIGHT   himself, themselves

3. Don't confuse pronouns in the possessive case with contractions.

POSSESSIVE PRONOUNS	CONTRACTIONS
its	it's (it is)
their	they're (they are)
your	you're (you are)
whose	who's (who is)

4. Don't use *here* after *this* or *there* after *that* as a modifier.

    WRONG   **this here** bag of peanuts, **that there** elephant
    RIGHT   this bag of peanuts, that elephant

CHAPTER 8

The Correct Use of Modifiers

COMPARISON AND PLACEMENT

Two parts of speech — an adjective and an adverb — are modifiers; that is, they describe or limit the meaning of another word. An adjective modifies a noun or a pronoun. An adverb modifies a verb, an adjective, or another adverb. (See pages 7 and 14.) As you learned in Chapter 3, prepositional phrases as well as many verbal phrases are also modifiers. In like manner, a clause is a modifier whenever it is used as an adjective or an adverb to describe or limit the meaning of another word in the sentence. (Review pages 61–77.)

In the following paragraph, taken from *Walden* by Henry David Thoreau, all modifiers (words, phrases, and clauses) are italicized. If you read this passage and omit the italicized modifiers, you can see how necessary modifiers are for vivid expression of ideas.

At length the jays arrive, *whose discordant screams were heard long before, as they were warily making their approach an eighth of a mile off,* and *in a stealthy and sneaking manner* they flit *from tree to tree, nearer and nearer,* and pick *up the* kernels *which the squirrels have dropped. Then, sliding on a pitch pine bough*, they attempt to swallow *in their haste a* kernel *which is too big for their throats and chokes them;* and *after great labor* they disgorge it, and spend *an* hour *in the endeavor to crack it by repeated blows with their bills.* They were *manifestly* thieves, and I had *not much* respect *for them;* but *the* squirrels, *though at first shy*, went *to work as if they were taking what was their own.*

The purpose of this chapter is to help you to use modifiers correctly and effectively.

Comparison of Modifiers

Adjectives state qualities of nouns or pronouns: a *small* house, an *attractive* girl, *good* health. You can show the degree or extent to which one noun has a quality by comparing it with another noun which has the same quality. For instance: *This house is smaller than that house.*

Similarly, you can show degree or extent by using adverbs to make comparisons: *I frequently go swimming at the beach, but he goes more frequently.*

8a. The forms of modifiers change as they are used in comparison.

There are three degrees of comparison: *positive, comparative,* and *superlative.* Notice below how the forms of modifiers change to show comparison.

POSITIVE	COMPARATIVE	SUPERLATIVE
small	smaller	smallest
often	oftener	oftenest
attractive	more attractive	most attractive
recently	more recently	most recently
good	better	best
bad	worse	worst

REGULAR COMPARISON

(1) A modifier of one syllable forms its comparative and superlative degrees by adding –er and –est.

POSITIVE	COMPARATIVE	SUPERLATIVE
short	shorter	shortest
slow	slower	slowest

(2) Some modifiers of two syllables form their comparative and superlative degrees by adding –er and –est; other modifiers of two syllables form their comparative and superlative degrees by means of *more* and *most*.

POSITIVE	COMPARATIVE	SUPERLATIVE
simple	simpler	simplest
foolish	more foolish	most foolish

When in doubt about which way an adjective is compared, consult an unabridged dictionary.

● EXERCISE 1.   Write the forms for the comparative and superlative degrees of these words:

1. gentle	6. worried
2. eager	7. cheerful
3. pleasing	8. careless
4. funny	9. lucky
5. sincere	10. idle

(3) Modifiers having more than two syllables form their comparative and superlative degrees by means of *more* and *most*.

POSITIVE	COMPARATIVE	SUPERLATIVE
obedient	more obedient	most obedient
gracefully	more gracefully	most gracefully

8a

● EXERCISE 2.   Orally give the superlative and the comparative degrees of *ignorant, typical, favorably, important, hopefully.*

(4) Comparison to indicate less or least of a quality is accomplished by using the words *less* and *least* before the modifier.

POSITIVE	COMPARATIVE	SUPERLATIVE
successful	less successful	least successful
frequently	less frequently	least frequently

IRREGULAR COMPARISON

Adjectives and adverbs that do not follow the regular methods of forming their comparative and superlative degrees are said to be compared irregularly.

POSITIVE	COMPARATIVE	SUPERLATIVE
bad	worse	worst
good ⎤ well ⎦	better	best
many ⎤ much ⎦	more	most

● EXERCISE 3.   Be prepared to give the correct forms of the comparative and superlative degrees when your teacher dictates the positive forms of the 5 adjectives and adverbs listed above.

● REVIEW EXERCISE A.   Write the comparative and superlative forms of the following modifiers. If you are in doubt about the words of two syllables, look them up in an unabridged dictionary.

1. young	8. patient	15. satisfying
2. respectable	9. exciting	16. secure
3. crooked	10. original	17. becoming
4. late	11. affectionate	18. well
5. heavy	12. good	19. settled
6. bad	13. mischievous	20. simply
7. methodically	14. easy	

Use of Comparative and Superlative Forms

8b. Use the comparative degree when comparing two things; use the superlative degree when comparing more than two.

The comparative form of a modifier is used for comparing two things, as these examples indicate.

1. This eraser is **better** than that one.
2. The traffic laws are **more strictly** enforced in town than on the open highway.
3. He is **more agreeable** than his twin sister.

The superlative form of a modifier is used for comparing three or more items:

1. Which freshman is **most likely to succeed?**
2. This road is the **roughest** of the three.
3. I had to report on the **least interesting** book in the library.

● EXERCISE 4.   Correctly using adjectives or adverbs, write 5 sentences comparing two things and 5 comparing more than two.

8c. Do not omit the word *other* when comparing one thing with a group of which it is a part.

It is incorrect to say, "She is smarter than any girl in her class," because obviously she too is a girl in her class, and she cannot be smarter than herself. You should say, "She is smarter than any *other* girl in her class."

WRONG   Emily walked faster than any girl in her group.
RIGHT   Emily walked faster than any **other** girl in her group.

WRONG   He is shorter than any boy on his team.
RIGHT   He is shorter than any **other** boy on his team.

8b-c

● EXERCISE 5. The following comparisons are illogical because of the omission of the word *other*. Orally supply the needed word so that the sentences will be logical.

1. This lake is larger than any lake in the state.
2. My dog is more courageous than any dog in our neighborhood.
3. Dr. Smith is more popular than any doctor in his community.
4. Jack is friendlier than any boy in his class.
5. I like Mark Twain better than any American writer.

8d. Avoid the double comparison.

A double comparison is one in which the degree is formed incorrectly by both adding *−er* or *−est* and using *more* or *most*.

WRONG   His story is more funnier than yours.
RIGHT   His story is **funnier** than yours.

WRONG   Janet is the most beautifulest girl I know.
RIGHT   Janet is the **most beautiful** girl I know.

● EXERCISE 6. Number on your paper from 1 to 10. Write the correct form of the incorrect modifiers, eliminating double comparisons.

1. Your poster is more prettier than mine.
2. Ralph was the most politest.
3. It is more darker outside now.
4. A pine tree grows more taller than a mesquite.
5. He is the most stubbornest child in the family.
6. About nine o'clock, the noise became more louder.
7. This is the most loveliest day!
8. Miss Adkins is the most finest teacher that I've ever had.
9. The patient is more worse than he was last night.
10. Then I made the most stupidest remark.

● REVIEW EXERCISE B. Number in a column on your paper from 1 to 20. If the sentence is correct, write a plus sign (+) after the corresponding number on your paper; if it is incorrect, write a zero (0). Be prepared to give the correct usage for each sentence that you label 0.

1. Of the two sisters, Martha is the most friendly.
2. This is the better of the two bicycles.
3. My paper got more red marks than any paper in the class.
4. Is he more unhappier than he was?
5. We drove more slowly than they did.
6. Of the four boys, Ted is the most laziest.
7. Suddenly the siren became more loud.
8. Your mistake was bad, but my blunder was worser.
9. We were undecided about which one of the two books was best.
10. Clara is younger than any other girl in the contest.
11. Your kitten is littler than mine.
12. Which one of the three is the more heavy?
13. Sally is more industrious than her brother.
14. The sky is bluer today than it was yesterday.
15. His suggestions were helpful, but yours are more practical.
16. That is good, but this is better.
17. Paul is the fastest runner of the two.
18. He is the most saddest clown in the circus.
19. This place is more suitable than any spot that we've seen so far.
20. Which dress is the most attractive — the pink gingham or the lavender organdy one?

Dangling Modifiers

8e. A phrase or clause which does not clearly and sensibly modify a word in the sentence is a *dangling* modifier.

When a modifying phrase containing a verbal comes at the beginning of a sentence, the phrase is followed

8d-e

by a comma; immediately after that comma should come the word that the phrase modifies. Notice below how the introductory phrases clearly and sensibly modify the words which follow the commas.

1. **Walking to school this morning,** I saw wisteria vines in full bloom.   [I did the walking.]

2. **After scratching his fleas for a while,** Fido lay down. [Fido scratched his fleas.]

The following sentences, however, contain *dangling* modifiers, which do not clearly or sensibly modify a word in the sentence.

1. **Walking to school this morning,** the wisteria vines which I saw were in full bloom.   [In this sentence, the vines were walking to school.]

2. **After scratching his fleas for a while,** Bill told Fido to lie down. [Here Bill, not the dog, scratched fleas.]

● EXERCISE 7.   After copying the following introductory modifiers onto your paper, complete the sentences so that each modifier will *clearly* and *sensibly* modify a word in your sentence.

EXAMPLE   1. **While talking on the telephone,** . . .
        1. **While talking on the** telephone, I forgot the cake in the oven.

1. While driving through the mountains, . . .
2. After waiting for over an hour, . . .
3. Encouraged by the coach, . . .
4. Failing to catch the ball, . . .
5. At the age of fourteen, . . .
6. Not expecting the interruption, . . .
7. Besides giving her a birthday party, . . .
8. By paying close attention in class, . . .
9. To avoid being caught in the rain, . . .
10. Trying to keep from laughing, . . .

CORRECTING DANGLING MODIFIERS

To correct a dangling modifier, you should either rearrange the words in the sentence or add words to make the meaning logical and clear.

WRONG   While flying over Vicksburg, the national military park came into view.

RIGHT   While flying over Vicksburg, we could see the national military park.

RIGHT   While we were flying over Vicksburg, the national military park came into view.

WRONG   To gain weight quickly, doughnuts are a good bedtime snack.

RIGHT   To gain weight quickly, you should eat doughnuts at bedtime.

RIGHT   If you wish to gain weight quickly, doughnuts are a good bedtime snack.

WRONG   Hopelessly baffled by the problem, our teacher was asked for the right answer.

RIGHT   Hopelessly baffled by the problem, we asked our teacher for the right answer.

RIGHT   Since we were hopelessly baffled by the problem, our teacher told us the answer.

● EXERCISE 8. Eliminate the dangling modifiers in the following sentences by rewriting each sentence so that each modifier clearly and sensibly modifies a word in the sentence. You will have to supply words.

1. Just after eating my lunch, the telephone rang.
2. When putting on lipstick, a mirror is needed.
3. To build a complicated model airplane, instructions must be followed.
4. After having a serious heart attack, the voters were concerned about the health of the mayor.
5. Strolling through the French Quarter, the cafés particularly impressed me.
6. Stepping on the brakes, the car skidded to the side of the road.

7. To make a dress, a pattern must be bought.
8. Being very hungry, this sandwich looks as good as fried chicken to me.
9. To go to Mexico, a vaccination certificate must be presented at the border.
10. When shaving, Mother often tells Dad about her plans for the day.

● EXERCISE 9. Many sentences below contain dangling modifiers; some do not. Number on your paper from 1 to 20. If a sentence is correct, write a plus sign (+) after the corresponding number. If it is incorrect, rewrite the sentence to eliminate the dangling modifier.

1. After saying grace, dinner was served.
2. To appreciate good music, you should learn to play an instrument.
3. While trimming the rosebushes this morning, a spider bit me.
4. Made of durable plastic, a child cannot easily break these toy trucks.
5. Glittering in the soft, silent moonlight, the water looked beautiful and seemed inviting to the boys.
6. Filled with high school students, the visitors could not find an empty seat in the auditorium.
7. While listening to the radio, I soon fell asleep.
8. While reading my assignment by the river, the wind kept blowing dust into my eyes.
9. When the bell was ringing, no one seemed to hear it.
10. Running across the meadow, my ankle was sprained.
11. To become a great athlete, physical endurance is necessary.
12. To become well informed, you should form the habit of reading newspapers and magazines.
13. To earn spending money, Mr. Levy gave me a job.
14. After mopping the kitchen, the baby woke up and began to cry.
15. After being in school all day, a long hike is refreshing.

16. Sitting up on its hind legs, the squirrel munched a nut.
17. When learning to swim, everything that one tries seems ridiculous at first.
18. While walking alone in the woods, it is good to hear the birds singing.
19. While eating his dog food, Dad noticed that Rover seemed hungry.
20. When trying to understand the meaning of a sentence, look at the little words, especially the prepositions and conjunctions.

Misplaced Modifiers

A dangling modifier, as the preceding exercises have shown, makes the meaning of a sentence absurd because the modifier either seems to modify a word which it cannot sensibly modify or is left without any word to modify at all. Just as damaging to the clear expression of ideas are misplaced modifiers.

8f. Modifying phrases and clauses should be placed as near as possible to the words they modify.

MISPLACED PHRASE MODIFIERS

The following examples of misplaced phrases show the importance of placing phrase modifiers as near as possible to the words they modify.

WRONG   The friendly policemen tell you what you are doing wrong with a smile. [Here *with a smile* seems to indicate how you are enjoying doing wrong.]

RIGHT   With a smile the friendly policemen tell you what you are doing wrong.

WRONG   Louise yearned to see the Mississippi River while in Arizona.

RIGHT   While in Arizona, Louise yearned to see the Mississippi River.

8f

WRONG   On the bottom shelf of the refrigerator, I finally found the cottage cheese.

RIGHT   I finally found the cottage cheese on the bottom shelf of the refrigerator.

● EXERCISE 10.   Rewrite the following sentences in order to eliminate the misplaced phrase modifiers. Decide what word the phrase should modify, and place the phrase near that word.

1. The orlon blouses were shown to us by the clerk on sale for $2.98.
2. In a cage at the dog pound, we felt very sorry for the little bulldog.
3. I read about the kidnapers who were found in this morning's paper.
4. The names of the men were called out by the announcer in the starting line-up.
5. I watched him make a thrilling touchdown on the forty-yard line.
6. He told us about roping and branding the steer in the school cafeteria.
7. Three freshmen were punished after the rules had been broken by the principal.
8. When only eight years old, my father persuaded me to become a teacher.
9. On the way to the grocery store, the streets seemed slippery.
10. The thief was arrested soon after the grocery store had been robbed by the police.
11. Inside the oven I noticed that the turkey was burning.
12. The long pass was not caught by the quarterback too high in the air to reach.
13. At the age of six, my mother taught me to get along with my teachers.
14. The governor agreed that the state should punish every driver who endangers the lives of others without delay.
15. A small group of boys were all watching a bright object in the sky on the school grounds.

16. I read about the Indian scalping him in the middle of the seventh chapter.
17. We had a real thrill when we saw a star fall through the telescope.
18. The explorer told us about seeing cannibals roast and eat a man at the bus station.
19. There is the package given to me by my aunt under the Christmas tree.
20. The florist sent the flowers to the house of the dead man in a hurry.

MISPLACED CLAUSE MODIFIERS

Place the clause as near as possible to the word it modifies. Notice below how the sentence has its meaning distorted by a misplaced clause modifier.

WRONG   **The dress is hanging on the clothesline that I have sewed on for weeks.**

Since the modifying clause *that I have sewed on for weeks* seems to modify *clothesline*, the sentence is ridiculous. The clause should be close to the word it modifies, as follows:

RIGHT   **The dress that I have sewed on for weeks is hanging on the clothesline.**

To correct misplaced clauses, you place the modifying clause as close as possible to the word it modifies.

WRONG   **There is a park beyond the city dump which is very beautiful.**

RIGHT   **Beyond the city dump is a park which is very beautiful.**

WRONG   **The convict quietly listened to the words of the judge, who was to spend the rest of his life behind bars.**

RIGHT   **The convict, who was to spend the rest of his life behind bars, quietly listened to the words of the judge.**

● EXERCISE 11.   Read each of the following sentences. Decide what word the misplaced clause should modify, and rewrite the sentence, placing the clause near this word.

1. I saw a large dog trotting behind the little boy that was growling as if he were getting ready to attack me.
2. We played in two old shacks between the post office and the bank which weren't being lived in at the time.
3. Birds were the main targets for our slingshots, which were eating chicken feed.
4. The boy is engaged to Ellen, who has a stubby mustache.
5. The diamond-shaped playing field was carefully marked off with a chalk line which was as green as the hills of Ireland.
6. Then the baby was placed on the bed by Mother, who was still contentedly sucking her bottle.
7. We rode in the car of our neighbor that has the long, sweeping tail fins.
8. I just saw the honor roll on the teacher's desk, which has your name on it.
9. We crossed the Mississippi River on a long bridge which was almost a mile wide.
10. The girls commented on my large brown eyes that sit across the aisle from me.

● REVIEW EXERCISE C.   The sentences below contain dangling modifiers and misplaced modifiers. Rewrite the sentences so that the meaning is clear.

1. I watched the farmer operate the tractor smelling the rich, warm fragrance of the freshly plowed fields.
2. She served sandwiches to Elmer and me, packed with pickles, garlic, tomatoes, and cheese.
3. Everyone was waiting for the teacher in English class.
4. Buried at the top of a mountain near Denver, I visited the grave of Buffalo Bill.
5. We didn't see the approaching tornado in the storm cellar.
6. After boiling for exactly three minutes, Emma poured cold water over the eggs.

7. The dead snake was brought into camp by a cub scout six feet long.
8. Trying to remember my lines, my heart pounded against my ribs.
9. After eating ten watermelons, the hostess asked us to go inside and play games.
10. Cleopatra died from the poison of an asp in love with Marc Antony.
11. The motel was recommended to us by a tourist with hot and cold running water, television, and a swimming pool.
12. To avoid the hot sun, our plans were to travel at night.
13. Flying at half-mast, my heart grew sad when I saw the flag.
14. After completing my homework, the doorbell rang.
15. At the lake we saw many mussel shells trying to catch minnows.
16. Hitless all afternoon, the fans shouted their joy as Red drove a hard ball into the outfield.
17. Stepping out into the blinding snowstorm, my teeth chattered, and my hands grew numb.
18. To hunt jack rabbits, my neighbor's oat field is a good place.
19. After knocking out the heavyweight champion, the referee proudly announced the winner.
20. At the traffic light we barely managed to stop the impatient hot rod that quickly turned from green to red.

● REVIEW EXERCISE D. Read the following paragraphs, carefully noticing the use of modifying phrases and clauses. Number on your paper from 1 to 25. If a sentence is correct, write a plus sign (+) after the corresponding number. If a sentence has errors involving modifiers, write a zero (0). Be prepared to give oral revisions of every sentence that you label 0.

1. Have you ever heard the story about an absent-minded professor who put a letter in his wife's mouth and kissed the mailbox good-by? 2. The typical professor, of

course, has done much worse than that in many other stories.   3. In my opinion, though, absent-mindedness is not a characteristic possessed by teachers only.   4. In fact, my friends and I were discussing our own absent-mindedness at a slumber party the other night.

5. Aline began the conversation by saying that she habitually "pulls the most dumbest of stunts."   6. Once while taking a shower, the doorbell began to ring.   7. Aline suddenly remembered that Rex was coming by at four o'clock in the shower.   8. "It couldn't be four o'clock," she mumbled as she looked at her watch.   9. Two hours later, when Rex finally did arrive, Aline's watch had stopped running.   10. After being completely overhauled by the jeweler a few weeks later, Aline had to pay ten dollars to replace rusty parts.

11. Aline's story reminded Doris of the time that she had made a similar mistake.   12. Then Doris told us about her particular variety of absent-mindedness while eating our midnight snack.   13. Every time that she day-dreams about Roscoe, she doesn't pay any attention to what she is doing.   14. For instance, the other day she wore shoes to all of her classes that didn't match.   15. After telling her that she had on one black and one red shoe, Doris went home at noon to put on a pair of mates. 16. That night, however, when she was taking her shower, she happened to look down.   17. Seeing that she had forgotten to take her shoes off, the water was turned off by Doris in a hurry.

18. After the laughter had subsided, Vivian told us about her "more funnier stunt"; last Wednesday about midnight, she was so sleepy that she couldn't see.   19. Stumbling into the bathroom, the mirror seemed to hold the image of a stranger, not that of Vivian.   20. Since her hair looked like a tired piece of steel wool, she decided to give herself a shampoo.   21. After putting some white goo from a handy jar all over her hair, warm water failed to produce a lather.   22. The more she scrubbed her hair, the worse it looked.   23. Finally, Vivian began to wonder what it was that made her hair so gummy in the jar.

24. After a while, she discovered what she had done.
25. While smearing on a second application, her eyes fell upon the label of the jar, which read "All-Purpose Face Cream."

ONLY and JUST ━━━━━━━━━━━━━━━━

Among the most popular words in our language, *only* and *just* are forever playing leapfrog with other words in a sentence. These modifiers can land almost anywhere — at the beginning, middle, or end of a line of words.

My dog barked at our neighbor.
> **Only** my dog barked at our neighbor.
> My dog **only** barked at our neighbor.
> My dog barked **only** at our neighbor.
> My dog barked at our **only** neighbor.
> My dog barked at our neighbor **only**.

Dad paid the debt.
> **Just** Dad paid the debt.
> Dad **just** paid the debt.
> Dad paid **just** the debt.
> Dad paid the **just** debt.

Read aloud each of the sentences above, noticing how the various positions of *only* and *just* cause you to stress different words in the sentences to convey meaning.

For fun, why don't you change the meaning of the sentences below by placing *just* and *only* in various positions?

Yesterday Ann mentioned his decision.
The judge talked about the foreman of the jury.

PART THREE

COMPOSITION

CHAPTER 9

Varying Sentences

BEGINNINGS, STRUCTURE, AND LENGTH

In music, in art, in life, monotony creates boredom. In your compositions, monotony of style — too many stringy sentences or too many subject-first sentences — can cause your reader to lose interest in what you have to say. The purpose of this chapter is to help you improve your style by varying the ways you construct sentences.

9a. Vary the beginnings of your sentences.

Although sentences which have the subject first may be grammatically correct, too many of them in one paragraph are monotonous. To avoid a common cause of dullness in writing, then, you should learn to vary the beginnings of your sentences.

Read the following paragraph, in which every sentence begins with the subject.

We have been studying table manners in our home economics class. Miss Melton is our teacher. She gave us five rules to study today after she had told us never to act greedy or make noise at the table. One of the most important rules was concerned with handling a napkin. You should not tuck a napkin under your chin. You should leave it instead on your lap. You should lay the napkin to the right of your plate after the meal. Miss Melton gave us several other pointers. A teaspoon should not be left in the glass or cup while you are drinking. You should not butter a whole slice of bread at once. You should break the bread, and you should butter only one bite at a time. Crackers should not be crumbled into chili. You should not dunk doughnuts into coffee. Miss Melton is going to tell us tomorrow about correct ways to use silverware at a formal dinner.

The sameness of the subject-first sentences in the paragraph above mars the effectiveness of the ideas. Compare the following style as you notice the varied beginnings of sentences.

In our home economics class, we have been studying table manners. Today, after she had told us never to act greedy or make noise at the table, Miss Melton, our teacher, gave us five rules to study. Among the most important rules was advice on handling a napkin. Instead of tucking a napkin under your chin, you should leave it lying upon your lap. After the meal, you should simply lay the napkin to the right of your plate. Miss Melton gave us several other pointers. For instance, while you are drinking, you should never leave a teaspoon in your glass or cup. Rather than butter a whole slice of bread at once, you should break the bread, buttering only one bite at a time. According to Miss Melton, it is bad manners to crumble crackers into chili and to dunk doughnuts into coffee. Tomorrow Miss Melton is going to tell us about correct ways to use silverware at a formal dinner.

As this paragraph shows, there are many ways to begin sentences. Instead of putting the subject first in every sentence, you can vary your style by starting with a modifying word, phrase, or clause.

(1) You may begin sentences with single-word modifiers.

Learn to use adjectives, adverbs, and participles at the beginnings of sentences.

9a

ADJECTIVES	**Wet** and **dirty,** Rags tracked across Mom's clean floor.
	Destructive and **dangerous,** the tornado ripped through Dallas.
ADVERBS	**Later** they decided to try finger painting.
	Cautiously we approached the icy bridge.
PARTICIPLES	**Whispering,** Betty told me the secret.
	Exhausted, we pitched camp for the night.

● EXERCISE 1. The sentences in this exercise (and in the following exercises) are good sentences. You are asked to revise them so that you will learn a variety of ways of expressing the same idea. The following sentences, all of which begin with the subject, contain a modifier that can be placed at the beginning of the sentence. Find this modifier, and write it on your paper.

1. The suitcase, torn and battered, now lies in the attic.
2. The rain suddenly stopped.
3. The ghost, reappearing, asks Hamlet to act at once.
4. Charles often reads himself to sleep.
5. Gertrude, lovable and obedient, has many talents.
6. This fine ball club, unbeaten and untied, has established a record at our school.
7. I enjoy washing the dishes sometimes.
8. Albert, stumbling, fell headlong into a deep gully.
9. Sally counted her money again.
10. We do not usually eat lunch this early.

● EXERCISE 2. Use the following modifiers to begin sentences of your own.

1. always	6. blushing
2. hungry	7. slowly
3. yawning and stretching	8. discouraged
4. occasionally	9. diluted
5. alone and friendless	10. unwillingly

(2) You may begin sentences with phrases.

To vary your sentences, begin some of them with prepositional, participial, and infinitive phrases.

PREPOSITIONAL PHRASES   **In the middle of the pond,** we caught a large bass and yanked it into the boat.
At the edge of town is a skating rink.

PARTICIPIAL PHRASES   **Taking my temperature,** the nurse smiled pleasantly.
Hypnotized by her radiant beauty, Homer sighed and surrendered to her charm.

INFINITIVE PHRASES   **To make a good impression,** you should be ready to go when your boy friend arrives.
To kill all of the termites, the men bored holes through the cement and poured poison beneath the porch.

● EXERCISE 3. The following sentences, all of which begin with the subject, contain phrase modifiers that can be placed at the beginning of the sentence. Recast each sentence by placing the modifying phrase at the beginning. (Remember that a modifying phrase should be placed as close as possible to the word it modifies.)

1. The jalopy began to fall apart, rumbling down Fifth Street.
2. We began playing ticktacktoe to make the time pass faster.
3. The train crossed the Missouri River at sunset.
4. I read a beginner's book on physics to find out about the laws of motion.
5. Ned, worried about his brother, began to pace the floor.
6. We were too tired to think at the end of the rehearsal.
7. Henry never makes below ninety on a test because of his thorough preparation.
8. The old barn stood vacant, surrounded by tall weeds

9. I don't know, to tell the truth, where she is now.
10. The wispy fog along the highway looks like gray ghosts prowling in the cold darkness, in the Smoky Mountains about midnight.

● EXERCISE 4. Write 10 original sentences that begin with modifying phrases. Include at least 2 prepositional, 2 participial, and 2 infinitive phrases. After each sentence, name the kind of phrase with which it begins.

● EXERCISE 5. Write 3 good sentences that begin with the subject; then recast each one twice by varying the beginning of the sentence.

EXAMPLE 1. I went to the library yesterday to find material for an oral report. [subject first]
1. Yesterday I went to the library to find material for an oral report. [single-word modifier]
1. To find material for an oral report, I went to the library yesterday. [infinitive phrase]

(3) You may begin a sentence with a subordinate clause.

EXAMPLES **After they had left the stadium,** Sue missed her purse.
Although David wanted to go with us, he decided that he should stay home and help his father.
When we were entering the theater, we met Hal and his girl friend.

● EXERCISE 6. The 10 simple sentences in this exercise begin with the subject. Using the examples above as a guide, add an introductory subordinate clause that is related to the main idea. Place a comma after each one of your introductory clauses. (You may find the list of subordinating conjunctions on page 77 helpful.)

1. I could not answer the riddle.
2. He noticed that she was unusually shy.
3. The sky began to clear.
4. He pushed his way to the ten-yard line.
5. I walked over to Bob's house.
6. The mouse raced toward the pantry.
7. I saw that the bed had not been slept in.
8. They decided to cancel the game.
9. She was determined to attract more attention.
10. We tried a different way to avoid working.

● REVIEW EXERCISE A. Rewrite each of the following sentences, changing the beginning as directed.

Begin these sentences with single-word modifiers:

1. We finally reached the Tennessee River Basin.
2. The large lakes, man-made, there have dams that control the flow of the Tennessee River.
3. Flood waters do not cause soil erosion in the region nowadays.
4. The Tennessee Valley Authority has certainly made many improvements since 1933.
5. Our family, vacationing, saw many other points of interest in the South.

Begin these sentences with modifying phrases:

6. Eskimos live in igloos during the winter.
7. They hunt wild game to provide food for themselves.
8. The hides of bears, stitched with the hair turned inward, are often used for clothing.
9. Eskimos use the hide of a walrus for making shoes.
10. The people in Arabia, unlike the Eskimos, have no difficulty keeping warm.
11. The Arabs wear flowing garments to protect themselves from the hot wind and sun.
12. They move about from place to place, seeking water and grass for their sheep and camels.
13. They use light, movable tents for shelter.

Begin the following sentences with subordinate clauses:

14. There are many plantations in Brazil because the mild climate is ideal for growing coffee.
15. The coffee thrives when the heavy rains fall during the winter months.
16. Men begin working when the golden berries fall from the trees in May.
17. The harvest will be a good one if heavy rains have not damaged the blossoms in September.
18. A long process of washing and drying is necessary before the coffee beans are ready to sell.
19. Trains haul tons of coffee to market after the workers have dried the beans for two months.
20. These crops bring prosperity to Brazil because the plantation owners seldom produce more coffee than they can sell.

● REVIEW EXERCISE B.   Every sentence in the following paragraph begins with the subject. Rewrite the paragraph to demonstrate that you have learned how to begin sentences with single-word modifiers, phrases, and clauses. Do not begin more than three sentences with the subject as you strive to make the paragraphs more effective through variety. (If you wish, add words of your own, but keep the main ideas intact.) You may combine sentences if you wish.

1. Frank and I always celebrate the Fourth of July together.   2. We usually either go to the lake for a swim or go on a picnic.   3. We decided this year, however, to take a boat ride up the river.   4. An outboard motor was out of the question because we didn't have much money. 5. We rented a light boat with two battered oars.   6. We started upstream, attacking the swift water like a couple of wood choppers clearing out underbrush.   7. The river, growing narrow, suddenly became shallow and made rowing a problem.   8. Frank decided that he would jump onto the bank in order to pull me in with a rope.   9. He missed his footing when he tried to leap from the boat.

10. The expression on his face, as he sat in the river, showed that only his feelings were hurt.   11. His clothes were soaked, and his shoes were full of mud.   12. He gradually fretted his way toward dry land, mumbling under his breath.   13. "We are going to the lake next year," he informed me.

9b. Vary the kinds of sentences you write.

Another common cause of sentence dullness is lack of variety in the kinds of sentences in a paragraph. Too many simple or compound sentences can make your style just as monotonous as too many subject-first sentences. Write a variety of sentences, using not only compound and simple sentences but also complex and compound-complex ones. (For a review of the four kinds of sentences, see pages 81–82.)

The style of the following paragraph is monotonous because every sentence is either simple or compound. Every idea, because of this sentence structure, is of the same importance as every other idea.

At present our only true names are nicknames. I knew a boy with peculiar energy, and he was called "Buster" by his playmates. This rightly supplanted his Christian name. Some travelers tell about an Indian. He was not given a name at first; he had to earn it, and his name was his fame. Among some tribes he acquired a new name with every new exploit. A man often bears a name for convenience merely. This is pitiful, for he has earned neither name nor fame.

Now compare the style of the following paragraph, which develops the same ideas with varying kinds of sentences.

At present our only true names are nicknames. I knew a boy who, from his peculiar energy, was called "Buster" by his playmates, and this rightly supplanted his Christian name. Some travelers tell us that an Indian had no name

9b

given him at first, but earned it, and his name was his fame; and among some tribes he acquired a new name with every new exploit. It is pitiful when a man bears a name for convenience merely, who has earned neither name nor fame.[1]

This paragraph is more emphatic because the style is more varied. There are 2 compound-complex sentences, 1 complex sentence, and 1 simple sentence.

Using subordinate clauses not only gives welcome variety to your writing but also helps you to show how ideas are related.

Study the following pairs of sentences. The first sentence in each pair is compound. The second sentence is complex. Notice that in the second sentence the relationship between ideas is clearer than in the first sentence. (The subordinate clauses are in heavy print.)

1. **The stain was old and stubborn; we tried to remove it by using a strong detergent.**
Since the stain was old and stubborn, we tried to remove it by using a strong detergent. [The idea in the introductory subordinate clause tells the *cause* of the idea in the main clause.]

2. **The school bus suddenly slowed down, and we saw the roadblock.**
When the school bus suddenly slowed down, we saw the roadblock. [The first idea expresses the *time* of the second idea.]

3. **I asked Mother to write a note about my illness, and then I could get permission to make up my schoolwork.**
I asked Mother to write a note about my illness **so that I could get permission to make up my schoolwork.**
[The second idea gives the *reason* for the first idea.]

● EXERCISE 7.   To show how the ideas are related, change each of the following sentences by using one

[1] From "Walking" by Henry David Thoreau.

of these subordinating conjunctions: *after*, *although*, *as soon as*, *because*, *before*, *if*, *since*, *when*.

EXAMPLES
1. My conscience began to trouble me, and I apologized to Marian.
1. Since my conscience began to trouble me, I apologized to Marian.

2. The temperature gauge pointed to the danger zone, but the motor was not damaged.
2. Although the temperature gauge pointed to the danger zone, the motor was not damaged.

1. My cut hand kept bleeding, and Mother took me to Dr. Bell's office.
2. Louise can entertain our guests Tuesday night, for she plays the piano beautifully.
3. The Chinese are acknowledged as the first printers, but Johann Gutenberg is credited with being the first European to print from a movable type.
4. The weather report on television warned us of the danger of freezing temperatures, and we hurriedly put antifreeze in the radiator of our car.
5. In Boston we visited the Old South Church, and then we went to see the Bunker Hill Monument.
6. Eleanor came into the room; she started looking for Henry.
7. I studied the lesson a long time; I wanted to make a good grade on the test.
8. My friends play soccer or baseball at my house, but they never abuse the lawn or the flowers.
9. We will sell popcorn and drinks at the concession stand, and we can make some money for the class.
10. I enjoy having a room of my own, and I try hard to keep it clean and attractive.

● EXERCISE 8. Rewrite the following paragraphs, which consist wholly of simple and compound sentences. To vary the style, change or combine some of the sentences into complex sentences. Do not, however, make all of the sentences complex since your purpose is to get variety.

1. A little dog lives near us, and her name is Tippy. She frequently comes over to play with my dog. She has four snow-white feet, and her coat is shiny black. I watch her cross the street. She reminds me of a little girl with fresh white gloves on. She seems ready for church on Sunday morning.

2. The music and thump of the drums grew louder, and the people lined up along the streets. In another minute the band would come around the corner. Finally, with a blast of brass, the high school band emerged from behind the buildings. The majorettes raised their feet high and proud like prancing horses. The girls were followed by the bandsmen. They were wearing blazing red jackets. The band led the parade of colorful floats. Cheers and claps came from the crowd. Every child stood watching with shining eyes. Each one dreamed of being in the school band someday.

3. Margie is always thinking of some kind of mischief. One day we were riding in a streetcar. It was during rush hour, and we stopped for about ten minutes. Traffic jammed the streets, and beside us was another streetcar, not two feet away. Margie noticed two boys quietly looking at us through the windows, and she suddenly had an idea. "Let's drive them mad by pretending. Let's act as though we're talking about them. They can't hear us, and they can only imagine things." At first we both stared at them, and then we started giggling and nodding to each other. We kept looking at them, and we talked and talked. Actually, we were not saying anything, but the boys grew very self-conscious. We started pointing at them, and then they began to squirm in their seats and frown at us. Our streetcar began to move forward slowly, and so we turned backward to stare at the boys in the other car. We could see them relax and breathe a sigh of relief. Then they tried to see us once more; we were still laughing, not of course at them, but at our own private little joke.

● REVIEW EXERCISE C. Write about 200 words sharing a funny story, true or imaginary, with your classmates. You may want to tell two or three short jokes that are among your favorite conversational pieces. As you write, pay close attention to your style. Underline all beginning phrases and clauses and all subordinate clauses.

9c. Vary the length of your sentences.

Since sentences of the same length are monotonous, you should strive to write some short sentences, some middle-sized ones, and some long ones. A series of short sentences often makes for a primer or babyish style. Long, stringy sentences are also a common cause of dullness.

(1) Avoid too many short sentences.

Although short sentences are useful for describing exciting action, a composition consisting entirely of short sentences gives the effect of being chopped up. There are too many sentences of this kind in the following paragraph.

We have a parakeet. He is learning to talk. We have taught him several words. For instance, he can say "Good morning, Pedro." Pedro is his name. He knows the names of James and Freda. Pedro can say "James is a freshman." He can also say "Freda plays a fiddle." During the Christmas holidays, he learned other sentences. One was "Santa Claus is fat and jolly." Another was "Lights are in the tree." Now Pedro often gets mixed up. He combines the phrases as he pleases. Yesterday he said, "Freda is a fat and jolly light. Santa Claus is a freshman." Once he said, "Santa Claus plays a fiddle."

Notice how these short, choppy sentences can be combined into longer, smoother sentences.

We have a parakeet named Pedro who is learning to talk. We have taught him several words, for instance, "Good morning, Pedro." He also knows the names of James and Freda, and can say "James is a freshman" and "Freda plays a fiddle."

Read through the rest of the paragraph and plan how you would revise it.

● EXERCISE 9. Combine each of the groups of short sentences below into one long sentence. Use any means you wish — compound verbs, modifying phrases, subordinate clauses, appositives, and so on. Make your long sentences read smoothly.

EXAMPLE   1. She put out the cat. She locked the doors. Then Hazel fell into bed for a long night's sleep.
          1. After putting out the cat and locking the doors, Hazel fell into bed for a long night's sleep.

1. Pinky grew impatient. He yowled at me. He wanted to go rabbit hunting.
2. I could not get my gun fast enough. Pinky then lifted both front feet. He stamped them on the ground in doggy defiance.
3. You can build up self-confidence. Read books and magazines. Become interested in other people.
4. A doctor uses a stethoscope. With it he listens to the heart beat. He also listens to the lungs.
5. The garage doors were tightly closed. Mr. Jones could not be aware of the presence of carbon monoxide. He died in a matter of minutes.
6. The world is full of parasites. A bug eats a gnat. A chicken eats the bug. We eat the chicken.
7. I soaked the stamps in water. Then I placed them in my album. I used little gummy hinges.
8. Jean is my girl friend. Last week she and I went to a dance at the country club. This is located near a beautiful lake.
9. Betsy likes loud music. She likes fast jazz. She is particu-

larly attracted by any album of records grownups don't like.

10. Joe is a handy man about the house. He can repair a broken window. He can also repair any electrical gadget.

● EXERCISE 10.   Use each group of facts below in one long sentence.

EXAMPLE   1. **Englewood: a city in Hackensack Valley, fourteen miles from Jersey City, near the George Washington Bridge.**

1. **Located in the Hackensack Valley, fourteen miles from Jersey City, Englewood is not far from the George Washington Bridge.**

1. My brother: graduated from high school last year, went to college, is now taking science courses, wants to enter medical school.

2. The car: air-conditioned, power steering, automatic transmission, power-adjustable seats, beautiful design.

3. Boxing match: September 21, at Yankee Stadium, Rocky downs Archie, ninth round, remains champion.

4. Disorderly room: scattered papers, empty coke bottles, dusty furniture, cigarette ashes, an overturned chair.

5. Midnight movie: Halloween, the Palace, a double feature, terrifying scenes, screams from the audience.

(2) Avoid long, stringy sentences.

When you strive to eliminate short, choppy sentences, you may make the mistake of writing long, stringy sentences. An occasional long sentence is good; it characterizes a mature style, and it adds both smoothness and variety to your compositions. The stringy sentence, however, in which main clauses are strung together with *and, but, for, or, nor,* is bad. To correct the stringy sentences in your compositions, use subordinating conjunctions and compound verbs.

STRINGY   Cleveland caught the pass, **and** he ran twenty-two yards, **and so** he made a first down.

BETTER   **After he had caught the pass,** Cleveland ran twenty-two yards and made a first down.

STRINGY   Janet went to the board, **and** she drew a map, **but** her directions were still not clear to the class.

BETTER   **Although Janet went to the board and drew a map,** her directions were still not clear to the class.

Sometimes it is better to break a long, stringy sentence into two or more sentences.

STRINGY   I read the assignment, **and** then I began making notes on cards, **for** I wanted to memorize the main points in the lesson, **but** the bell rang, **and** I was not through, **and so** I had to carry my heavy book home.

BETTER   **After reading the assignment,** I began making notes on cards **so that** I could memorize the main points in the lesson. **Since I was not through when the bell rang,** I had to carry my heavy book home.

● EXERCISE 11.   Revise the following stringy sentences by using subordinating conjunctions (see page 77) and compound verbs. Some of the very long sentences should be broken into two or more sentences.

1. An accident occurred at the busy intersection, and several persons were injured, and then the police decided to put up a traffic light.
2. Gertrude has beautiful red hair, for she brushes it daily, but my hair is stubby and dull-looking, for I often go swimming in the hot sun.
3. A small child may swallow a dozen aspirins, or he may wander out into the street, for he is not old enough to think for himself, and adults must make decisions for him.
4. Fever is usually the first sign of the measles, and the

eyes soon grow red, or the eyelids swell, and later the sneezing and coughing make a person think that he has a cold.

5. I have a hard time talking to girls, but I am not at all bashful around boys, for they are interested in sports, outdoor fun, cars, but girls are different, for all they want to talk about is clothes or boys.

6. I had put the grease in the popcorn popper, and then I had to answer the telephone, and I returned to the kitchen and found the grease on fire, and I thought that the water from the faucet ought to put it out, and so I put the flaming pan of grease under the running water, and a sudden explosion of hot steam gushed to the ceiling, but I was not badly burned, and the house didn't catch fire.

7. The trouble with New Year's resolutions is that they are always broken, for people make too many of them, or they hope for impossible reform, and they often try to become perfect all at once.

8. We are all creatures of habit, and bad habits are hard to break, but a person can make one resolution a year, and he can concentrate on that one aim, and then he can keep it.

9. Aunt Maggie is a terrible driver, and the family tries to help her keep her mind on the road, and the best way is to remain silent, for one day we were talking and pointing out attractive dresses in the store windows, and she started looking and at the same time driving on the wrong side of the street, and four cars threatened to annihilate us.

10. Another time, about sunset, she was driving along Main Street, but she was creeping, going only five miles an hour, and other drivers tried to honk us forward, or they shouted at us when passing, and Aunt Maggie kept leaning forward, for she was trying to see, and then she turned on her headlights in the broad daylight, and we reminded her that the sun had not quite gone down, and then she remembered that she was still wearing her sunglasses.

● REVIEW EXERCISE D.   After you have reviewed every rule in this chapter, write a composition about 300 words in length. Concentrating on your ideas, write the first draft of your composition. Then revise the first draft, keeping in mind the need for a lively style to keep your reader interested. As you write the final draft of your paper, demonstrate your ability to use varied, emphatic sentence structure. Be sure that you vary the beginnings, kinds, and lengths of your sentences.

You might want to write about what you would like to be for a day. At one time or another, everyone deceives himself by thinking that he would like to fill someone else's shoes. What would you like to be for a day? A football hero or a movie star? The governor of New York or a grower of wheat in Kansas? Perhaps you would like to be a parakeet or your neighbor's lap dog. Should you choose this subject, your title might well begin with "I Wish I Were . . ."

You may enjoy writing about your ideas of an ideal person — a parent, teacher, class president, or friend. An interesting composition could be based upon your ideas of an ideal place or thing — a school, home, church, textbook, automobile, or holiday.

CLICHES: THEIR ORIGIN AND USE ────────

Cliché is a French and an English word that means "stereotype." A cliché is a worn-out expression or a trite phrase, like *water over the dam* or *It's a small world*.

The origins of many clichés are interesting. Take, for example, the familiar "You stole my thunder" or "You'll play thunder." In the late nineteenth century, William Roberts (in articles in the *Book Worm* as well as in the *Dictionary of National Biography*) called attention to the origin of this cliché by singling out an anec-dote in Cibber's "The Life of John Dennis." John Dennis, a dramatist in the eighteenth century, once gave a very bad play that the managers soon took off the stage. One thing, however, about Dennis's play was excellent — a thunder machine that he had rigged up for exciting sound effects. Recognizing the value of this contraption for making thunder, the managers later stole the thunder for their production of *Macbeth*. Furious because of the theft, Dennis indignantly pro-tested: "The villains will play my thunder but not my plays." And thus a cliché was born.

However interesting the derivations of clichés may be, these stale, timeworn expressions do not give sparkle to a composition. They have lost their original luster; too familiar and overworked, they no longer have vitality. In your compositions, then, avoid clichés such as *stealing thunder, an ax to grind, a bone to pick, bury the hatchet, wipe the slate clean,* or *make a beeline.*

CHAPTER 10

Writing Paragraphs

THE STRUCTURE OF A PARAGRAPH

Your long compositions should be divided into paragraphs. Set off by themselves by means of spacing and by indenting the first line, these paragraphs are guides for the reader. When he reads a paragraph, he finds a discussion of one topic. When he starts reading a new paragraph, he knows that there will be a small change of topic — a moving on to a new idea, a change in time or place, or a shift in emphasis.

If you frequently see "¶" or "no ¶" (symbols meaning "Begin a paragraph here" and "Do not begin a paragraph here") in the margins of your graded compositions, you are doing one of two things. Either you are forgetting to start a new paragraph when you change to a different topic, or you are chopping your thoughts into too many divisions. Either way, you confuse your reader because your ideas are not properly paragraphed. Study this chapter so that you will learn how to write unified, fully developed paragraphs.

10a. A paragraph is a series of sentences developing one topic.

As a unit of thought, a paragraph contains a group of related sentences developing one central idea.

This topic is usually, but not necessarily, stated in a "topic sentence" somewhere in the paragraph.

As you read the following paragraph, taken from Christopher Morley's essay "On Going to Bed," notice that every sentence is related to "the shadow," or the lack of enthusiasm about going to bed.

It is a sad thing that as soon as the hands of the clock have turned ten the shadow of going to bed begins to creep over the evening. We have never heard bedtime spoken of with any enthusiasm. One after another we have seen a gathering disperse, each person saying (with an air of solemn resignation): "Well, I guess I'll go to bed." But there was no hilarity about it. It is really rather touching how they cling to the departing skirts of the day that is vanishing under the spinning shadow of night.[1]

The Topic Sentence

10b. A topic sentence states the one topic of a paragraph.

The topic sentence of the above paragraph is: "It is a sad thing that as soon as the hands of the clock have turned ten the shadow of going to bed begins to creep over the evening." This sentence contains the controlling idea of the whole paragraph. The topic sentence usually, though not necessarily, comes at or near the beginning of a paragraph. The other sentences develop the idea expressed by the topic sentence.

10c. Every sentence in a paragraph should be closely related to the topic.

A paragraph is a unit. Any sentence in a paragraph which does not relate to the topic of that paragraph spoils the unity and should be taken out.

[1] From *Pipefuls* by Christopher Morley. Copyright, 1920, 1948, by Christopher Morley. Published by J. B. Lippincott Company.

10 a-c

The following paragraph contains a sentence that is not related to the topic sentence. As you read the paragraph, notice how this sentence, printed in italics, spoils the unity. Every other sentence except this one tells about protecting cotton crops from destructive pests.

A farmer who depends upon raising cotton for a livelihood must protect his crops from destructive pests. According to Mr. Fred Rudd, who plants hundreds of acres of cotton every year, the insects that do the greatest harm to cotton plants are the boll weevil, the cotton worm, the cotton aphid, and the red spider. To combat boll weevils, which eat both cotton bolls and seeds, Mr. Rudd uses calcium arsenate. Calcium arsenate also protects his crops from cotton worms, which stunt the growth of the stalks by eating the leaves. Mr. Rudd always watches out for other parasites, like cotton aphids; they not only suck the juice from the leaves but also do damage to the open cotton boll. When necessary, he uses nicotine sulfate, combined with hydrated lime, as a weapon against aphids. To kill red spiders, which sometimes feed on the leaves, Mr. Rudd dusts his fields with sulfur. *In the United States, sulfur is used in manufacturing matches, medicines, paper, and many other products.* By getting rid of these common pests, Mr. Rudd, like other successful farmers, gets a good yield of cotton from each acre.

The topic of the following paragraph is the beauty of a perfect day. Every detail should relate to this central idea. Which sentence in the paragraph gets off the subject?

All of the elements of nature must have contrived to produce such a perfect day. It was a day that made everything seem possible and anything wonderful. The sun didn't shine down — it drew one up to it. Every blade of grass was saturated with light. The wind whipped the leaves in the trees and then parted the wildflowers as it ran through them. In the wintertime I have to stay indoors so much that

I like to be outdoors in the spring and summer. It was a day when every living cell seemed to vibrate with the joy of life as the sun and wind had a glorious frolic with the earth.

● EXERCISE 1. In each of the following paragraphs, there is one sentence that is not closely related to the topic. Find this sentence, and copy it on your paper.

1

I never know what to do with my hands when I am in an awkward situation. For instance, when I am making an oral report in history class, I have trouble with my hands. Sometimes I self-consciously clasp them behind me so that they won't show. At other times, I hide them in my pockets and start jingling coins noisily. A good speaker does not have disconcerting mannerisms — such as saying "uh" at every pause, pacing back and forth, or looking out the window instead of at his audience. I can understand why Napoleon went through life as a one-armed man, why he always kept his other hand safely buried beneath his coat.

2

When our English teacher asked the class to give a specific example of a generally known truth, I chose "Honesty is the best policy." Elmer and I had learned the day before that dishonesty brings nothing but trouble. We were taking a science test. The first question asked us to list three important minerals and to give their uses. Since I hadn't read my assignment, I took a peek at Percy's paper and copied his answer: "mineral jelly used for canning, mineral wells used for naming cities, and mineral oil used for sick cats and children." In the meantime, Elmer slyly stole the information from me for his paper. After class, laughing and bragging in the hall, we told Percy to keep on studying the assignments so that we could pass our tests. Percy didn't laugh; he just pointed over our shoulders. Behind us stood Mr. Courtland, who had heard every word. A wonderful science teacher, Mr. Courtland often umpires our baseball games after school. After giving us a lecture on honesty, he sentenced us to make a detailed summary of the chapter on minerals, to draw pictures of sulfur beds, and to report orally on the means of conserving oil, mercury, and silver. Needless to say, Elmer and I have learned that dishonesty carries heavy penalties. Honesty is the only sensible policy.

3

There is hardly a more exciting way to travel than by ship. Perhaps it is the complete isolation from land or the feeling of living in another world inhabited only by the passengers on board which makes one so ready for adventure. Of course, sometimes I get bored because every day is alike; it is as monotonous as riding a train across barren wastelands. What a thrill it is to wake early in the morning and go up on deck to see nothing but water sparkling in the morning air! It's fun to sight an occasional gray hump of land away in the distance. All day the ship breaks through the water with a burst of foam, and although her journey seems endless, there are no tracks in front of or behind her. At night the ocean around becomes a dark world with only one moonlit path to nowhere.

4

Yesterday Ann, Jean, and I went to the beach. Arriving about two o'clock, we parked the car, flung open the door, and leaped out, running over the sand with our bare feet. Then we spread out a large blanket and sprawled out side by side to let the hot rays of the sun turn our white skins to golden red. In a little while, Jean, by far the smallest girl in the group, jumped up and bellowed, "Let's take a dip! Last one in is a rotten egg!" Of course, Jean was the rotten egg. Lately Jean has been dieting; she eats very few sweets and starches. In the water, we dived for shells and pretended that we were graceful ballet dancers. At five o'clock, when we were exhausted, it was moved and seconded that we leave the beach and go eat.

5

Even though they know that speed is the main cause of traffic accidents, many Americans still enjoy racing toward death on the highway. Rather than be late for a round of golf or a week's visit with relatives, drivers speed around sharp curves, pass other cars on steep hills, and squeeze in and out of a line of cars. Frequently the oncoming drivers, taken by surprise, must swerve to the shoulder of the road or crash headlong into a speeding automobile on the wrong side of the road. Newspapers are filled with the gory details of mangled bodies found in car wrecks that occur because of slick highways, faulty brakes, or drivers falling asleep at the wheel. The speeder is a daredevil who gambles that he will not become a statistic in the files of the state highway department. A menace to society, he must "make good time," even though he risks his own life and endangers the lives of others who must share the highway with him.

The Development of a Paragraph

To develop a paragraph, you usually supply additional information to make clear the meaning of the topic sentence. Let's read another one of Morley's paragraphs in order to observe the way in which a topic sentence may be developed. In his essay "On Making Friends," the writer makes the point in this paragraph that it takes time to make friends. His topic sentence begins the paragraph: "Emerson is right in saying that friendship can't be hurried." You know immediately that he is going to discuss this one idea. And, as you would expect, every other sentence in the paragraph shows how time ripens friendships.

Emerson is right in saying that friendship can't be hurried. It takes time to ripen. It needs a background of humorous, wearisome, or even tragic events shared together, a certain tract of memories shared in common, so that you know that your own life and your companion's have really moved for some time in the same channel. It needs interchange of books, meals together, discussion of one another's whims with mutual friends, to gain a proper perspective. It is set in a rich haze of half-remembered occasions, sudden glimpses, ludicrous pranks, unsuspected observations, midnight confidences when heart spoke to candid heart.[2]

10d. A paragraph may be developed by specific details — facts, examples, incidents, etc. — which support the topic sentence.

In Morley's paragraph specific details like "interchange of books," "meals together," "ludicrous pranks," and "midnight confidences" give meaning and interest to the sentences developing the topic.

Generalizations, however, do just the opposite. They often make dull reading. Compare the following two paragraphs that develop the same topic sentence.

GENERAL

Whenever you buy a gift, you should always consider the interests of the receiver. Whatever the occasion, you should remember what a person likes when you buy him a present. That way you can buy an appropriate gift. If you select something that he can enjoy or use, he will appreciate it. If you get a present that does not interest him, then your choice of a gift is a poor one.

SPECIFIC

Whenever you buy a gift, you should always consider the interests of the receiver. For example, if you are buying a birthday present for a friend who likes to read detective stories, you might select *The Adventures of Sherlock Holmes* or *The Case of the Red Rooster*. If, on the other hand, you are choosing a gift for your little cousin who likes to play "cowboys and Indians," you might decide upon a cap pistol, a toy sheriff's badge, or an Indian suit. Similarly, if you

[2] From *Pipefuls* by Christopher Morley. Copyright, 1920, 1948, by Christopher Morley. Published by J. B. Lippincott Company.

must choose a gift for your mother on Mother's Day, you should remember that she especially likes new things for her kitchen. You can please her by buying a novelty cooky jar or a new gadget for slicing potatoes.

The second paragraph is more interesting and convincing than the first one. The specific details in the second paragraph are three particular examples of choosing definite gifts after a consideration of the exact interests of each receiver.

(1) Use examples to develop a paragraph.

The method of developing a paragraph by giving specific examples is easy to learn. After you have stated your topic sentence, you can support it with examples that are closely related to your central idea. As you read the following paragraph, notice how each example develops the topic sentence in heavy print.

A rumor of some unaccountable phenomenon had preceded Mr. Hooper into the meetinghouse, and set all the congregation astir. Few could refrain from twisting their heads toward the door; many stood upright, and turned directly about; while several little boys clambered upon the seats, and came down again with a terrible racket. There was a general bustle, a rustling of the women's gowns and shuffling of the men's feet, greatly at variance with that hushed repose which should attend the entrance of the minister.[3]

● EXERCISE 2.   On page 204 are skeletons of paragraphs. Choose two of them and plan how you would develop them by completing the unfinished statements. Then copy the two paragraphs. As you complete each statement, you will be developing the topic sentence with specific examples.

[3] Adapted from "The Minister's Black Veil" by Nathaniel Hawthorne.

10d

1

When the projector broke down during the most exciting scene of the movie, the audience grew restless. At first, everyone groaned in unison. Then several impatient people put on their coats and left the theater. Some older persons .... Many children who suddenly became aware of the popcorn popper in the lobby .... A few noisy boys sitting near the front .... Of course, my friends and I ....

2

Yesterday's storm caused great damage in Centervale. First of all, lightning knocked out the city's electrical power. Then, as the squall line moved across the downtown area, strong winds lashed .... These gusts were accompanied by large hailstones, which .... Causing the most damage, however, the torrential rains......................

3

Spring cleaning started at our house last Saturday. Immediately after breakfast, Mother took down the Venetian blinds and .... Dad spent the morning in the basement; his job .... By noon my brother Sandy had finished................ ...... After I had cleaned the floors for hours, I .... At one o'clock, the family had ....

4

Everything went wrong at the dress rehearsal of the junior play. To begin with, Ann Miles, the heroine, arrived forty minutes late. Just as soon as the rehearsal got under way, the prompter...................... During the second act, two of the actors forgot...................... At the end of the play, the stagehand who was supposed to pull the curtain...................... Finally, Miss Stephens, the director, announced......................

● EXERCISE 3.   Choose one of the following topic sentences and develop it into a paragraph. By answering the questions in brackets, you can make your paragraph interesting with specific details or examples. Use the topic sentence as the first sentence of your paragraph.

1. Money cannot buy the best things in life. [What exactly are the "best things" in life? Who can possess or enjoy these things? Where? When?]

2. There are several kinds of smiles. [Can you name three or four kinds of smiles? How does each one differ from the other? Do your friends or acquaintances smile at different things?]

3. Spring is the loveliest season of the year. [What happens in the spring? Why, exactly, is it the loveliest of all seasons?]

4. Walking down the hall today, I heard many interesting sounds. [When did you notice the sounds — between classes, during the noon hour? Can you give specific details about each sound? How do these noises reflect the personalities and activities of the teachers and pupils?]

5. Ninety-five per cent of the things we worry about never happen. [Can you apply this common saying to your own experiences? Are you a chronic worrier? Can you point out two or three things that once caused you needless anxiety? Can you convince your reader, by your specific illustrations, that worrying is senseless?]

6. There is a difference between a man and a gentleman. [What are the main characteristics of a gentleman? How does he look? What does he say? How does he behave? Can you answer all of these questions by telling about a gentleman you know?]

(2) Use incidents from your experience to develop a paragraph.

Another way to develop a paragraph is to select an incident or two from your experiences that will support and explain your topic sentence. The following is an example of this type of development.

Experience has taught me to be afraid of electricity, for I have been severely shocked twice. Once a wall plug in my bedroom wasn't working; so I decided to take it apart and tighten the wires. Since I forgot to turn off the electricity before making repairs, I got a hard jolt when I stuck my screw driver into live wires. This first shock did not frighten me much; I merely scolded myself for not remembering to throw the main switch. The second time, however, was different. When our automatic percolator wouldn't work early one morning, I started loosening screws and adjusting all movable parts of the electric coffeepot. Angry because it wouldn't work, I forgot to unplug the cord. When I began to tinker with the thermostat, my knife slipped. Fire sizzled into the air, and electricity shot through my arm, numbing it to the elbow. Finally the fuses blew out and shut off the current. As I tried to rub life back into my arm, I noticed that the tip of my pocketknife was melted. Because of these two experiences, I fear electricity and no longer expose myself to its dangers.

● EXERCISE 4.   Answer any one of the following questions by writing a paragraph clearly expressing your ideas. First write a clear topic sentence; then develop it by giving additional information — specific details, examples, or incidents from your experience.

1. What is your opinion of space travel?
2. What does "a well-rounded personality" mean?
3. What is your idea of a perfect evening?
4. What do you like about your favorite course?
5. What are two good ways to make friends?
6. Why do you fear something?
7. Why do airplanes sometimes crash?
8. Why do you like holidays?
9. How can a person learn to swim?
10. How does a compass work?
11. What is radar?
12. How can one develop an appreciation of bebop?

10e. Make a working plan for developing the topic sentence into a paragraph.

As you have now learned, a paragraph is a unit containing a series of closely related sentences developing one central idea. To organize your thoughts effectively, you should learn to make a working plan. Morley's paragraph on page 201 reveals a plan like this.

TOPIC   Friendship can't be hurried.
DETAILS   needs time to ripen
            shared experiences and memories
            exchanges of books
            meals
            pranks
            discussions, confidences

As you write your plan of a paragraph, keep your topic sentence firmly in mind so that every detail will be closely related to your central idea. Suppose, for example, that you are to write a paragraph on this topic: "Everyone in my family likes to read different kinds of books." Your details should give the names of the members of your family and should tell exactly what each one likes to read. By holding strictly to the topic sentence, you will not list details about the reading taste of a friend or a teacher or someone else, nor will you ramble off to favorite radio or television programs. Notice how the details below stick closely to the topic sentence.

TOPIC   Everyone in my family likes to read different things.
DETAILS   Brother — comics
            Sister — novels
            Mother — magazines about housekeeping
            Father — how-to-do-it-yourself books
            I like science fiction.

10e

● EXERCISE 5.   Choose 2 of the following topic sentences, and for each write a plan for a paragraph. First, copy the topic sentence, and then list details to support it.

1. Stealing bases is an art.
2. My friends have a strange assortment of pets.
3. I like to watch people as they walk along a crowded street.
4. We were not expecting company.
5. My little brother is always pretending.
6. I never tire of going to the zoo.
7. The guest room was beautifully furnished.
8. Some programs on television are educational.
9. I have definite opinions about billboards on the highways.
10. Everyone should develop his sense of humor.

● EXERCISE 6.   Using one of the plans that you prepared for Exercise 5, write a well-developed paragraph. Make your specific details interesting as you develop the topic sentence.

● EXERCISE 7.   After making a plan, write below it an interesting, well-unified paragraph based upon any one of the following topic sentences.

1. The mumps made me miserable.
2. I like my teachers.
3. Teen-agers have their own ideas about good music.
4. I believe in miracles.
5. Sometimes I don't like myself.
6. You can tell a great deal about a person by the way he handles money.
7. It's fun to teach an animal new tricks.
8. A good breakfast is easy to cook.
9. Some promises are easy to make and hard to keep.
10. There are several reasons why I like Sundays.

Connectives in a Paragraph

In writing paragraphs, you need to bridge the gaps between sentences so that your paragraphs will read smoothly. To do this, you may use connectives such as these: *first, second, third, finally, next, at the same time, similarly, likewise, therefore, however, for this purpose.* Words like *one, other, another, that,* and *it* are also useful for bridging the gaps between sentences because they refer the reader to preceding ideas.

Read the following two paragraphs and notice how the words in heavy print link ideas.

Suppose you go into a fruiterer's shop, wanting an apple. **First,** you take up **one,** and on biting it, you find it is sour; **then** you look at it and see that it is hard and green. You take up **another one,** and **that** too is hard, green, and sour. The shopman offers you a **third.** Before biting it, **however,** you examine it and find that it is hard and green. **Therefore,** you immediately say that you will not have it, as it must be sour, like those that you have already tried.

Nothing can be more simple than **that,** you think. If you will take the trouble to analyze and trace out into its logical elements what has been done by the mind, **however,** you will be greatly surprised. **In the first place,** you have performed the operation of induction. You have found that, in two experiences, hardness and greenness in apples went together with sourness. **It** was so in the **first** case, and **it** was confirmed by the **second. True, it** is a very small basis, but still **it** is enough to find sourness in apples where you get hardness and greenness. You found upon **that** a general law that all hard and green apples are sour; and **that,** as far as it goes, is a perfect induction.[4]

● EXERCISE 8. Write a paragraph explaining clearly step by step how to do one of the following:

1. How to buy a good used bicycle
2. How to make a map

[4] Adapted from *Collected Essays* (1893) by Thomas Henry Huxley.

3. How to catch fish
4. How to get a date
5. How to clean a gun
6. How to give a speech
7. How to develop a good memory
8. How to win at checkers (or any other game)
9. How to build a model airplane
10. How to make good grades
11. How to train a dog
12. How to sell magazines
13. How to grow potatoes (or any other plant)
14. How to enjoy studying
15. How to behave in the cafeteria
16. How to diet
17. How to stay awake in class
18. How to plan a party
19. How to decorate a kitchen (or any other room)
20. How to predict the weather

● REVIEW EXERCISE A. Write a paragraph beginning with one of the following topic sentences. Put into practice what you have learned in this chapter. After you have written your paragraph, ask yourself these questions about it:

Does the topic sentence clearly state the central idea of the paragraph?
Have I given enough details to develop the topic fully?
Are these details interesting and specific?
Does every sentence in the paragraph relate closely to the topic sentence?
Do connective words help to clarify the explanation as they bridge the gap between ideas?

1. The weather is changeable.
2. Everyone in my class has spring fever.
3. There are several ways to spoil a child.
4. I believe that lasting friendships are based upon good character.

5. Western movies are healthy entertainment for young people.
6. Only a few snakes are poisonous.
7. A hurricane can do great damage.
8. There is a right way to put on make-up.
9. Conversation is an art.
10. Anyone can learn to play volleyball.
11. I have trouble making decisions.
12. There are many ways to use leftovers.
13. I know three good "icebreakers" for a party.
14. If you know how, you can build a fire without using a match.
15. The way that a thermometer works is interesting.
16. Uranium is an important element.
17. The rules of water baseball are similar to those of regular baseball.
18. I notice other people's eyes.
19. Limestone has many uses.
20. There is an art to taking good colored snapshots.

● REVIEW EXERCISE B.   Study the following paragraphs so that you can discuss them in class. Be prepared to give the topic sentence or the central idea of each paragraph if it does not have a topic sentence and to tell what kind or kinds of details are used to develop it: facts, examples, incidents.

1

Sonar is the name of a sound detector that locates the position of submarines or mines. Like AWOL, NATO, and CARE, the word *sonar* is made up of the first letters of the words it stands for: "*so*und *na*vigation *r*anging." To detect a submarine, sonar sends out inaudible sound waves. When these strike an object, the vibrations bounce back to the sonar, which shows by the pattern of echoes where the object is. Because of the ability of this apparatus to locate distant objects under water, the United States Navy found sonar especially useful for detecting the positions of enemy submarines during World War II.

2

Two rope handles located at the balancing point of a folded stepladder make it a lot more convenient to carry singlehandedly. One handle is fastened to each part of the ladder so that when both are gripped, the ladder cannot spread apart. Sash cord is used as a handle in the step portion and inserted through holes and knotted at the ends. The other handle is of lighter drapery cord and held with two staples. The sash-cord handle actually carries nearly all the weight while the smaller one serves mainly to keep the legs of the ladder together.[5]

3

Suppose that you were going to paint a picture of a hillside on a windy day. There are two ways you might go about it. One would be to paint a blade of grass and then another blade of grass and then another, until you had put down all the blades of grass you could see, sketched in the rest of the hillside, and were ready to start on the trees, limb by limb, and then the clouds — with a stray butterfly thrown in for good measure. If you could do all of this accurately, reproducing exactly the perspective and color, you would have produced something known as "photographic realism." The other way of going at this picture would be to paint *what you really see* when you look at that hillside; that is, not when you dissect the scene to do a realistic painting of it, but when you look at it for the pure pleasure of seeing that hillside on a windy day. You don't see the grass blade by blade.[6]

4

We had a remarkable sunset one day last November. I was walking in a meadow, the source of a small brook, when the sun at last, just before setting, after a cold gray day, reached a clear stratum in the horizon, and the softest, brightest morning sunlight fell on the dry grass and on the

[5] Reprinted from "Rope Handles on Stepladder Make It Easier to Tote," by permission of *Popular Mechanics*, April, 1957.

[6] Adapted from "Caval-Comment," *Literary Cavalcade* magazine, by permission. Copyright, 1956, by Scholastic Magazine, Inc.

stems of the trees in the opposite horizon and on the leaves of the shrub-oaks on the hillside, while our shadows stretched long over the meadow eastward, as if we were only motes in its beams. It was such a light as we could not have imagined a moment before, and the air was so warm and serene that nothing was wanting to make a paradise of that meadow. When we reflected that this was not a solitary phenomenon, never to happen again, but that it would happen forever and ever an infinite number of evenings, and cheer and reassure the latest child that walked there, it was more glorious still.[7]

5

There are very few moments in a man's existence when he experiences so much ludicrous distress, or meets with so little charitable commiseration, as when he is in pursuit of his own hat. A vast deal of coolness, and a peculiar degree of judgment, are requisite in catching a hat. A man must not be precipitate, or he runs over it; he must not rush into the opposite extreme, or he loses it altogether. The best way is: to keep gently up with the object of pursuit, to be wary and cautious, to watch your opportunity well, get gradually before it, then make a rapid dive, seize it by the crown, and stick it firmly on your head: smiling pleasantly all the time, as if you thought it as good a joke as anybody else.[8]

[7] From "Walking" by Henry David Thoreau.
[8] From *Pickwick Papers* by Charles Dickens.

CHAPTER 11

Writing Compositions

PLANNING AND WRITING

You learned in Chapter 10 how to write a paragraph. When you write a composition, about the only difference is quantity. Instead of developing only one topic sentence (such as one paragraph on being afraid of electricity), you develop several topics that are closely related (for instance, three paragraphs on three fears — electricity, high places, deep water). In other words, a paragraph is a series of sentences explaining one topic sentence; whereas a composition is a series of paragraphs explaining one subject.

As you write compositions, follow the suggestions in this chapter, which will help you not only to choose and limit a subject but also to organize and develop your ideas effectively.[1]

Selecting a Subject

11a. Choose a subject that you know something about.

If you try to handle a subject that you know very little about or one that doesn't interest you, you are almost sure to write a poor composition. In searching

[1] The instructions in this chapter apply only to expository writing; for rules regarding narrative writing, see Chapter 13, pages 274–96.

for a subject, select one that you know something about. When you have something to say, you will enjoy writing the composition, and you can easily gain your reader's interest.

● EXERCISE 1.   Below are 10 subjects for compositions. Choose 3 that you know something about and that interest you. Or, if you prefer, list 3 subjects of your own that you would enjoy writing about.

1. making a dress
2. fishing
3. student government
4. sports
5. popular music

6. color television
7. automobiles
8. problems of teen-agers
9. choosing a career
10. wonder drugs

11b. Limit the subject.

Having chosen a subject for an interesting composition, ask yourself: Is the subject narrow enough for a short theme? If not, how can I limit it? For compositions of only two or three pages, you cannot handle a big subject well. In fact, you should learn to choose a *part* of a subject to write about.

Suppose, for instance, that you chose, in Exercise 1, to write on "fishing." This general subject includes all kinds of fishing, in fresh water and in salt water, as well as all ways of fishing, from cane poles to harpoons. It also includes every type of fish, from a crayfish to a whale, and every kind of bait, from earthworms to mullet. To cover the general subject "fishing" in a brief composition is impossible. If, however, you limit this subject by choosing only a part of it, you can handle the subject well in a short paper. For example, you could fully develop such limited topics as "How to Catch Bass," "Four Tips on Fresh-Water Fishing," "Using a Spinning Reel," "The Differences in Artificial Lures," or "A Tangle with a Stingaree."

11
a-b

Notice how the following general subjects are sub-divided into more limited topics.

GENERAL SUBJECT	Automobiles
LIMITED TOPICS	The Art of Washing a Car
	The Best Low-priced Car on the Market
	How to Clean a Carburetor
	Kinds of Mufflers
	Recent Improvements in Automobile Tires
GENERAL SUBJECT	High School Activities
LIMITED TOPICS	An Experiment in Science Class
	Making Posters During Fire-Prevention Week
	How We Organized a Club
	The Value of a Field Trip
	Marching with the School Band
GENERAL SUBJECT	Entertainment
LIMITED TOPICS	The Best Program on Television
	Planning a Hobo Party
	How I Learned to Skate
	Four Kinds of Movie Actors
	Why I Like to Watch High School Plays

● EXERCISE 2. Number from 1 to 10 on your paper. For each general subject below, give a limited topic that is narrow enough for a good, short composition.

1. Sports in High School
2. Family Life
3. Hunting
4. Interior Decoration
5. Travel
6. School Publications
7. Races
8. Airplanes
9. A Summer at Camp
10. Part-Time Jobs

● EXERCISE 3. Before continuing your study of this chapter, try your hand at writing a brief composition. Select an interesting subject that you know something about. Perhaps you will choose one of those listed in Exercise 1 or Exercise 2. Limit your subject so that you can develop your ideas well in 300 words or less. Writing this composition will help you to understand better the advice given on the following pages.

11c. Determine the purpose of your composition.

When you take a particular attitude toward a subject, you can define your purpose easily. Take, for example, the general subject "Baseball." What do you think about baseball? If you like baseball better than any other sport, show your reader why it is your favorite sport. If you want to write about pitching, show your reader how a person can develop this skill. If, on the other hand, you don't like baseball, you can write a composition showing its drawbacks as a sport. Topics indicating these various attitudes are: "What I Like About Baseball," "How to Become a Good Pitcher," and "Baseball Is a Dull Sport." As you can see, determining your purpose helps you to limit the subject.

● EXERCISE 4.   Choose 5 of the limited topics that you wrote for Exercise 2. Then show what your purpose would be in writing a composition on that subject.

EXAMPLE   1. **On Being an Only Child**
            1. **The Advantages of Being an Only Child**

● EXERCISE 5.   Below is a list of limited topics. Number from 1 to 10 on your paper. After the appropriate number, write what your purpose would be in writing about each topic.

EXAMPLE   1. **The Characteristics of a True Friend**
            1. **To show that a true friend is dependable, un-selfish, and loyal**

11c

1. What I Dislike About Cleaning House (or the yard)
2. How to Enjoy Being Sick
3. Advice to a Practical Joker
4. Why I Am a Football Fan (or any other kind of fan)
5. The Characteristics of a Good Leader
6. What I Can Do Well
7. Why I Want to Be an Engineer (or anything else)
8. How to Live with a Siamese Cat (or any other animal)
9. Three Things That I Fear
10. Dressing for Different Occasions

11d. Plan your composition before writing it.

An outline will help you organize your ideas. It will also make the actual writing of your composition much easier because, after making an outline, you know exactly what you are going to say and when you are going to say it. Before you begin your outline, however, you should take these preliminary steps.

(1) List your ideas.

As soon as you have chosen a limited subject and have decided upon your purpose, make a list of your ideas. Write them down as they come to you as rapidly as you can, without worrying too much at this time about the value of the ideas or where you would include them in your composition. Later, when you are organizing, you can cut out those which you decide not to use. The important thing is to see what material you have to work with.

FIRST LIST OF IDEAS

Title of Composition My Pet Peeves
Purpose To define and give examples of my pet peeves

long assignments, especially on Friday
women's hats
homework in general
hate to play bingo
any dull game
also games like musical chairs
my older brother's "I told you so"
having to go to bed early

arguing about TV channels
riding with a back-seat driver
interruptions when I am talking
a show-off at a party
nagging hostesses
boring talks in assembly
hate preparing oral reports
get stage fright

(2) Group related ideas under headings.

After you have made a list of your ideas, you are ready to group them so that your plan will gradually develop into a few larger divisions. How you group them will depend upon the subject. Some topics, especially those dealing with a process, are easily arranged in chronological (time) order. Other topics also fall into a chronological pattern; for example, *morning, noon, night,* or *childhood, youth, maturity, old age.* For all subjects, however, you should group your ideas according to the phase of the subject they deal with.

IDEAS FOR THE COMPOSITION ON "MY PET PEEVES"
GROUPED UNDER HEADINGS

I. At home
arguing about TV channels
hearing "I told you so"
having to go to bed early

II. At school
homework
assignments on Friday
preparing oral reports
boring assembly programs

11d

III. At parties
  dull games
  bingo
  musical chairs
  nagging hostesses
  a show-off

(3) Arrange ideas in order.

Your next job is to arrange the ideas in the order in which you will discuss them in your composition. Some subjects will require a certain order. For example, if your composition gives instructions on how to assemble the parts of a model airplane, you will need to follow a chronological order. If, on the other hand, you are writing about your reasons for joining the Scouts, you may arrange your ideas with the most important coming last and the least important first.

Sometimes the material under one heading is necessary for understanding the material under one of the other headings. For instance, if you are explaining how to process a roll of film, you will first need to point out the differences between panchromatic and orthochromatic film (one heading) because the kind of film determines whether or not a person should develop the negatives in complete darkness (another heading). You would have to put the first heading before the one which depends upon it.

If the ideas themselves do not determine the order in which they should come, you may decide yourself upon the most interesting and the clearest arrangement.

(4) Make an outline.

Arranging your ideas in a definite order is the first step in making an outline. Besides indicating the order in which ideas come, an outline often shows their relative importance. You will have main headings and subheadings under them. For most of the compositions you will write, a *topical* outline will be satisfactory. A topical outline is one in which the various items are topics, not complete sentences.

Remember that an outline is a working plan, the first step in writing the composition. Do not try to be literary or to crowd in too many details here. The language of the outline should be simple and clear. Use as few words as possible for each topic to make your meaning clear and to show the organization of your ideas.

TOPICAL OUTLINE

"My Pet Peeves"

Purpose To define and give examples of my pet peeves

I. At home
   A. Hearing "I told you so"
   B. Arguing about TV channels
   C. Going to bed early
II. At parties
   A. Dull games
      1. Bingo
      2. Musical chairs
   B. A show-off
   C. Nagging hostesses
III. At school
   A. Boring assembly programs
   B. Homework
      1. Assignments on Friday
      2. Preparation of oral reports

11e. Observe rules for form in making an outline.

(1) Place the title (and the purpose) above the outline. It is not one of the numbered or lettered parts of the outline.

(2) Use Roman numerals for the main topics. Subtopics

11e

are given capital letters, then Arabic numerals, then small letters, then Arabic numerals in parentheses, and then small letters in parentheses. Study this outline form:

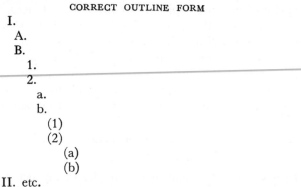

CORRECT OUTLINE FORM

I.
  A.
  B.
    1.
    2.
      a.
      b.
        (1)
        (2)
          (a)
          (b)
II. etc.

(3) Indent subtopics. Indentions should be made so that all letters or numbers of the same kind will come directly under one another in a vertical line.

(4) There must always be, under any topic, more than one subtopic.

Subtopics are divisions of the topic above them and you cannot divide anything into fewer than two parts. If you find yourself wanting to use a single subtopic, rewrite the topic above it so that this "sub idea" is included in the main topic.

WRONG C. Hostesses
          1. Those who nag
RIGHT   C. Nagging hostesses

(5) For each number or letter in an outline, there must be a topic.

For example, never write IA or A1.

(6) A subtopic must belong under the main topic beneath which it is placed. It must be closely related to the topic above it.

WRONG   A. Dull games
            1. Bingo
            2. Not enough refreshments

(7) Begin each topic with a capital letter.

You may place a period after each topic or you may not. But be consistent. If you use a period after one topic, use a period after all of them.

(8) The terms *Introduction*, *Body*, and *Conclusion* should not be included in the outline.

Of course, you should have an introduction and a conclusion in your composition, but the terms are not topics that you intend to discuss. Therefore, they should not be listed as topics in the outline.

● EXERCISE 6.   The following form for an outline contains several errors. After you have found them, write the letters and numbers in correct outline form on your paper.

    I. A.
       B.
   II. A.
  III. 1.
       2.
          (a)

● EXERCISE 7.   Copy the skeleton outline given at the right below, and then place each of the topics in the list at the left in its proper position. The title is listed among the 12 topics.

By obeying school rules	*Title:*
With teachers	I.
With classmates	A.
By being interested in schoolwork	B.
How to succeed as a freshman	II.
Sense of humor	A.
Listening in class	B.

Attendance	III.
By developing likable characteristics	A.
Wide range of interests	B.
Behavior	IV.
Doing homework	A.
By co-operating with others	B.

● EXERCISE 8.   The items in the unsorted list of ideas below can be grouped under the 4 main headings given before the list. On your paper write these main headings leaving several blank lines beneath each; then under each, list the topics which properly belong there. Number, letter, and arrange in a correct outline.

TITLE   What I Like About My Home Town

MAIN HEADINGS   location
school
entertainment facilities
people

UNSORTED LIST   friendly
near a large city
charitable
superior library
parks
on a river
well-trained teachers
in the mountains
modern classrooms
recreation center
well-balanced curriculum
theaters

● EXERCISE 9.   Decide on answers to the questions in one of the following numbered items. Then write a topical outline based upon your answers. Group your subtopics properly under the main headings, and follow the correct form of an outline.

1. Which do you think makes the best pet — a dog, cat, parakeet, or monkey? Why?
2. According to your knowledge and experience, does your school have an adequate physical education program?
3. What are three good ways to make friends?
4. What have you learned in the ninth grade about mathematics?
5. Before joining a club, what three or four things should a person consider? Why?
6. Do high school athletics encourage sportsmanship, school spirit, and teamwork? How?
7. What are the main characteristics of a good speaker? Of what importance are preparation, voice, and delivery?
8. What are the necessary steps in getting ready for school, for church, or for a camping trip?
9. In your opinion, what are the most interesting attractions of a state or county fair — the midway, acrobats, motorcycle or automobile races, exhibits? Why?
10. How have your friends influenced your thinking? Which three or four friends have influenced you most? In what ways?

● EXERCISE 10.   Write a topical outline of any one of the subjects listed in Exercise 5, page 218.

● EXERCISE 11.   Write a composition of about 300 words based upon the outline you wrote for Exercise 10.

Introduction, Body, and Conclusion

11f. Every composition has a beginning, a middle, and an end.

When you begin to write a composition, you should keep in mind the fact that you will need an introduction (beginning), a main discussion of the topics in your outline (middle), and a conclusion (end).

11f

(1) The introduction should be interesting and should give the purpose of the composition.

The first sentence of your composition should gain the interest of the reader so that he will want to read more. One of the best ways to create interest is to give the reader a feeling that you know what you are writing about. Begin your discussion with pertinent facts that are closely related to your title and your purpose.

In view of what you have just read, which one of the following sentences is better for starting a composition on pet peeves? Why?

1. I am going to write about my pet peeves; of course, everybody has pet peeves, and mine are like everybody else's in many respects.
2. A telephone ringing at two o'clock in the morning, a hole in my pocket, a thunderstorm on a picnic, a fly in my soup — these are only four of my pet peeves.

Besides creating interest, you must in your introduction make clear your purpose or the central idea of your composition. Be sure to include any necessary facts. Usually one paragraph is enough for the introduction.

Below are two introductory paragraphs for the same composition. Why is the second paragraph better than the first one?

1. Although I don't know very much about color television, I'll try to write a composition about it. I will have as my purpose the idea that color television is here to stay.
2. Whether the scene is a radiant sunrise in New England or the bright spectacle of a Notre Dame football game during half time, color television captures the beauty of reality. Millions of Americans will soon be able to afford the pleasure of watching color television because of the recent developments by scientists working with picture tubes, electron guns, and glowing chemicals.

(2) The body should state and develop the main points in the outline.

The body is really the composition itself; it will make up about three-fourths or more of your paper. Usually there will be several paragraphs in the body.

It may be that in the body of your composition you can devote one paragraph to each main heading in the outline, using the subtopics as specific details to develop the main heading. Notice below how a paragraph can be built upon a main heading with its subtopics.

TITLE   Characteristics of a Good Football Player

ONE HEADING

  IN THE OUTLINE   II. Speed
                     A. Quick running
                     B. Fast thinking

Speed is an important requirement in football; a good player not only has to run fast but also has to think fast. For example, Floyd Scott, a star on the freshman squad, can run fifty yards in eight seconds, even when dodging or angling. He can catch the ball and race to pay dirt before the referee knows what has happened. Floyd can also think fast. Always alert for breaks, he is the first to snatch up a fumbled ball and the last to be caught in the arms of a tackler. As Coach Abbott has often said, "Floyd has the makings of a great ballplayer because he can outrun and outthink any other player on the field."

Your development of each main heading in your outline, then, is the body of your composition.

(3) The conclusion should clinch the main points made in the body of the composition.

The conclusion may summarize what you have said in the body. A summary should not, as a rule, be a mere *listing* of the main points. It should be a restate ment of the main idea and should leave the reader with a feeling of completeness, as of a job now finished. The conclusion is usually stated in one paragraph.

● EXERCISE 12. Write a composition of about 300 words based upon the outline that you prepared for Exercise 9. Write a brief and interesting introduction that states your purpose; carefully develop each paragraph in the body of your composition with specific examples and details; and write a short concluding paragraph. When you hand in your paper, be sure to include your outline.

● EXERCISE 13. Read the passage below and divide it into the introduction, the body, and the conclusion. To do this you will have to decide where paragraph divisions should be made. You should be able to find 5 paragraphs. Number from 1 to 5 on your paper and copy the first and last words of each paragraph. Then tell whether each paragraph belongs in the introduction, body, or conclusion.

Americans have great faith in the modern facilities for travel. No matter what happens, they believe in the intrinsic worth of the automobile, train, and airplane. Especially fond of the automobile, my Uncle Alex bought a new roadster last year. When he traveled over the Alcan Highway, however, he knocked a hole in the gas tank, ruined three tubeless tires, and burned out a rod. When he finally arrived in Alaska, he had to sell the wreck. Even so, a week later, he bought another car, just like the one he had sold. My father likes trains as well as Uncle Alex likes cars. A few months ago, when going to El Paso, Dad chose to ride the "Rocket." This train jerked its way across the desert, each jolt aggravating Dad's appendicitis. In Albuquerque he had to have an emergency operation. When Dad left the hospital, he traveled on to El Paso— by train. Although Mr. Barnes, my next-door neighbor, does not enjoy riding trains, he does like to travel by air.

In fact, he owns a cub plane. Last June, when flying to Memphis, he hit terrific air pockets, suddenly lost control of his machine, and plunged into a cow pasture. Upon regaining consciousness, he mumbled to his doctor, "Wonder if my plane can be patched up as well as my collarbone." Like every other American I know, each of these men believes in the future of the automobile, train, and airplane. Nothing — not even experience — can shake his faith in modern methods of fast transportation, for it is a faith based on a firm confidence in American ingenuity and know-how.

11g. Use specific details, incidents, and anecdotes to develop the paragraphs of your composition.

As you learned in Chapter 10, you can develop paragraphs by using specific details and incidents from your experience. Anecdotes or very short stories can also be useful for explaining an idea.

Read the following composition, noticing how the writer develops each paragraph. Pay special attention to the story in the introductory paragraph, which gains the reader's interest as it leads into the main discussion of the personality of crowds.

CROWDS

The bull pawed the ground until hot, angry clouds of dust almost hid him from the crowds watching the bullfight. It had been a long, hard battle, and the matador was tired; but the bull could not be conquered. The shouts of "*Olé*" had become fewer as the matador deftly parried the bull again and again, and soon a change of feeling could be sensed in the crowd. Then, with a deep rumble, the cry of "*Indulto*" rose until the bull ring trembled. The crowd, which had been applauding the matador a few minutes before as he tried to give the deathblow to the bull, was now asking for the brave, proud animal to go free.

Often a fellow human being does not fare as well as the bull. Our history books are full of incidents where crowds

11g

have committed atrocious crimes against humanity. Many times these acts were done by people who knew better, as in the Salem witch trials. Although we are always inspired by a great crowd ready to face and fight any obstacle in order to win freedom from tyranny, the world still shudders at the hysteria of the French Revolution, when people let animal instincts take the place of intelligent judgment.

What is the infectious mental quality which causes people to be drawn into a mass opinion as in the above instances? Each person has his own thoughts, emotions, and opinions, and yet en masse a group can exhibit one definite personality — a happy party, an angry mob, a cheering audience, or a frightened gathering. There is a crowd instinct which makes us do things we would not do on our own. Perhaps it is a feeling that the crowd is to blame, not we, which lets our conscience rest.

Because the power of a crowd is almost unlimited, it is well for us to try to develop a strong core in our being which can discern when we are just "going along with the crowd" or really believing in our hearts that a group action is right. — *Carmel Fleming Coleman*

● EXERCISE 14. Write about 300 words on any one of the following subjects. Word your own title as you decide upon your purpose. After making an outline, write the composition, carefully developing each paragraph with interesting details, incidents, anecdotes, or stories that will help to clarify your main ideas.

1. White lies
2. The personality of the freshman class
3. Antics of a blue jay (or any other animal)
4. The party-line telephone
5. Voices on the street (in the hall, in a stadium)
6. Building a raft (campfire, birdhouse, diving board)
7. What makes girls giggle
8. Why boys need pockets
9. Ways to succeed as a debater
10. What a microscope can reveal

11. A stroll through a factory
12. Memories of my childhood
13. Creating my own designs
14. It pays to be courteous
15. The value of basketball (or any other sport)
16. A good listener
17. What is good luck?
18. Tricks of memory
19. The promises of advertisers
20. The language of dogs (cats, flowers, birds)

11h. Use linking expressions to bridge the gaps between paragraphs.

You have already learned that bridging the gaps between ideas within a paragraph is essential for good writing (see page 209). The very same words that connect ideas within a paragraph can help you bridge the gaps between paragraphs.

Become familiar with the following list of linking words so that you can use them to make your thoughts flow along smoothly. If you will make it a habit to use one of them in the first sentence of a new paragraph, you can clearly show the reader the relationship between the paragraph he is starting and the one that he has just read.

LINKING EXPRESSIONS

therefore	on the other hand	in the next place
thus	after all	next
consequently	such	meanwhile
as a result	instead	soon
accordingly	furthermore	later
similarly	moreover	finally
likewise	in fact	in spite of this
besides	for instance	also
nevertheless	an example of this	in addition
however	at first	in other words
on the contrary	at last	then

11h

When you write an explanatory composition, in which ideas are often arranged in chronological (time) order, you will find transitional expressions like *first* (*second*, *third*, etc.), *next*, *meanwhile*, *soon*, *later*, *then*, *finally* especially useful. (Avoid the overuse of *then*.)

As you read the following paragraphs, notice how the author uses linking words that express time in order to bridge the space between the ideas of one paragraph and those in the next.

Eight years ago, when Enid Larson came to Carmel High, biology was virtually a dead subject. Only one year of it was offered, and only 30 out of 300 students took that. The "laboratory" boasted a single display: a pretty arrangement of sea shells purchased from a gift shop.

At first, the students didn't know what to make of their new teacher. They kept asking, "When do we study animals?" She kept replying, "When you bring them in." Months passed without the class's studying a single animal.

Finally a boy brought in a strange, hard object shaped like a cocoon. He found from the reference shelves that it was a pellet regurgitated by a barn owl to dispose of indigestible wastes. Opening it before his awed classmates, the boy sorted out a collection of tiny bones that started the whole class doing detective work. It took them two weeks to identify the skull of a gopher and the bones of meadow mice and shrews.

The boy **later** went back to the reference shelves to prepare a painstaking paper on the food of predatory birds. His report on the great extent to which the barn owl aids man in checking our destructive rodent population was the first lesson Miss Larson's students ever had on the balance of nature. They were fascinated, and they reacted by swamping the laboratory with specimens of plant and animal life, whose behavior and interrelationships they proceeded to study.

Within two years, more and more students were electing the course, and a second year had to be offered. Word got around: "She's fabulous." Students finally petitioned the Board of Trustees for a third year, and until recently Carmel High School was offering the state's only three-year sequence in biology. Miss Larson now teaches six crowded classes a day.[2]

● EXERCISE 15.   In a magazine that you may cut up, find an article that has numerous linking expressions. Underline these expressions, and then paste the article neatly on your paper. In class, be able to point out the ways that the author of the article bridges the gaps between paragraphs.

11i. In the first sentence of a new paragraph, you may refer to the thought in the preceding paragraph.

You can bridge the gap between paragraphs by using words such as *this*, *that*, *those*, *these*, *such*, *other*, *another*. Suppose, for example, you are writing a composition about the traits of a person you admire. You have just finished a paragraph about his consideration for other people, and now you are ready to begin a discussion of his ability to hold his temper. You may bridge the gap between these ideas by starting the second paragraph with: "*Another* praiseworthy characteristic is his ability to hold his temper."

A second method of making the change to another idea in a new paragraph is to refer directly to the preceding paragraph by mentioning again the principal idea in the preceding paragraph. For instance: "Tom is not only considerate of other people but also even-tempered in dealing with his associates." Another

[2] From "The Teacher Who Won't Answer Questions" by Frances V. Rummell. Reprinted from the *Reader's Digest*, April, 1957. Quoted by permission of the *Reader's Digest*.

11i

234   *Writing Compositions*

way to do this is: "Just as important as his consideration for others is his ability to hold his temper."

Every time that you go from one paragraph to a
new one, you should use either a linking expression
or a linking reference in order to make a skillful
and clear connection between the ideas of the paragraphs.

● EXERCISE 16. Assume that the first sentence in
each pair below is the last sentence of one paragraph and that the second is the first sentence of the
next paragraph. Your job is to rewrite the first sentence of the second paragraph so that it will include
a linking expression or some other device to bridge
the gap between the ideas.

EXAMPLES   1. a. I found that visiting the Grand Canyon
                  was an unforgettable experience.
               b. The Yellowstone National Park is filled
                  with nature's wonders.
            1. **Although the Grand Canyon impressed me with
               its beauties, the Yellowstone National Park has
               an even greater variety of the wonders of
               nature.**
            2. a. Clean hands and fingernails, then, are
                  essential to good grooming.
               b. A person should pay attention to the ap-
                  pearance of his clothes.
            2. **A well-groomed person also pays attention to
               the appearance of his clothes.**

1. a. Of course, this kind of stamp collecting can be a
      very expensive hobby.
   b. Building model airplanes does not require much
      money.
2. a. Certainly boats built for racing should be made of
      sturdy materials.
   b. The engines of the racing boat should be capable
      of seven thousand revolutions a minute.

3. a. Perhaps I shall someday realize this secret ambition by riding in the caboose of a freight train.
   b. I have always wanted to wear a pair of blue jeans to a formal party.
4. a. In other words, a calf roper must have proper equipment.
   b. He should use "horse sense" as he practices roping a calf.
5. a. As this incident illustrates, my parents usually understand my personal problems.
   b. My friends sometimes do not care about what troubles me.
6. a. A person who can sew can therefore design her own clothes.
   b. She can make pretty things for her home.
7. a. As these figures show, a boy can earn a great deal of spending money by delivering newspapers.
   b. A girl can make several dollars a week by baby-sitting.
8. a. The band finished its performance with the "Wagon Wheel" stunt.
   b. Two high school girls began to twirl flaming batons.
9. a. You can see that my mother has a wonderful sense of humor.
   b. My father takes pride in telling the truth at all times.
10. a. It was certainly a lot of fun playing these games outdoors.
    b. We enjoyed the entertainment indoors.

SUMMARY OF THE STEPS IN WRITING A COMPOSITION

(1) Choose an interesting subject that you know something about.
(2) Limit the subject and determine your purpose.
(3) Organize your ideas by making an outline.
(4) Write your composition, keeping in mind the following:
   (a) Create interest and state your purpose in the introductory paragraph.

(b) Develop one idea in each paragraph in the body of your composition. Use specific details, incidents, stories, examples. Connect your paragraphs with linking expressions.

(c) Write a concluding sentence or paragraph.

A CHECK LIST FOR WRITING COMPOSITIONS

The check list below is for use *before* and *after* you write; use it to remind yourself of the techniques of good writing and to help you detect weaknesses in your writing.

(1) Does my outline clearly and logically develop my subject?

(2) Does every idea stick to the title and carry out my purpose?

(3) Is my composition properly divided into well-constructed paragraphs?

(4) In developing each paragraph, have I been generous with interesting, specific details?

(5) Are my paragraphs properly tied together with linking expressions?

(6) Are all of my sentences clear, grammatically correct, and varied?

(7) Are my punctuation and spelling accurate?

(8) Can I improve the choice of words?

● EXERCISE 17. Read the following informal essay. Then, as you consider the "Steps in Writing a Composition" and the "Check List" above, decide whether or not the essay meets the requirements for a good composition. In class, be able to discuss intelligently (1) the selection and limitation of the subject, (2) the organization of the ideas, and (3) the division into paragraphs. Also be able to point out (4) the purpose of the essay, (5) the topic sentence of each paragraph, (6) the links between paragraphs, and (7) the parts of the composition — introduction, body, and conclusion.

THE GUM-WATCHER'S CLUB

I have just made a survey of gum chewers for the gum-watching club that I'm going to start at my school. This survey will teach prospective members how to spot all kinds of gum chewers, who may fit into one of three categories: gum clickers, rotary rovers, and independents.

The gum clickers, or rabbit chewers, are an endurance test. Just sit near one for a few minutes, and you will find yourself betting as to whether the next click will be louder than the last one or as to which side of the jaw the click will come from. After a while, it gets to be torture, like a tap dripping. A prospective member in my gum-watching club must pass the initiation test by sitting near a gum clicker for at least thirty minutes.

Next on my list, the rotary rovers move the gum round and round, deliberately and slowly, with a look of cowlike contemplation. The first rotary rover I catalogued was a lovely teen-age girl who floated down the stairs in clouds of a frothy formal and sweet perfume. As she reached the bottom step, the munch-munch of gum took away every illusion. Her date came to meet her with nervous jaws — gum clicker — above a perfectly placed necktie. Away they went, each trying to outdo the other in gumnastics.

Finally, there are the independents. They can't decide which way they want the gum to go and cause me much anxiety. After I have catalogued them as rabbit clickers, they suddenly switch to a rotary action and foul up my statistics. Secretly, they don't want to be caught chewing gum. In fact, the independent I questioned slowly moved his piece of gum to one side (where I suspected he placed it securely on a wisdom tooth) and mumbled something about "onions for lunch."

The chewers in each category give a different reason for chewing gum. Typical reasons are: "It's relaxing," "Helps me think," "Cleans my teeth." Should any member of my gum-watching club ever succumb to this propaganda, I have devised the following methods to break the habit: (1) Take a long, honest look at yourself in the mirror while you are chewing. (2) Have a dentist temporarily wire your jaw hinges so that they can be stopped from the continual up, down, in, and around movement when you feel the urge for a chew coming on. — *Carmel Fleming Coleman*

SUGGESTIONS FOR WRITING COMPOSITIONS

1. *Write a composition dealing with your special knowledge.*

What do you know that most of your classmates are not aware of? What's your special kind of knowledge? Do you know what makes an airplane fly or why a cat is supposed to have nine lives? Then share this information with your friends. Perhaps you are a lover of games. If so, you can probably write a composition on how to play badminton, Chinese ping-pong, straddle ball, or some other lively game. Don't hide your talents under a bushel by pretending that you have nothing to say. If you know how to tie knots, how to administer first aid, how to solve cryptograms, how to take apart a hi-fi set, how to do hem-stitching or Italian drawn work, you can write a good composition on what you know how to do. As you choose a subject, keep in mind that a composition on riding a bicycle or doing homework can be just as interesting, if not more so, than a paper on the function of spark plugs or on the nature of cosmic rays. Some suggested topics are listed below. You may change one of them; or you may think of something different.

1. Four Kinds of Guns
2. Soapbox Derbies
3. How the Olympics Began
4. How to Give a Home Permanent
5. How to Get the Most out of a Hi-Fi Set
6. What I Know About Static Electricity
7. How We Hear
8. Building Air Castles
9. The Art of Finger Painting
10. Taming a Wild Kitten
11. How Paper Is Made

12. Sailing in Choppy Waters
13. Caring for Babies
14. The Habits of the Opossum
15. Mountain Climbing
16. Tide Levels
17. Dance Steps
18. New Medical Discoveries
19. Patterns of Change in Styles
20. Sunspots Influence the Weather

2. *Write a composition dealing with your ideas or beliefs.*

What are your ideas and beliefs? Do you believe that boys should learn how to cook? What do you think about pay-as-you-watch television? How do singing commercials on radio or television impress you? Are you superstitious about walking under a ladder, eating black-eyed peas on New Year's Day, crossing your fingers, or picking up a pin? What changes do you think science will make in our homes during the next ten years? What do you suppose schools will be like in 1985? What is your idea about life after death? Can you imagine what living on the moon would be like? Below is a list of topics about which you may have strong beliefs.

1. Fortunetellers
2. I Believe in Education
3. Going Dutch
4. Putting Ideals into Action
5. Deliver Me from Flattery!
6. Three Dangers of Self-satisfaction
7. The Evils of Gossip
8. New Year's Resolutions
9. The Power of Music
10. How Belief Makes a Big Difference
11. Money: A False Value
12. Keeping Up with the Joneses
13. I'm an Optimist
14. Premonitions
15. Why I Respect Curiosity
16. Will There Be Laughter in Heaven?
17. The Future of Motion Pictures
18. Work Is a Blessing, Not a Curse
19. I'll Always Believe in Santa Claus
20. Love Isn't Blind

3. *Write a composition giving your critical opinions.*

It is all right to use a composition as a kind of steam valve to air your views on what's wrong with people, with your school, your community, or the world. Your criticism of what you don't like or what you think isn't fair or right can make an interesting theme.

Of course, it is much easier to criticize than it is to offer an answer to a problem. Your reader, however, will be more apt to accept the validity of your fault-finding when you do present a possible solution.

If you choose, then, set forth a problem in your introduction; next give three or four critical opinions in the body of your composition; offer a solution to the problem in your concluding paragraph. The following topics are suggestions.

1. Juvenile Delinquency in My Town
2. The Rules Should Be Changed
3. Away with Supervision!
4. Down with Examinations!
5. My Quarrel with High School Athletic Contests
6. What's Wrong with School Publications
7. Why Students Play Hooky
8. Capital Punishment Is Wrong
9. The Curse of Atomic Power
10. No Required Courses in High School
11. My Pet Peeve
12. The Grading System Isn't Fair
13. Misleading Advertisements
14. Let's Stop Exchanging Gifts on Christmas
15. Holiday Slaughter on Our Highways
16. Why Assign Homework?
17. I Object to Some Forms of Discipline
18. Why I'd Like to Run Away to a Deserted Island
19. Is Everyone Blind to His Own Faults?
20. What I Don't Like About Myself

4. *Write a humorous composition.*

Different from the serious essay which attempts to convince the reader by logical arguments, the humorous composition entertains the reader by a light, playful consideration of a subject that is often too ridiculous for serious treatment.

"The Gum-Watcher's Club" on page 237 is an example of the humorous composition. The classification of gum chewers is amusing, the idea of organizing a gum-watcher's club is absurd, and the suggested remedy of using wire hinges for a gum-chewer's jaws is preposterous. Yet these very ideas make the composition fun to read. Because of the gentle humor, the reader smiles his way from the first sentence to the last period.

As you write a humorous composition, you should not strive to produce rollicking laughter, which is better suited to slapstick comedy on the stage or screen. Instead, write a light essay that is pleasant to read, one that is mildly amusing.

Also remember the importance of consistency of tone. Do not shift to a serious treatment of an idea at any time. For instance, if you are showing that a dog ought to have at least one flea that keeps him company and affords him a delightful pastime, do not drift into a serious discussion of the ways to rid the dog of fleas. Throughout your composition, stick to your purpose, which is to entertain the reader with pleasant humor.

Perhaps the following titles will give you ideas for writing an original humorous composition.

1. Three Kinds of Laughter
2. These Amazing Movie Heroes
3. Ways to Waste Time
4. Ignorance Is Bliss
5. The Importance of Appearing Wise
6. What I Admire About Myself
7. All Girls (Boys) Are Alike

8. A Classification of Women Drivers
9. Learn to Swim in Three Easy Lessons
10. You Too Can Be a Modern Artist
11. Ways to Impress a New Teacher
12. The Art of Cramming for a Test
13. The Pains of Growing Up
14. Things I Never Notice
15. Listening to Soap Operas
16. My Dog Solomon
17. Gadgets That I'm Going to Patent
18. Eccentric Relatives
19. The Art of Making Excuses
20. A Liar's Bench on a Fishing Pier

SUGGESTED TOPICS FOR COMPOSITIONS

Places

1. Exploring a Cave
2. Curiosities in a Museum
3. Drive-in Movies
4. A Modern Turkey Farm
5. In the Corridor of a Hospital
6. The Lights of Broadway
7. My First Glimpse of Niagara Falls
8. These Amazing Motels
9. Legends About My State
10. The Lincoln Tunnel
11. Sights Along the Seashore
12. Sailing Down the Hudson River
13. A National Park
14. The Plan of Our Library
15. Visiting a Zoo
16. My Favorite View
17. A Crowded Beach
18. A Day in the Mountains
19. The Comforts of a Station Wagon
20. The School Grounds at Night

School

1. Students Need a Code of Conduct
2. The Problem of Copying Homework
3. Stage Hands Are Artists
4. Controlling Hall Traffic
5. Unidentified Flying Objects
6. Learning Parliamentary Procedure
7. Going Out for Track
8. What My Science Book Doesn't Tell Me
9. Better Never Than Late
10. In Study Hall
11. Getting on Good Terms with a Typewriter
12. I Like Foreign Languages

13. The Joys of Learning to Sew
14. Working with a Compass
15. My Favorite Subject
16. Rummaging Through the Lost and Found Department
17. Working Together on Halloween Night
18. Planning an Amateur Show
19. Our High School Orchestra
20. The Latest Fad at School
21. Presenting a One-Act Play
22. Learning About Nature's Laws
23. The Value of Mathematics
24. My School's Policies
25. An Important Class Meeting
26. Burning the Midnight Oil
27. We Learn Good Manners
28. Parents' Day
29. An Experiment in Shop
30. Mass Vaccinations
31. We Put Out a School Paper
32. Raising Money for Group Projects
33. What I Admire About Teachers
34. Games During the Lunch Hour
35. What Sports Teach Youth

Personal

1. My Declaration of Independence
2. The Importance of Self-discipline
3. My Reading Tastes
4. I Didn't Believe It!
5. No Mother Is Like My Mother
6. Dad Knows All the Answers
7. I Had Twenty-five Cents
8. Selecting a New Dress
9. Idleness Is My Imagination's Workshop
10. What I Learned as a Scout
11. One Freshman's Opinion
12. A Fragment from My Diary
13. Advice I Never Take
14. Among My Souvenirs
15. Why I Gave Up Short Cuts
16. Adventures of a Would-be Hero
17. Why I Can't Save Money
18. My Grand Entrance
19. A Struggle with My Conscience
20. Learning How to Dance

21. Why I Like Folk Songs
22. My Impressions of the Ocean
23. Three of My Secret Ambitions
24. The Life and Death of a Daydream
25. My Luck Often Runs Out
26. Self-examination
27. Am I Gullible!
28. What I Like (Dislike) About Girls (Boys)
29. Controlling My Temper
30. Three Things I Cherish
31. I Learned How to Say No
32. Traditions in My Family
33. What School Spirit Means
34. My Good Intentions
35. What I've Learned from Watching Television
36. I Always Do Things the Hard Way
37. If I Were a Newspaper Editor
38. My Sense of Humor
39. Why I Hate Alarm Clocks
40. My Interest in Pets

Occasions

1. A Family Reunion at Thanksgiving
2. Exploring the Attic
3. Fun in an Amusement Park
4. Winning a Prize at the Fair
5. Wrapping Gifts
6. When to Be Silent
7. How to Skate on Thin Ice
8. Arranging Flowers
9. On Making a Tape Recording
10. An Hour in a Bargain Basement
11. Christmas at Our House
12. Prize Fights
13. Are Wrestling Matches "Fixed"?
14. Sleeping Outdoors
15. An Unlucky Winner
16. My First Ride in an Airplane
17. Traveling by Pullman
18. An Addition to Our Family
19. A Birthday to Remember
20. The Day Unexpected Relatives Moved In
21. The Night the Lights Went Out
22. Dad Gives Advice
23. Celebrating the Fourth of July
24. Going to Church on Easter
25. A Decision That Changed My Life

People

1. Characteristics of a Popular Teacher
2. Portrait of a Friend
3. The Way to a Girl's Heart
4. Are Young People Still "Going to the Dogs"?
5. Two Heads Are Not Better Than One
6. Bad Habits of My Best Friend
7. The Wisdom of Little Children
8. Audiences Have Personalities
9. Bores I Have Known
10. Two's a Crowd
11. A Stranger I'll Never Forget
12. My Admirable Aunt
13. Memories of My Grandfather
14. Four of a Kind
15. A Churchman I Respect
16. My Curious Kid Sister
17. My First-Grade Teacher
18. An Eagle Scout
19. Life Among the Freshmen
20. The Voices in My Family
21. A Practical Joker
22. A Man of Action
23. Blondes Are Not Dumb
24. A Person I'd Like to Know Better
25. Mr. Happy-Go-Lucky Meets Serious Sam

Hobbies

1. A Bird's-Eye View of My Scrapbook
2. Collecting Old Coins
3. Saving Coupons
4. Raising Vegetables
5. How to Care for a Pet Alligator
6. Photography Is My Hobby
7. Making Home Movies
8. The Art of Sailing
9. Learn to Bind Your Own Books
10. I'm a Bird Watcher
11. My Glass Menagerie
12. How to Handle a Bow and Arrow
13. I Collect Picture Post Cards
14. Making Old Furniture Look Like New
15. Water Skiing
16. I Work with Wood
17. A 4-H Project
18. My Favorite Pastime
19. I Learned to Play the Harmonica
20. Joining the Weather Watchers

CHAPTER 12

Writing Letters

FRIENDLY LETTERS, SOCIAL NOTES, BUSINESS LETTERS

In school or out of school, at the age of seven or seventy, you practice the art of writing letters — whether you write to a pen pal in the Philippines, a friend on vacation, a relative in the hospital, a mail-order clerk in Chicago, or a businessman in your home town. Generally speaking, the letters you write may be divided into three classes: (1) the friendly letter, (2) the social note, and (3) the business letter.

Four Tips on Writing Letters

No matter what kind of letter you write, you should remember to do these things:

1. *Make your letter clear.*

Remember that when your letter is read, you will not be there to explain what you mean. In order not to leave out important details in a business letter, plan what you are going to say and how you are going to say it. Furthermore, if you will think about what you are going to say *before* you write a friendly letter, then you can avoid many careless errors that often interfere with clarity.

246

2. *Write an attractive letter.*

Take pride in the appearance of your letter. A letter represents *you*. If you send a neat and clearly written letter, the receiver will respect you as a considerate person. On the other hand, if you mail a messy letter, then your reader's opinion will drop accordingly. Especially is this true in the business world. Many times a businessman receives letters from people whom he has never met and never will meet. The writer is judged entirely by his letter. If a businessman receives a messy, illegible letter, he naturally assumes that the writer either doesn't know any better or doesn't care enough to take the time to make the letter readable and attractive.

3. *Use correct English, punctuation, and spelling.*

A letter filled with errors in writing will not only lead the reader to believe that you are uneducated but will also mar the clear expression of your ideas. Run-on sentences, mistakes in usage like "he done" or "for Joe and I," and misspelled words like "dosen't" or "truble" will never make a good impression upon your reader.

4. *Be yourself.*

Above all else, be natural. Don't make your letters sound like an English teacher or a clever friend of yours. Moreover, don't be a slavish imitator of models of letters in textbooks. Originality is always better than imitation. There are few better ways of reflecting your personality than a letter written by you, in your own style, saying what you want to say.

The Friendly Letter

The friendly letter is informal, casual, and personal. It is the kind of letter you write to your family and friends. Although there are no rigid, inflexible rules for writing friendly letters, you should learn to follow a few widely accepted practices.

12a. Choose stationery and ink that are appropriate for friendly letters.

Use letter stationery, preferably white or lightly tinted. Writing on paper that is gaudy or that reeks with perfume is considered poor taste. Do not write a letter of any kind on lined paper.

Instead of using a pencil, you should always write in ink, which is much easier to read and is more attractive on the page. Use blue, black, or blue-black ink. If you like green, purple, or red ink, use it for writing to only your closest friends; never use it for writing to a new acquaintance or someone else that you do not know very well. It is all right to type friendly letters, but be sure to sign your name in ink. If you type your letter, do not strike over letters or make messy erasures on your paper. Whether you type or use longhand, always be neat.

12b. Observe standard practices regarding the arrangement of the pages of a friendly letter.

You should arrange your letter so that your reader can easily follow your train of thought. Pay special attention to the margins, page order, and spacing.

Margins

Be sure to have even margins on both sides of the page. Don't run lines or afterthoughts up and down the margins. If you must add something you forgot to include, use a postscript (P.S.). Also remember that margins at the top and bottom of the page are just as important as those at the sides.

Page Order

If you use folded stationery and if your letter is more than two pages long, use the page order of a book. Write the second page on the back of the first page. If your letter is only two pages long, however, write your second page on the third page of your stationery. Before you mail the letter, check to see that each page is in the proper order.

Spacing

Always have *at least* two lines of your last paragraph on the last page of your letter. Never finish your last paragraph on one page and then put the closing and signature on the next.

12c. Learn the proper form for the five parts of a friendly letter.

The parts of the friendly letter are the *heading, salutation, body, closing,* and *signature*. The form below shows where these parts are placed upon the page.

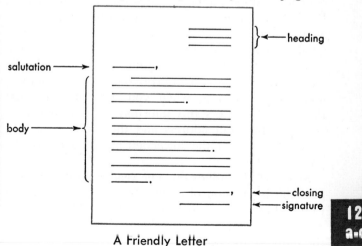

A Friendly Letter

12
a-c

1. *The Heading*

Placed at the top right-hand corner of the page, at least a half-inch from the top, the three lines of the heading give your address and the date. The first line contains your street address, the number of your rural route, or your post office box number. The second line has the name of your town, followed by the postal zone number if there is one, and the name of your state. A comma is placed after the zone number, between the town and the state. The third line gives the month, day, and year that the letter is written; a comma comes after the day of the month.

There are two styles for writing the heading:

BLOCK STYLE	INDENTED STYLE
4801 Live Oak Street	R.F.D. 2
Dallas 4, Texas	Fulton, Arkansas
April 26, 19—	June 4, 19—

The rules for the heading are, of course, flexible, depending upon the person to whom you are writing. For instance, if you are writing to your father, who is away for a few days on business, then certainly you would not need to give him your home address, and "Tuesday morning" or "Friday night" might be enough for the date. You give your complete address and the exact date when you are not sure that the receiver knows this information. If you prefer, you may put your address and the date at the end of the letter — in the lower left-hand corner of the page.

Since, in the minds of some readers, abbreviations give the impression of careless haste, it is better not to use abbreviations. If you do use them, however, be consistent by abbreviating the word *Street* as well as the name of the state.

2. *The Salutation*

Your salutation greets the reader. The usual form is the word *Dear* followed by the name of the person to whom you are writing. A comma comes after the salutation.

EXAMPLES   Dear George,
               Dear Sis,
               Dear Mr. Nelson,

3. *The Body*

The body is the letter itself. Be sure to divide your letter into paragraphs, making clear indentions of the first lines. If you type your letter, double space below the salutation, between paragraphs, and before the closing.

4. *The Closing*

Among the many appropriate closings for a friendly letter are: *Sincerely yours, Sincerely, Love, With love, Affectionately*. Do *not* use formal phrases, such as *Very truly yours* or *Respectfully yours*, which are found in business letters. Notice that only the first word of the closing is capitalized.

Do not try to be clever with such worn-out quips as "Yours till a weeping willow weeps." Also avoid using trite phrases like "Hoping to hear from you soon." These are poor substitutes for the conventional and more acceptable closings.

5. *The Signature*

Whether you type your letter or write it in longhand, always sign your name below the closing. Write legibly, and do not trail off into the space reserved for the right margin.

12d. Address the envelope correctly.

Place your own name and address in the upper left-hand corner of the envelope. Do *not* give yourself a title such as "Miss" or "Mr."

You do, however, always use a title like *Mr.*, *Mrs.*, *Miss*, *Dr.* before the name of the person to whom you are writing. (Notice that *Miss*, which is not an abbreviation, is never followed by a period.) Place his or her name and address on the lower half of the envelope, about midway between the ends.

Do not use such abbreviations as *St.*, *Ave.*, *Rd.* on the envelope, and do not abbreviate the name of the state. You may write the name of the state on a separate line.

Lynn Melton
4139 South Rockford Street
Tulsa, Oklahoma

              Miss Helen Barnes
              8 Hillvale Circle
              Knoxville 19
              Tennessee

12e. Make the content of your friendly letters lively and interesting.

The most important things for you to remember when writing friendly letters are *to be yourself* and *to say what you mean*. Certainly this book cannot tell you what to say in your letters. After all, a friendly letter is like a conversation, and your letters should be filled with lively, original comments that reflect your interests and personality.

There are, however, several "do's" and "don't's" that you should keep in mind as you write friendly letters.

1. *Write about those things that will interest your reader.*

Just as a good speaker considers his audience, a good letter writer remembers the interests of the person to whom he is writing. Your friend Bill may enjoy hearing about your recent hunting trip; whereas your Aunt Martha may be more interested in canning strawberries. If you are writing to your grandmother, she will probably want to know the news about your family and the progress you're making at school. When you are corresponding with friends of your own age, write about what you and they usually talk about when you are together. In short, make the content of your letter appropriate to the receiver.

2. *Be specific.*

Generalizations are always dull. A sentence like "School is about the same" is never so interesting as one with specific details, such as "At school, Miss McMahan is still harping about our errors in spelling, and Jerry Cates keeps on making up different excuses for dragging in late to math class every morning." Telling in detail about a definite incident at home is always more interesting than a lazy comment like "The family is fine."

3. *Don't gossip.*

Talking about mutual friends is always interesting and appropriate. Do not, however, make sarcastic remarks or repeat malicious gossip. Instead, look at your friends' good characteristics as you speak of what they say, where they go, and what they do.

12
d.e

4. *Don't ask too many questions.*

Don't start your letter with a series of questions like "How goes it with you? Are you still going out with Larry? Has your father started teaching you to drive yet? Are you and he still arguing about money? What have you been doing lately? Why don't you write to me more often?" (The answer to the last question is rather obvious.) The person to whom you write wants a letter from you, not a nosy questionnaire.

5. *Write a strong last paragraph.*

When you plan a composition, you often save the most important point until the last; and when you write a letter, you should make the last paragraph especially interesting. Don't suddenly stop with "I've got to go eat now," "No more news," or "I'll see you in my dreams." Instead, you might suggest that your friend plan to visit in your home or that you may have other interesting news to report in your next letter, after the ball game on Friday or the dance on Saturday. Or you might make reference to something you would like to hear about when your friend answers your letter.

● EXERCISE 1. Number from 1 to 10 on your paper. Seven of the following sections of a friendly letter are incorrect; three are correct. If a part is correct, write a plus sign (+) after its proper number. If a part is incorrect, write a zero (0) after the appropriate number.

1. *Heading:*   May 22, 19—
                 261 Main Street
                 Greenville
2. *Closing:*   With love,
3. *Salutation:* Dear John:
4. *Closing:*   Very truly yours,

5. *Heading:*   P.O. Box 692
                Claremont, California
                August 23, 19—
6. *Salutation:*   Harry —
7. *Salutation:*   Dear Mr. Blake,
8. *Last sentence in the body:*   "Time to eat — no more news anyway."
9. *Closing:*   Sincerely Yours,
10. *Closing:*   Yours till the Milky Way rains milk,

● EXERCISE 2.   After studying the proper form for the five parts of a friendly letter on page 249, close your book and draw lines on a sheet of paper showing where these parts are placed upon the page. Be especially careful about spacing and about correct punctuation of the lines representing the heading, salutation, and closing. In the margins of your paper, label each part of the letter.

● EXERCISE 3.   After drawing two envelopes on your paper, use the following information as you correctly address these "envelopes." (You will not use every word given below.)

1. *Sender:*   Miss Jane Black, Boulder, Colorado, P.O. Box 297
   Receiver: Mr. Robert Cleveland, 1112 Rose Boulevard, Postal Zone 12, Utah, Salt Lake City
2. *Sender:*   Mr. Thomas Flanders, New York City 13, 81 Waverly Place, New York State
   Receiver: Miss Florence White, Grand Rapids, Zone 6, Michigan, 336 East High Street

● EXERCISE 4.   You probably either owe someone a letter or know someone who would like to hear from you — a homesick friend who moved away from your town last month, a shut-in relative who reads every letter a dozen times, or perhaps a pen pal abroad whom you know only through correspondence. Write that letter today as an assignment in English. Follow the rules in this chapter as you write the heading, salutation, closing, and signature. Make your content lively, as you write specifically about your experiences that the reader will enjoy hearing about. Write in ink on regular letter stationery. Address the envelope properly, including your complete return address. Put your letter into the envelope, and hand it in to your teacher. *Do not seal the envelope.* After your teacher has written comments in the margins and has returned the letter to you, then you can copy your letter and mail it if you wish.

The Social Note

The social note is a short letter usually written for one of the following purposes: (1) to extend an informal invitation; (2) to accept or decline an informal invitation; (3) to thank someone for a gift or for entertaining you.

The form of the social note is very much like that of a friendly letter. The address and the date are either in the top right-hand corner or the lower left-hand corner of the page. The salutation is simply *Dear ——*, and the closing is usually *Sincerely yours* or *Sincerely.*

The social note may be written on regular note paper, on correspondence cards, or on personal note paper.

THE INFORMAL INVITATION

12f. Include all necessary information when you extend an informal invitation.

Although the form and the content of an invitation are very similar to those of a friendly letter, you do have to be careful to include the following information: (1) your full address; (2) the date, time, and place; (3) any necessary explanation regarding the kind of affair it is to be.

2132 Elkton Place
Greenwich, Connecticut
June 20, 19—

Dear Joyce,

    Dad, Mom, and I are getting ready for a trip to Garden City to visit my Uncle Howard. We plan to arrive there in time to go to Coney Island on July 2.

    Since you live right on our route, it would be very convenient for us to pick you up and take you with us. Are you interested? We could really have a lot of fun!

    If you can go, have yourself and your suitcase ready shortly before noon on July 2. You can tell your mother that you'll be back home before dark on July 3.

                Yours sincerely,
                Mary

An Informal Invitation

REPLYING TO THE INFORMAL INVITATION

12g. Answer an invitation by accepting gracefully or by refusing courteously.

Any time that you receive a written invitation, good manners require that your acceptance or refusal be

12
f-g

written. No matter what your decision may be, you should always show that you are glad you were invited. If you accept, show your pleasure. If you decline, then refuse graciously, with regret and with courtesy. In every letter that you write, politeness is important, and especially so when you accept or decline an invitation.

When you refuse an invitation, you should give a good reason for not accepting. Do not be offensively vague with sentences such as "Sorry I can't make it because I'll be busy."

As you read the following notes, notice the courteous tone of the letters.

20 Main Street
Rye, New York
June 23, 19—

Dear Mary,
　　It will be wonderful to go with you to Coney Island! As I count the days, I can hardly wait for the time to get here. I'll be ready when you arrive the morning of July 2.
　　　　　Affectionately,
　　　　　Joyce

A Note of Acceptance

20 Main Street
Rye, New York
June 23, 19—

Dear Mary,

I'm very sorry that I have to turn down your invitation. I'd give anything if I could go with you to Coney Island, but Dad needs me at the store. Since nearly all of his clerks are on vacation, I have to stay around to help out.

I hope that you and your family have a grand trip.

Sincerely,
Joyce

A Note of Refusal

● EXERCISE 5.   Write an informal invitation to your grandparents asking them to spend a week end with you and your family during the spring vacation. You may suggest a convenient bus or train that they might take.

● EXERCISE 6.   Write a note accepting an invitation to a party in your honor — for example, a going-away party or a birthday party.

● EXERCISE 7.   Write a letter refusing an invitation to Thanksgiving dinner with a friend who lives in a neighboring town. Express your regret courteously, and give a definite reason for being unable to accept. Be sure to express your appreciation of the invitation.

THE THANK-YOU NOTE

12h. Write courteous thank-you notes promptly.

Never fail to acknowledge a gift. When someone thoughtfully remembers you with a present, let him know that you appreciate it. Write a thank-you note within a week after you receive the present, and be sure to mention what it is. If you say merely "Thanks for the gift," the sender may think that you have forgotten what he sent or that you have no use for the gift.

After you have been entertained at someone's home, you should write a prompt thank-you letter; this note, often called a "bread-and-butter" letter, is addressed to your hostess. You should thank her for her hos-

---

321 *Fifth Street*
Park Manor, Illinois
December 30, 19—

Dear Fred,

> *Thanks a million for the belt. I really do like its unusual design and the large, sturdy buckle. Did you and Dad by any chance get together? The belt exactly matches the boots he got me for Christmas.*
>
> *I'm about ready for school to start again. Aren't you? It'll be fun to show off my new belt to all my friends.*

Sincerely,
Tom

A Thank-You Note

pitality and say what a good time you had. Show your appreciation of her kindnesses; in your letter, you might mention some of the things that you liked especially well during your visit.

● EXERCISE 8. Write a thank-you note to a friend who has sent you a birthday gift. Be sure to mention the gift by name.

3865 Fairview Road
Shreveport, Louisiana
September 7, 19—

Dear Mrs. White,

It was great to spend a whole week in the country with you and Don. I surely did have fun. Riding old Ned, helping Mr. White round up the cows, driving over to Marshall, seeing you work miracles with your "Dutch Oven" — everything was a real treat for me. Thank you for having me in your home.

Sincerely,
Steve

A Bread-and-Butter Note

● EXERCISE 9. Write a bread-and-butter note to a hostess who has entertained you over the week end. While you were visiting a friend, your hostess (your friend's mother) invited several people in for a party so that you would enjoy your visit more than usual

She also cooked your favorite dishes and provided you with tickets for a show on Saturday afternoon. Tell her in your bread-and-butter note that you had a good time, and show her that you appreciate her hospitality.

The Business Letter

The letters that you write to a place of business or to a person in a firm are business letters. Whether you are ordering merchandise or making a request, you should make your business letters short and to the point as you state your purpose clearly and courteously.

STATIONERY AND APPEARANCE

12i. Choose appropriate stationery for business letters.

When you write a business letter, never use the folded or pastel stationery that you use for friendly letters or social notes. Businessmen much prefer that you write on an $8\frac{1}{2} \times 11$-inch plain white sheet. Enclose your letter in a white business envelope.

12j. Make your business letters attractive and easy to read.

A neatly typed letter is more legible and therefore more quickly read than a handwritten one. If you write the letter by hand, however, use your very best penmanship. Do not expect a businessman to try to decipher or decode your letter; he doesn't have the time. Also be sure to space your letter attractively, leaving wide margins as you do for friendly letters. (See page 248.)

FORM

12k. Learn the proper form for the six parts of a business letter.

In addition to the five parts of a friendly letter, the business letter has an *inside address*, which is identical with the outside address on the envelope.

The semi-block form is a popular type of business letter. As the following model shows, the first line of each paragraph is indented; and the heading, closing, and signature are begun just to the right of the middle of the page. (The pure block form, which has no indentations of the first lines of paragraphs, is also acceptable for business letters.)

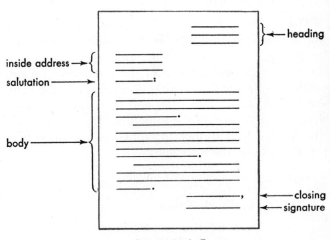

inside address →
salutation →
body →
heading
closing
signature

Semi-block Form

Carefully notice the spacing of the parts of the business letter above. It is centered on the page, with approximately the same margin at the top as at the bottom and with the same margin on each side of the

**12
i-k**

page. If you type your business letters, double space after the inside address, after the salutation, between paragraphs, and after the last line of the last paragraph.

1. *The Heading*

Beginning no less than one inch from the top of the page, put your *complete* address and the *full* date in the upper right-hand corner of the page. It is better to write this heading without abbreviations.

EXAMPLES   685 Lawton Street   R.F.D. 1
            Dayton, Ohio   *or*   Billings, Montana
            October 9, 19—   May 3, 19—

2. *The Inside Address*

The inside address is placed several spaces (at least four if you are typing) below the heading, and should be flush with the left-hand margin. It should include the full name and address of the company you are writing to. If you are writing to a person in the firm, use his full name and title, with a comma between the two if they are on the same line. If the name and title are too long to look attractive on the same line, put the title on the next line.

EXAMPLES   Acme Insurance Company
            P.O. Box 9721
            Topeka 14, Kansas

            Dr. Frank Harmon, Director
            Hunt County Tuberculosis Association
            Greenville, Texas

            Mr. David Yates
            Assistant to the Manager
            Ace Manufacturing Company
            451 North Fifth Street
            Weberville, Pennsylvania

Manager, Hotel Lexington
Lexington Avenue at Forty-eighth Street
New York 17, New York

3. *The Salutation*

The salutation is placed two spaces below the last line of the inside address and flush with the left-hand margin. The proper salutation for a letter written to a firm is *Gentlemen* followed by a colon. *Dear Sirs* is also used. When writing to an individual within the firm, the correct salutation is *Dear Mr. ——* (or *Mrs.* or *Miss*). If you are writing to a professional man or woman, use his title (*Dr.*, *Professor*, etc.) instead of *Mr.* A colon always follows the salutation.

EXAMPLES   Gentlemen:
Dear Dr. Harmon:
Dear Mr. Yates:
Dear Sir:

If you know the name, use it in both the inside address and the salutation. If you don't, then use *Dear Sir* (for one individual), *Dear Sirs* or *Gentlemen* (for a firm).

4. *The Body*

The form of the body of a business letter is the same as that of any letter. If your letter is very short (7 lines or less), you may double space the entire body of the letter. When you are typing a longer letter, however, you normally single space the paragraphs and double space between them.

5. *The Closing*

The closing comes between the body of the letter and the signature. The closings that you use for friendly letters are *not* appropriate for business letters. In business letters, appropriate closings are limited.

```
                                249 Trinity Street
                                Richmond, Virginia
                                March 18, 19--

                                     6

      Mr. E. F. Akin, Secretary
      Chamber of Commerce
      Glendale, Wyoming

      Dear Mr. Akin:

           Will you please send me information about
      the points of interest in and around Glendale?
      I would especially appreciate a map of the town
      as well as tips on good hotels or tourist courts.

           My family and I will spend the first week
      of June in Glendale. Will you be having a rodeo
      or another special event then?

                                Yours truly,

                                Edward Collins

                                Edward Collins
```

A Business Letter

Very truly yours, *Yours truly*, and *Yours very truly* are the ones most frequently used. *Sincerely yours* and *Yours sincerely* are also correct. The closing is placed just to the right of the center of the page, two spaces below the last line of the body of your letter. It is followed by a comma.

Do not end your letter with old-fashioned phrases such as "I beg to remain," "Hoping to hear from you soon, I am," or "Thanking you in advance, I am." End the body of your letter with a *period*, not a comma; then begin your closing.

EXAMPLES   Very truly yours,
            Yours sincerely,

6. *The Signature*

Sign your full name to your letter. Do *not* put *Miss* or *Mr.* before your name. If an unmarried woman is writing to a stranger, however, she may place *Miss*, in parentheses, before her signature so that the receiver of the letter will know how to address his reply.

EXAMPLE   *(Miss) Mary Jane Fiske*

A signature should always be handwritten. If your letter is typewritten, type your name flush with the first letter of the closing and far enough (usually four spaces) below to allow room for your signature.

121. Address the business envelope correctly.

Your envelope should have the same address on it as the inside address on your letter. Although you may put your return address on the back of the envelope, the post office prefers that you place the return address in the upper left-hand corner of the envelope, as follows:

```
Edward Collins
249 Trinity Street
Richmond, Virginia



              Mr. E. F. Akin, Secretary
              Chamber of Commerce
              Glendale, Wyoming
```

121

12m. Fold your letter to fit your envelope.

There are two kinds of standard business envelopes, for either regular mail or air mail: $6\frac{1}{2} \times 3\frac{1}{2}$ inches and $9\frac{1}{2} \times 4\frac{1}{2}$ inches. You should fold your business letter (on the standard $8\frac{1}{2} \times 11$-inch sheet) to fit the size of the envelope you are using.

For the large size, the letter is folded only twice. First, fold the bottom of the page up about four inches. Second, fold the top of the letter down, leaving about a half-inch at the bottom so that it will be easy to open.

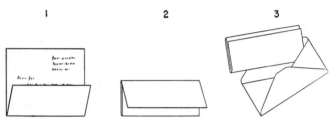

If your envelope is small, fold your letter up from the bottom to within a quarter of an inch of the top; then fold the right side over a third of the way; finally, fold the left side over, leaving about a fourth of an inch so that it can be opened easily.

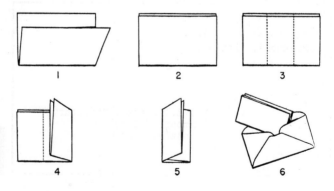

● EXERCISE 10. Copy in the proper form and arrangement on the page the business letter given below.

1. *Heading:* 311 East Houston Street, Luling, Texas, November 1, 19—

2. *Inside Address:* Mr. Walter T. Wiley, Business Manager, All-Occasion Greeting Cards, 115 Browder Street, Chicago 11, Illinois

3. *Salutation:* Dear Mr. Wiley

4. *Body:* As the secretary of the freshman class at Luling High School, I am writing to you to find out more about the offer that you are advertising in the Dallas *Morning News.* Since my class is working to raise money for the "Toys for Tots" campaign, we are interested in selling your Christmas cards. Will you please send me more information about the kinds of cards you have, the price range, and the percentage of profit made on each box sold.

5. *Closing:* Very truly yours

6. *Signature:* Charles Evans

● EXERCISE 11. Using either a small or a large business envelope, properly address the letter that you copied for Exercise 10. Be sure that the return address is accurate, and use no abbreviations (except for *Mr.* before the name of the person addressed). Also be sure that the address on your envelope is identical with the inside address on your letter. Next, fold your letter to fit the envelope; do not seal the envelope. (See page 268 for directions on folding and inserting the letter.)

12n. Make your letters of request simple and clear.

A request letter asks for information from the company or businessman to whom you are writing. It is a good idea to make your first sentence state your request. The other sentences can give further details. The business letter on page 266 is an example of the request letter.

● EXERCISE 12. Write to any place of business (a fence company, a bakery, a ready-to-wear store, a publishing firm, a jewelry store) requesting information about a particular product. Ask for circulars describing the merchandise and listing the prices.

● EXERCISE 13. Thumb through one of your favorite magazines, noticing the advertisements. Choose a firm that interests you, and write a letter of request. A steel company, for example, may send you circulars about the uses of steel. A manufacturer of flour may give away a recipe book. A travel bureau may have interesting, free pamphlets available. Some companies may have information that will help you in making reports in your classes at school. (Don't mail the letter unless you are really in need of the information.)

12o. Write order letters that contain complete and accurate information.

Although printed order blanks and "clip-it-out-and-mail" coupons are growing in popularity, there are still times when you need to write a letter ordering merchandise.

When writing an order letter, you should list the items you wish, one below the other, with complete information (style, size, price, catalogue number, or trade name) about each item. The price should be put at the right-hand side (flush with the right-hand margin). Each price should be placed directly under the one above so that the column of figures will be easy to add. List the cost of shipping, if you know it, and include it in the total, unless you know that the firm pays for shipping. Also be sure to say how you are paying for the order — by check, money order, C.O.D.

```
                                    R. F. D. 2
                                    Burnet, Ohio
                                    April 30, 19--


        Ajax Auto Supply
        6890 Clifton Road
        Dayton, Ohio

        Gentlemen:

            Will you please send me the following merchandise
        as advertised in your spring catalogue:

        1 pr. swimming fins, Cat. No. S20, adjustable
            straps, heavy duty                              $2.39

        2 skull caps, Cat. No. B261, one blue (size 7)
            and one red (size 6½), at 40¢ each                .80

        1 bicycle mirror, Cat. No. M45, small (4 by
            2), chrome trimmed                                .75
                                                            $3.94

            I enclose a money order for $4.14 to cover the cost
        of the order and the postal charge of $.20.

                            Yours very truly,

                            Byron Moore
                            Byron Moore
```

An Order Letter

● EXERCISE 14.   Write an order letter to Academy Novelty Company, P.O. Box 3975, Los Angeles, California, for the following merchandise: 2 green Wizard shirts, one size 15 and the other size 34, at $5.98 each; one OO-GA whistle, at 49¢; 6 yellow

Bond pencils, with the name "Skippy" printed in gold, at 7¢ each; and 1 set of Canton carving knives, with white handles, at $7.50. You are enclosing a money order to cover the total cost as well as an extra $.25 for postage.

THE ADJUSTMENT LETTER

12p. Write courteous adjustment letters.

When filling an order, businessmen sometimes make mistakes, and sometimes you make errors or leave out important information in your order letter. An adjustment letter is one that you write after an error has been made.

When you are trying to straighten out a mistake, by all means be courteous. Your adjustment letter should

R. F. D. 2
Burnet, Ohio
May 5, 19--

Ajax Auto Supply
6890 Clifton Road
Dayton, Ohio

Gentlemen:

In my letter of April 30, I ordered a pair of heavy-duty swimming fins with adjustable straps. Advertised on page 26 of your spring catalogue, these fins are numbered S20. This morning, however, I received a deep-sea diving helmet, which I am returning to you by parcel post. I'll appreciate your exchanging the helmet for the fins.

Yours truly,

Byron Moore

Byron Moore

An Adjustment Letter

not have curt remarks like "Can't you read? Why didn't you send me what I ordered?" or "I'll never buy another thing from your store." Always be polite as you explain what happened and as you ask for an adjustment.

Also be very prompt about correcting a mistake. Don't wait two or three weeks before you exchange an article or complain about not receiving something that you ordered.

● EXERCISE 15. Let's suppose that the Academy Novelty Company (see Exercise 14, page 271) failed to send you the six pencils that you ordered; moreover, you received blue shirts instead of green ones. It has been four days now since you received the package, and you still have had no word from the company about the missing pencils or a refund of your money. Write an adjustment letter.

12p

CHAPTER 13

Writing Stories

ESSENTIAL ELEMENTS IN NARRATIVES

Do you know how to tell a good story? Can you write a story? Storytelling is one of the oldest skills in the world. People have always enjoyed telling about things they have seen, heard, or experienced, and there has always been an audience to listen. Good storytellers are popular because they are entertaining. They make interesting letter writers. If you can write a good story of almost any length, you can use your skill to enrich other types of composition. Moreover, there is great satisfaction in being able to catch and hold the attention of an audience by voice or pen. Storytelling is fun.

13a. Learn how to find story material.

If you keep your eyes and ears open for story material, you will never have to say to your teacher or classmates, "I couldn't think of a story to write." To begin with, you are frequently hearing good jokes and anecdotes which either are stories in themselves or can be made into stories. Every day you see many incidents which, with a little imagination, you can develop into interesting stories. Your own personal experiences, those you enjoy telling to your friends, can be elaborated and written down in story form. Things you read, especially the daily paper, will suggest stories.

The storyteller has a wide range to choose from. In *length*, he may decide upon anything from a brief anecdote to a full-length novel. In *content*, he may choose personal experience, true stories, fanciful or romantic tales, folklore, biography, or history. As to *type*, his narrative may range from a more or less formless sketch to a mystery story with a highly complicated plot. As an inexperienced storyteller, you should begin with some of the simple forms.

(1) Learn to tell a joke entertainingly.

One of the shortest and easiest types of narration is the humorous anecdote or joke. It is also one of the most useful, since it enlivens ordinary conversation and is used frequently by speakers to brighten speeches and arouse bored audiences. Most jokes should end right at the climax or "punch line." Any further talk or explanation destroys the effect.

EXAMPLES

1

First hunter: You there, Bill?
Second hunter: Yes.
First hunter: You all right?
Second hunter: Yes.
First hunter: Then I've shot a bear.

2

A clerk at the hosiery counter was waiting on a customer. Another woman interrupted to ask, "Where can I find neckwear?"

"Aisle C," replied the clerk.

The second woman did not go away. She stood right where she was while the clerk completed her sale. Then she spoke impatiently.

13a

"Are you going to find out where neckwear is located?"

"Aisle C," repeated the clerk.

"That's what you said the first time," said the woman angrily. "You ought to be reported." And off she flounced — but not in the direction of Aisle C.

"The customer is always right," muttered the clerk as she turned to wait on the next one.

Here is another version of the hunter story:

Once upon a time there were two hunters who were out on a bear hunt. Suddenly one of them called to the other, "Are you there, Bill?"

"Yes," replied the second hunter.

"Are you all right?"

"Yes," answered Bill again, wondering what was the matter with his companion.

"Then," said the first hunter, "I've shot a bear."

Why is the first version so much better than the second?

Read the second joke aloud just as it is. Now try it without the last sentence. Which way is more effective? Is there any better place to stop? Can you think of a more interesting conclusion?

● EXERCISE 1.   Tell the second story as if you were the clerk telling it at home or to other clerks during the lunch hour.

● EXERCISE 2.   After giving yourselves twenty-four hours to think about it, take half an hour in class for a joke-swapping period. Afterwards write the joke that amused you the most. See if you can make it even funnier than the way it was told.

(2) Learn to tell an anecdote interestingly.

The personal anecdote is usually a small joke or an amusing incident from the writer's experience. Anecdotes may involve other persons, however, or they may be stories you have read or heard. They may be pathetic or even tragic rather than humorous, and no matter how short, they can make a strong impression. Most families have a treasury of anecdotes. Mothers are especially apt to cherish little stories of amusing things their children say or do. Don't neglect your grandparents, either, as a source of anecdotes about the "good old days."

EXAMPLES

1

One of the family jokes that my mother loves to tell is about the time she chased me under the bed with a hairbrush. Then she called my father. He came striding in and got down on his hands and knees to snake me out, so I moved over and said, "Gosh, Pop, is she after you, too?"

2

My father died in a mine explosion. I remember my mother's face as I stood beside her in the black of night with the light of the rescuers' lanterns falling on her white cheeks and haggard eyes. It frightened me to see her look like that. It was not my mother's face at all. When they brought my father's body up in the cage, my mother moaned a little and collapsed in a dark heap. I put my hand on her shoulder. That was the moment when I grew up.

● EXERCISE 3. Tell in class a personal anecdote that you recall because it was funny, exciting, joyful, or just interesting.

● EXERCISE 4. Write a brief anecdote of a more serious nature like the second example. Without using much action, try to create a single impression of fear, sorrow, homesickness, pain, or some other emotion.

● EXERCISE 5. One of the following topics may suggest a personal anecdote that you have forgotten. Write one this time that has some action, but keep it short and lively. Do not write more than two or three short paragraphs.

1. Unexpected company
2. A big scare at camp
3. When my mother cut my hair
4. My first high heels
5. A skunk under the porch
6. My first merry-go-round
7. My mother and the magazine agent
8. Dad and the power lawn mower
9. I broke Mother's prize vase
10. An adventure on stilts

(3) Learn to use the story material in actual incidents.

An incident is a small happening. Your own daily life is full of incidents. Some are so unimportant that you scarcely notice them, and others make such an impression that you remember them all day long and perhaps relate them at the evening meal at home. Something may happen that brightens or shadows your whole day. The boy whom you have been admiring at a distance for weeks catches up with you on the way to school, carries your books for all to see, and asks you to meet him for a coke after school. Or it may be the other way around. You learn that the boy whom you considered your own personal property has asked someone else to the Frosh Hop. Either way it is an incident and part of your daily life. You can write about it because it is true and real to you. Your success in story writing depends to a considerable extent upon your ability to write convincing incidents, either real or imaginary. You do your best writing about things that are familiar to you.

Frequently during the day you become aware of part of someone else's story. On a bus you overhear a conversation that arouses your curiosity. You see two persons quarreling violently on a street corner. What is their relationship? What are they quarreling about? A student speaks rudely to a teacher and is sent to the principal's office, or an inexperienced teacher humiliates a student before the rest of the class so that you cringe in sympathy. All of these little happenings involving yourself or others are incidents and can be made into stories.

Just to get a feeling for incidents, think back over your day so far, or about yesterday. What incidents stand out in your mind? What happened while you were dressing? Did you break a shoelace? (What happened as a result?) Did you discover that someone else was wearing your favorite tie or sweater? (Did you have time to battle for it?) What happened at breakfast? Did anything exciting occur in your home room or in any of your classes, in assembly, or in the cafeteria? If you work after school, did anything about your job amuse or bore you? Take it from there for the rest of the day.

13b. Consider characters, action, and setting when writing a story.

(1) Make your characters interesting.

Nearly all human beings are interested in other human beings. We like to know what makes other people "tick." Life is full of problems, conflicts, and minor difficulties. We are most concerned with our own, of course, but we do like to know how other people meet theirs. The most popular movies deal with individuals and their problems. Magazines are full of success stories. Most of the failures turn up in police reports of crime and accident in the newspapers. A reporter who can find a "human interest" angle in a news item is valuable to his paper.

13b

If you want to make a character come alive for your readers, answer the questions you as a reader would ask. What does he look like? Where does he live? What does he do? Why does he do it? (This is called *motivation* and it is important.) What does he think about common human problems? The best way to show character is not just to pin on a label like *stupid*, *generous*, *cruel*, *shy*, or *lazy*, but to show the character doing something that indicates that trait.

EXAMPLE   Jim Corris was lying in a cool, grassy spot under the big elm tree. His hat was tipped over his eyes to keep out the sun as well as the sight of his shovel, which suggested work. Feeling thirsty, he opened one eye to see where his Thermos bottle was. It was out of reach. Jim closed his eye and stayed thirsty.

● EXERCISE 6. Think of a well-liked student whom you know. What characteristics make him or her popular? Write a short incident which shows why he is popular. Don't describe the person or tell what you think of him. You keep out of the story. Let the character's actions speak for themselves.

● EXERCISE 7. Try to recall some older person who has made a strong impression on you. Was it a doctor, a nurse, a minister, a Scout leader, or a relative? Write an incident showing what that person did or said that changed your way of thinking, inspired you to work harder, or started you on the way to some profession. Stick to the one incident that made the greatest impression on you.

● EXERCISE 8. Who is your favorite book character? Which of his characteristics do you most admire (courage, honesty, a sense of humor)? From the book recall an incident which illustrates his character and write it in your own words.

● EXERCISE 9. Think over some of the popular people in sports, the movies, or television. Write an incident which seems to you characteristic of that person. You don't have to like him. You could write a good sketch that shows a certain player or actor to be a conceited, self-centered publicity-hunter.

(2) Fill your story with action.

Interesting characters are all very well, but they can't just sit around and look interesting. They must do something or have something done to them. There must be action in a story just as in a movie. When a moving picture becomes "talky," the audience grows restless. They want action. So does the reader. It can't be just any kind of action, however. It must be true to life. Whatever a character does must be something that such a person *would* do in similar circumstances. Any action, moreover, must contribute something to the story. It must not be put in just for padding, nor should it interrupt the main action of the story. If you are in the midst of an exciting horse race, for example, you must not interrupt it to describe some minor action in the grandstand unless that action has some strong bearing on the plot.

This is probably a good place to consider the matter of tense. Verbs are the words that give action and liveliness to your stories, and you should be able to use them well. Most stories are told in the *past tense*. Occasionally, however, a story can be made more exciting by using the *narrative present tense*.

EXAMPLE   Now the runners *are* on their mark. The on-
lookers *are* suddenly quiet. The starter *raises* his
arm. After a tense moment, the gun *barks* and

the men *are* off. One of them *pulls* away from the others. Head up, elbows back, his legs working like pistons, he *pounds* along the track and *crosses* the line a good ten feet ahead of his nearest rival. The band *plays*, the crowd *cheers*, and he *collapses* into the waiting arms of his friends. The race *is* won.

Whichever tense you choose for your story, be consistent in your use of it. Do not shift unnecessarily and carelessly from past to present or from present to past.

● EXERCISE 10.   In about 200 words, write an incident that involves rapid, exciting action such as an accident at the end of a stock-car or motorcycle race. When one car rams a wall and catches fire, what do the other contestants do? What do the spectators do? How does the race end? Use some other form of contest if you like.

(3) Make the setting clear and interesting.

Every story has a *scene* or *setting*. The setting is the time and place of the action. Even the least important incident has to take place somewhere, sometime. Before you start to write, you must choose your characters and decide upon a setting. If you are lucky enough to have traveled a bit, you may select a scene somewhat remote from your classroom. If you do, be sure that you stayed in the place long enough to write about it convincingly. But don't scorn the home scene. There are hundreds of good stories everywhere about you. All you need is a sharp, observant eye and ear. It is not sufficient, however, just to describe a scene faithfully. The good storyteller shows what effect the setting has upon the characters. Note the difference in the two examples that follow. The first describes just what the eye can see. In the second a sympathetic imagination supplies the invisible.

EXAMPLES

1

The study hall was long and narrow, with blackboards on one side and windows on the other. The teacher usually sat at her desk correcting papers while the boys made paper airplanes and the girls passed notes to each other.

2

Carol sat in the third seat in the row near the blackboard. How she hated that seat! How she hated Bill Nevins, who sat in front of her making paper airplanes and turning around to grin at her like an ape! Like an ape — that's exactly what he is, she thought to herself with satisfaction. Carol liked exact description. How she hated that silly Myrtle Evans, who sat behind her and spent the whole period writing notes to the boys! She wished she sat in the row near the window — in the back seat where nobody could sit behind her — where she could look out at the trees and the hills beyond, and where she could not hear the slap, slap of turning papers as Miss Dentman stolidly corrected them and placed them in little piles of E's, D's, and C's. There were no A's and very few B's. Carol was usually a B.

● EXERCISE 11. Make a list of at least ten places in your school, home, and community environment that would make possible settings for interesting action. Such a list could include the post office, the library, the skating rink, the rumpus room, the gymnasium, and the tennis court.

● EXERCISE 12. Write two short sketches (about 150 words each), one about a character of your own age and one about a much older or much younger person such as your grandfather, the school janitor, or your baby sister. In each case, place the character in a familiar setting and show how he is affected by it. Show what emotions are aroused in the character by the setting, such as fear, hatred, pleasure, grief, or boredom. If you can't dredge anything out of your memory, try one of the suggestions below. Be sure to select one that you know something about.

1. A small child in a dentist's office
2. A mother washing dishes
3. A hungry teen-ager at the end of the cafeteria line
4. An old man watching a ball game
5. A boy "on the bench" hoping for a chance to play
6. A baby sitter on her first job
7. A man waiting to ask the boss for a raise
8. A boy waiting for his date while her father entertains him
9. A new girl standing near her locker hoping that someone will speak to her

13c. Base your story on an interesting situation, preferably one involving conflict.

The word *situation* as used in storytelling means the relationship of your characters to each other and to their environment at the beginning of the story. They may hate each other and be paired off at a dance; they may love each other and be separated by parents or circumstances. They may be caught in crooked deals or perform heroic deeds, but whatever the situation, it is the basis of your story. The most interesting and exciting storytellers usually put their characters in a situation that involves conflict of some sort. The conflict may be between one man and another, as in stories of the prize ring, or between one man and a gang. It may be man fighting against nature, as in pioneer stories, or conquering the sea or the air. It may be man against society, a conflict between criminals and the law, as in the ever popular mystery and detective stories. Whatever the conflict, the situation presents the criminal just as he is being arrested, the champion on the floor taking the count, or the hunter lying helpless in the snow with a broken leg and no means of getting help. In a long story, the situation may change from time to time, but at your stage of experience, stick to a single situation.

● EXERCISE 13.   Below are four suggestions for incidents stressing situation. Choose the one that interests you most and build it up into a short, readable story of about 200 words.

1. A boy is practicing his speech for assembly before the mirror in his room. He is in the midst of an eloquent gesture when his little sister bursts in with one of her friends.
2. A baby sitter making a routine check of a baby in his crib finds the child breathing heavily and feverish. The parents had told her that they were going to an address on Arnold Park. They had written the address on a piece of paper and she had put it into one of her schoolbooks. Now in her excitement she can't find it.
3. A young girl is in a large department store choosing her first formal dress for a very important dance. She has found one that exactly suits her, and now she is waiting anxiously for her mother, who will arrive shortly and make the decision.
4. The score is 7–6, with thirty seconds to play. Oak Hill High must make that extra point or go home humiliated. A tie is better than defeat. Everything depends on Jimmie Hale, the quarterback, who is going to try for the point himself.

● EXERCISE 14.   Write an incident, preferably from your own experience, paying particular attention to the situation. Use only two or three characters. Place them in a believable situation and make them behave as normal people would in such a case. Work on your final sentence. Put a punch in it.

13c

13d. Keep the story interesting throughout.

The bards and minstrels, who were the chief story-tellers in former times, often acted out their stories or accompanied themselves on a musical instrument like a harp or a lute. They caught the attention of their audience by means of a crashing chord and worked their stories up to a climax of excitement or drama. Then they finished quickly lest they lose the interest of their audience. When you write a story, your first problem is to catch the reader's attention in the very first sentence. You have to use words to get the same effect as the minstrel's strings. Your next problem is to hold your reader's interest, and your third, to stop yourself before you spoil the whole thing. Many a good tale is ruined by stringing it out too long. Read the following examples. Decide upon at least three ways in which the second one is better.

1

I am going to tell you about something that happened on my way to school this morning. It was raining, and I was wearing my raincoat and trying to keep my books from getting wet. At the corner of Main Street and West Elm Street I heard a loud noise. It was an ambulance. A lot of people were standing around, and someone was on the ground. The policemen held the people back while they put the person in the ambulance. He was on a stretcher. I don't know who it was.

2

Hey! Wait for that light! No, I'm not going chicken, but I saw an accident this morning right on this corner, and I'm still shaking. An old man started away from the curb before the light changed. Wham! A car hit him and dragged him three or four feet along the street. A crowd gathered. Police came and in no time an ambulance rolled up. I saw them put the old man in. His face was gray and there was blood all over his clothes. That was enough for me! Believe me, I'll never jump a light again.

● EXERCISE 15. Take one of the suggestions below as your opening sentence and complete the incident.

1. "James Wilson, you march right into the living room and tell your father where you've been."
2. "Put up your hands. This is a stick-up!"
3. "*One*, two, three, *one*, two, three! Terrible! Take it again."
4. "Oh, for goodness' sake, don't look like that! What have I done to you?"
5. Quietly, quietly, inch by inch, he pulled himself across the damp grass toward the lighted window.

● EXERCISE 16. Below are five possible conclusions. What kind of incident does each suggest? Choose one and write an imaginary story that might have ended that way. You need not use the exact words as a final sentence; maybe something better will occur to you.

1. She turned the key in the lock, walked down the steps, and, without once looking back, went forward into a new life.
2. "Gosh," muttered Ricky, "*that* was a narrow escape."
3. "And don't you ever darken this door again!" Well, that sounded final. As the door banged, old Big John shrugged his shoulders and started off down the street whistling softly.
4. "Good-by," said Janet, her voice just a little shaky. "You'll write, won't you?" But she knew he wouldn't. This was the end.
5. "Time to get ready, Miller." It was the last mile. Well, he had it coming to him. He'd been expecting it. Now it was here. This was it.

13d

13e. Write natural dialogue.

We learn a great deal about the characters in a story from what they say to each other. Dialogue should be natural and spontaneous. In the following example, note that occasionally a sentence is introduced indicating action or emotion, but in general the feelings of the characters are expressed only by what they say.

"Well, look who's here! If it isn't Mr. Touchdown, U.S.A.!"

"Aw, forget it, Jeanie. I can't help it if the kids got a little excited. After all, we *did* beat North High —"

"You mean *you* beat North High all by yourself — and you let that painted-up cheerleader kiss you!" Jeanie could hardly keep the tears out of her voice.

"Oho! So you're jealous! Well —"

"I am not jealous. If you want a painted blonde with Kurlash on her eyelashes, you can have her. And you needn't come over tonight because I won't be home. I'm going to the movies with Howard Mason."

"Howard Mason!" Gerry fairly snorted. "*That* rhomboid! Why, he hasn't even got a head on his shoulders! All he has is a metal box full of slide rules and formulas and figures."

"He's a mathematical genius. That's what Mr. Lochran calls him. Don't you dare —"

"Aw, come on, Jeanie. You're not going anywhere with that T-square Tommy. The gang's going down to Larry's at eight. I'll pick you up at seven forty-five."

Jeanie's heart began to beat more normally. She hoped that Gerry wouldn't find out that she hadn't even seen Howard.

"Howard's all right, Gerry Cummings. Why, I think he's the best —"

"Sure he is, but you're not going anywhere with him." Gerry grinned. "See you at seven forty-five. No Kurlash, remember!"

● EXERCISE 17.   Place two characters in a situation which has in it some elements of conflict. Write enough dialogue between the two to let the reader know what the situation is and how the conflict is decided or comes to an end.

● EXERCISE 18.   Select one pair of characters from the following list, and write some believable dialogue between them. No matter who has the last word, make the speech sound final.

1. Two boys arguing about which one can lick the other
2. A lady and her hairdresser
3. Two girls raving about a movie actor
4. A father and son on the subject of using the family car
5. A teen-ager and a younger brother deciding which television progam to watch

13f. Consider the various points of view from which a story may be told.

You have probably at some time had an experience like this. Something occurs at school that will require careful reporting at home. Perhaps you were sent to the principal's office for talking too much in class, or you got into a fight with another fellow during football practice. You know that you will have to tell your parents, so all the way home you rehearse the story in order to make it sound as unimportant or as favorable to you as circumstances will permit. Maybe you are lucky enough to find your mother at home and you get a chance to tell her the tale from your point of view. Then your father arrives. He has met the coach or the principal or the boys' adviser and heard a very different story. Or your sister bursts in to tell the tale as she heard it. You discover that the same facts can sound very different when told from different viewpoints.

13
P.f

● EXERCISE 19. Write your version of one of the incidents suggested above as you planned it on the way home. You will, of course, write in the first person, using the word *I*. That is often the most effective way to tell a story and is necessary when a character is obliged to defend himself.

● EXERCISE 20. Write your sister's version of the same incident. She will, of course, use the third person, as is usual in storytelling. She will speak of you as *he* or use your name. Her version is not likely to be as sympathetic as yours.

● EXERCISE 21. Decide on what subjects the following pairs of characters might possibly have widely differing points of view. Choose one pair and write an incident to illustrate the difference. Work in some dialogue.

1. A mother and a teen-age daughter
2. A ballplayer and an umpire
3. A crook and his partner in crime
4. A teacher and a parent
5. A freshman and the school janitor

Stories to Write

A good source of story material is the news item of the lighter sort, often used by editors to fill columns. Below is a compact item of this type with a good punch line.

> PALMER, NEB. — A woman called the Palmer Post Office with a complaint: The substitute mail carrier was bothering her dog.
>
> "The regular man gets along just fine with him, so it must be this new man's fault," she said.

"Where was your dog when this incident occurred?" asked the postal employee, filling out a complaint blank.

"Right out in the front yard under a tree," the woman replied.

"And where was the postal carrier?"

"Up in the tree."

● EXERCISE 22. Expand the above item to about twice its length. Tell it as if you were the postal employee who took the message telling it to the other postal clerks after he had hung up the receiver. Or tell it from the point of view of the substitute carrier.

● EXERCISE 23. Read the incident given below and then carry out the directions that follow it.

DALTON, PA. — Ten-year-old Richard Mullen got out of school yesterday, sniffed the balmy spring air — the temperature was 73 — and decided to do some climbing.

Richard scrambled 40 feet up a cliff near his home and got stuck.

He shouted for a half-hour before Joseph Snyder and William McGurrin heard him. Snyder obtained a rope, dropped it from the top of the cliff, and told the boy to tie it around his waist. Then Snyder lowered the boy to McGurrin at the foot of the cliff. By this time the place was alive with police and curious people.

Gasped young Richard: "I'll never climb again."

Make a story out of the above incident. Use more dialogue. What might Snyder and McGurrin have said to Richard and to each other while they were working out his rescue? What did Richard say? Give him a better speech at the end.

● EXERCISE 24. Read the incident given below and then carry out the directions that follow it.

CHICAGO, ILL. — Gusty winds brought a shower of money — as well as rain showers — on Michigan Avenue yesterday.

The money — $610 in 10's, 20's, and a $100 bill — came from the purse of Mrs. Pearl North, 39, as she was walking near the Drake Hotel. She was unaware her purse had opened until a man shouted, "Lady, your money is blowing out!"

Mrs. North frantically ran after the bills, which whipped down sidewalk and gutter and blew across the street in front of buses and cars. Two other women ran to help her. The women, dodging traffic, rounded up $410. The missing money included the $100 bill.

Mrs. North said she had the money in her purse because she intended to pay her life insurance premium.

The item above could easily be expanded into three or four hundred words. You might begin with Mrs. North at home, putting her money into her purse and planning her shopping trip. (You need not stick to the life insurance. That could be only one of her errands.) Put in some dialogue as the women return, breathless, with the money. End with what Mr. North said when she had to explain what he had already read in the evening paper. You could have an enterprising young reporter among those who collect Mrs. North's money.

● EXERCISE 25. Read the incident given below and then carry out the directions that follow it.

SARASOTA, FLA. — Two rattlesnakes slithered out of an overturned box at a snake-handling demonstration yesterday, frightening some thirty spectators.

Snake handler "Texas" Jack Miller leaped from his lecture platform and grabbed the rattlers as they wriggled within five feet of the crowd. Miller picked the snakes up by their tails and dropped them back in the box before they could coil and strike.

In the above item you have less to work with. You have one character and a situation. Build a story out of what you have. Who is "Texas" Jack? Where did he get the snakes? Where is he giving the demonstration? Is he one of the attractions at a county fair? Why is he doing this kind of work? What does he say or do to attract an audience? Include the "spiel" that he uses. Create a sense of excitement and suspense as the box tips over and the snakes escape. See if you can invent a good conclusion without any help.

● EXERCISE 26. Here is a humorous newspaper story that needs a little polishing. Pretend that you wrote it yourself and that you are now making your final revision. Improve the paragraphing, make the sense clearer in the phrases in heavy print, and strengthen the last paragraph.

Imagine finding yourself face to face with a snorting bull in a field rimmed by an electrified fence.

You have just landed there by parachute from an airplane. There are yards and yards of blood-red parachute silk draped over the landscape and you are smack in the middle.

Such was the predicament of Bill Wedekind. He had no inkling when he went to Municipal Airport late yesterday to practice parachute jumping that he was almost to become history's first air-borne matador.

The wind changed when Bill jumped. Instead of coming down gently on the airfield, he got blown into a farm field and came to light in a billow of red silk in the hostile neighborhood of the bull.

Wedekind said that he sat there waiting for the bull to go away. The bull didn't budge but stood 20 feet distant and gazed back. Occasionally, he snorted.

"Don't be scared," Wedekind said he reminded himself. "After all, you have a knife."

He said that he pulled it out, looked at the two-inch blade. Then he put it away and looked at the bull.

Along about this time, he noticed the fence. He also noticed that it was electrified.

He smiled reassuringly at the bull and tried to gather in all that red silk. But there was too much of it.

Then he began edging toward the fence. The bull looked on with interest.

Wedekind reached the fence. He scrambled through but says that he doesn't remember how he avoided the live wires.

The Longer Story

So far you have been writing very short stories. Now it is time to try your hand at a longer one (400–500 words). The story which follows will serve as a model of the longer story. It involves a personal experience told in the third person and in the past tense. Note that there is only one important character and that the situation is simple. There is enough action to maintain interest with a minimum of dialogue, and the ending is satisfying. Read and discuss it with your classmates.

THE WINNER

As the day for the big swimming carnival approached, Jim Morris found each class period getting longer. He felt responsible for the success of Splash Day this year, because he was in charge of most of the arrangements. Up until the last minute, Jim worked at selling tickets, supervising banana-tree decorations, and practicing for the 100-yard free-style. He knew he could win it. In fact, just the other day, Mr. Phillips, the coach, had stopped him in the hall and said, "We're counting on you to win the free-style next Saturday, Jim." All he'd been able to do was grin, but inside he felt good.

He had that same "good feeling inside" on the day of the carnival, as he stood on the edge of the open-air pool. Waiting for the starting gun, Jim noticed the colors in the water as it crinkled in the sunlight. There was the signal! Sp-p-p-lash! Bodies hurled themselves into the water. Then came the hurting whack of a confused dive, for one of Jim's feet slipped as he pressed to make a fast start. Many people stood up to see what had happened. Others called out. Mr. Phillips knew that Jim would finish the race, although he was hopelessly behind.

Jim was the last one to get out of the water, and he wished there were some way for him to go through the bottom of the pool to the dressing room. But he knew that he had to face the spectators and that they would see the violent red of his face, although they would not be able to see the burning tears in his eyes. His embarrassment was almost more than he could bear as he called himself the biggest fool in the world.

Standing up, he heard cheering and noisy clapping. Voices shouted, "Hard luck, Jim!" "Wonderful carnival, Jim!" "Don't worry, Jim!" He saw that everyone was clapping for *him*, Jim Morris, fool swimmer who had messed up everything. He couldn't believe it, and his face grew a deeper red. Then, Mr. Phillips was walking toward him. He put his arm around Jim's shoulder and said, "You didn't win, boy, but this whole afternoon is your big win. It's a great success, and we're all grateful to you."

All Jim could do was grin. The "good feeling inside" was coming back again, and as he looked down into the water he saw that the ripples were made up of smiles.

— *Carmel Fleming Coleman*

● EXERCISE 27. Write a story of 400–500 words, based on some experience of your own or of some other person. The story above stresses feelings rather than action. Put more action into yours if you like.

CHAPTER 14

Taking Notes
and Writing Reports

METHOD AND CONTENT

You are often required to take notes and write reports on what you read. Your history teacher may have you read and report on current events. Your science teacher may ask you to go to the library to gather facts about magnetism or electronics and then to write a report on your findings. In any class, when you are taking a test, you must often summarize what you have read in your textbook.

This chapter will show you how to take notes and how to write summaries or reports based upon those notes. You will learn to find the most important facts in what you read and to write the information in your own words.

Taking Notes

14a. As you read, take notes on index cards.

To write a report on a particular subject, you will probably need to read more than one article. You should get a package of 4 × 6-inch index cards, and use these to take notes as you read. Use a separate

14a

note card for each item — newspaper story, magazine article, or portion of a book.

On the first line of the card, write the author's name (if given), the title of the article, and the name of the magazine, newspaper, or book. When you record the author's name, give the last name first. Enclose titles of chapters and articles in quotation marks, and underline book and magazine titles. On the second line, give the date of publication and the page numbers. Use the rest of the card, of course, for notes needed for your report.

14b. Write most of your notes in your own words. Put quotation marks around everything you copy.

The purpose of note-taking and report-writing is to show clearly that you understand what you read. You can do this best by using your own words. You should do very little copying. If you find a few important lines useful as a direct quotation in your report, copy the *exact* words, and be sure to use quotation marks. As you take notes, however, you should remember that too many quotations weaken a report.

14c. Jot down the most important ideas.

To catch the most important ideas in an article, look for topic sentences. The topic sentence, as you know, states the main idea of the paragraph. The sentences that follow give details. You should pay special attention to topic sentences, because they not only give important information but also guide you in your choice of the supporting details that best clarify the main ideas.

Below is an article about Paul Bunyan. As you read each paragraph, notice the topic sentence that introduces the specific examples.

PAUL BUNYAN [1]

Paul Bunyan was a legendary lumberjack of great size and strength. He was the hero of many stories told in North American lumber camps. The legends disagree about his place of birth. Some say that he was born of French parents on Prince Edward Island, Canada. Others say that he was born in Maine, of American parents. His great logging operations took him through the Middle West and the Northwest. Among his wonderful feats of strength were many changes in the geography of North America. The legends say that he made the Allegheny and Rocky Mountains, the Mississippi and other rivers, the Grand Canyon, Old Faithful Geyser, and many other natural wonders. His constant companion and helper was Babe, the Blue Ox, born in the Winter of the Blue Snow. The Blue Ox, the stories claimed, could drink rivers dry.

Paul was noted for solving difficult problems with little effort. It was said that to grease his large pancake griddle, he had boys skate on it with slabs of bacon fastened on their feet. He made a handle of woven grass for his ax. Then he swung it in a circle and cut all the trees around him at one sweep. He used his buckskin harness in various ways. On rainy days it stretched so that the Blue Ox arrived at camp while the load of wood which he was supposed to haul remained in the forest. But when the sun came out, the harness shrank so that it drew the load into camp and the animal did not have to work at all.

Paul Bunyan stories are humorous chiefly because of their exaggeration. For example, the Blue Ox's shoe was so heavy that the blacksmith carrying it sank knee-deep into solid rock at every step. Often the stories were matter-of-fact but highly exaggerated. For example, a hill was so

14
b-c

high that one man took a week to see the top. But seven men, if they all worked together on it, could see the top in one day. These Paul Bunyan "tall stories" were most popular among lumbermen from about 1850 to 1900, but new ones have been added through the years. There are stories of how Bunyan helped to build Bonneville Dam, and how he carried on logging operations by airplane.

The first paragraph, which deals with Bunyan as a legendary figure, tells about particular legends. Notes on this paragraph should be sure to mention this main topic and to include a few details that support and define the topic.

"Paul Bunyan," *World Book Encyclopedia,* II
    1957, pages 1064-1065

<u>Legends</u> about Paul Bunyan - giant
    Origin uncertain - born in Maine or Canada
    Was lumberjack in Middle West & Northwest
    Supposedly changed American geography,
        making rivers, Rockies, etc.
    "Babe" was his Blue Ox - also tremendously
        big, according to legends

Note Card

● EXERCISE 1.   Using the above note card as a guide, take notes on the second and third paragraphs of the article about Paul Bunyan. First, jot down the main topic of each paragraph; then list details supporting the topic. Be sure to use *your own words,* and do not try to include *all* of the information. After you have checked to see that you have included the most important ideas, hand in your notes to your teacher.

● EXERCISE 2. As you read the following article, look for the main ideas of the author. Write these ideas, in your own words, on a note card. Include notations on only a few of the specific details.

BLIZZARDS FROM SPRINKLERS COVER SLOPES WITH SNOW [2]

Ski-resort owners across the country, watching their profits melt away in cloudless skies, are resorting to a new technique — making their own snow. To create blizzards, they stretch two hose lines up the ski slope, one carrying water and the other compressed air. Under high pressure the water and air mix inside a sprinkler, and the mixture is ejected in a fine mist. All nature must do is provide a temperature a few degrees below freezing and presto — snow! The flakes can be coarse or fine, depending upon the proportion of water to air.

Some resorts have permanent installations buried below the frost line. At others, men drag the sprinklers from place to place to distribute the snow evenly.

Out on Moonridge Mountain, near Big Bear, Calif., there's a six-man crew working to cover a slope the size of four football fields. The snow makers brew their blizzards at night, building a foot-deep base on the first cold night, then adding six or eight inches each ensuing night to keep the slope in good shape following the activities of skiers during the day.

One group of men, calling itself the "pneumonia detail," occasionally throws vegetable dye into the water system, just to amaze the customers. Sure enough, out comes colored snow.

Writing Reports That Summarize

14d. Make your reports short.

In most of your reports, you are required to condense material that you have read. A report that

[2] Reprinted by permission of *Popular Mechanics*, February, 1957, page 9.

14d

summarizes an article should be about one-third the length of the article itself. If you are reporting on information that you have gathered from several sources, the length of your paper will vary according to the scope and purpose of your assignment, but you should always be concise in your wording and in your direct statement of points. You must choose your words so that you can get the maximum amount of meaning into the minimum space.

Usually you will find that your summary is too long in its first draft and that you will not need to use all of your notes. If it is too long, reduce it to the proper length as you revise your work.

● EXERCISE 3.   Since the article about Paul Bunyan (page 299) is 382 words long, a summary of it should not have more than 127 words. The following summary (263 words) is far too long. Read it and decide which details and examples should have been omitted. Then rewrite the summary in a concise, to-the-point manner.

There are many legends about Paul Bunyan. According to these legends, he was a giant among lumberjacks. Legends about his birth are contradictory. It is said by some writers that Paul Bunyan was born in Maine, and it is said by other writers that he was born in Canada. Therefore, the origin of this legendary giant is uncertain. Legends are more consistent about where he lived; they say he was a lumberjack in the Middle West and Northwest. Paul Bunyan and his Blue Ox did all kinds of things. They supposedly changed the geography of America by making rivers and by making mountains like the Rockies.

In fact, Paul could do almost anything he wanted to do. He didn't have any trouble figuring out a hard problem. When he wanted his griddle greased so that he could have pancakes, he put bacon on some boys' feet. Then he had them skate across the griddle. He also used grass for the handle of his ax. He could cut down lots of trees this way. He also used a harness that would shrink when it rained. He rigged this up so that his Blue Ox wouldn't have any work to do.

Stories about Paul Bunyan are very exaggerated. That is what makes them funny. For instance, legends say that it took a man a whole week to see the top of a high hill. Although these stories were very popular during the last half of the nineteenth century, there are some modern legends saying he performs his duties as a lumberjack by using an airplane.

14e. Give only the "heart" of the article on which you are reporting.

Only the main ideas go into your report. Omit repetitions, minor details, illustrations, and most adjectives. Above all, do not subordinate or leave out the author's main points and dwell upon interesting but insignificant ideas.

● EXERCISE 4. The following summary of "Blizzards from Sprinklers Cover Slopes with Snow" is of acceptable length (66 words), but it is a distorted version of the original. The selection of ideas is poor, and the emphasis is wrong because the summary does not give the heart of the article. After you have reread the article on page 301, rewrite the summary below so that it will stress the author's main ideas. (Do not use more than 70 words in your revised summary.)

When high pressure is applied to hoses containing compressed air and water, an attached sprinkler will eject a spray of water. At freezing temperatures, the drops of water quickly turn to snowflakes. The size of the flakes is determined by the amount of air mixed with the water. Once a crew in California, the "pneumonia detail," produced colored snow by putting some dye into the water.

14e

14f. Use your own words, not those in the article you read.

If you use long phrases or whole sentences from an article, you are merely copying, not writing a summary. If you cannot put the ideas in your own words, you do not understand what you have read. Use your dictionary to look up words that you do not know. If you carefully take notes in your own words as you read, it will be easier to write the summary. Be sure that you thoroughly understand an article before you begin to summarize its main ideas in your own words.

● EXERCISE 5.   Read carefully the following article. Take notes on index cards and write a summary from your notes. Do not copy anything from the article.

HELP ON CELLULOID [3]

It was only planned as an eleven-minute film, but seldom has a moviemaker run into a more temperamental star. The actor was a bobcat that obviously had no intention of doing what he was told. He broke out of his cage, fled up a tree, fought so violently when lassoed that he broke his neck and died. Reported the frustrated moviemaker to his employer, Encyclopædia Britannica Films, Inc.: "I am now without a cat to work with. I very much regret having to report so much trouble, but it seems to go with this kind of work."

For twenty-eight years E.B.F. has been wrestling with "this kind of work" to bring to the world's classrooms some of the best educational films ever made. It is the largest producer of school movies, distributes them not only in the U.S. but to fifty-five foreign nations. Though no money-maker, it has as impressive a board of advisers as any corporation going — former Senator William Benton, Econ-

[3] Courtesy *Time*, copyright Time, Inc., 1957.

omist Beardsley Ruml, onetime Assistant Secretary of Defense Anna M. Rosenberg, Psychologist George Stoddard, President Robert Hutchins of the Fund for the Republic, and Social Scientist Ralph Tyler. Last week it was sporting another big name: Chairman-elect Adlai E. Stevenson.

Three Ears for One. Founded by Western Electric in 1929, the company that was to become E.B.F. was just struggling along until well after the Britannica took over. Teachers had balked at using movies in their classes, and pupils never seemed to take them seriously. Spurred by the success of the armed services with audio-visual education during World War II, the company sent out forty experts to proselytize in schools. The experts taught pupils how to run projectors, talked thousands of teachers into experimenting with films. The E.B.F. staff went through 109 standard elementary textbooks, this year drew up detailed guides on how some of its films could be tied in with appropriate chapters. The whole idea, says E.B.F.'s President Maurice Mitchell, was to get the teacher to use "the right film at the right time. Nothing can replace the teacher, but there are some things a film can do that a teacher can't."

Through E.B.F., millions of students have been able to witness such wonders as the growth of a plant from seed to blossom in a matter of minutes. They have seen the human heart in action, been whisked through the ages of history. To make one film on hearing, the E.B.F. staff worked eighteen months, used the ears of three corpses to show the ear's inner workings. Each script gets a thorough examination by experts, but it is primarily up to producer and photographer to present the facts with imagination.

Tepees & Châteaux. One photographer waited an entire week to shoot a burrowing owl going into a hole and coming out again. Another cameraman was speared by a savage while working along the Amazon. In making a film called *Indian Family of Long Ago*, experts had to teach the actors, some Sioux from South Dakota, how to put up tepees, pack a travois (a primitive sledge), and shoot bows and arrows. When Producer Milan Herzog made his series on medieval life, nothing would do but to shoot it in real

141

French châteaux that had been especially decorated with priceless furniture and tapestries from museums.

Because of the current teacher shortage, E.B.F. thinks that its influence will grow even greater. Last week it began to distribute a 162-session physics course by the University of California's Harvey White — the first full-length, high school physics course ever put on film. The series is to be used not merely to supplement the work of the high school teachers. It is primarily meant for an estimated 14,000 high schools that have no trained physics teacher at all. With other such projects in the works, E.B.F. may not only become more and more influential, but for hundreds of schools it may well become downright indispensable.

14g. In writing a report, use the point of view of the author of the article you have read.

Your own opinion does not have a part in the summary of another person's article. As you report his main ideas, hold to his point of view. *Do not add any opinions or ideas of your own.*

● EXERCISE 6. Carefully read the following poor attempt to summarize "Help on Celluloid." Be able to point out in class how these paragraphs depart from the point of view of the author of the article. Be prepared to show (orally) how you would revise the paragraphs in order to take out all opinion. (You can begin by striking out "The title means.")

The title means that students are being taught by movies made by the Encyclopædia Britannica Films, Inc. This company, which has a very capable staff, is doing a wonderful job of making educational films.

The first paragraph gets the reader's interest by talking about a bobcat that didn't co-operate with a movie-maker. It showed me that the work is dangerous, too. Just as interesting to me was the part about the man who stood around for a week watching a burrowing owl.

I think that these films are a good answer to any teacher shortage and that they provide excellent, educational entertainment for students in crowded classrooms.

This project is similar to the ones being made with television. In these experiments, one person can teach hundreds of pupils who watch several television screens in various rooms. Actually, these films could be put on television, and the two projects combined would be very effective.

Like E.B.F.'s President Mitchell, though, I am convinced that "Nothing can replace the teacher."

CHECK LIST FOR WRITING REPORTS

1. Is the report short — less than one-third the length of the article?
2. Have I included the main ideas and the important details?
3. Have I used my own words?
4. If I have copied any phrases, are they enclosed in quotation marks?
5. Have I held strictly to the author's point of view?

● EXERCISE 7.   Read the following article, carefully taking notes on the most important ideas. Then write a report based upon your notes. After you have written it, check your work by answering the questions in the check list above.

TORNADO RECORD SHOWS
HUMANLIKE AMBITIONS [4]

DENTON, APRIL 13 (AP) — A professor who's spent thirty years gathering tall tornado tales says tornadoes are "pretty much like people."

"They have their likes and dislikes, whims and ambitions, their impulses good and bad," says Dr. Howard C. Key, North Texas State College English professor.

From folklore he has gathered, Dr. Key

4 Reprinted by permission of Wide World Photos, Inc.

14g

made this psychoanalysis of tornadoes' personalities:

1. Tornadoes are partial to infants. He has collected thirty-two stories about miraculous preservation of infants. One tornado in southeastern Kansas about fifty years ago gathered a six-week-old baby out of its cradle and deposited him unscathed but plastered with mud in a haystack a mile away.

2. They regard flowers. Houses and furniture have been scattered over many acres, but a vase of roses will be left undisturbed on the living room table. Dr. Key has this story from Arkansas, Oklahoma, Texas, and Louisiana.

3. Twisters don't care for chickens. One storm picked thirty chickens absolutely clean and left them bolt upright, but dead, on their perches. Another popped a rooster into a jug, leaving only his head sticking out.

4. Tornadoes are musically inclined. Dr. Key gave this account of Colonel William Porter, who was carried away in an 1893 twister at Cisco.

"He found that instead of running toward the back room as he intended, he was waving his arms and legs somewhere in mid-air. Seconds later he slammed into some object that felt like a wire fence. Then he heard music and decided he was either dead or dying.

"It was their new player piano, the kind that had to be pumped with foot pedals. The suction of the storm had somehow started it going and it was appropriately playing 'Nearer My God to Thee.' Both Mr. Porter and the piano were lodged in a big pecan tree 50 yards away. Neither was much damaged."

5. Tornadoes can be accommodating. One lady in a farm town had written her sister in Ponca City, Okla., 35 miles away. The letter was lying stamped and addressed on the dining room table and disappeared when the storm struck. The letter fell uncanceled in Ponca City in the yard of a neighbor only a block away from its intended address.

6. Tornadoes like to show off. An eastbound Northern Pacific locomotive was uncoupled from its freight cars by a twister, which set it down full steam ahead on a parallel track headed west. Tornadoes in East Texas and Arkansas have turned cast-iron washpots inside out. One in Central Kansas forty years ago whipped together the branches of a 60-foot cottonwood tree and dropped a cast-iron wagon wheel over it the way you would put a ring on your finger.

"The worst mistake tornadoes have ever made was to venture into New England in 1954," Dr. Key said. "Up until that time tornadoes had been running wild all over the rest of the United States and people had been accepting them — like measles.

"But not New Englanders. They immediately set up a public howl and demanded that Congress do something. So now, through special appropriations to the U.S. Weather Bureau, the awful eye of science has been turned upon these murderous intruders. And justice is about to be done."

Dr. Key is apparently optimistic about the results. He doesn't own a storm cellar.

Model Report

THE ORIGIN OF COMICS

About 20,000 years ago primitive men told humorous stories
by carving pictures on the walls of caves. As Dr. Charles F.
Gosnell, a New York librarian, once said, "There seems to be a
fundamental human urge" for comic drawings that are frequently
"rustic, rural, and crude."

Although comics have a long history, the funnies printed
in modern newspapers are not yet a hundred years old. According to Coulton Waugh, the comic strip began in America on
February 16, 1896, when R. F. Outcault published his "Yellow
Kid" in the New York World. Outcault made two significant con-
tributions to the development of the comic strip: by creating a
popular comic character and by putting conversations inside the
cartoon rather than as a caption on the outside of the picture.
Americans loved laughing at Outcault's kid, whose words (like
"I AM PLAYIN DIS GAME AN I DONT WANT NO FRESH MUG TE GIMME ANY
TIPS SEE") were printed across his gawky yellow nightgown.

Frank Luther Mott credits Rudolph Dirks, not Outcault,
with creating the first "true comic strip." Unlike Outcault,
who used a single cartoon for one adventure of the "Yellow
Kid," Dirks developed a series of six pictures for each adventure of his "Katzenjammer Kids," which started as a colored,
half-page Sunday feature of the New York Journal in early 1897.

Ten years passed, however, before comics became regular
daily features of newspapers. Mott names H. C. ("Bud") Fisher
as the first artist to establish a comic strip running six days
a week. The daily adventures of Fisher's "Mutt and Jeff" were
first printed in the San Francisco Chronicle in November, 1907.

References
    "Comics Have Existed for 20,000 Years," Science News
      Letter, October 1, 1955, page 217.
    Mott, Frank Luther, American Journalism (1947), pages
      585-587.
    Waugh, Coulton, The Comics (1947), pages 1-2, 5.

● EXERCISE 8. By looking through magazines, the table of contents of one of your textbooks, or the index of a good encyclopedia, find at least two interesting articles on any one of the following subjects. Be sure that they deal with related phases of the subject and can be appropriately covered in one report. As you read these articles, take notes upon which you can base a report summarizing the main ideas of the articles. At the end of the report, list the articles that you have read. Your note cards are to be handed in with your report.

Before writing study the model on page 310.

atomic-powered airplanes	sailboats
stringed instruments	New Zealand
erosion	ceramics
pantomimes	Rockefeller Center
fossils	sound waves
radioactivity	automatic telephones
winter sports	solar batteries
Crater Lake National Park	Industrial Revolution
diamonds	landslides
mural painting	circulation of blood
Roman roads	diesel engines
forestry	guided missiles
deep-sea life	cosmic rays
rockets	volcanoes
Orville Wright	corn belt
Korean War	dairy farming
uranium	Richard E. Byrd
meteors	Navaho Indians
ocean travel	irrigation
Louisiana Purchase	hydroelectric power
Monroe Doctrine	fatigue
Thomas A. Edison	respiratory system
Stamp Act Congress	emotions
Stonewall Jackson	etiquette

PART FOUR

AIDS

TO GOOD

ENGLISH

CHAPTER 15

The Library

THE CARD CATALOGUE AND REFERENCE BOOKS

One characteristic of an educated person is that he either knows what you ask him or can tell you where you can find the answer. Since very few people are "walking encyclopedias," and since even the most learned individual does not know everything, we have to depend upon our libraries to provide us with easily accessible information that we want to know. This chapter will show you how to find that information.

The Card Catalogue

15a. Learn the system of cataloguing books in your library.

To find a book quickly, you ought to know how the books are arranged in your library.

FICTION

In most libraries novels and stories (fiction) are placed in alphabetical order according to the names of the authors. Suppose, for instance, that you want to find Owen Wister's *The Virginian*. First, ask your librarian where the shelves of fiction are. Then look on these shelves for books whose authors' last names

314

begin with *W*. In alphabetical position among these will be Wister's *The Virginian*.

NONFICTION: THE DEWEY DECIMAL SYSTEM

Books that are not fiction are organized and arranged according to the Dewey Decimal System (a system developed by Melvil Dewey, an American librarian).

In the Dewey system, all books are numbered and grouped according to ten subject classes. The classifications with the numbers that stand for them are as follows.

000–099	General Works (encyclopedias, periodicals, book lists, books about the library) (In some libraries the letter *R* appears before the number.)
100–199	Philosophy (psychology, conduct, personality)
200–299	Religion (Bibles, theology, mythology)
300–399	Social Sciences (economics, government, education, law, holidays, etiquette, folklore, legends, fairy tales)
400–499	Language (grammars, dictionaries, books about foreign languages)
500–599	Science (general science, mathematics, chemistry, physics, astronomy, geology, biology, botany, animals)
600–699	Useful Arts (engineering, agriculture, health, television, aviation, home economics, business, manual training)
700–799	Fine Arts (sculpture, painting, photography, motion pictures, music, sports, recreation)
800–899	Literature (poetry, drama, essays, histories of literature)
900–909 930–999	History (ancient, modern, United States, world)
910–919	Travel (geography)
920–929	Biography (Some libraries use the letter *B* or the number *92* for a book about one person's life.)

15a

Whenever a new book is added to the library, the librarian writes on the spine of the book its proper number. If the book is about birds, he uses 598.2. If it is a history of the United States covering the Colonial Period, he uses 973.2. Because all books on the same subject are grouped together according to number, you can easily find every book on a particular subject in your library, once you know the number of the subject you are looking up.

The Subdivisions

Within each of these main classifications are numerous subdivisions. For example, if you are looking for a play by Shakespeare, the general subject is "literature," which is numbered from 800 through 899. The exact number for English drama is 822, and the number for Shakespeare is 822.3. Then there are other numbers indicating the date of the edition and other facts about the book. Your librarian can explain further details of this remarkable, but complex, classification of books; the main facts given here are enough to show you how the system works.

15b. Learn to use the card catalogue.

In your library there is a chest of small drawers containing cards. Each card in this file represents a book that the library owns.

The Call Number

The number of the classification of a book is known as the *call number*. To find this number, you look in the upper left-hand corner of the card in the card catalogue. (See the illustration on page 317.)

The call number is useful to you in two ways.

1. You can find out the location of books on the library shelves of any particular number classifica-

tion. By going at once to the shelves containing books with the number of the one you want, you can, in a few moments of looking, find your book.

2. In a large library where books are kept in the "stacks" so that you cannot look for the book yourself, you give the librarian the call number of the book you want, and he will send for it.

In the card catalogue, the cards representing books are arranged alphabetically. Three cards are usually entered for the same book: the *author card*, the *title card*, and the *subject card*.

THE AUTHOR CARD

You may find any book by looking it up under the author's name, which is printed at the top of the author card. You will find filed together cards for all books by the same author. For instance, if you have read one book by Charles Dickens and if you would like to know what other books by Dickens are in your library, you will find cards for all of them arranged in alphabetical order according to titles under the name "Dickens, Charles," which is printed at the top.

914.3   **Boehle, Bernd,** 1906-
       Handy guide to Western Germany; a reference book for travel in the Germany Federal Republic.   Sloane 1957 [c1956]
         488p illus maps

           Original German edition published 1954. This translation first published in England 1956
           From the Black Forest to Upper Bavaria, from the Lower Rhine to the North Sea, the scenic, historic, and artistic attractions of Western Germany are described. Climate, food specialities, and accommodations are considered. All methods of travel are covered fully. Tips about currency and a chapter on architecture are also included. (Publisher)
           Sightseeing vocabulary: p19

    1   Germany—Descrip-   tion and travel   i Title   914.3
    1-25-57   (W)   The H. W. Wilson Company

Author Card

15b

In the card catalogue, you will find cards for books *about* an author filed *behind* the cards for books *by* him.

THE TITLE CARD

At the top of the title card is the title of the book. If you wish to find out whether a certain book is in your library and you don't remember the author's name, look for the title card. Its proper alphabetical position is determined by the first word of the title unless the first word is *the, an,* or *a,* in which case the book will be listed under the second word of the title.

Handy guide to Western Germany

914.3   Boehle, Bernd, 1906-
Handy guide to Western Germany; a reference book for travel in the Germany Federal Republic.   Sloane 1957 ₍c1956₎
488p illus maps

Original German edition published 1954. This translation first published in England 1956
From the Black Forest to Upper Bavaria, from the Lower Rhine to the North Sea, the scenic, historic, and artistic attractions of Western Germany are described. Climate, food specialities, and accommodations are considered. All methods of travel are covered fully. Tips about currency and a chapter on architecture are also included. (Publisher)
Sightseeing vocabulary: p19

1   Germany—Descrip-   tion and travel   I Title   914.3
1-25-57   (W)   The H. W. Wilson Company

Title Card

THE SUBJECT CARD

Books are also catalogued according to the subjects they deal with. If, for example, your hobby is taking pictures and you are interested in how prints are developed, you could look for those cards listed under the subject "Photography."

GERMANY—DESCRIPTION AND TRAVEL

914.3 Boehle, Bernd, 1906-

Handy guide to Western Germany; a reference book for travel in the Germany Federal Republic. Sloane 1957 [c1956]

488p illus maps

Original German edition published 1954. This translation first published in England 1956

From the Black Forest to Upper Bavaria, from the Lower Rhine to the North Sea, the scenic, historic, and artistic attractions of Western Germany are described. Climate, food specialities, and accommodations are considered. All methods of travel are covered fully. Tips about currency and a chapter on architecture are also included. (Publisher)

Sightseeing vocabulary: p19

1 Germany—Descrip- ◯ tion and travel I Title 914.3
1-25-57 (W) The H. W. Wilson Company

Subject Card

"SEE" AND "SEE ALSO" CARDS

A "see" card refers you to another part of the catalogue for the information you are seeking. For instance, suppose you want to find and read *Life on the Mississippi* by Mark Twain. You look for the author card under "T." Instead of finding a card for your book there, you may find a card saying "See Clemens, Samuel Langhorne," since this is the real name of Mark Twain. The "see" card, then, directs you to a different part of the card catalogue, in this instance to the "C" file, where the book you want is listed.

A "see also" card refers you to other subjects closely related to the one you are looking up. For example, if you are looking up "Cows," you may find a card saying "see also Milk-Production." Looking up "Milk-Production," you can probably find more books that will help you find out about cows.

SUMMARY OF INFORMATION IN THE CARD CATALOGUE

1. *The call number,* showing the location of the book on the shelves of the library

2. *The author,* his full name as well as the date of his birth and — if he is no longer living — the date of his death
3. *The title,* publisher, place of publication, date of publication, occasionally a brief statement about the contents of the book, the number of pages, and whether the book has illustrations
4. *References* to other books or subjects, where appropriate

● EXERCISE 1.   Referring to the list on page 315, which shows the Dewey system of classification, give the range of numbers for the subjects listed.

EXAMPLE   1. **mythology**
           1. **200–299**

1. geography
2. aviation
3. poetry
4. psychology
5. music

6. encyclopedias
7. Canadian history
8. dictionaries
9. biography
10. sports

● EXERCISE 2.   Number from 1 to 12 on your paper. By using the card catalogue in your library, look up the following information:

A. Find the cards for each author below, and list the title of one of the books he has written. If there is no card for an author's name, write "not in our library" after the proper number.

1. Hamlin Garland
2. Daniel Defoe
3. Jonathan Swift

B. By looking up title cards, find out whether or not the following books are in your library. If they are, give the authors; after each name, write the date of his birth and of his death (if given). If you do not find the title in the card catalogue, write "not in our library" after the appropriate number.

4. *Northwest Passage*
5. *The House of the Seven Gables*
6. *Our Town*

C. By looking for subject cards, find the number of books your library owns on each of these subjects.

7. metals
8. hygiene

D. Give the title, author, call number, and date of publication for:

9. a favorite novel
10. a book of nonfiction

E. Find and list the title and the author of a book *about* the following:

11. Benjamin Franklin
12. William Shakespeare

Reference Books

15c. Learn to use the *Readers' Guide.*[1]

To find a magazine article on any subject, you use a most valuable book known as the *Readers' Guide to Periodical Literature*, which indexes all the articles, poems, and stories in more than a hundred magazines. A list of these magazines is given in the front of each volume of the *Readers' Guide*. This reference book is published every two weeks from September through June, and monthly in July and August. Every year the separate issues are combined into one volume, and every three years into a larger volume.

Study the sample entries taken from the *Readers' Guide* on page 322. As you can see, the magazine articles are listed by subjects (like HIBERNATION) and

[1] Copies of "How to Use the *Readers' Guide to Periodical Literature* and Other Indexes" may be obtained from the H. W. Wilson Company, 950–72 University Avenue, New York 52, New York. This pamphlet contains useful explanations, sample pages from the *Readers' Guide*, and a section entitled "Questions and Problems."

Another useful, though more complex, pamphlet is *The Cataloguing and Indexing Services*, also supplied by the H. W. Wilson Company (the first 50 pamphlets are free; 4¢ is charged for each copy over the first 50).

15c

Sample Excerpt from *Readers' Guide* [1]

HIBERNATION
What the groundhog really tells us. J. K.
   Lagemann. il Coronet 41:80-2 F '57
Winter sleep. H. Loftin. il Sci N L 71:48
   Ja 19 '57
HICKENLOOPER, Bourke Blakemore
Is present federal policy in civilian atomic
   energy field sound? excerpt from address,
   July 12, 1956. Cong Digest 36:18+ Ja '57
HIDDEN river; drama. See Goetz, R. G. and
   Goetz, A.
HIGBEE, Alma Robison
First crocus; poem. Nature Mag 50:80 F '57
Winter sycamores; poem. Nature Mag 50:101
   F '57
HIGH fidelity sound systems
Audiophilia; excessive passion for hi-fi sound
   and equipment. Time 69:44 Ja 14 '57
Power requirements for hi-fi. D. Hafler. il
   diag Radio & Tv N 57:44-5+ Ja '57
Realistic high fidelity. H. A. Hartley. il tabs
   diags Radio & Tv N 55:39-42 Ap; 46-7+ My;
   43-5 Je; 56:59-61+ Jl; 42-4+ Ag; 72-4+ S;
   43-5+ O; 51-3+ N '56; 57:64-6+ Ja; 51-3+
   F '57
West Coast hi-fi shows. Radio & Tv N 57:
   159 F '57
HIGH school students
Principal is a short-order cook. M. Feinberg.
   il Coronet 41:64-5 F '57
Teachers should know us. il Nat Educ Assn J
   46:40-1 Ja '57
HIGH school students, Mentally superior
Perishable resource. il Time 69:79 Ja 14 '57
HIGH schools
              Honors courses
What's happening in education? W. D. Bout-
   well. Nat Parent Teach 51:15 F '57
HIGH SIERRA wilderness area. See Sierra
   Nevada, California
HIGHWAY safety. See Roads—Safety devices
   and measures
HILBERRY, Conrad
Diver; poem. Atlan 199:54 F '57
HILL, Emily
Child's the thing. Nat Educ Assn J 46:36-7
   Ja '57
HILL, Lister
Interview. por U S News 42:131-2 Ja 11 '57
HILL, Lucienne
(tr) See Anouilh, J. Waltz of the toreadors
HILL, William Silas
Interview. por U S News 42:134 Ja 11 '57
HILLER helicopters (firm)
Hiller expansion due to new R&D work. Avia-
   tion W 66:109 Ja 21 '57
HILLIS, Margaret
Portrait
   Mus Am 77:16 Ja 1 '57
HILLSIDE architecture
Skyscraper for a family. il Vogue 129:194-7
   F 1 '57
Two-story modern makes sense. H. H. Cobb.
   il plans Am Home 57:96-8 F '57

[1] Reproduced by permission of the H. W. Wilson Company.

by authors (like HILL, Emily). The *Readers' Guide* gives information about each article by using easy-to-read abbreviations (like "Ja 19" and "il," meaning "January 19" and "illustrated"). A key to these abbreviations is given at the front of the *Readers' Guide*. As the entry "HILL, Lucienne" shows, "see" references are used. Moreover, if you look up a subject like MEAT, you will find "see also" references to related topics like "Buffalo meat" and "Sausage."

Of course, finding out what articles have been published on a certain topic will be of little help to you unless you can get the magazines in which the articles appear. Whether you can do so depends upon whether your library takes the magazine and whether it has back numbers of it. Usually you will find near the *Readers' Guide* a list of the magazines which your library takes. The list will also tell you which back issues are available.

● EXERCISE 3. After referring to the "Key to Abbreviations" and to the "List of Periodicals Indexed" at the front of the *Readers' Guide*, give the meaning of each of the following:

1. Sci N L	5. v	8. abr
2. cond	6. Je	9. +
3. 54:320–56	7. Sch & Soc	10. por
4. Atlan		

● EXERCISE 4. Find in the *Readers' Guide* one article listed under any 5 of the following subjects. For each article, give the title, author (if given), magazine, date, and page numbers. Place a check (√) before each article that can be found in your library.

EXAMPLE　1. Winter
(*Entry:* Deep North, U.S.A.; photographs. map Fortune 55:109–20 Ja '57)

1. "Deep North, U.S.A."
Fortune, January, 1957, pages 109–20

1. Boats	5. Roads	8. Airplanes
2. Comics	6. Petroleum	9. Painting
3. Furniture	7. Thomas Jefferson	10. Basketball
4. Mexico		

● EXERCISE 5.   Select someone you want to know more about (a television star, a great fighter or pilot or explorer, the President of the United States) *or* something that interests you (a hobby, cooking, helicopters, stars). Then thumb through several volumes of the *Readers' Guide* in order to find 5 magazine articles about the topic you choose. Make a list of these articles, giving complete information about each one, as you did for Exercise 4.

15d. Become familiar with the kinds of information found in reference books.

Reference books contain brief, informative articles on various subjects. You should not only know where the reference books are shelved in your library but also learn what they have in them. In every library there are six main types of reference books: dictionaries, encyclopedias, biographical dictionaries, atlases, almanacs, and reference books on specific subjects such as literature, authors, etc.

DICTIONARIES

The most used reference books, as you know already, are dictionaries. In fact, the unabridged and abridged dictionaries are so important that a separate chapter in this book describes their use (see pages 333–49).

You may not, however, be acquainted with a different kind of dictionary that is a serviceable tool for writing compositions: *Roget's Thesaurus of the English Language*, which in the latest edition is in dictionary form. *Thesaurus* means "treasury," in this instance a "treasury of words." Suppose, for example, that you have used the word *good* many times in a composition. To avoid needless repetition and to find other words to express your meaning, you could look up *good* in the *Thesaurus* and find over a hundred words you could use in place of *good*. Cross references will reveal an even wider choice of related words.

ENCYCLOPEDIAS

Ever since you were in elementary school, you have no doubt used encyclopedias, which consist of a collection of articles (alphabetically arranged) on almost all subjects within man's knowledge. You will find that encyclopedias become even more useful to you as you grow older. In addition to the abundance of printed information in encyclopedias, there are valuable illustrations which would be hard to find in any other place.

To find information on a subject in the encyclopedia, you should use the guide words at the top of the pages as well as the guide letters on the back of each volume. If you depend wholly upon this method of looking up material on a certain subject, however, you may not find other important information. If you will look in the index, you will see that your subject is probably discussed in several volumes, and you can then refer to *all* of the material on your topic. The index is usually located in the last volume of the set.

Although encyclopedias are rewritten and revised continuously, you may find (by looking on the title page) that the encyclopedias in your library were published several years ago. Even so, you can still find up-to-date information in the annual or yearbook, which many encyclopedias publish every year. If

15d

your library buys any of these yearbooks, you can use them to find out about the most recent events and latest developments in your subject.

There are five well-known encyclopedias that you should learn to use:

Collier's Encyclopedia
    20 volumes
    Index in Volume 20
    ~~Publishes *Collier's Yearbook*~~
Compton's Pictured Encyclopedia
    15 volumes
    One third of space is pictures
    Fact index (which itself gives information) at end of each
        volume
    Publishes a yearbook and an annual supplement
Encyclopedia Americana
    30 volumes
    Index in Volume 30
    Publishes *Americana Annual*
Encyclopædia Britannica
    24 volumes
    Index and atlas in Volume 24
    Publishes *Britannica Book of the Year*
World Book Encyclopedia
    19 volumes
    Reading and Study Guide in Volume 19
    Publishes an annual

Compton's Pictured Encyclopedia and *World Book Encyclopedia* are written especially for younger readers.

BIOGRAPHICAL DICTIONARIES

Although encyclopedias give biographies of important persons, there are many special books that print the lives of famous men and women.

The Dictionary of American Biography is especially useful when you are looking for information about Americans. It contains excellent lives of famous

Americans who are no longer living. The set has twenty volumes.

Current Biography, which is published monthly in pamphlet form, is the best source of information about persons prominent in the news. The monthly pamphlets are bound into a book each year. By using the cumulative index in each issue, you can locate biographies of persons in the news in previous months. There are frequently pictures of the persons whose lives are given.

Another important reference book is *Who's Who*, which contains information about famous English men and other distinguished figures in other parts of the world. A similar reference book is *Who's Who in America*, which contains information — parentage, important dates, positions held, main achievements, books written, present address — about famous Americans. *Who's Who* is published annually, and *Who's Who in America* is published every two years. Remember that these particular books have information on *living* persons only and that they give only the essential facts of a person's life.

Unlike *Who's Who* and *Who's Who in America*, Kunitz's reference books about authors give much "human-interest" information. These books also have pictures of writers. If your library owns this series, you will find the books valuable tools in your study of literature.

Stanley J. Kunitz:

Authors Today and Yesterday

Stanley J. Kunitz and Howard Haycraft:

The Junior Book of Authors (about writers of juvenile literature)
British Authors of the Nineteenth Century
American Authors 1600–1900
Twentieth Century Authors
Twentieth Century Authors. First Supplement

ATLASES

An atlas is much more than just a book of maps. It contains a vast amount of information about the cities and countries of the world — facts about population, resources, industries, natural wonders, climate, exports and imports, history. You should know where in your library the atlases are located. You should also take time to familiarize yourself with one or more of these atlases:

The Britannica Atlas
Collier's World Atlas and Gazetteer
Goode's World Atlas
Hammond's Standard World Atlas
Rand McNally — Cosmopolitan World Atlas

ALMANACS

Almanacs are full of information on current events. They also contain much of historical interest: facts, dates, statistics, sports records, etc. The two most useful almanacs are *The World Almanac and Book of Facts* and the *Information Please Almanac*. Both of these books are published annually.

REFERENCE BOOKS ABOUT LITERATURE

Bartlett's *Familiar Quotations*, the most famous of all collections of quotations, is useful when you want to know (1) the author of a quotation; (2) the name of the literary work in which it appeared; (3) the complete quotation of which you know only a part; (4) a few famous lines from any author. This book is arranged chronologically by authors and has alphabetical indexes of authors and quotations. You use the author index in the front of the book to find the number of the page that contains quotations from his works. If you know the quotation or a part of it, you can use the index in the back of the book to find its author or the full quotation. Suppose, for instance, you want to find out who wrote

> When Duty whispers low, *Thou must*,
> The youth replies, *I can*.

You should look under *duty*.

If you want a quotation on a certain subject, Stevenson's *Home Book of Quotations* is especially useful. The quotations in this book are arranged by subjects. For example, if you want a quotation about *Thanksgiving*, *nature*, or *time*, you will find many quotations listed under each of these topics, which are arranged so that you can find them easily. However, if you are looking for the author of a quotation, the information would be easier to find in Bartlett's book.

Granger's *Index to Poetry and Recitations* tells you where you can find almost any poem or popular prose passage you wish. It does not, however, *contain* poems or recitations. Granger's *Index* lists poems and recitations according to subjects, titles, and authors. You can use this reference book, then, to find out where you can find a certain literary work, what poems or recitations have been written on a particular subject, and who wrote a certain work. You will *not*, however, find the poem or recitation itself in Granger's *Index*.

When you are hunting for the poem itself, you can look for it in Stevenson's *Home Book of Verse* as well as his *Home Book of Modern Verse*. These large volumes contain many well-known poems. The books are indexed by author, by title, and by first line. The poems are classified under general headings like "Love Poems" or "Familiar Verse." This classification helps you when you want a poem on a certain subject but have no single poem or author in mind.

SUMMARY

DICTIONARY OF SYNONYMS
  Roget's Thesaurus of the English Language
  Webster's Dictionary of Synonyms and Antonyms

ENCYCLOPEDIAS
  Collier's Encyclopedia
  Compton's Pictured Encyclopedia
  Encyclopedia Americana
  Encyclopædia Britannica
  World Book Encyclopedia

BIOGRAPHICAL DICTIONARIES
  American Authors 1600–1900
  Authors Today and Yesterday
  British Authors of the Nineteenth Century
  Current Biography
  The Dictionary of American Biography
  The Junior Book of Authors
  Twentieth Century Authors
  Twentieth Century Authors: First Supplement
  Who's Who
  Who's Who in America

ATLASES
  The Britannica Atlas
  Collier's World Atlas and Gazetteer
  Goode's World Atlas
  Hammond's Standard World Atlas
  Rand McNally — Cosmopolitan World Atlas

ALMANACS
  Information Please Almanac
  The World Almanac and Book of Facts

REFERENCE BOOKS ABOUT LITERATURE
  Bartlett's *Familiar Quotations*
  Granger's *Index to Poetry and Recitations*
  Stevenson's *Home Book of Modern Verse*
  Stevenson's *Home Book of Quotations*
  Stevenson's *Home Book of Verse*

● EXERCISE 6.   According to your teacher's instructions, select any of the reference books listed above,

and find out what kind of information the book contains and how the material is arranged.

● EXERCISE 7. Go to the library and find the shelves of encyclopedias, atlases, and almanacs. After you have looked up each of the following items, write after the appropriate number on your paper the name of the reference book you used. Do not use the same title twice.

1. a list of national parks
2. a picture of Michelangelo and pictures of his art
3. illustrations of Archimedes' principle of specific gravity
4. a list of points of interest in Kansas
5. types of face make-up used for motion pictures
6. the origin and development of polo
7. a discussion and illustrations of the development of three kinds of mosquitoes
8. the statistics of baseball last year
9. the population of Vermont
10. a map of Sweden

● EXERCISE 8. Disregarding unabridged and abridged dictionaries, as well as encyclopedias, decide what reference book would be best to use for looking up the following. Number from 1 to 10 on your paper. After the corresponding number, write the title of the reference book.

1. a picture and biography of Mickey Mantle, a baseball player for the New York Yankees
2. the names of the five states that bound Nevada
3. a list of quotations about *silence* and *umbrella*
4. a quotation from the works of Rudyard Kipling
5. a biography of Paul Revere
6. a book listing synonyms for *activity*
7. a brief list of facts about John Mills, an English actor
8. a brief biography of Walt Disney
9. the complete poem "The Raven"
10. a book containing a limerick by Edward Lear beginning "There was an Old Man in a boat"

● EXERCISE 9.   Suppose that you have been assigned reports on the following subjects. Give for each subject the names of at least two reference books that you would use.

1. Salk's anti-polio vaccine
2. the purification of city water
3. Henry W. Longfellow
4. the climate of Africa
5. the Lewis and Clark expedition

CHAPTER 16

The Dictionary

HOW TO USE DICTIONARIES

The most important reference book of all is the dictionary. If you are in doubt about the pronunciation of a word, looking for the name of the capital of New Hampshire, wondering about how to write a Roman numeral, or trying to learn about the kinds of triangles, the stinger of a yellow jacket, the location of Alcatraz, or the identity of William Edward Parry, you should turn to a good dictionary. If you think that a dictionary only defines and spells words correctly, you are not making full use of this valuable reference book. To find information quickly and easily, you should know in detail about the various kinds of knowledge that dictionaries contain.

16a. Become familiar with the differences among dictionaries.

Generally speaking, there are two kinds of dictionaries: the unabridged and the abridged.

The Unabridged Dictionary

In every library *Webster's New International Dictionary* is placed on a convenient stand for quick and easy reference. This big dictionary contains most of the words in the language and gives very detailed information about them. On page 335 is an excerpt from *Webster's New International Dictionary* showing three entries for the word *corner*. Following the word its origin or derivation is given in brackets. Notice all of the other information given about *corner* — the classification of the parts of speech, the distinction between the synonyms *corner* and *angle*, the quotations illustrating the usages, the cross references (Cf.) to other words in the dictionary, the labels printed in italics showing the levels of usages, and the special meanings of the word *corner*.

The Abridged Dictionary

Since an abridged dictionary is shortened, it is much smaller than an unabridged dictionary. You will find that your students dictionary, though it does not contain detailed information or list all words, is adequate for most purposes.

Three of the most popular dictionaries used in high school classrooms are the *Webster's Students Dictionary*, the *Winston Dictionary for Schools*, and the *Thorndike-Barnhart High School Dictionary*. These dictionaries contain essentially the same information, but they are arranged differently and do have differences in indicating pronunciation of words. You should carefully examine the dictionary that you use most frequently so that you can find in a moment the particular information that you are looking for.

WEBSTER'S STUDENTS DICTIONARY

More than 57,000 words are arranged alphabetically in the body of *Webster's Students Dictionary*. (See the sample entries on page 336.) Along with these words are special articles, tables, and many illustra-

Sample Entries from
Webster's New International Dictionary [1]

cor'ner (kôr'nĕr), *n.* [ME., fr. OF. *corniere*, fr. ML. *corneria*, fr. L. *cornu* horn, end, point. See HORN.] **1.** The point or place where two converging lines, sides, or edges meet; an angle, either external or internal; specif.: **a** The place of intersection of two streets. **b** An angular part of anything at the meeting point of two of its sides or edges. **c** The space between meeting lines or walls, close to the vertex of the angle; as, the chimney *corner*. **d** A position from which escape by retreat is impossible; a position of great and unavoidable difficulty or embarrassment, as in a discussion; as, to drive a person into a *corner*. **e** A cornerpiece separated or remaining from anything else. **2.** A secret, remote, or out-of-the-way place; a nook.

> This thing was not done in a *corner*.   *Acts* xxvi. 26.

3. An edge or extremity; the part farthest from the center; hence, any quarter or part; esp., a quarter of the earth; one of the four quarters or directions.

> From the four *corners* of the earth they come.   *Shak.*
> Oh, the wind in that *corner*?   *Shak.*

4. A piece designed to form, occupy, mark, protect, or adorn a corner of anything, as a leather or metal cap for the corner of a book; also, a design for a corner ornament or a stamp, type, or the like, for impressing it. **5.** *Association Football.* A corner kick. **6.** *Baseball.* Either of the angles of the home plate nearest the pitcher. **7.** *Card Playing.* A player or position in a game in which several play, considered as being at a corner of the table; as, to play whist at ten cents a *corner*. **8.** *Com. & Exchanges.* The state of things produced by a person or persons who buy up the whole or the available part of any stock or species of property, thus compelling those who need such stock or property to buy of them at their own price; as, a *corner* in flour or cotton. Cf. EN-GROSS; see TRUST, *n.*, 11, *Note*.

Syn. — CORNER, ANGLE. In common usage, CORNER applies to the space included or the projection formed by the convergence of the actual sides of a material structure; as, the *corner* of a box, a table, a room, a house; a street *corner*; a chimney *corner*; to drive into a *corner*. ANGLE has usually the more technical sense of the space included between, or the degree of inclination of, two converging lines or planes; as, a right *angle*; the *angle* of the faces of a crystal; the walls forming the *corner* met at an obtuse *angle*. *Angle* is also used in the sense of a sharp projection; as, "We rub each other's *angles* down" (*Tennyson*); cf. *corner*, in "I let my head against the sharp *corner* of the table."

cor'ner (kôr'nĕr), *v.; * COR'NERED (-nĕrd); COR'NER·ING. *Transitive:* **1.** To provide with corners. **2.** To put or set in a corner. **3.** To drive into a corner or into a position of difficulty or embarrassment; as, to *corner* a person in argument. **4.** *Com. & Exchanges.* To get command of (a stock, commodity, etc.), so as to be able to put one's own price on it; as, to *corner* the shares of a railroad stock; to *corner* petroleum. **5. a** To take (one) round a corner. **b** To round (a turn) in racing. *Colloq.* **6.** In turpentine orcharding, to cut a wide chip from each half or each corner of (a box) with an ax. ——, *Intransitive:* **1.** To form, have, or come to, a corner or angle; as, the spot where three States *corner*. *U. S.* **2.** *Com. & Exchanges.* To make a corner.

cor'ner, *adj.* **1.** Situated at a corner; as, *corner* grocery. **2.** Used or fitted for use in a corner; as, a *corner* brace.

[1] By permission. From *Webster's New International Dictionary*, Second Edition, copyright 1934, 1939, 1945, 1950, 1953, 1954, 1957 by G. & C. Merriam Co.

Sample Entries from *Webster's Students Dictionary* [2]

grov′el (grŏv′′l; grŭv′′l), *v. i.;* GROV′ELED (-′ld) or
-ELLED; -EL·ING or -EL·LING.   [fr. ME. *grovelinge,*
adv., on the face, prone.]   **1.** To creep or lie, face
down, on the ground, esp. in fear or humility; to
cringe or crawl abjectly.   **2.** To take pleasure in
what is low, base, and despicable.

grow (grō), *v. i.;* GREW (grōō); GROWN (grōn); GROW′-
ING.   [AS. *grōwan.*]   **1.** To spring up and develop
to maturity.   **2.** To thrive; flourish.   **3.** To increase in size, strength, force, understanding, or
other way.   **4.** To become; as, to *grow* pale.   **5.** To
become united by or as by growth; as, two trees
which have *grown* together. — *v. t.* **1.** To cause
to grow; to cultivate.   **2.** In the passive, to be
covered with a growth; as, land *grown* with trees.
3. To develop, as a taste or liking. — **grow′er,** *n.*

growl (groul), *v. i. & t.*   To utter or express with a
growl or growls. — *n.* The deep threatening sound
made by a surly dog; hence, a grumbling or rumbling sound; esp., a low muttered complaint.

grown (grōn), *past part.* of GROW.

grown′-up′ (grōn′ŭp′; 2), *adj.*   Adult; *Colloq.,* characteristic of adults.

grown′up′ (grōn′ŭp′), *n.*   *Colloq.* An adult.

growth (grōth), *n.*   **1.** A growing; increase; esp., pro-
gressive development from beginning to maturity.
2. A stage or condition in growing; size.   **3.** That
which has grown or is growing; produce; product;
hence, result.   **4.** A morbid formation, as a tumor.

grub (grŭb), *v. i.;* GRUBBED (grŭbd); GRUB′BING.
[ME. *grubben, gruben.*]   **1.** To dig laboriously, as
for a root.   **2.** To plod; drudge. — *v. t.* **1.** To
clear or break up (land) by digging.   **2.** To root out
by digging; as, to *grub* up a root. — *n.* **1.** Any
thick wormlike larva, as of a beetle.   **2.** A drudge;
plodder.   **3.** *Slang.* Food. — **grub′ber,** *n.*

grub′by (grŭb′ĭ), *adj.;* -BI·ER; -BI·EST.   [fr. GRUB.]
Grimy; dirty. — **grub′bi·ness,** *n.*

grub′stake′ (grŭb′stāk′), *n.*   *Western U. S.* Supplies
or funds given to a prospector on the promise of a
share in his finds. — **grub′stake′,** *v. t.*

Grub Street.   A London street (now Milton Street)
described by Dr. Johnson as inhabited by hack
writers; hence, hack writers as a group.

grudge (grŭj), *v. t.*   [ME. *grutchen, gruchen,* to grum-
ble, fr. OF. *groucher.*]   To be reluctant to give or
allow to have; as, to *grudge* a penny to a beggar;
to begrudge; envy; as, he *grudged* him his success.
— *n.* Sullen, ill-tempered malice; a feeling of ill
will. — **Syn.** See RESENTMENT. — **grudg′ing·ly** (grŭj′-
ĭng·lĭ), *adv.*

---

[2] By permission. From *Webster's Students Dictionary,* copyright 1938,
1943, 1945, 1950, 1953, 1956 by G. & C. Merriam Co.

tions. Printed at the bottom of each page is a key to the symbols given for pronouncing words. In the front of the dictionary are several special sections: a detailed guide to pronunciation, spelling rules, "Correct English Usage," notes explaining labels and symbols used in the dictionary, and a key to all abbreviations. In addition there is a section on new words that have recently come into usage. By looking in the back of the dictionary, you can find a list of abbreviations used in writing, a chart showing the meaning of symbols (used in mathematics, medicine, etc.), and a section entitled "Proper Names: Geographical and Biographical." Throughout the pages of this dictionary are scattered full-page, colored illustrations of things such as popular breeds of dogs and the wildflowers found in America.

WINSTON DICTIONARY FOR SCHOOLS

With 1700 pictorial illustrations and almost three dozen full-page colored plates and maps, the *Winston Dictionary for Schools* includes over 46,000 words especially selected for young people. (See the sample entries on page 338.) At the bottom of each page in the main body is a key to pronunciation. The first few pages of this dictionary tell you how to use the book, explaining spelling, pronunciation, and abbreviations. In the appendixes are a table of weights and measurements, a list of monetary units, a chart of signs and symbols (used by astronomers, the United States Weather Bureau, etc.), signal codes, a list of the Presidents of the United States, and special information on places, including population figures, in the United States and foreign countries. The *Winston Dictionary for Schools* ends with a "Concise Atlas of the World," which features many colored maps.

Sample Entries from
Winston Dictionary for Schools [3]

Ach·er·on (ăk′ẽr-ŏn), *n.* in Greek and Roman mythology, one of the rivers of Hades; hence, Hades itself.

a·chieve (*à*-chēv′), *v.t.* [achieved, achieving], **1,** to gain or get by effort; as, to *achieve* success; **2,** to accomplish; as, he *achieved* a difficult feat.

    Syn. do, fulfil, execute, win.

a·chieve·ment (*à*-chēv′mĕnt), *n.* **1,** accomplishment; completion; as, the *achievement* of one's purpose; **2,** something accomplished through bravery or skill; a great or heroic deed; as, the discovery of radium was a scientific *achievement.*

A·chil·les (*à*-kĭl′ēz), *n.* the greatest Greek warrior in the Trojan War.

ach·ing (āk′ĭng), *adj.* painful; throbbing with pain; as, an *aching* jaw.

ach·ro·mat·ic (ăk′rō-măt′ĭk), *adj.* without color:—**achromatic lens,** a lens through which light passes without being split up into the colors of the spectrum.

ac·id (ăs′ĭd), *adj.* sharp or biting to the taste, as vinegar; sour:—*n.* **1,** a sour substance, often liquid; **2,** in chemistry, that which combines with a base to form a salt.

a·cid·i·ty (*ă*-sĭd′ĭ-tĭ), *n.* sourness.

ack—ack (ăk′॰ăk′). *n.* antiaircraft fire, especially that from rapid-firing guns.

ac·knowl·edge (ăk-nŏl′ĕj). *v.t.* [acknowledged, acknowledg-ing], **1,** to admit as real or genuine: as, to *acknowledge* a fault or a signature; **2,** to respect; recognize; as, to *acknowledge* Dickens as a great novelist; **3,** to admit the receipt of: express thanks for; as, to *acknowledge* a letter or a gift.

    Syn. avow, grant, allow, concede.

ac·knowl·edg·ment or **ac·knowl·edge·ment** (ăk-nŏl′ĕj-mĕnt), *n.* **1,** a declaration or admission that something is true or genuine; **2,** an expression of appreciation; as, an *acknowledgment* of a gift or favor.

ac·me (ăk′mē), *n.* the highest point; perfection; as, her dancing was the *acme* of grace.

---

[3] *Winston Dictionary for Schools*, copyright 1957, The John C. Winston Company, Philadelphia, Pa.

THORNDIKE–BARNHART HIGH SCHOOL DICTIONARY

To find out exactly how the *Thorndike-Barnhart High School Dictionary* staff arranges and edits its materials, you should carefully read "Outstanding Features of This Dictionary," which is printed in the preface. Instead of having appendixes, this dictionary contains more than 75,000 entries — common words, abbreviations, proper names, etc. — in one alphabetically arranged list, which is the body of the dictionary. (See the sample entries on page 340.) In the front of the book you can also find instructions on using the *Thorndike-Barnhart High School Dictionary;* this section includes important information on spelling, pronunciation, definitions, and word origins. For explanations of correct grammar and for distinguishing between troublesome words like *affect* and *effect*, the "usage notes," which are printed at the end of various entries, are especially helpful.

● EXERCISE 1. Carefully study the table of contents at the front of your dictionary. Examine all sections that you are not familiar with. Be prepared to discuss in class the various divisions of your dictionary, explaining as you go along what these sections contain.

● EXERCISE 2. Referring to the dictionary that you use most frequently, tell *where* you would look to find the following. If your dictionary does not contain information about an item below, tell where you would look for it in an unabridged dictionary.

1. the correct pronunciation of a word
2. an abbreviation (like C.O.D. or Ph.D.) commonly used in writing
3. the explanation of an abbreviation used in your dictionary
4. information about a famous person

Sample Entries from
Thorndike-Barnhart High School Dictionary [4]

Mo ses (mō′ziz or mō′zis), *n.* in the Bible, the great leader and lawgiver of the Israelites who led them out of Egypt.

mo sey (mō′zi), *v.,* **-seyed, -sey ing.** *U.S. Slang.* **1.** shuffle along. **2.** saunter; amble. [Am.E; origin uncertain]

Mos lem (moz′ləm or mos′-ləm), *n., pl.* **-lems** or **-lem,** *adj.* Mohammedan. Also, **Muslem, Muslim.** [< Arabic *muslim* one who submits < *aslama* submit. Related to *salaam.*]

Mosque

mosque (mosk), *n.* a Mohammedan place of worship. [< F < Ital. < Arabic *masjid* < *sajada* prostrate oneself]

mos qui to (məs kē′tō), *n., pl.* **-toes** or **-tos. 1.** a small, slender insect. The female gives a bite or sting that itches. There are many kinds of mosquitoes; some kinds transmit malaria; some transmit yellow fever. **2.** a light, fast British bomber. [< Sp. *mosquito,* dim. of *mosca* < L *musca* fly]

mosquito boat, a fast motorboat, carrying a gun or torpedo.

Mosquito. Line shows actual length.

moss (môs or mos), *n.* **1.** any of various very small, soft, green or brown plants that grow close together like a carpet on the ground, on rocks, on trees, etc. **2.** any of various similar plants. [OE *mos* bog] **—moss′like′,** *adj.*

Mos sa degh (môs′ä′deg′ or mü′sä′dēk′), *n.* **Mohammed,** born 1880, Iranian statesman, prime minister of Iran from 1951 to 1953.

moss back (môs′bak′ or mos′bak′), *n.* *U.S. Slang.* person whose ideas are out of date. [Am.E]

moss rose, a cultivated rose with a mosslike growth on the calyx and stem.

moss y (môs′i or mos′i), *adj.,* **moss i er, moss i est. 1.** covered with moss: *a mossy bank.* **2.** like moss: *mossy green.* **—moss′i ness,** *n.*

most (mōst), *adj.* (*used as superlative of* **much** *and* **many,** *with the comparative* **more**), *n., adv.* **—***adj.* **1.** the greatest quantity, amount, measure, degree, or number of: *The winner gets the most money.* **2.** almost all: *Most children like candy.* **3. for the most part,** mainly; usually. **—***n.* **1.** the greatest quantity, amount, degree, or number: *He did most of the work.* **2. at most** or **at the most,** not more than. **3. make the most of,** make the best use of. **—***adv.* **1.** in or to the greatest extent or degree: *Which hurt most?* **2.** *Informal.* almost; nearly. [OE *māst*]

➤ **most, almost.** *Most* is the common informal clip of *almost: A drop in prices will appeal to most everybody.* It would be used in writing conversation and in informal style, but is ordinarily out of place in written English. ➤ See **more** for another usage note.

5. information about a place (like Iceland or Georgia)
6. the origin of a word
7. a new word
8. a picture of Gothic architecture
9. a map of the Hawaiian Islands
10. the years during which the American Revolution was fought

Kinds of Information in Dictionaries

16b. Learn what your dictionary tells you about words.

Refer often to the sample pages from the unabridged and abridged dictionaries (pages 335, 336, 338, 340) as you study the following.

1. *Spelling*

When you don't know how to spell a word, you can look it up in the dictionary, which is the authority on correct spelling. If a word may be spelled two ways — like *acknowledgment* and *acknowledgement* — the dictionary gives the preferred spelling first.

If there is a spelling problem connected with forming the plural of a word or about adding a suffix (like *-ed*, *-ing*, *-ness*), the dictionary shows you how to spell these words. Examples are: *achieve*, *achieving*, and *grubbed*, *grubbiness*.

● EXERCISE 3. Number from 1 to 10 on your paper. Find the answers to the following questions in your dictionary.

A. What is the preferred spelling for the following?

1. neighbor, neighbour
2. flunkey, flunky
3. lodestar, loadstar
4. draught, draft
5. catalogue, catalog

16b

B. Correctly add the suffix listed on the right to the word
on the left:

6. funny   est
7. refer   ed
8. usual   ly
9. happy   ness
10. travel   ing

2. *Capital Letters*

If you are not sure about capitalizing a word, the
dictionary will help you. Notice on pages 336 and 338
the capitalized words like *Grub Street* and *Acheron*.
Some words, like *democratic*, may or may not have a
capital, depending upon how you use the word.
Usually *democratic* is listed as an uncapitalized common adjective; however, when the *particular* party is
designated in the list of definitions, then a capital is
used — "*Democratic* party." Sometimes, however,
when a word is commonly used as a proper name,
it is listed with a capital — for example, *Kodak*. When
the word *kodak* is applied to cameras in general, *not
cap.* appears.

● EXERCISE 4. Check your dictionary to find out
whether (or when) the following words are capitalized.
If the words may be used both ways, write sentences
illustrating both uses.

1. mercury   5. president   8. scot
2. mumbo jumbo   6. escalator   9. republican
3. bible   7. arab   10. state
4. god

3. *Syllables*

Whenever you need to divide a word at the end
of the line, you should split it between syllables only.
The dictionary divides all words into syllables: for instance, *ac cu rate* is divided into three syllables.

If your dictionary should use a small dot or dash to show the breaks between syllables, *do not confuse this dash or dot with the hyphen*. Be sure that you know what the hyphen looks like in your dictionary by looking up such words as *mother-in-law* or *ack-ack*.

● EXERCISE 5. Divide the following words into syllables. Check your work in the dictionary.

1. preliminary
2. old-fashioned
3. impractical
4. forevermore
5. recognize

4. *Pronunciation*

To show how a word is pronounced, the dictionary uses *diacritical markings*, which indicate the sounds of vowels, and it respells the word using certain consonants to mean certain sounds. Dictionaries differ somewhat in the marking system they use. As you learn to master your dictionary's method of showing the correct pronunciation of a word, you will need to refer to the pronunciation key (usually given at the bottom, or the top, of each page).

Your teacher may wish to have you learn the common pronunciation markings now so that in your dictionary practice you will be able to understand how to pronounce any word you look up. If so, you should turn to pages 349–54, where you will find further explanation and exercises.

5. *The Part of Speech*

Every word listed in the dictionary is followed by an abbreviation telling what part of speech the word is. Since many words may be used as more than one part of speech, you may find the part of speech given before the various definitions within the longer entry. Study the sample pages, noticing how these abbreviations are used to indicate the parts of speech.

n.	noun	*pron.*	pronoun
v.	verb	*prep.*	preposition
adv.	adverb	*interj.*	interjection
adj.	adjective	*conj.*	conjunction

● EXERCISE 6.   Look up these words in your dictionary, and classify each one according to its part of speech. (If a word may be used as three or four parts of speech, write each use after the proper number on your paper.)

1. not	5. forward	8. out
2. regular	6. play	9. base
3. row	7. jerk	10. beside
4. court		

6. *Derivation*

Your dictionary also tells you the derivation or the origin of a word. To indicate the languages from which a word has come, abbreviations like *L.* (Latin) and *F.* (French) are used. The meanings of these and other abbreviations are given in the key to the abbreviations at the front of the dictionary. Look on page 335, and notice the origin of *corner*, and on page 336 for the derivation of *Grub Street*. Notice, too, that *grudge* comes from the Middle English language and an Old French word. Knowing the derivation of a word can sometimes help you remember its meaning.

● EXERCISE 7.   Write after the proper number on your paper the origin of each word listed below. If your student dictionary does not give the derivations, go to an unabridged dictionary. If a word is unfamiliar to you, learn its meaning when you look up its origin.

1. kaleidoscope	5. sponsor	8. pince-nez
2. sympathy	6. exorbitan.	9. procrastinate
3. phosphorous	7. chlorophyll	10. pinch hitter
4. sporadic		

7. *Meaning*

Of course, you know that a dictionary defines words. But do you make full use of its definitions? When a word has many different meanings, do you seek out the particular definition that you are looking for? Notice on page 335 the different meanings for *corner* as a noun. There is a great difference between "driven into a *corner*" and "a *corner* in wheat." Again, as you can see on page 338, there are three meanings for the verb *acknowledge*. These are indicated by numbers.

Some dictionaries place the oldest meaning first; others list the meanings in the order of their use, the most common meaning being given first. Either way, you will need to look over the many definitions until you find the one that fits the sentence in which you have found the word.

● EXERCISE 8. Number from 1 to 10 on your paper. Look up the exact meaning of each italicized word in these sentences, and write the meaning after the corresponding number.

1. Now I will *pose* for a snapshot.
2. His attitude seems to be a *pose*.
3. On the counter was a novelty key *ring*.
4. The *rings* indicated that the tree was twenty years old.
5. The *kite* lives on snails.
6. When the breezes are not too strong, sailors use *kites*.
7. The third *volume* in the series is the most useful.
8. The *volume* control on my radio is broken.
9. When did Spain's *civil* war end?
10. He wasn't even *civil*.

8. *Labels Showing Usage Levels*

The dictionary indicates usage levels with labels such as *Slang*, *Colloq*. (colloquial), *Obs*. (obsolete, no longer in common use), *Dial*. (dialect), *Bib*. (Biblical).

Notice the italicized labels before the definitions on page 336. When a word has no label showing a level of usage, the word is *standard English* and can be used correctly in both speaking and writing.

When you are writing a composition, you should be careful to avoid using words that are labeled *Slang*. Moreover, for very formal writing, you should not use any word labeled *colloquial*. Notice on page 336 that a word may be standard English when it has one meaning (like *grown-up* ways) and yet be colloquial English when it has a different meaning (several *grownups*). When a word is labeled *colloquial*, it is not *wrong* (like the illiterate *ain't*); rather it is right for informal writing and for conversation.

● EXERCISE 9.   Look up the following words in your dictionary to see whether or not they are standard English. If you find no label anywhere in the definitions of a word, write "standard" on your paper after the proper number. If you find a label indicating a special classification, write the label on your paper, using the abbreviations found in your dictionary.

1. pep   5. hydrogen   8. bug
2. snooze   6. blob   9. stratum
3. smithereens   7. case   10. note
4. cosmos

9. *Synonyms and Antonyms*

A synonym is a word having almost the same meaning as the word being defined: *calm, serene.* An antonym is a word having the opposite meaning: *hot, cold.* Frequently, you will find a small paragraph set aside not only listing synonyms but also showing the distinctions of meanings. Look, for instance, at the entry *grudge* on page 336. Notice the "Syn. See RESENTMENT." When you want to choose the exact word for your meaning, your dictionary, with its listing of synonyms and its cross references, will help you find the word.

● EXERCISE 10. Look up the following words in your dictionary, and make a list of the synonyms and the antonyms given for each word.

1. freedom   3. shrewd
2. laughable   4. rough

10. *Illustrations*

If the meaning of a word can best be shown by a picture, the dictionary may give an illustration. If, for example, you are studying gauges or the ancient Pyramids, the chances are that you can find these illustrated in your dictionary.

16c. Find out what your dictionary tells you about people and places.

In your dictionary the names of people and places are either listed in a special biographical, geographical, or "proper names" section, or listed in the main body along with all other words. You can easily discover which method your dictionary uses.

To learn what your dictionary can tell you about a person, look up *David Livingstone*. First of all, of course, you find his name correctly spelled, and you can see how to pronounce it. In parentheses you find 1813–1873, the dates of his birth and death. Next is information about his nationality, which is Scottish. Finally, you learn why he became famous, that he was an explorer in Africa. Should you look up the name of a President, you would find the dates of his term of office. Your dictionary also has interesting information about people in the Bible (Moses, Lazarus) as well as about mythological and literary characters (Hercules, Robin Hood).

16c

Now look up the name of a place — say *Hwang Ho, Patmos,* or *Richmond* — in your dictionary. Notice that you can find out (1) how to spell and pronounce the word; (2) what it is (city, river, island); (3) where it is; (4) how big it is; (5) why it is important. Very frequently information about history and government is given.

● EXERCISE 11. *Speed and Accuracy Test.* When your teacher gives the signal, look up the answers to the following questions in the dictionary you have. Write the answers on your paper. Accuracy is more important than speed, but speed *is* important. Your speed shows to some extent your knowledge of the dictionary.

1. Where is Madagascar?
2. When did Christopher Columbus die?
3. How high is Mount Everest?
4. When was Charles Dickens born?
5. What is the Hydra?
6. How deep is Lake Huron?
7. What was the nationality of John Drinkwater?
8. How long is the Panama Canal?
9. Who was Merlin?
10. Where is Gatun Dam?

● REVIEW EXERCISE. Number from 1 to 10 on your paper. By using your dictionary, correctly answer each of the following questions.

1. What is the correct syllable division of *hypochondriac?*
2. Which is the preferred spelling — *moustache* or *mustache?*
3. When, if ever, is the word *state* capitalized?
4. What part of speech is *please?*
5. Is *nincompoop* slang?
6. What is the origin of the word *jujitsu?*
7. What is the meaning of the word *ossify?*
8. What is the meaning of NCO?
9. Who was Alfred Bernhard Nobel?
10. Is it correct to use the word *swell* as an adjective in formal writing?

Pronunciation

16d. Learn the dictionary method of showing pronunciation.

Some dictionaries use a special system for showing how words are pronounced. For instance, the *Thorndike-Barnhart High School Dictionary* has these markings:[5]

hat, āge, cãre, fär; let, ēqual, tèrm; it, īce; hot, ōpen, ôrder; oil, out; cup, pùt, rüle, ūse; ch, child; ng, long; th, thin; ŦH, then; zh, measure; ə represents *a* in about, *e* in taken, *i* in pencil, *o* in lemon, *u* in circus.

Diacritical marks not given here may be found in a "Complete Pronunciation Key" at the front of the book.

Webster's unabridged dictionary, as well as other student dictionaries, uses a different system of diacritical marks.

VOWEL SOUNDS

The long straight mark (macron) over a vowel indicates that the vowel is pronounced as it is named. For instance, the name of the letter *e* is the sound of that letter when it is written ē, as in the word *eel*. Pronounce the following: ā, ē, ī, ō, ū. The sound of ū is *yew* as in *cūbe*, not *ōō* as in *cōōl*.

The macron with a vertical (˝) means the sound is that of the name of the letter, but in pronouncing the letter, you speak somewhat more rapidly. Notice the difference between the pronunciation of *gō* and *ôbey'*.

The short curved mark (˘) over a vowel is called the *breve*. It indicates that the sound is "shortened." Study these sounds indicated by the breve:

ădd ĕnd ĭll ŏdd ŭp

[5] From *Thorndike-Barnhart High School Dictionary*, edited by Clarence L. Barnhart and E. L. Thorndike. Copyright © 1957, 1952, by Scott, Foresman and Company, and used with their permission.

16d

Knowing the meaning of the breve and the macrons will help you pronounce many words. To get the correct pronunciation of any word in the dictionary, however, you need to learn the markings used for other vowel sounds. To interpret these markings, all you have to do is refer to the key that is printed at the bottom (or the top) of each page in the dictionary. Read the words in the key below, noticing as you go along the diacritical markings:[6]

āle, chăotic, câre, ădd, ăccount, ärm, ȧsk, sofȧ; ēve, hẹ̄re, ĕvent, ĕnd, silĕnt, makẽr; īce, ĭll, charĭty; ōld, ŏbey, ôrb, ŏdd, sôft, cŏnnect; fōōd, fŏŏt; out, oil; cūbe, ûnite, ûrn, ŭp, circŭs, F. menü

CONSONANT SOUNDS

Nearly all of the twenty-one consonants in the language are pronounced just as they are named. A few, however, as the following key shows, do present special difficulties.[7]

chair; go; sing; then, thin; natŭre, verdŭre; ᴋ = ch in G. ich, ach; F. boɴ; yet; zh = z in azure

Pronunciation markings not given in this key may be looked up in "A Guide to Pronunciation" in the front of the dictionary.

The dictionary uses respelling to indicate the sounds of some consonants. Look up these words in your dictionary: *can* and *city*, *echo* and *chagrin*, *gem* and *gum*. Notice how the differences in the sounds of *c*, *ch*, and *g* are shown.

[6] By permission. From *Webster's Students Dictionary*, copyright 1938, 1943, 1945, 1950, 1953, 1956 by G. & C. Merriam Co.

[7] By permission. From *Webster's Students Dictionary*, copyright 1938, 1943, 1945, 1950, 1953, 1956 by G. & C. Merriam Co.

ACCENT

In words of several syllables, one syllable is accented or stressed more than the others. This accented syllable is shown by an accent mark (′) placed immediately after and above it: *for′est, pro mote′, per fec′tion.* In long words there may be two accented syllables, one of which receives greater stress than the other: *in′stru men′tal, e lec′tric′i ty.* The main, heavier accent is shown by the heavier accent mark. The secondary, lighter accent is shown by the lighter accent mark. Sometimes dictionaries use a double accent mark in light type (″) for the secondary accent: *e lec″tric′i ty.*

Sometimes the same word may be accented in different ways, depending upon how the word is used. The words below show how the accent shifts when the words are used as different parts of speech.

con′test [noun]	con test′ [verb]
per′fume [noun]	per fume′ [verb]
pro′ceeds [noun]	pro ceeds′ [verb]

As *proceeds* shows, the meaning of a word may change completely with a change in accent. Other examples of change in meaning with change in accent are: *con sole′* and *con′sole, in′cense* and *in cense′.*

● EXERCISE 12. Using the key on page 350, write the vowel markings above the vowels in these common words. Place accent marks in the words of more than one syllable. (Final silent *e,* of course, cannot be marked.)

1. choose
2. low
3. rot
4. die
5. in deed
6. jack et
7. pro duc tive
8. se cu ri ty
9. shad y
10. spec u late

● EXERCISE 13. Using the keys to both vowels and consonants, rewrite with diacritical markings, respellings, and accents each of the following words as you think the dictionary might rewrite them to show pronunciation. When you have finished, check your work in the dictionary.

1. clum sy
2. cha os
3. fo li age
4. skel e ton
5. ges ture
6. im me di ate
7. ad vise
8. pho to graph ic
9. pneu mo ni a
10. choir

● EXERCISE 14. Look up the following words, which are commonly mispronounced. Copy each word onto your paper with the diacritical markings as shown in the dictionary. Practice pronouncing the word correctly after your teacher has approved your interpretation of the diacritical markings. Learn the meaning as well as the pronunciation of any unfamiliar word.

1. chasm
2. admirable
3. condolence
4. motorcycle
5. biography
6. culinary
7. via
8. stomach
9. remembrance
10. exquisite

WORDS COMMONLY MISPRONOUNCED

By means of the diacritical markings given below, figure out how the following commonly mispronounced words should be pronounced. Practice saying these words correctly.

accept ăk·sĕpt′
alias ā′lĭ·ăs
almond ä′mŭnd
architect är′kĭ·tĕkt
arctic ärk′tĭk
athlete ăth′lēt
attacked ă·tăkt′
auxiliary ôg·zĭl′yȧ·rĭ

bade băd

because bē·kôz′
blackguard blăg′ärd

café kȧ·fā′
candidate căn′dĭ·dāt
cello chĕl′ō
cement sē·mĕnt′
champion chăm′pĭ·ŭn
chasm kăz′m
children chĭl′drĕn

column kŏl'ŭm

comparable kŏm'pȧ·rȧ·b'l

coupon kōō'pŏn

creek krēk

curiosity kū'rĭ·ŏs'ĭ·tĭ

deaf dĕf

diphtheria dĭf·thēr'ĭ·ȧ

discretion dĭs·krĕsh'ŭn

docile dŏs'ĭl

drowned dround

elm ĕlm

everybody ĕv'ẽr·ĭ·bŏd'ĭ

extraordinary ĕks·trôr'dĭ·nẽr'ĭ

faucet fô'sĕt

film fĭlm

further fûr'thẽr

futile fū'tĭl

genuine jĕn'û·ĭn

geography jê·ŏg'rȧ·fĭ

geometry jê·ŏm'ê·trĭ

gesture jĕs'tūr

gibberish jĭb'ẽr·ĭsh

gigantic jī·găn'tĭk

government gŭv'ẽrn·mĕnt

grimy grīm'ĭ

handkerchief hăng'kẽr·chĭf

height hīt

hundred hŭn'drĕd

impious ĭm'pĭ·ŭs

indicted ĭn·dīt'ĕd

infamous ĭn'fȧ·mŭs

influence ĭn'flōō·ĕns

introduce ĭn'trô·dūs'

Italian ĭ·tăl'yăn

italics ĭ·tăl'ĭks

just jŭst

length lĕngth

library lī'brĕr'ĭ

mischievous mĭs'chĭ·vŭs

municipal mû·nĭs'ĭ·păl

museum mû·zē'ŭm

pathos pā'thŏs

perform pẽr·fôrm'

perhaps pẽr·hăps'

perspiration pûr'spĭ·rā'shŭn

poem pō'ĕm

preferable prĕf'ẽr·ȧ·b'l

probably prŏb'ȧ·blĭ

quantity kwŏn'tĭ·tĭ

raspberry răz'bĕr'ĭ

recognize rĕk'ŏg·nīz

rinse rĭns

strength strĕngth

superfluous sû·pûr'flōō·ŭs

telegraphy tê·lĕg'rȧ·fĭ

theater thē'ȧ·tẽr

veteran vĕt'ẽr·ăn

wash wŏsh

wrestle rĕs'l

● EXERCISE 15.   *Oral Drill.* Practice reading the following sentences *aloud*, correctly pronouncing the italicized words.

1. The *athlete* walked *across* the stage to *accept* the trophy from the former *champion*.
2. The policeman *bade* the *blackguard* to *recognize* the *strength* of *municipal government*.
3. *Everybody* in my class wants to see the *extraordinary film* now showing at the Palace *Theater*.
4. The words in *italics* say that this *coupon* can be exchanged for a *genuine* leather billfold.
5. Going *further*, the *veteran* aroused our *curiosity* by talking about the *height* of the *gigantic column* and the depth of the *chasm*.
6. At the *museum*, we were *introduced* to a *deaf* guide, whose *gibberish* we didn't understand.
7. After walking on the wet *cement*, the *mischievous children just* disappeared *because* they feared punishment.
8. Covered with *perspiration*, I *washed* a large *quantity* of *grimy* clothes, *rinsing* each garment twice.
9. Under the *elm* tree near the *creek*, we were *attacked* by yellow jackets.
10. This afternoon I'll *probably wrestle* with my *geometry* assignment and will *perhaps* study *geography* in the *library*.

CHAPTER 17

Vocabulary

LEARNING AND USING NEW WORDS

Before you start to work on enlarging your vocabulary, take the following test to see how good your vocabulary is now. The words in the test were taken from books commonly read by ninth-grade students. What percentage of these words do you know?

Diagnostic Test

Number from 1 to 25 on your paper. After the proper number, write the letter of the word which is nearest in meaning to the italicized word at the left.

1. *amends* a. repairs b. payment c. changes
2. *assiduous* a. diligent b. foolish c. sour
3. *benevolence* a. laziness b. surliness c. kindliness
4. *capacious* a. large b. careful c. careless
5. *condolences* a. buses b. packages of freight c. expressions of sympathy
6. *discrepancy* a. difference b. noise c. enmity
7. *exasperated* a. breathed b. irritated c. outlined
8. *feign* a. pretend b. make c. invent
9. *grueling* a. exhausting b. cereal c. questioning
10. *haven* a. paradise b. snow c. shelter
11. *illustrious* a. picturesque b. wearisome c. famous
12. *lull* a. the bottom of a ship b. grain c. a calm
13. *misgivings* a. feelings of distrust b. feelings of generosity c. feelings of friendship

355

14. *mottled* a. mixed b. spotted c. confused
15. *nimbly* a. slowly and carefully b. quickly and actively c. without feeling
16. *ominous* a. threatening b. hungry c. existing everywhere
17. *plaintive* a. weedy b. melancholy c. restless
18. *presume* a. forewarn b. assume c. prepare
19. *reprimands* a. warnings b. scoldings c. gifts
20. *seethe* a. plant b. boil c. scrape
21. *tawny* a. brownish b. shady c. lazy
22. *unscrupulous* a. dishonest b. unhurried c. not ready
23. *unseemly* a. incoherent b. unprepared c. improper
24. *waning* a. decreasing b. crying c. rising
25. *weird* a. speedy b. mysterious c. empty

17a. List new words with their meanings in your notebook, and use them in speech and writing.

When you learn a new word, list it in your notebook with its meaning. Use it in speech and writing as often as you can in order to make it a permanent part of your vocabulary. Begin now by listing any words that were new to you in the diagnostic test. Keep a special section of your notebook for this purpose; after each exercise in this chapter, add to the list all words you did not know. Add any other words you learn from day to day.

Ways to Learn New Words

17b. In determining the meaning of a word, consider the context, the situation, and the resemblance to other words you know.

Context

If you did not know the meaning of the word *pedestrian* in the sentence, "The pedestrian appeared," the only way for you to find out its meaning would be to look it up in the dictionary, since the sentence gives no clue to the meaning. Sometimes you can guess at the meaning of a word you read from the surrounding words, or *context*. For example, in the following sentence it is quite clear that *pedestrian* means "person who goes on foot; walker": *Because there was no sidewalk, pedestrians had to be careful to avoid the cars.*

Situation

You may guess the meaning of a new word you hear by observing the situation in which it is used. If a walker is dodging cars on a busy thoroughfare and an onlooker says, "Look at that foolish pedestrian," you can guess the meaning of *pedestrian* quite easily.

Resemblance to Words You Know

A third way of guessing the meaning of a word is by noting resemblance to another word, either in English or in another language. If you know that *pedal* means "referring to the foot or feet," for example, you may guess that *pedestrian* means "one going by foot." Check your guesses by referring to the dictionary, however, or you may make mistakes.

● EXERCISE 1. Number from 1 to 10 on your paper. Copy each italicized word in the following passage, and write next to it what you think it means. Write either a definition or a *synonym*, which is another word meaning about the same thing. When you have completed the exercise, check with dictionary meanings, rewrite those you had wrong, and restudy the context which you missed. Add new words to your notebook list.

Although our team had played a good game, the second half of the ninth inning found our (1) *adversaries* holding

17
a-b

a three-run lead, and this seemed too big for us to (2) *surmount*. Our hope (3) *diminished* further when our first batter flied out to center, but it revived a little when Frank, our pitcher, hit a double. Our opponents decided to use (4) *strategy*, and they gave an (5) *intentional* base on balls to George, our third batter. Excitement reached a (6) *climax* when Eddie, the fourth man up, hit a sharp grounder which the second baseman was unable to (7) *intercept*. (8) *Subsequent* events were almost too quick to follow. With the bases full, Joe, our catcher, hit a home run, and the (9) *frenzied* spectators rushed out on the field and carried him with wild (10) *acclaim* to the clubhouse.

● EXERCISE 2. Number on your paper from 1 to 20. Next to the proper number write the italicized word and, after it, the correct synonym from the three words at the right.

1. the *agility* of the monkey — cuteness, nimbleness, brightness
2. *averring* his innocence — asserting, proving, denying
3. *chided* by the dean — advised, rebuked, honored
4. the *covetous* old man — learned, generous, greedy
5. in a *disheveled* state — sad, joyous, disorderly
6. *drastic* treatment — extreme, skillful, technical
7. the *elation* of success — height, joy, position
8. *flaunt* the flag — furl, salute, wave
9. his *hectic* condition — feverish, discouraged, weary
10. an *indulgent* father — cruel, conscientious, lenient
11. the *listless* dog — vicious, gentle, inactive
12. in *meditative* mood — thoughtful, active, resolute
13. a *perceptible* change — desirable, noticeable, slow
14. a *portly* figure — graceful, stout, erect
15. to *retrieve* the treasure — hide, recover, steal
16. a *somber* day — dark, bright, short
17. to *surmise* the truth — conceal, tell, guess
18. a *trivial* matter — secret, petty, significant
19. his *unflinching* attitude — generous, unyielding, hypocritical
20. the *valiant* general — proud, veteran, brave

17c. When you look up a word in the dictionary, find the meaning appropriate to the context.

As you know, a word may have several different meanings. The dictionary must give all these meanings. When you are looking up a word in the dictionary, you must keep in mind the context in which you found the word and then choose the meaning which fits this context. For example, suppose you read this sentence: *He dispatched his captives quickly and painlessly.* The meaning of this sentence depends upon the meaning of *dispatched.* When you look the word up in the dictionary, you will find at least three meanings: (1) to send away, as to *dispatch* a messenger; (2) to put to death; (3) to dispose of speedily, as business. The appropriate meaning in the context of your sentence is the second meaning — to put to death. He put his captives to death quickly and painlessly.

● EXERCISE 3. Number from 1 to 10 on your paper, and copy the ten nouns below. By referring to the dictionary, write the meaning next to each word. Each of the nouns fits into one of the blanks in the following sentences. Since the dictionary gives several meanings for a word, you must select the meaning which best fits the sentence in the exercise. After the meaning, write the number of the sentence in which the noun fits.

1. agitation	6. locale
2. auditor	7. mimic
3. charlatan	8. perfectionist
4. dilemma	9. première
5. discord	10. stamina

1. Because he was a(n) ——, he was seldom satisfied with the work he did.
2. The —— offered the patent medicine as a cure for almost every ailment.

3. The vibration of the pump in the tank created a(n) —— which disturbed the fish.
4. The cross-country run demands great ——.
5. As the comedian imitated well-known people, it became apparent that he was an excellent ——.
6. Many motion-picture stars attended the ——.
7. The business dissolved because of —— among the partners.
8. When the —— went over the accounts, he found several errors.
9. Choosing a college sometimes presents a(n) ——.
10. Quebec is the —— of Willa Cather's *Shadows on the Rock*.

● EXERCISE 4. Number from 1 to 10 on your paper, and copy the following adjectives. By referring to the dictionary, write a definition or a synonym next to each word. Each of the adjectives fits into one of the blanks in the paragraph below. After the meaning, write the number of the blank in which the adjective fits.

1. alien	6. oppressive
2. cosmopolitan	7. palatial
3. immune	8. quaint
4. medieval	9. spacious
5. monotonous	10. towering

New York is a city of great variety. The numerous foreign sections lend a(n) _(1)_ atmosphere which makes it impossible for a stranger to feel completely _(2)_. _(3)_ modern structures like the Empire State Building and the United Nations Building stand within a short distance of the _(4)_ architecture of the Cathedral of St. John the Divine and St. Patrick's Cathedral. _(5)_ parks stretch above the _(6)_ caverns of the crowded subways. The _(7)_ houses of the wealthy in the Sutton Place area contrast with the _(8)_ old dwellings of Greenwich Village. No one can complain that life in this city of busy variety is _(9)_, and few can be _(10)_ to its vivid appeal.

● EXERCISE 5. Number from 1 to 10 on your paper, and copy the following verbs next to the numbers. By referring to the dictionary, write the meaning next to each verb. Each of the verbs fits into one of the blanks in the sentences below. After the meaning, write the number of the sentence in which the verb fits. You may use any tense needed to fit the meaning of the sentence.

1.	acquiesce	6.	mollify
2.	connive	7.	pervade
3.	disrupt	8.	renounce
4.	infringe	9.	transfigure
5.	instigate	10.	wrest

1. The Duke of Windsor —— his right to the English throne.
2. Despite the efforts of the chairman, the meeting was —— by the disorderly club members.
3. When the twelfth member ——, the jury declared the defendant guilty.
4. As the old lady listened to her grandson singing, her face was —— by joy.
5. The barons —— power from the tyrannical King John at Runnymede.
6. As he wiped the coffee from the coat of the angry diner, the waiter tried to —— him.
7. The perfume of honeysuckle —— the June night.
8. Some of the town officials —— at the gambling.
9. Those who —— upon the rights of others abuse their own privileges.
10. An army group tried unsuccessfully to —— a rebellion in the small nation.

17d. Use the word which conveys the precise meaning and impression that you want to give your reader or listener.

The English language is rich in synonyms. Although synonyms have the same broad meaning, each one has its own shade of difference. Using the word that conveys the precise meaning that you intend makes for clear and effective writing. The richer your vocabulary, the better able you will be to choose the exact word.

● EXERCISE 6.   Number on your paper from 1 to 10. For each sentence below, select the most appropriate synonym for the word *walk* from the following list. Use a different word in each sentence. You may use any tense needed to fit the structure of the sentence. Write that word next to the number, and be prepared to explain in class why each word is most appropriate. If you are in doubt, use your dictionary.

amble	stride
march	stroll
pace	tramp
plod	tread
promenade	wander

1. The referee picked up the ball, —— back ten yards, and put it on our thirty-yard line.
2. Over a thousand veterans —— in the Memorial Day parade.
3. —— the deck of a large ocean liner is an exhilarating experience.
4. In his haste he —— ahead of his companions through the crowded street.
5. The horse —— slowly along the path as his rider enjoyed the scenery.
6. Unaware of the surroundings, the blissful couple —— slowly, arm in arm.
7. The cows had —— a path to the stream.
8. The happy boy on his vacation —— idly along beside the brook.
9. Hoping to make up the lost time, the hikers —— resolutely through the woods.
10. The weary workman, lifting each foot with obvious effort, —— up the hill.

● EXERCISE 7. Number from 1 to 10 on your paper. Refer to the dictionary for the exact meaning of each adverb. Then answer each of the questions below by writing the most appropriate adverb next to the number of the question which the adverb answers.

barbarously	grotesquely
comprehensively	nocturnally
defiantly	reluctantly
ferociously	reverently
genially	ungraciously

1. How did the tiger bare his teeth at the visitors in the zoo?
2. How did the tourists stand at the tomb of the unknown soldier?
3. How did the Goths and Vandals act when they sacked and burned the city of Rome?
4. How did the nervous patient approach the dentist's chair?
5. How did the scarecrow stand in the cornfield?
6. How did the master of ceremonies smile as he greeted the contestant in the quiz contest?
7. How did the cornered rat glare at the cat?
8. How did the weary housewife greet the unexpected guests at dinnertime?
9. How did the well-prepared student answer the examination questions?
10. When do owls hunt for prey?

● EXERCISE 8. Number from 1 to 20 on your paper. Next to each number, write the letter of the correct synonym for the italicized word. Refer to the dictionary.

1. *abate* a. worm b. lessen c. return
2. *avert* a. green b. avoid c. open
3. *defile* a. scrape b. line c. make dirty
4. *durable* a. lasting b. hot c. tired
5. *encounter* a. meet b. table c. reach
6. *falter* a. fail b. hesitate c. need

7. *futile*   a. old   b. frail   c. useless
8. *gaudy*   a. general   b. useful   c. showy
9. *intricate*   a. complicated   b. interior   c. pretty
10. *laconic*   a. slow   b. funny   c. concise
11. *manifest*   a. strong   b. reveal   c. displace
12. *poise*   a. composure   b. beauty   c. pride
13. *potency*   a. pretense   b. strength   c. view
14. *realm*   a. bone   b. kingdom   c. coin
15. *repel*   a. drive back   b. bring forward   c. hide
16. *requisite*   a. necessary   b. late   c. early
17. *symbol*   a. something played in a band   b. something growing   c. something standing for something else
18. *turbulent*   a. ancient   b. young   c. violent
19. *ultimate*   a. final   b. aged   c. reliable
20. *vogue*   a. confused   b. fashion   c. quiet

● EXERCISE 9.   Number from 1 to 10 on your paper. Next to each number, write a word from the list below which conveys the idea of the sentence having that number. Use the dictionary to find the meaning of each word.

complacent	garrulous
considerate	inquisitive
diffident	obstinate
discriminating	obtuse
gallant	volatile

EXAMPLE   1. Little children are always exploring new places and picking up strange objects.
   1. **inquisitive**

1. The boy was slow in grasping the point and in understanding things.
2. Sir Walter Raleigh put his cloak in the mud for Queen Elizabeth to walk on.
3. The boy felt shy speaking for the first time in class.
4. The successful man was very pleased with himself because of his accomplishments.
5. The young lady changed rapidly from one interest or mood to another.
6. Rip Van Winkle talked a great deal in his old age.

7. With taste and good judgment, the shopper chose the articles she bought.
8. Sherlock Holmes wanted to know all the circumstances surrounding crimes.
9. Robinson Crusoe was stubborn about wanting to go to sea again despite the troubles he had encountered on his first voyage.
10. Aladdin was kind and thoughtful to his mother after he found the magic lamp.

17e. Learn to understand and use literary terms.

High school students are frequently asked to discuss books or plays. The words in the following exercise will help you to carry on a literary discussion with intelligence and clarity.

● EXERCISE 10. Number from 1 to 10 on your paper. If necessary, look up in the dictionary the numbered words in column A. Write the letter from column B which is appropriate for the numbered word in column A.

A	B
1. atmosphere	a. the main story
2. comedy	b. the main character
3. foreshadowing	c. an unchanging conventional character
4. plot	
5. protagonist	d. the main subject or idea of a literary work
6. setting	
7. soliloquy	e. a hint of something to come
8. stereotype	f. speech by an actor alone on a stage
9. theme	g. the color or feeling pervading a literary work
10. tragedy	h. a play making fun of something
	i. a serious play having an unhappy ending
	j. a historical literary work
	k. a play with a happy ending
	l. the place and time of a literary work

17e

● EXERCISE 11. Number from 1 to 10 on your paper. If necessary, look up in the dictionary the numbered words in column A. Write the letter from column B which is appropriate for the numbered word in column A.

A	B
1. biographical	a. painfully moving or touching
2. didactic	b. freely imaginative and fanciful
3. farcical	c. appealing to the emotions by sensationalism and exaggeration
4. fictitious	
5. hackneyed	d. ridiculous, absurd, improbable
6. melodramatic	e. ornate in style
7. poignant	f. attacking or ridiculing a custom, habit, or idea
8. realistic	
9. romantic	g. of a person's life
10. satirical	h. overused, commonplace, stale
	i. clear and simple
	j. representing life in literature as it actually is
	k. intended to instruct, teacherlike
	l. not real, imaginary, made-up

Prefixes and Roots

When you look up a word in the dictionary, you often find older words listed as the origin. English has borrowed words from almost all languages, but particularly from Latin and Greek. Sometimes one Latin or Greek word element is found in many English words. Knowing the meaning of a Greek or Latin word element gives you an understanding of a great many English words.

These word elements may be the part of a word that comes first, called the *prefix;* they may be the main part, called the *root;* they may be the part added at the end, called the *suffix.* Many words have only one or two of these parts, but some have three. Consider the word *semiannual*. This word is composed of the prefix *semi–*, meaning "half" in Latin; the root *–annu–*, meaning "year" in Latin; and the suffix *–al*, from a Latin word meaning "pertaining to." The word *semiannual* means "pertaining to an event that occurs every half year." (The same root may show a vowel change in different words. In "biennial," for example, *–enni–* is the same root as *–annu–*, although two of its letters are changed.)

17f. Learn some of the common Latin prefixes and roots.

The following word parts from Latin are commonly used in English words. If you learn the meaning of these prefixes and roots, you will be able to figure out the meaning of a great many words in which they occur.

LATIN PREFIX	MEANING	LATIN ROOT	MEANING
ad–	to, toward	cise	cut
bi–	two	fide	faith
con–	with	ped	foot
in–	into	spec	look
intra–	within	voc	call

● EXERCISE 12. Number from 1 to 5 on your paper. Write the prefix and its meaning and the root and its meaning for each word in the numbered list below. Then write the meaning of the whole word. Use your dictionary if necessary.

EXAMPLE **submarine = sub (under) + mare (sea) = underwater boat**

1. biped
2. incise
3. confide

4. advocate
5. introspect

17f

Here are some other commonly used Latin prefixes and roots. Before you do the exercises below, try to think of words in which these parts appear. Can you see a relationship between the meaning of the part and the meaning of the whole word?

LATIN PREFIX	MEANING	LATIN ROOT	MEANING
ab–, abs–	off	cadere	fall
re–	back, again	cide	kill
sub–	below, under	dic, dict	say, speak
		hom	man
		pond	a weight
		prob	prove
		sed	seat
		tenere	hold
		tract	draw
		vert, vers	turn

● EXERCISE 13. Number from 1 to 10 on your paper. For each italicized word below, write the part or parts derived from Latin and their meanings. Then write the meaning of the word as it is used in the phrase. Use your dictionary if necessary. Ignore the suffixes in this exercise.

EXAMPLES
1. *dictate* letters
1. dict (speak) = speak letters for someone to write down
2. *subtract* the balance
2. sub (below) + tract (draw) = withdraw or take away the balance

1. the *cadence* of her voice
2. a detective from the *homicide* division
3. faultless *diction*
4. act of *subversion*
5. a *ponderous* elephant
6. on *probation*
7. *retract* the statement
8. *abstain* from food
9. a *versatile* musician
10. a *sedentary* job

17g. Learn some of the common Greek prefixes and roots.

There are many words in English which are derived from Greek words. Study the following list of common prefixes and roots.

GREEK PREFIX	MEANING	GREEK ROOT	MEANING
auto–	self	aster	star
di–, dia–	between	chir	hand
hydr–	water	dox	opinion
micro–	small	geo	earth
ortho	right, straight	graph	write
sym–	together	logue; logy	discourse; science of (something)
tri–	three		
		nomy	law
		phobia	dread of
		phone	sound
		pod	foot

● EXERCISE 14. Number from 1 to 10 on your paper, skipping a line after each number. Copy the italicized words below. After referring to your dictionary, write the part or parts derived from Greek and their meaning. Then write the meaning of the word as it is used in the phrase. Ignore the suffixes in this exercise.

EXAMPLE 1. a case of *hydrophobia*
   1. **hydro (water) + phobia (dread) = a case involving a dread of water**

1. marked by an *asterisk*
2. an *autograph* collector
3. granted *autonomy*
4. treated by a *chiropodist*
5. a *dialogue* in the play
6. studying *geology*
7. examining a *microphone*
8. an *orthodox* believer
9. a flutist in the *symphony*
10. standing on a *tripod*

17g

● EXERCISE 15. As your teacher dictates them, write the meaning of each of the following Latin and Greek prefixes. Then write a word in which the prefix appears. Be prepared to explain the relationship between the meaning of the prefix and the meaning of the word.

1. ab–	6. di–, dia–	11. micro–
2. ad–	7. sub–	12. ortho–
3. auto–	8. hydr–	13. re–
4. bi–	9. in–	14. sym–
5. con–	10. intra–	15. tri–

● EXERCISE 16. As your teacher dictates them, write the meaning of each of the following Latin and Greek roots. Then write a word in which the root appears. Be prepared to explain the relationship between the meaning of the root and the meaning of the word.

1. aster	10. graph	19. prob
2. cadere	11. hom	20. sed
3. chir	12. logue, logy	21. tenere
4. cide	13. nomy	22. tract
5. cise	14. ped	23. vers
6. dict	15. phobia	24. vert
7. dox	16. phone	25. voc
8. fide	17. pod	
9. geo	18. pond	

17h. Learn the origins of words as an aid to re-membering meaning.

(1) Words with interesting histories.

Study the origin of each word when you look it up in the dictionary. For example, in the entry for the word *candidate* you will find the following: [L. *candidatus*, clothed in white]. *L.* means "Latin," and *candidatus* is the Latin word from which *candidate* comes.

The explanation of this word origin is that in ancient Rome candidates wore white robes. Many other words, like the ones in the following exercise, have interesting stories connected with them.

● EXERCISE 17. Number on your paper from 1 to 10. Next to the appropriate number, write the italicized word. By referring to the dictionary, write the definition of each word and the language of its origin. Be prepared to explain the origin orally in class.

1. The *assassination* of the Austrian Archduke touched off the explosion of World War I.
2. Electronic machines now do in a few seconds *calculations* which would take mathematicians months or years to complete.
3. Exhibits of armor in museums remind us of the days of *chivalry*.
4. Diogenes, a famous *cynic*, used a lantern in daylight as he searched for an honest man.
5. The workman *detonated* the explosive, and the rock split.
6. Yellow fever has been *eradicated* through the work of Walter Reed.
7. The disloyal citizen was *ostracized* by his fellow townsmen.
8. The *supercilious* senior ignored the freshmen.
9. *Tantalizing* odors from the kitchen made the hungry boys' mouths water.
10. The gypsy fortuneteller was decked out in heavy, *tawdry* jewelry.

(2) Foreign words in English.

You have seen that many English words have a foreign origin. In addition to these, many foreign expressions have become part of the English language. Sometimes their pronunciation becomes "Anglicized," while their spelling remains as it was in the original language. Examples of such expressions are *en masse*,

17h

meaning "in a group," *joie de vivre*, meaning "joy in living," *tête à tête*, meaning "a private conversation between two people." If you are alert to such expressions in your reading and listening, you will find that your vocabulary is growing in this direction.

● EXERCISE 18. Ten familiar foreign expressions are given below in column A. Number from 1 to 10 on your paper. Refer to the dictionary and copy next to each number the letter of the appropriate meaning from column B. Write the name of the language from which the expression comes.

A	B
1. cliché	a. the best people
2. de luxe	b. the masses
3. elite	c. witty replies
4. hoi polloi	d. a midday rest
5. incognito	e. a meal at a fixed price
6. patio	f. a marble floor
7. repartee	g. with name concealed
8. siesta	h. timeworn expression
9. table d'hôte	i. never satisfied
10. terra firma	j. an inner court
	k. solid earth
	l. elegant

● REVIEW EXERCISE. Number from 1 to 50 on your paper. Next to each number, write the letter of the correct synonym.

1. *acclaim*　a. acquire　b. applause　c. desire　d. land
2. *agitation*　a. shaking　b. evidence　c. readiness　d. structure
3. *assiduous*　a. dry　b. balanced　c. diligent　d. near
4. *auditor*　a. one who paints　b. one who resembles　c. one who denies　d. one who checks accounts
5. *aver*　a. assert　b. evade　c. compare　d. approach

6. *benevolence*   a. kindly feeling   b. sensation of flying
   c. health   d. wealth
7. *biped*   a. animal with two feet   b. bison   c. pedigree
   d. three-footed stand
8. *charlatan*   a. bus   b. Scottish plaid   c. medicine
   d. quack
9. *cliché*   a. lock   b. timeworn expression   c. broken
   machine   d. small group
10. *condolences*   a. winter snows   b. carriages   c. looks
    of annoyance   d. expressions of sympathy
11. *cynic*   a. bird   b. picturesque   c. sneerer   d. tourist
12. *didactic*   a. tightened   b. knocking   c. teacherlike
    d. flowerlike
13. *discord*   a. heavy rope   b. distortion   c. friendliness
    d. disagreement
14. *disheveled*   a. chinaware   b. packed   c. rumpled
    d. partial
15. *exasperated*   a. arranged   b. annoyed   c. decorated
    d. enervated
16. *falter*   a. fail   b. hesitate   c. rise   d. transport
17. *frenzied*   a. wearied   b. carried   c. excited   d. with
    carved edges
18. *grotesquely*   a. gracefully   b. unnaturally   c. orderly
    d. ornately
19. *hectic*   a. feverish   b. colorful   c. stout   d. emphatic
20. *incise*   a. look into   b. cut into   c. sharpen   d. intend
21. *indulgent*   a. inventive   b. soft   c. polite   d. lenient
22. *intricate*   a. complicated   b. clever   c. ingenious
    d. interesting
23. *lull*   a. sailboat   b. period of calm   c. carve   d. yeast
24. *meander*   a. walk rapidly   b. examine   c. wander
    d. untie
25. *mimic*   a. argue   b. assert   c. exhibit   d. imitate
26. *mottled*   a. sickly   b. saturated   c. intensified
    d. spotted
27. *ominous*   a. altogether   b. hungry   c. threatening
    d. disappearing
28. *ostracized*   a. banished   b. enrolled   c. combined
    d. distracted

29. *patio*   a. inner courtyard   b. Spanish food   c. tower   d. hinged box
30. *plaintive*   a. weedy   b. tiresome   c. mournful   d. unusual
31. *poise*   a. gem   b. composure   c. intelligence   d. reflection
32. *première*   a. first in a contest   b. opening performance   c. irritable   d. foolish
33. *probation*   a. connection   b. decision   c. courage   d. test
34. *quaint*   a. odd   b. know   c. scene   d. ugly
35. *reluctantly*   a. quickly   b. seriously   c. unwillingly   d. gladly
36. *reprimands*   a. revisions   b. reproofs   c. results   d. remembrances
37. *retrieve*   a. reconcile   b. overlook   c. combine   d. recover
38. *satirical*   a. well-dressed   b. genuine   c. ironical   d. inactive
39. *seethe*   a. stitch   b. view   c. boil   d. confuse
40. *soliloquy*   a. dock   b. diamond   c. separate   d. speech alone
41. *stamina*   a. endurance   b. part of a flower   c. startle   d. a stone wall
42. *strategy*   a. planning   b. tiling   c. leveling   d. pitcher
43. *supercilious*   a. high-ranking   b. generous   c. youthful   d. haughty
44. *symphony*   a. climbing plant   b. orchestral composition   c. style of architecture   d. type of government
45. *table d'hôte*   a. writing desk   b. level space   c. meal at a fixed price   d. high area
46. *tawdry*   a. gaudy   b. gay   c. bashful   d. friendly
47. *terra firma*   a. vegetable   b. solid ground   c. old ruin   d. new building
48. *tripod*   a. triple-coated   b. three-buttoned   c. stumbling   d. three-legged stool
49. *unseemly*   a. unlike   b. ungrateful   c. improper   d. impassable
50. *volatile*   a. wishful   b. fickle   c. flying   d. dull

Word List

The following list of 300 words has been selected from ninth-year books. It should form the basis of your vocabulary study for the year. When you have mastered the exercises in this chapter, you will know over 200 of the words. Use the list for further dictionary work and review.

abate	avert	complacent
abject	avid	complement
absolve		comprehensively
abstain	axiom	condolences
acclaim	barbarously	confide
acquiesce	benevolence	
adversary	biographical	conjecture
advocate	biped	connive
agility	bizarre	considerate
agitation	broach	cosmopolitan
	brusque	cosmos
alien	cadence	covetous
amble	calculation	cynic
amends		dedicate
appraisal	candid	defiantly
apprehend	capacious	defile
arbitrary	casual	
ascribe	chagrin	de luxe
assassin	charlatan	deplore
assiduous	checkmate	dialogue
asterisk	chide	didactic
	chiropodist	diffident
atmosphere	cite	digress
auditor	cliché	dilemma
auspices		diminish
autocracy	climax	dingy
autograph	cognizant	disaster
automation	collaborate	
autonomy	comedy	discord
aver	companion	discrepancy

discriminating
disheveled
disrupt
dissect
drastic
durable
elation
elite

equation
equilibrium
erroneous
ethical
exasperated
excoriate
exploitation
extort
falter
farcical

feign
ferociously
fictitious
figurative
flaunt
foreshadowing
fortitude
fossil
frenzied
futile

gallant
garrulous
gaudy
gauntlet
genially
geology
glibly
gloating

gratify
grill

grotesque
grueling
guise
hackneyed
haggard
haven
havoc
hectic
hoi polloi
homicide

illustrious
immune
impact
impute
inalienable
incidentally
incise
incognito
indomitable
indulgent

infringe
ingenious
innovation
inquisitive
insatiable
insidious
instigate
integrate
intentional
intercept

intimate
intricate
introvert
laconic

laudable
legitimate
listless
locale
lull
lurid

manifest
march
marital
martial
meander
medieval
meditative
melodramatic
merge
microtome

mimic
misgivings
mollify
monopoly
monotonous
mottled
mystic
nimbly
nocturnally
novice

obstinate
obtuse
obvious
odious
ominous
omnivorous
oppressive
orthodox
oscillate
ostracized

pace
palatial
palliate
patio
perceptible
perfectionist
pertinent
pervade
plaintive
planetary

plod
plot
poignant
poise
ponderous
portly
potency
preclude
première
presume

priority
probation
promenade
propriety
prospective
protagonist
pugnacity
pulverize
quaint
random

ravage
realistic
realm
refuted
regime
rejuvenate
reluctantly

renounce
repartee
repel

reprimands
requisite
reticence
retract
retrieve
reverently
romantic
satellite
satirical
sedentary

seethe
servile
setting
siesta
sinister
solicitude
soliloquy
somber
sordid
spacious

specific
spurn
stamina
stereotype
sterile
strategy
stroll
subsequent
subside
sundry

supercilious
surmise
surmount

swan song
symbol
symphony
syndicate
table d'hôte
tantalizing
tawdry

tawny
terra firma
terse
theme
towering
tragedy
tramp
transcend
transfigure
tread

tripod
trivial
turbulent
ultimate
unflinching
ungraciously
unscrupulous
unseemly
valiant
vehemently

versatile
violation
virile
vogue
volatile
voluntary
vouchsafe
vulnerable
waning
wrest

PART FIVE

SPEAKING

AND

LISTENING

CHAPTER 18

Speaking Before Groups

CONTENT AND DELIVERY OF SPEECHES

As a high school student, you will often have to speak before groups of your schoolmates. Besides taking part in class discussions, you will also speak at club meetings, make committee reports, announce events at assembly programs, and stir up enthusiasm at athletic rallies.

The boy or girl who can speak well is admired by his fellow students and is often elected to office in a club or other school organization. The ability to speak easily and naturally will help you to succeed in school and later in your chosen business or profession.

Speaking before groups is easy if you have some training and experience. In this chapter you will learn how to handle some of the most common speech situations you will meet in high school.

Preparing the Speech

18a. Choose an appropriate topic.

If you are asked to speak before a group, you will probably find that the hardest part of your assignment is deciding on something to talk about. You may waste hours looking for a topic and finally select one about which you know little and care less.

(1) Your topic should be one about which you have firsthand information.

Start your assignment by selecting a subject about which you already know a great deal. Choose one with which you have had direct experience. For example, if your hobby is pigeons, talk about their care and breeding, and the fun of racing your homers in national contests. If you own a sailboat, explain how to handle it. If you have just gone on an overnight hike, tell about your experiences. A girl who attends a dancing school might describe various ballet steps. A boy who owns a jalopy might explain how he put it together. As a high school student once phrased it, "Speak in your own back yard!"

When you talk from firsthand experience, you are not at a loss for ideas, you speak more fluently, and you infect your listeners with your own enthusiasm.

(2) Your topic should be one which will interest your listeners.

As a general rule, a subject which you find interesting will interest your listeners if they are the same age as you.

Before deciding on your topic, however, ask yourself whether it will capture the attention of your audience. Consider your listeners' age, likes and dislikes, backgrounds, and special interests. Your own classmates might like to hear a talk on your record collection or your experiences in a summer camp, while an alumni group might be more interested in your plans for a career. A group of parents might like to hear you talk about teen age problems, while an

18a

athletic team might prefer to hear how you trained during the summer for the coming football season.

● EXERCISE 1.   List 5 subjects which you feel competent to speak about because of your experience. In a sentence or two for each topic, explain the nature of your experience.

EXAMPLES   How to Sail a Boat.   I have a 14-foot sailboat which I have been sailing for the past two years. I have received expert instruction in sailing from my father.

Figure Skating.   I enjoy ice skating and hope someday to try out for the Olympic team. Last winter I spent an average of two hours daily practicing figure skating.

● EXERCISE 2.   Number in a column on your paper from 1 to 7. List after each number two topics which might appeal to each of the groups below.

1. your home-room class
2. high school biology club
3. basketball team
4. school assembly
5. Boy Scouts
6. movie fan club
7. dramatic society

18b. Have a definite purpose when you speak.

Speaking without a purpose is like blindly shooting off a shotgun. You may hit something — but not what you intended.

Aim your speech. Know beforehand what result you want to bring about. Your purpose may be:

1. to inform
2. to convince
3. to impress
4. to entertain
5. to move to action

Suppose, for example, you are going to speak to your English class on the topic of automobiles. What you say depends largely on your purpose.

If your purpose is *to inform*, you may discuss what a buyer should keep in mind before purchasing a second-hand car, the way a carburetor works, or the proper method of waxing or polishing a car.

If your purpose is *to convince*, you may discuss the advisability of equipping automobiles with safety belts and other protective devices.

If your purpose is *to impress*, you may compare the number of automobiles in this country with the number in other countries or tell about the unusual features that will probably appear in future cars.

If your purpose is *to entertain*, you may talk about amusing adventures you have had while touring with your family or friends.

If your purpose is *to move to action*, you may argue that a driver-training course should be included in your school curriculum and ask your listeners to sign a petition to the principal to that effect.

After deciding on your topic, determine your purpose and always keep it in mind when preparing your talk.

18c. Gather material for your speech.

After you have settled on your topic and purpose, your next step is to gather material.

Resist the temptation to run to the library to consult reference books and magazine articles. This should be the final step in gathering material. If you read what others have written before you do your own exploring and thinking, your talk may lack originality. It may be a summary of what others have said rather than an expression of your own experiences and thoughts

18
b-c

(1) Explore your own background.

What do you already know about your subject? (You probably know more than you suspect.)

(2) Observe.

Keep your eyes and ears open for material bearing upon your topic. You will run across bits of usable information while conversing with friends, listening to radio programs, viewing television programs, or reading newspapers.

(3) Question.

Ask additional information of someone who knows a great deal about your topic. Your parents, a doctor, a service-station owner, or a local merchant may have expert knowledge.

(4) Read.

After you have followed the three steps listed above, consult encyclopedia articles, books, and magazines. Record pertinent information on note cards for easy reference.[1]

Always have far more material than you can use. A good speaker is an authority on his subject — even though he uses less than half of what he has at hand.

Your speech should grow gradually. It cannot be prepared overnight. Mull it over, changing it mentally, adding and discarding ideas. New thoughts will come to you at odd moments — while walking to school, waiting for a bus, chatting with friends, dressing, and even while doing your homework. This kind of preparation is a slow process but it results in thorough knowledge of subject matter and in self-confi-

[1] See instructions on taking notes in Chapter 14, pages 297–300.

dence. Make it a practice to jot down thoughts as they come to you.

● EXERCISE 3. Select a topic for a three-minute talk to your English class. Make a list of the sources of information you intend to consult, using the following headings.

1. Your own experience (*Describe it.*)
2. Persons you are going to interview and questions you will ask them.
3. Encyclopedias (*Name the encyclopedia, the title of the article, volume, and number.*)
4. Magazine articles (*Consult the Readers' Guide. Name the magazine, title and author of article, volume, and number.*)
5. Books (*Consult the card catalogue. List titles and authors.*)
6. Newspapers (*List the newspapers and dates of publication.*)

18d. Arrange your material by preparing an outline.

Your final step in preparation is to arrange the material you have gathered.

If you have jotted down your notes on index cards, each idea on a separate card, you can easily put them in sequence. Lay aside those for which you have no need.

An outline for a short speech should rarely cover more than one side of a page and should include only your main points.[2] See the examples below.

TRAINING A DOG

Purpose To inform
  I. The importance of training
     A. Value to dog
     B. Value to owner
 II. Housebreaking

18d

[2] For a treatment of outlining, see pages 218–25.

III. Advanced training
    A. Training for hunting
    B. Training in obedience
IV. Things to avoid
    A. Coddling
    B. Overfeeding

EXTRACURRICULAR ACTIVITIES

Purpose   To convince

I. Every high school boy and girl should join a school club or team.
    A. Clubs and teams add enjoyment to high school life.
        1. Interscholastic competition is fun.
        2. Club exhibits and projects are rewarding.
    B. Clubs give pupils an opportunity to develop their hobbies and interests. (Examples: Stamp Club, Chemistry Club)
    C. Clubs give pupils an opportunity to meet their teachers informally.
II. Join a club now.
    A. Our student council is trying to increase club membership.
    B. Every boy is invited to try out for a school team. (Name the teams.)
    C. All pupils are urged to join at least one school club. (Name some clubs.)
    D. Apply for membership — now! (Tell how to join.)

● EXERCISE 4. Prepare an outline for a three-minute speech. Here are some suggested topics.

1. Earning Money After School
2. An Adventure I Once Had
3. The Best Movie I Ever Saw
4. Summer — Gone but Not Forgotten!
5. Why Study Latin?
6. The Man (or Woman) I Most Admire
7. My Hobby
8. A Popular Sport
9. Cats
10. Foods I Like
11. Stock-Car Races
12. Academic or Vocational High School?

18e. Prepare a conclusion which leaves your audience with the central idea of your talk.

Amateurs do not know how to end a speech. They drift to a halt weakly like a motorboat that has run out of gas. End strongly. The conclusion is your last chance to drive home main ideas.

You can conclude by summarizing the important points you have covered.

Our ball team should have a good season. Most of last year's players are back; we have some promising new-comers; the pitching staff is strong; and we have the best coach in Staunton County.

If you're looking for an interesting hobby, take up bowling. It's good exercise because it develops every muscle in the body. It's good fun because you can join our school bowling club and bowl with other girls and boys of your age. It's inexpensive because the local alley has a reduced rate for high school students. Rip Van Winkle loved to bowl. So will you!

Or you can conclude by urging action.

By joining our General Organization, you will help sponsor our school clubs and teams. You will have a voice in student government. You will build school spirit. Join now. Sign up with your class delegate.

Don't miss our school play. It's going to be a lot of fun. "Time Out for Ginger" is a rollicking comedy with an all-star cast. Get your tickets while there are still some available.

Delivering the Speech [3]

18f. Overcome nervousness.

You should be pleased that you are nervous before beginning to speak. Nervousness is a sign that your

[3] Refer to "Pronunciation and Enunciation" at the end of this chapter, pages 403–08.

18
e-f

body is keyed for action. A race horse is nervous; a dray horse is not. Every good public speaker is on edge before he starts, even though he may have had years of experience in talking before groups. Experienced actors and actresses readily admit that they are tense before stepping on the stage.

Some nervousness is desirable. What you must guard against is *excessive* nervousness or stage fright, which prevents free movement or coherent thinking.

Here are some practical suggestions for preventing stage fright.

(1) Know your subject thoroughly.

Begin your preparation well in advance of the day on which you are scheduled to speak. Mull over your topic, talk about it with your parents and friends, and read as much as you can about it. When you know your material thoroughly, you will gain self-confidence.

(2) Practice.

Rehearse your talk before a full-length mirror, bedpost, or empty chair. Do not commit your talk to memory. (You may, however, memorize the first and last sentences so that you can get off to a smooth start and come to a graceful finish.) Each time you practice, your words will be different although the sequence of ideas will be the same. Practice will also give you self-confidence.

(3) Keep your purpose in mind.

Forget about yourself. Think of what you want your listeners to believe, feel, or do.

(4) Relax!

Yawn, breathe deeply, let yourself go limp for a moment or two before you mount the platform.

Move about. Movement drains off tension.

18g. Talk to your listeners.

Look your hearers in the face. Let your gaze move smoothly over your audience so that each listener gets the impression you are talking directly to him.

Remember that you are not reciting or exhibiting. You are *communicating.*

18h. Stand and move naturally and easily.

Stand easily erect, feet a few inches apart, weight mainly on the ball of one foot, shoulders level, arms hanging naturally at your sides.

Your posture will change as you express different ideas and as you move about the platform. Move when there is an important change in thought. You should not pace back and forth like a caged animal, nor should you remain as stolid as a statue. Move smoothly and normally but not excessively.

● EXERCISE 5. Practice good standing posture before a full-length mirror, using the instructions given above as a guide. Move from one spot to another easily and smoothly.

● EXERCISE 6. Deliver the speech for which you made an outline in Exercise 4.

Kinds of Speaking Situations

TELLING AN EXPERIENCE

You have had experiences different from everybody else's. Some of them were quite unusual and others

18
g-h

were dull. Which would your classmates like to hear about? Obviously, they will be more interested in your unusual experiences. People like to hear of happenings which are strange, exciting, or surprising.

18i. Relate experiences which are unusual or otherwise interesting.

Listeners like to hear about unexpected occurrences. Here are some hints to enliven your accounts of personal experiences.

(1) Begin with action.

Long, explanatory openings are unnecessary and dull. Start in the middle of things.

1

When I awoke one night in camp and found a snake coiled at the foot of my bed, I was a bit upset.

2

I did not stop to think when I saw smoke pouring out of the window of my neighbor's house. I rushed to the phone and shouted, "I want to report a fire!"

3

Sauntering home from the movies late one night, I was startled when two men dashed out of a store and scrambled into a waiting car. Inside the store I could hear someone screaming, "Help!"

(2) Use direct conversation.

The exact words of a speaker are more interesting and lively than an indirect statement. Compare these two versions of the same incident.

1

A pawnbroker explained that he displayed unredeemed saxophones, banjos, tubas, and shotguns together in his window, because after a man bought a sax or tuba, his neighbors bought shotguns.

2

A pawnbroker loaded his show window with unredeemed saxophones, banjos, tubas — and shotguns. "Very interesting display," commented a friend, "but does it sell merchandise?"

"Does it!" enthused the pawnbroker. "One day a fellow buys a sax or tuba. Two days later his neighbors buy the shotguns." [4]

(3) Maintain suspense.

Include details and episodes that keep your listeners in suspense. Lead to a climax. Do not reveal the ending too soon.

(4) Use action-packed verbs.

A good storyteller chooses verbs that are specific rather than general because they help a listener to see, feel, and hear.[5]

GENERAL   The boy **walked** into the classroom.
SPECIFIC   The boy **strolled** (**sidled, limped, burst, dashed, slouched**) into the classroom.

GENERAL   The plane **rose** into the sky.
SPECIFIC   The plane **zoomed** (**roared, lurched, shot**) into the sky.

● EXERCISE 7. Relate an unusual experience you have had or have heard about. It may be exciting, amusing, or both, but the incident or its outcome should be unusual. Be sure you begin with action,

[4] From *Life of the Party* by Bennett Cerf (Hammond and Hammond, London, England). Reprinted by permission.
[5] For a detailed discussion of the use of exact words, see Chapter 17, pages 361-63.

18i

392 **Speaking Before Groups**

use conversation and specific verbs, and maintain suspense.

● EXERCISE 8. Relate an unusual incident in the life of a famous man or woman. The following list is suggestive only.

1. Dwight D. Eisenhower	7. Helen Keller
2. Colonel Charles Lindbergh	8. John Paul Jones
3. Robin Hood	9. Nathan Hale
4. Admiral Richard Byrd	10. Socrates
5. T. E. Lawrence of Arabia	11. Thomas Edison
6. Richard the Lion-Hearted	12. Napoleon

PARTICIPATING IN CLASS DISCUSSION

In high school more than in elementary school, students learn from one another. There is more class discussion. In high school you teach yourself to a great extent.

The teacher is a guide. He stimulates interest, assigns topics for study, conducts discussions in an orderly manner, and explains difficulties.

Every class offers an opportunity for you to learn from the other pupils and for them to learn from you. When your teacher asks a question, direct your reply not only to him but to your classmates. When you recite, you are helping others to understand. You have a responsibility to them, and they in turn have a responsibility to you.

In other words, every class is an experience in sharing. When you and your classmates exchange ideas, all benefit. You comprehend more clearly and are better able to apply what you learn.

When everyone participates, a class discussion is lively, interesting, and profitable. Dull periods occur when only a few join in class discussion or when replies are inaudible, irrelevant, or directed to the teacher rather than to the group.

18j. Observe good etiquette in classroom discussion.

Do not wait to be called upon. If you have something to say which might clarify a point under discussion, raise your hand, wait until you are recognized by the teacher, and speak so that all can hear. Voluntary recitations make a class stimulating if they are pertinent, audible, and clearly expressed.

When someone else is speaking, listen attentively — as you would like to be listened to. It is rude to fidget or to allow yourself to be distracted. Listen — and think!

Keep in mind the following points of good etiquette:

1. Do not wave your hand while another person is speaking. Wait until he has finished before indicating that you wish to speak.

2. Do not prompt.

3. Do not laugh at or rudely correct another's mistake.

4. Do not contradict. Instead of saying "You're wrong" or "That's not true," say instead "May I question that statement?" or "I may be in error, but I think . . ."

● EXERCISE 9. Listen carefully to recitations in all of your classes. On the basis of your observation, draw up a list of "Do's and Don't's for Classroom Speakers." Compare your list with those of your classmates and compile a class list for guidance.

● EXERCISE 10. In your English or speech class explain a problem that you are going to discuss in your science or hygiene class — for example, the meaning of pasteurization, artificial respiration, how a lightning rod works. Use the blackboard and make

18j

your explanation so clear that everyone understands easily.

DELIVERING A COMMITTEE REPORT

In many high school classes, committees of students handle various phases of a large problem. For example, if the class is studying traffic congestion, one committee might concern itself with the causes of traffic congestion, another with its effects, and a third with community efforts to lessen it.

After studying a problem, a committee submits an oral as well as a written report to the class. The chairman is responsible for delivering the oral report.

18k. When you deliver a committee report, give a brief summary of the main points in your own words, and acknowledge the sources of quoted material.

Do not read your manuscript word for word. Hold it in your hand for reference but do not subject your listeners to a verbatim reading. Instead, summarize the report in your own words.

To do this effectively, you must practice beforehand. Stand before a chair or mirror in your own room and *communicate* the content of your report to an imaginary audience. Do this several times to acquaint yourself with the sequence of ideas. Each time you will use different words, but such changes of phrasing are desirable because they give your report a flavor of spontaneity.

Be careful to stay within your time limit. Those points of your report which you do not touch upon in your formal presentation may come up during the question-and-answer period. If they don't come up, omit them.

If you quote from an article or book, be sure to give credit to the source of your material. To pretend that somebody else's thoughts are your own is a form of deception called plagiarism. Recast another person's ideas into your own language if you wish, but do not employ somebody else's words without acknowledging his authorship.

● EXERCISE 11. As chairman of a committee, deliver an oral report to your class. Pay attention to the hints given above; try to put them into practice.

● EXERCISE 12. Listen attentively to a committee report given in one of your classes. Offer constructive suggestions for improvement, considering such matters as the following:

1. Was the content of the report sound? Did you agree with the findings and recommendations? Why?
2. Did the speaker rely too much on his manuscript?
3. Did he stay within his time limit?
4. Was the report couched in the writer's own language? If quotations were used, were sources credited?

MAKING EXPLANATIONS

In school and out of school you will find it necessary to explain how to make something or how an instrument operates. For instance, you may need to explain how to construct a model airplane, bake a cake, sail a boat, catch a fly ball, or figure skate. You may need to explain how a transistor, barometer, carburetor, or electric toaster works. Make your explanations so clear that your listeners will understand easily.

18l. In making explanations, know your subject and present it clearly and interestingly.

You cannot explain clearly unless you understand clearly. If you say, "I know what I want to say but

18 k-l

I can't explain it," you are in error. The reason you cannot explain is that your own understanding is foggy. Know your facts thoroughly. Become an expert on your topic before you try to explain it to others.

(1) Prepare an introduction which will capture attention.

An experienced speaker spends time in preparing an arresting opening. Lincoln, for example, planned his introductory remarks very carefully. So did Daniel Webster, Franklin D. Roosevelt, and Sir Winston Churchill. Every able and convincing speaker knows the value of an effective beginning. A good beginning makes your listeners regard you and your topic favorably.

You may open your talk with a question.

What is hi-fi?
Have you ever kept a snake for a pet?
What is the correct way to swim the backstroke?
Do you know how forecasters predict the weather?

You may arouse curiosity by a story.

About the turn of this century an Englishman named Sayce was wandering through Turkey when he saw some crumbling ruins quite unlike any he had seen before. Thousands of travelers had passed these ruins but none had stopped to examine them carefully. Because Sayce was intellectually curious he discovered a forgotten empire. Twenty centuries after Christ he discovered a mighty empire that had existed twenty centuries before Christ!

You may use an exhibit.

I wonder how many of you know what this object is. It looks like some kind of meter. In a way it is. It is a Geiger counter.

You may show how your subject affects the health, wealth, comfort, or future of your hearers.

Here's a gadget that will save you hours of work every month.

I'm going to show you how you can save a good part of your monthly allowance.

Many people diet themselves to death. They don't know the difference between a nutritious meal and a fattening one.

You may jolt your hearers with startling facts.

Two out of every five pupils who enter high school never finish.

More people were killed last year by automobiles than were killed by guns in World War II.

(2) Develop your explanation in an orderly fashion, using diagrams, illustrations, or models if they are helpful.

Begin with what your listener knows and advance step by step to new ideas. If you are trying to explain jet propulsion, for example, demonstrate how an inflated toy balloon will suddenly shoot forward if you release your fingers from the mouthpiece and let the air escape. Then show how this principle is applied to jet-propelled airplanes.

When describing a process, arrange the steps in order of performance. "First, you do this. (*Demonstrate*.) Next, you do this. (*Demonstrate*.)" And so on until you complete the procedure.

A blackboard sketch will often help make your explanation clear. To save time, draw the diagram before class begins. When you refer to the diagram, do not turn your back to your audience.

In addition to a diagram — or, sometimes, in place of it — bring an illustration to class. Your school librarian may have a file of illustrations from which you can borrow appropriate pictures. An actual model, if you have one, is even more helpful. For example, if you are talking about building model airplanes, bring one along to show its construction. If you are talking about hemstitching or finger painting, exhibit samples to show what you mean.

(3) Explain technical terms.

Explain any words or expressions that may be unfamiliar to your hearers. For example, words like *baste, octane, watt, guy wire, condenser, inboard motor*, and similar terms should be clarified.

(4) Be brief but complete.

Lengthy explanations bore and confuse. Say only as much as is necessary to make your meaning clear. A good explanation answers as many of the following questions as are applicable: What? Why? How? When? Where? Who?

● EXERCISE 13. In a three-minute speech explain how to make one of the following. Use a diagram, illustration, or model to make your meaning clear.

1. marionette	9. basketball court
2. draperies	10. baseball diamond
3. scooter	11. end table
4. stool	12. patchwork quilt
5. scrapbook	13. hooked rug
6. Argyle socks	14. wallet
7. sweater	15. doghouse
8. skirt	16. model airplane

● EXERCISE 14. In a three-minute speech explain the operation of any one of the following devices.

1. burglar alarm
2. carburetor
3. spark plug
4. saxophone
5. kettledrum
6. barometer
7. thermostat
8. guitar

9. pressure cooker
10. telegraph key
11. sewing machine
12. ball-point pen
13. battery
14. doorbell
15. telephone
16. jet propulsion

MAKING AN ANNOUNCEMENT

18m. In making an announcement include all the essential information. State it briefly, clearly, and forcefully.

A good announcement answers such questions as: What? When? Where? How? How much? Why? To avoid misunderstanding, you should

1. Repeat the essential information.
2. Speak distinctly.

Fellow students, do you want to have the time of your life? Once a year your General Organization holds a skating party in Metropolitan Roller Rink on Staunton Street near Wykoff Avenue. Last year 600 boys and girls from our high school attended. If you were one of the lucky ones who were there, you know that everyone had a wonderful time.

This year's skating party will be held on Wednesday, April 17, from seven to ten in the evening. Tickets are fifty cents and may be purchased from your class delegate.

Since the rink accommodates only 600, only that number of tickets can be sold. Get yours right away if you don't want to be disappointed.

Remember: The date is Wednesday, April 17, the tickets are fifty cents, and the event is our annual skating party, the biggest event of our school year!

18m

● EXERCISE 15.   Make an announcement about one of the following to your class. Provide the necessary details. When you have finished, your listeners will tell you whether your announcement was clear, interesting, complete, and forceful.

1. school dance	8. tryouts for a team
2. athletic event	9. cake sale
3. musical concert	10. Open School Night
4. play	11. Career Night
5. boat trip	12. charity drive
6. club meeting	13. Christmas party
7. graduation rehearsal	14. arts and crafts exhibit

GIVING TRAVEL DIRECTIONS

Many people do not know how to direct a stranger to his destination. They give directions which are confusing, obscure, or even erroneous. Giving directions is an everyday speech situation which you should know how to handle.

18n. Give travel directions only when you are sure of your information. Do not hesitate to admit ignorance or uncertainty.

(1) Make the directions simple.

If several routes are possible, describe the one which is easiest to follow even though it may be the longest.

(2) Refer to permanent or easy-to-recognize landmarks along the route.

(3) Tell the approximate distance or the time required.

(4) Be sure your listener understands your directions.

If such terms as *north*, *south*, *east*, and *west* seem to confuse your listener, use such expressions as *turn right, continue straight ahead, bear left at the fork in the road*.

(5) If the route is complicated, draw a rough map.

● EXERCISE 16.   Working in pairs, dramatize situations in which one member requests travel directions and the other gives them. The following are sample situations; you can devise others of your own.

1. A stranger asks directions to your school from the center of town.
2. A driver asks the way to the next town.
3. A tourist wants to know the way to a historic site.
4. A visitor asks the way to the town hall.

TALKING ABOUT CURRENT EVENTS

Current happenings of local, state, national, or international significance are suitable subjects for talks before groups. So, too, are events in the fields of science, music, art, sports, education, business, and literature.

18o. **When speaking about current events, choose happenings that are important and likely to affect the lives of your listeners.**

Your talk should be more than a restatement of a news item. It should express a fresh and original viewpoint.

A current-events talk may be divided into two parts: (1) a statement of the facts; (2) an interpretation of the facts.

Where can you obtain the facts? News accounts in reputable newspapers or news magazines provide a source of material. So do radio and television broadcasts. For background information consult histories, encyclopedias, and atlases in your school or local library.

18
n-o

Your interpretation of the facts should be original. What results will follow from the situation? Why is it dangerous, important, or unique?

● EXERCISE 17. Deliver a three-minute talk on an important current event. Prepare an outline to guide you when speaking.

TALKING ABOUT BOOKS, MOVIES, AND TELEVISION PLAYS

18p. A report on a book, movie, or television program should include a description of your subject and your estimate of it.

When you speak before a group about a book you have read, your purpose is to tell enough about it so that your listeners may decide for themselves whether they want to read it. A book report includes at least two elements: (1) a description of the plot or contents; (2) your estimate.

When discussing fiction, do not reveal the entire plot, because by doing so you deny your listeners the pleasure of discovering the outcome for themselves. Tell just enough to whet interest. You may describe an exciting or amusing scene in detail or, if you wish, read it aloud when it is short, so that your listeners can judge for themselves whether the book has merit.

It is generally advisable to describe the appearance and traits of the main characters. Show how they act under certain circumstances and indicate how they change during the course of the story.

In addition to touching upon the plot and characters, discuss some of the following topics in your report. Do not try to include them all.

1. Title and author
2. Setting (time and place)
3. Climax

4. Style (vocabulary, ease or difficulty of reading, narrative or descriptive skill)
5. Comparison with the motion-picture version
6. Comparison with other books by the same author
7. Comparision with other books by different authors dealing with the same subject
8. Humor (Illustrate by reading a few paragraphs aloud.)
9. An incident that reveals character
10. A brief account of the author's life
11. The theme (What, if anything, is the author trying to show? For example, the difficulties of adolescence, the suffering caused by war, the need for child labor laws.)
12. Your opinion of the book (Do not be satisfied with a statement such as "I enjoyed the book immensely" or "I thought the book was dull." Explain why you found it interesting or boring. Was it because of the style, plot, vocabulary, setting? Was the story too fanciful or too realistic?)

In reporting on nonfiction, consider such topics as:

1. Title and author
2. Scope (What are the main topics?)
3. Style (Are the explanations interesting? clear?)
4. Usefulness (What useful information have you learned from reading it? Discuss an event, discovery, problem, or topic in detail.)
5. Your estimate of the book (Why did you find it interesting or dull?)

In reporting on a biography, discuss some of these points:

1. Title and author
2. The life, achievements, and personality of the subject of the biography
3. The obstacles he faced and overcame
4. Your reasons for admiring (or disliking) him
5. Your estimate of the book

18p

● EXERCISE 18.   Read and report orally to your class on a novel, biography, drama, or work of non-fiction which your teacher has approved in advance. Prepare an outline to guide you when speaking.

● EXERCISE 19.   Assume that you are standing before a microphone. In your own words relate an incident from a book that you have read. Make your narration so lifelike that your hearers will imagine the event is occurring at that very moment and that they are there. For example, describe the storming of the stockade in *Treasure Island* or the storming of Torquilstone Castle in *Ivanhoe*.

The suggestions offered for book reports apply in large part to discussions about movies and television plays. There are, however, some aspects of a motion picture that seldom enter into a book review. For example:

1. Cast (Who played the leading roles? Were the actors well cast?)
2. Acting (Who gave the best performances? Was the acting natural and effective? In which scenes was the acting most memorable?)
3. Photography (Color or black and white? Artistic or run of the mill?)
4. Settings (Lavish? Simple? Appropriate?)
5. Costumes (Attractive? Authentic?)
6. Sound (Clear? Muffled?)
7. Diction (Was the actors' speech distinct? Was dialect used effectively?)
8. Comparison with novel (How does the motion picture differ from the novel of the same name? Are the changes justified?)

● EXERCISE 20.   Orally review a good movie or television play that you have recently seen.

Pronunciation and Enunciation

When a speaker mispronounces a word, you are distracted. Your attention wanders from the thought he is conveying to his mispronunciation. Mispronunciation interferes with communication.

18q. Learn the ways by which you may improve your pronunciation.

(1) Listen to good speakers.

Radio and television announcers, public speakers, actors and actresses, and teachers generally are acceptable models to imitate.

(2) Refer to the dictionary.

Keep a dictionary at home on your desk so that you may readily check the pronunciation of unfamiliar words. The diacritical marks at the bottom of each page will help you determine correct pronunciation.[6]

(3) Do not omit syllables.

● EXERCISE 21. Pronounce all the syllables in each of the following words.

1. electric	8. finally	15. poetry
2. family	9. suppose	16. generally
3. different	10. diamond	17. average
4. ideal	11. actually	18. giant
5. geography	12. occasionally	19. jewel
6. mystery	13. champion	20. cruel
7. memory	14. accidentally	21. company

18q

[6] For this topic, see Chapter 16, pages 319–50.

(4) Do not add syllables or sounds.

● EXERCISE 22. Pronounce each of the following words as one syllable only. (For example, do not say *elum* for *elm*.)

1. elm	5. down	9. male
2. film	6. known	10. sale
3. helm	7. blown	11. bale
4. realm	8. grown	12. gale

● EXERCISE 23. Pronounce each of the following words, taking care not to add any sounds. (For example, do not say *athalete* for *athlete*.)

1. umbrella	5. grievous	9. burglar
2. idea	6. ticklish	10. translate
3. lightning	7. draw	11. laundry
4. chimney	8. hindrance	12. athlete

● EXERCISE 24. With the aid of a dictionary, learn the correct pronunciation of the following words.[7]

absolutely	drama	khaki
admirable	faucet	laboratory
alloy	February	orchestra
ally	final	parliamentary
almond	finale	particular
alternate	finance	penalize
banquet	forbade	positively
champion	forehead	recipe
chastisement	formerly	regular
column	gesture	romance
comfortable	government	Roosevelt
corps	hearth	salve
coupon	horizon	secretive
creek	hospitable	solemnity
decade	influence	tribunal
diphtheria	interesting	usually

[7] Word list prepared for ninth grade by New York State Speech Association.

18r. Improve your enunciation by sounding your words clearly and avoiding the unnecessary use of *and* and *ur*.

Enunciation refers to distinctness of utterance. A speaker may pronounce a word correctly — that is, use correct stress and vowel quality — yet mumble or mouth it so that it cannot be heard clearly.

For clean-cut enunciation, vigorous lip, tongue, and jaw action is necessary. Practicing such old-fashioned nonsense sentences as the following helps develop clear enunciation.

Betty Botta bought a bit of butter.
"But," said Bet, "this butter's bitter.
If I put it in my batter,
It will make my batter bitter."

Peter Piper picked a peck of pickled peppers.

Prunes and prisms, prunes and prisms.

The big black bug bit the big black bear.

Truly rural, truly rural.

Tent tops and ten tops and ten dented tent tops.

Five wives wearily weave bright red rugs.

Theophilus Thistle, the successful thistle sifter, successfully sifted some thistles.

She sells sea shells by the seashore.

● EXERCISE 25.   A common fault is the substitution of *–n* for *–ng* as, for example, *swimmin'* for *swimming*. List 20 words ending in *ng* and practice saying them singly and in sentences.

● EXERCISE 26.   The final consonant combinations in the following words are difficult to pronounce. Practice until you can say each word clearly and easily.

18r

1. breadth	10. lengths	19. twelfths	28. faiths
2. width	11. respects	20. months	29. myths
3. hundredth	12. acts	21. folds	30. accepts
4. lifts	13. sects	22. fields	31. precepts
5. wafts	14. facts	23. builds	32. depths
6. shifts	15. tracts	24. adjusts	33. precincts
7. crafts	16. mists	25. masks	34. tastes
8. tufts	17. tests	26. desks	35. asks
9. hyacinths	18. fifths	27. youths	36. tenths

● EXERCISE 27.   Practice the following pairs of words, being careful not to substitute *d* for *t* as, for example, *led her* for *letter*, or *t* for *th* as *true* for *through*.

1. riding	writing	10. true	through
2. medal	metal	11. taught	thought
3. bidden	bitten	12. tinker	thinker
4. pedal	petal	13. boat	both
5. madder	matter	14. tent	tenth
6. padding	patting	15. tick	thick
7. beading	beating	16. tree	three
8. boding	boating	17. tow	throw
9. biding	biting	18. tie	thigh

A common fault among beginning speakers is to link each sentence with the one preceding by means of *and*. At the end of each sentence, stop! Begin each new sentence cleanly.

Another common fault is the use of *ur*. The repeated use of this sound between words or sentences is annoying. Avoid it.

CHAPTER 19

Using the Telephone

MAKING AND RECEIVING CALLS

Alexander Graham Bell spoke into the mouthpiece of a crude mechanism. "Mr. Watson, come here. I want you." From an adjoining room, his excited assistant came running. The telephone was born! The date was March 10, 1876; the place, Boston, Massachusetts.

Today there are approximately 55 million telephones in the United States, one for every three people. They carry more than 200 million messages every day. The telephone plays such an important part in our social and business affairs that everyone should know how to use it effectively.

Making Telephone Calls

19a. Plan your call.

The person you call will understand your message more easily if you have clearly in mind what you want to say. Since you always have a specific purpose for calling, you must plan your call in advance so that it will accomplish your purpose quickly. If you are going to talk about several things, jot them down to prevent forgetting and rambling.

Be sure you have the correct telephone number. If you are doubtful, check it in the directory. It is good

19a

practice to keep at hand a list of the numbers you call frequently.

Call Information only if you cannot find the number you want in the directory.

19b. Use the directory accurately.

A telephone directory is divided into two sections: an alphabetical directory and a classified directory. In large cities, these directories may be separate books.

THE ALPHABETICAL DIRECTORY

The alphabetical directory contains alphabetical listings, indented listings, and cross-referenced listings.

Alphabetical Listings

As you might expect, the alphabetical directory lists names in alphabetical order. To help you locate a listing quickly, two guide words are printed in heavy black type at the top of each page. The first guide word is the first listing on the page; the second is the last listing on the same page. Suppose you were trying to locate a listing for *Lennox*. As you leaf through the directory, you notice at the top of a page the guide words **Lee — Levine** and immediately you know that the listing you want will be found in alphabetical order on that page.

Indented Listings

Merchants, businessmen, and professional people often list their home telephone numbers directly below their business or office listings. Departments, divisions, and branches of large corporations are frequently given under a main listing. These are called indented listings.

EXAMPLES   **Gallo's Meat Markets**
Branches —
100 Main . . . . PResdnt 2–7618
37 Mackay Av . . . . GEdny 4–1162
761 Haven Blvd . . . . SOuth 8–1941

Wechsler John   MD   82 Clntn MAin 4–1751
Res   172 King . . . . TOwn 7–2442

Cross-referenced Listings

Names which are pronounced the same way are often spelled differently. When this is the case, the telephone directory refers to alternative spellings. For example, the listing for SMITH may say, "See also SMYTH, SMYTHE." The listing for COHEN may say, "See also COAN, COEN, COHAN, COHN, CONE, KOHN." These are called cross-referenced listings.

"The" as the first word of a name is ordinarily omitted. For example, "The New York Times" is listed as **NY TIMES.** A firm may insert an additional listing for the convenience of directory users.

EXAMPLE   New Yorker Magazine pblctn
The New Yorker pblctn

Government Listings

The number and type of governmental listings vary from community to community. Generally, governmental agencies are listed under three main categories — federal, state, and local (county and municipal governments). Look for governmental listings under the name of the governmental unit. For example, if you are a resident of New York State and want to find the telephone number of the Bureau of Motor Vehicles in your town, look under the listing **New York — State of.** The telephone number of a public school is listed under the city or town in which the school is located.

19b

EXAMPLES   BOSTON, CITY OF
     SCHOOL COMMITTEE
     SCHOOLS
       ABRAHAMS HENRY
       ADAMS SAML

UNITED STATES GOVERNMENT
     AGRICULTURE DEPT OF —
     AIR FORCE DEPT OF THE —
     COURTS —
     INTERNAL REVENUE SERVICE —[1]
     POST OFFICE DEPT —
     WEATHER BUR —

NEW YORK — STATE OF
     ARMORIES —
     CIVIL SERVICE DEPT OF —
     CONSERVATION DEPT OF —
     EDUCATION DEPT OF —
     HEALTH DEPT OF —
     LABOR DEPT OF —

SUFFOLK COUNTY OFFICES
AND INSTITUTIONS
     BOARD OF HEALTH —
     FIRE DEPT —
     POLICE DEPT —
     SANITATION DEPT —

THE CLASSIFIED DIRECTORY

The classified directory, often referred to as the Yellow Pages, lists business concerns by products and services. You will find, for example, such listings as the following:

       Automobile driving instruction
       Bicycles and repairs

[1] In some cities, the Internal Revenue Service is listed under the Treasury Department.

Cleaners and dyers
Drugstores
Hairdressers
Lawyers
Meat markets
Piano tuning and repairing
Records — phonograph
Tuxedos — for hire

By using the classified directory you can easily find out where to purchase a particular product or obtain the service you need. The classified directory also lists nationally advertised products and indicates where they may be bought locally.

● EXERCISE 1.   Using the guide words to help you, look up the telephone numbers of listings given by your teacher. Write them clearly and legibly.

● EXERCISE 2.   Copy an indented listing from the directory.

● EXERCISE 3.   Find alternate spellings of their names as well as alternate listings for as many of the following as are given in your directory: McCauley, Kelly, Green, Burke, Ginsberg, Housman, Rice, Russo, Gray. Are the names of some of your classmates cross-referenced?

● EXERCISE 4.   Find the telephone numbers of the following government agencies in your community.

Department of Agriculture (federal)

Police Department (city)

Army Recruiting Station (federal)

Department of Education (state)

Municipal Court

County Court

Library (city)

Internal Revenue Service (federal)

Board of Health (city)

19c. Learn to place several kinds of calls correctly.

EMERGENCY CALLS

The cover or the first pages of the alphabetical directory give instructions for calling an ambulance, summoning a policeman, reporting a fire, and obtaining other emergency help. These instructions vary from community to community. Find out the procedure for your community and write out the directions. The usual procedure in an emergency is to dial or call the operator and say:

> "I want to report a fire."
> "I want a policeman."
> "I want an ambulance."
> "I want the Coast Guard."

If you can't stay at the telephone, tell the operator where the help is needed.

LOCAL AND OUT-OF-TOWN CALLS

If you are not using a dial phone, give the number to the operator clearly. If you dial your calls, lift the receiver and listen for the dial tone, a steady humming sound. Dial the number carefully. Letters on the dial are printed in black and numbers in red. When dialing, be careful to distinguish between the letter "O" and the numeral "0" and between the letter "I" and the numeral "1."

If you make an error in dialing, or if your finger slips, hang up the receiver for a few seconds; then pick it up, wait for the dial tone, and dial the complete number again.

Long-distance calls are usually handled by the operator. However, in some parts of the country these calls can be dialed directly. They are of two kinds: station-to-station and person-to-person.

A *station-to-station* call is to a given telephone number. The person calling speaks to whoever answers. Charges begin when the called telephone answers.

A *person-to-person* call is directed to a particular person. Charges begin when the person is reached. Person-to-person rates are higher than station-to-station rates.

When you place an out-of-town call, give the operator the city, state, and number you want. If you are placing a person-to-person call, add the name of the person you are calling.

EXAMPLES "I'd like to call Cleveland, Ohio. Laurelton 7–7674."

"I'm calling Cleveland, Ohio. Laurelton 7–7674. I'd like to speak to Mr. Stevenson."

Rates for out-of-town calls are lower every day after 6 P.M. and all day Sunday because the demand for telephone service is not so heavy at these times.

You may place an out-of-town call "collect." This means that the cost of the message is paid by the person receiving the call. If you wish to place a collect call, tell the operator and give her your name and number. Before she permits the conversation to start, she will ask the person who answers whether he will accept the charges.

Large business concerns usually handle telephone calls through switchboards. If you make a call to such a firm, ask the switchboard operator to connect you with the extension, office, department, or person to whom you wish to speak.

EXAMPLES "Extension 143, please."

"May I speak to Mr. Phillips, please."

"Will you please connect me with the Employment Office."

"The sporting goods department, please."

19c

In many localities, the telephone company will gladly send a representative to schools to demonstrate correct telephone technique.

WRONG NUMBERS

Wrong numbers annoy everybody — the person calling, the person called, and the telephone company. You can cut down on them by pronouncing numbers distinctly when you use a manual phone and by dialing carefully when you use a dial phone. If you dial a wrong number, recheck the directory to verify the number you want, or dial the operator and ask her to get the number for you.

If you are answered by someone who seems not to be the person you are calling, do not say, "What is your number?" or "Who is this?" Say instead something like, "Is this Orchard 5624?" or "May I speak with ——?"

If you reach a wrong number, express regret even though you may not be at fault.

EXAMPLES   "Sorry. I've called the wrong number."
"I beg your pardon. I have the wrong number."

TELEGRAMS

Since most telegrams are sent by telephone, it is important to know the different types of telegram service and the correct way of sending a telegram.

A "straight" telegram comprises no more than 15 words at a basic rate. It is dispatched immediately.

A night letter comprises no more than 50 words at a basic rate. It is dispatched at night for morning delivery.

A day letter comprises no more than 50 words at a basic rate. It is dispatched at the convenience of the company.

In all three types of telegrams, additional words may

be included at an additional charge. Wording telegrams provides excellent practice in using language. Every word should be meaningful and well chosen.

The procedure for sending a telegram is as follows:

1. Write the telegram, night letter, or day letter. Count the words. In counting the words, do not include the name and address of the person to whom the telegram is sent or the signature of the sender, as there is no charge for this information.

2. Check in your directory to see whether to dial Western Union directly or to ask the operator to connect you.

3. When the Western Union operator answers, give the name and address of the person to whom you are sending the telegram; then dictate the telegram carefully.

4. Give your name, address, and telephone number.

5. Check carefully while the operator repeats your message.

● EXERCISE 5. Working in pairs and using dummy or imaginary telephones, demonstrate correct procedure in sending the following telegrams. Limit your message to 15 words (if it is a straight telegram) or 50 words (if it is a day or night letter).

1. Message of congratulation to a friend on his birthday
2. Request to a sporting goods manufacturer for immediate delivery of uniforms for a school team (The uniforms were ordered three weeks ago.)
3. Congratulations to a coach upon his team's winning a championship

19d. When making a social call, be considerate of others.

Long, gossipy conversations prevent others from using the telephone and stop incoming calls which

19d

may be urgent or important. Aside from their cost, lengthy telephone conversations annoy others at home who cannot help overhearing them. If you are speaking on a party line, remember that others on your line may want to use the telephone.

If the operator requests you to get off a party line to allow an emergency message to reach another person, do so immediately. The emergency may be a call for a doctor, an ambulance, or fire apparatus. Good citizenship requires immediate compliance with the operator's request. Some states have passed laws requiring callers to get off a party line at the operator's request in an emergency.

19e. When making a business call, be business-like.

(1) Identify yourself immediately.

A telephone call is like a personal visit. When you visit a friend, he recognizes you when he opens the door. If a stranger answers the doorbell, you identify yourself immediately so that your name may be announced to the person you wish to see. So it is with telephone calls. It is courteous, time-saving, and informative to identify yourself immediately.

EXAMPLES   "This is Beacon Service Station, Irving Johnson speaking. May I speak to Mr. Darcy, please?"

"Is Mr. Greenbriar there? Mr. Herman calling."

"This is Ed Thomas. May I speak to Joe, please?"

(2) Have materials at hand to help you conduct a call without unnecessary delay.

A capable clerk or executive has at hand all he needs to help a call go smoothly. If he wants information, he has paper and pen or pencil ready. If he is going to inquire about many matters, he lists them to avoid overlooking any.

Similarly, if a student is calling about photographs for the school yearbook, he may find out beforehand such information as the number of students in the class, the time and place where the photographs are to be taken, the sizes required, and the date when delivery is expected.

(3) Call only at appropriate times.

Do not call too early in the morning or too late at night. Doctors dislike being called late in the evening, clergymen just before a service, and housewives at meal-preparation time.

(4) End calls appropriately.

The caller is responsible for bringing his call to a close. If you are the caller, leave a favorable impression by expressing thanks or regret, whichever is appropriate, addressing the person by name, and closing with "Good-by."

EXAMPLES   "Thanks a lot, Mrs. Reeves. Good-by."
"Thank you, Mr. Barton. I'll definitely call you on Wednesday morning. Good-by."
"Thank you for returning my call, Eileen. Good-by."

● EXERCISE 6.   Working in pairs and using dummy or imaginary instruments, conduct the following telephone conversations:

1. Make an appointment with a doctor, dentist, or beautician.
2. Find out the time of the feature film presentation at a local theater.

19e

3. Obtain a homework assignment from a friend.
4. Order groceries.
5. Place an order with a department store for an item advertised in a newspaper.
6. Schedule a club meeting with the club secretary.
7. Cancel an appointment with a photographer.
8. Request an interview with a prospective employer.
9. Give information for inserting an advertisement in a newspaper.
10. Check the time of arrival of a train.
11. Plan a trip or picnic with a friend.
12. Inquire about a sick friend.
13. Arrange for a baby sitter.
14. Invite a friend to a party.
15. Reserve train or airplane accommodations.

● EXERCISE 7. Working in pairs, demonstrate how to make the following long-distance calls:

1. A station-to-station call
2. A person-to-person call
3. A collect call

● EXERCISE 8. Imagine yourself a telephone company lecturer. In a three-minute talk discuss "wrong numbers," explaining why they are a source of trouble to the telephone company as well as to subscribers, how to prevent them, and how to deal with them in a satisfactory and courteous way.

● EXERCISE 9. Working in pairs, demonstrate good business practice in making a telephone call. Invent situations which provide an opportunity for showing:

1. How to identify yourself
2. The value of having the necessary materials at hand
3. Ending a call pleasantly

Answering Telephone Calls

19f. Be courteous and efficient when answering telephone calls.

(1) Answer promptly.

Answer the telephone as soon as you can. Hold the mouthpiece about an inch from your lips and speak directly into it.

(2) In a business situation, tell who you are immediately.

When answering a call in an office, identify yourself immediately, just as you should do when making a call. An efficient employee avoids the time-wasting use of "Hello" when answering the telephone. Instead, he identifies himself by stating his name, company or department, or telephone number. Sometimes he uses a combination of these — depending upon what is most helpful to the person calling.

EXAMPLES   "Mr. Jones" or "Mr. Jones speaking."
"Hall Brothers, Mr. Edwards speaking."
"This is Tim Fagan."
"This is Endicott 4726."
"Hardware Department, Miss Duffy speaking."
"Principal's office, student speaking."

(3) Take notes on the call if necessary.

When you answer either a social or a business call, it is helpful to have a pad at hand on which to jot notes. Your notes will aid you in restating the problem, organizing facts, or summarizing information you have received. They are a record, too, of promises you have made. For example, jot down travel directions or the place, date, and time of an appointment.

19f

(4) Offer to take a message when the person called is not in.

When you take a message, you create a pleasing impression and you save the caller the cost of another call.

When you take a message, be sure to record:

1. The caller's name and telephone number (Verify the spelling of the name. Repeat the number to be sure it is correct.)

2. The date and time the message was received

3. The complete message (Write it legibly. Repeat it to the caller to be sure it is accurate.)

4. Your name

19g. Return promptly all calls received in your absence.

If a person calls when you are out, return his call promptly regardless of whether it is a social or a business call. Courtesy requires that you do this. So does good business policy.

Using Voice and Diction Effectively

19h. Be pleasant and clear when speaking on the telephone.

In a telephone conversation you reveal yourself solely through your voice, what you say, and how you say it. A cheerful voice is a valuable asset. Just as you like a smile when you greet a friend or meet a stranger, so do callers like to speak to persons who sound natural and cheerful. It is satisfying to speak to persons who are gracious and understanding.

(1) Speak distinctly.

If a caller says, "I'm sorry, I didn't hear what you said" or "What did you say?" you should take the question as a hint to speak more distinctly. Check the tendency to slur and mumble. Form your words more crisply.

(2) Speak at a rate which is easily understood.

Speak at a normal conversational rate over the telephone. If you hurry, you will slur your words and have difficulty in making yourself understood.

Some information should be given more deliberately, such as lists, numbers, names, information that the listener is writing down, foreign or unusual words or expressions.

(3) Use polite language.

Address callers by their names, together with their titles when appropriate. When you address people by their names, you sound a personal as well as courteous note — "Mr. Hurley," "Dr. Miles," "Mrs. Curtis," "Edna," "Joe," and so on. Likewise "Sir" and "Madam" are in good taste in business calls.

Little expressions such as the following help create good feeling:

"Thank you."	"Please."
"I'm sorry."	"I shall be glad to."
"I beg your pardon."	"May I help you?"

● EXERCISE 10. Working in pairs and using demonstration telephones, carry on the following telephone conversations.

1. Several days ago you ordered a number of items from a department store which have not yet been delivered. You call the department store to inquire about the delay.
2. You call your friend to arrange a meeting with him. He is not in, but his brother offers to take the message.

**19
g-h**

3. The secretary of the club of which you are president was absent from the last meeting. You telephone to dictate to her the names and addresses of several new club members.
4. You ask a friend for the homework assignment in mathematics. He dictates several problems to you.
5. As chairman of a dance committee, you call a local store to order decorations.
6. A water pipe in your home is leaking. Your mother asks you to call a plumber. You select a plumber from the classified directory, call him, but learn that he is out on a job.

● EXERCISE 11. Analyze the following telephone conversations. Explain which of the two conversations is the better and why.

1

"Hello."

"Hello. Is this Mr. White's office?"

"Yes."

"May I speak to Mr. White?"

"Who is calling, please?"

"Mr. Glasser."

"One moment, Mr. Glasser."

(The secretary says to Mr. White, "Telephone, Mr. White.")

"Hello."

"Hello. Are you Mr. White?"

"Yes."

"Mr. White, this is Mr. Glasser."

2

"Mr. White's office. Mrs. Harrison speaking."

"Mrs. Harrison, this is Mr. Glasser. May I speak to Mr. White?"

"One moment, please, Mr. Glasser. I'll put him on."

(The secretary says to Mr. White, "Mr. Glasser calling, Mr. White.")

"Good morning, Mr. Glasser. This is Mr. White."

PART SIX

MECHANICS

CHAPTER 20

Capital Letters

LEARN THE RULES OF CAPITALIZATION

You should capitalize the first letter of a word when you have a *reason* for doing so — that is, if the word falls under one of the six rules for capitalization in this chapter. If you depend upon guesswork, you will not only fail to capitalize words correctly but also use unneeded capital letters.

20a. Capitalize the pronoun *I* and the interjection *O*.

WRONG o my! i think i've lost my watch!
RIGHT **O** my! **I** think **I**'ve lost my watch!

20b. Capitalize the first word of any sentence.[1]

WRONG cross your legs so that one foot will not touch the floor. then tap the tendon just below the kneecap. your light blow will cause a "knee-jerk reflex." this reflex action indicates that the nerves of your lower spinal cord are in good working order.

---

[1] For exercises in recognizing the beginning of a sentence, see pages 95–97.

RIGHT   **Cross your legs so that one foot will not touch the floor. Then tap the tendon just below the kneecap. Your light blow will cause a "knee-jerk reflex." This reflex action indicates that the nerves of your lower spinal cord are in good working order.**

● EXERCISE 1. Make a list of the 10 words that should be capitalized in the following paragraph. Be sure to capitalize the words you list. [CAUTION: A capital letter does *not* follow a semicolon.]

since it was the first warm day of spring, I decided to go barefoot. it was wonderful to feel the fresh grass crumple beneath my feet as I walked through the pasture. strolling down by the mill pond, I looked at the budding wild-flowers and watched the white clouds playing tag in the sky. suddenly, however, for some unknown reason, I looked down at my right foot; perhaps a sixth sense warned me of approaching danger. not two inches from my right foot was a water moccasin! his head was lifted. his fangs shot toward my toes. quickly I pulled my bare foot backward. was I scared! i ran almost a half mile before I realized that I had escaped those deadly fangs.

20c. Capitalize proper nouns.

A proper noun is the name of a *particular* person, place, or thing. How a proper noun differs from a common noun, which is not capitalized, may be seen from the following list.

COMMON NOUNS	PROPER NOUNS
girl	Mary Kelly
country	France
automobile	Chevrolet

Remember that common nouns name a type. For example, *mackerel* or *trout* is a common noun because it is merely a type of fish.

**20
a-c**

● EXERCISE 2. Below is a list of common nouns; for each one, give 2 proper nouns.

EXAMPLE   1. **city**
          1. **Boston, New Orleans**

1. teacher	6. town
2. magazine	7. lake
3. continent	8. pioneer
4. freshman	9. college
5. author	10. newspaper

(1) Capitalize geographical names.

CITIES, TOWNS   **Louisville, New York City, Boise**

COUNTIES, TOWNSHIPS   **Harrison County, Sheffield Township**

STATES   **Arizona, South Dakota, New Hampshire**

CONTINENTS   **North America, Europe, Africa**

COUNTRIES   **United States of America, Spain, Mexico**

ISLANDS   **Philippine Islands, Staten Island**

BODIES OF WATER   **Pacific Ocean, Hudson Bay, Gulf of Mexico, Caribbean Sea, Lake Erie, Missouri River, Barton Creek**

SECTIONS OF THE COUNTRY   **the East, the Southwest**

▶ NOTE   Do *not* capitalize *east, west, north,* and *south* when these words merely indicate directions: a **south** wing of the building, on the **north** shore, traveling **east,** looking toward the **west.**

MOUNTAINS   **Cumberland Mountains, Pikes Peak, Black Hills**

STREETS   **Cedar Lane, Shelby Boulevard, Seneca Avenue, West Twenty-first Street** [In a hyphenated number, the second word begins with a small letter.]

PARKS   **Carlsbad Caverns National Park, Cleburne State Park**

As you study the list above, notice that the complete name is capitalized. Words like *Street, Mountains, River,* and *Park* are capitalized because they are a part of the proper names. If these words are *not* part of a proper name, they are *not* capitalized. Compare the following lists:

COMMON NOUNS	PROPER NOUNS
attending high school	Hamilton High School
on the avenue	Clayton Avenue
across the river	St. Lawrence River

● EXERCISE 3. Number from 1 to 20 on your paper. In each of the following items you are to choose the correct one of the two forms. After the proper number on your paper, write the letter of the correct form (*a* or *b*).

1. a. He lives in Kansas city.
   b. He lives in Kansas City.
2. a. We crossed the Rio Grande river.
   b. We crossed the Rio Grande River.
3. a. My dog is a terrier.
   b. My dog is a Terrier.
4. a. Paul will soon enter High School.
   b. Paul will soon enter high school.
5. a. Mr. Ames attended Harvard university.
   b. Mr. Ames attended Harvard University.
6. a. City streets in the west are often wide.
   b. City streets in the West are often wide.
7. a. Yellowstone National Park has many geysers.
   b. Yellowstone national park has many geysers.
8. a. Go two blocks and turn South.
   b. Go two blocks and turn south.
9. a. The city of Columbus is the capital of Ohio.
   b. The City of Columbus is the capital of Ohio.
10. a. The wind changed from the South to the East.
    b. The wind changed from the south to the east.
11. a. We are proud of our State parks.
    b. We are proud of our state parks.
12. a. I live on Forty-Fifth Street.
    b. I live on Forty-fifth Street.
13. a. The headquarters are in Travis County.
    b. The headquarters are in Travis county.
14. a. I go to Wake Forest High School.
    b. I go to Wake Forest high school.

15. a. Where is your cocker spaniel?
    b. Where is your Cocker Spaniel?
16. a. She drives a red convertible.
    b. She drives a red Convertible.
17. a. I have a map of the Hawaiian Islands.
    b. I have a map of the Hawaiian islands.
18. a. New York City is the largest city in the east.
    b. New York City is the largest city in the East.
19. a. The Great Salt Lake is near the Nevada border.
    b. The Great Salt lake is near the Nevada border.
20. a. He teaches at Bay Path junior college.
    b. He teaches at Bay Path Junior College.

● EXERCISE 4. Copy the following sentences, inserting capitals wherever needed.

1. in geography class i have been learning about north america.
2. in the united states there are many coal mines — in the allegheny mountains as well as in the rockies.
3. deposits of iron ore are found around lake superior, and many oil fields are in illinois, kansas, oklahoma, louisiana, texas, and california.
4. i've learned that the miles of railroad tracks in the united states outnumber those of russia, france, england, canada, brazil, and argentina put together.

● EXERCISE 5. Write a paragraph of about 100 words telling a stranger about a town or city that you know well. Give its exact location (the county, state, section of the country), and name some of its streets. Also tell him about the points of interest — parks, dams, lakes, mountains — that your state is proud of. Be sure to capitalize all of the geographical names that you use in your description.

(2) Capitalize names of organizations, business firms, institutions, government bodies, ships, planes, brand names of business products, special events, items on the calendar, races, and religions.

ORGANIZATIONS   American Red Cross, National Boxing Association, Boy Scouts of America

> ▶ NOTE: Do *not* capitalize the members of a class (*freshman, junior, sophomore, senior*) unless part of a proper noun. Do *not* capitalize the word *party* in referring to political parties: *Republican party*.

> EXAMPLE   A freshman cannot go to the Junior-Senior Banquet.

BUSINESS FIRMS   Imperial Biscuit Company, Western Union, Academy Department Stores, Inc.

INSTITUTIONS   United States Naval Academy, Columbia University, Radcliffe College, Fairmont High School, Bellevue Hospital

> ▶ NOTE: Do *not* capitalize words like *hotel, theater, college,* and *high school* unless they are part of a proper name.

Kenmore **High School**	a **high school** teacher
Waldorf-Astoria **Hotel**	a **hotel** in New York
Ritz **Theater**	to the **theater**

GOVERNMENT BODIES   Congress, Federal Bureau of Investigation, House of Representatives [Usage is divided on the capitalization of such words as *post office* and *courthouse.* You may write them either way unless the full name is given, when they must be capitalized: *Kearny Post Office, Victoria County Courthouse.*]

SHIPS, PLANES, BRAND NAMES OF BUSINESS PRODUCTS, AND OTHER THINGS HAVING PARTICULAR NAMES   the *Mayflower,* the *Spirit of St. Louis* (airplane), the Statue of Liberty, the Purple Heart, Kodak, Tabasco, Palace Theater, Empire State Building

> ▶ NOTE: Do *not* capitalize the noun which often follows a brand name: *Thermos jug, Wizard appliances, Plymouth coupe*

EVENTS   Kentucky Derby, Gulf Coast Track and Field Championships, Parents' Day

HISTORICAL EVENTS AND PERIODS   French Revolution, Boston Tea Party, Middle Ages, World War II

CALENDAR ITEMS   **Saturday, December, Easter, Mother's Day**

▶ NOTE: Do *not* capitalize the names of the seasons unless personified: *summer, winter, spring, fall. Here is Spring in her green dress.* [Some newspapers do not follow this practice.]

RACES AND RELIGIOUS GROUPS   **Chinese, Negro, Methodist, Baptist**

● EXERCISE 6.   Copy the following, using capitals wherever needed.

1. a theater across the street
2. tuesday night, june 18
3. mediterranean sea
4. a hospital in albany
5. in high school
6. husky dog food
7. the sinking of the *lusitania*
8. world war I, the "war to end wars"
9. seniors in the spring
10. allandale high school
11. a few negroes
12. miami valley country club
13. fuller brushes
14. on christmas eve
15. a presbyterian
16. new york yacht club
17. ford motor company
18. chevrolet truck
19. colonial period
20. the supreme court

● EXERCISE 7.   Correctly use each of the following words in sentences of your own.

1. high school
2. High School
3. senior
4. Senior
5. hotel
6. Hotel
7. post office
8. Post Office
9. south
10. South
11. college
12. College

20d. Capitalize proper adjectives.

A proper adjective is an adjective formed from a proper noun.

PROPER NOUNS	PROPER ADJECTIVES
England	English
France	French
Spain	Spanish
America	American
Rome	Roman

● EXERCISE 8. Number from 1 to 10 on your paper. List an appropriate proper adjective for each blank below. (Use a different adjective each time.)

1. —— language
2. —— industry
3. —— citizens
4. —— cheese
5. —— numerals
6. —— fried potatoes
7. —— shepherd dog
8. —— calendar
9. —— cat
10. —— tribes

20e. Do not capitalize the names of school subjects, except the languages and course names followed by a number.

EXAMPLES   Spanish, French, English, German
geography, home economics, general science
Geography I, Home Economics II

● REVIEW EXERCISE A. After you have reviewed the five rules for capitalization (20a–20e), read the following paragraphs and find the errors in capitalization. List in a column on your paper all words requiring capitals. When the capitalized words belong together, list them together: *Ohio River*, *United States Military Academy*. Number your list by sentences. Do not list words already capitalized.

EXAMPLE   1. Last saturday we shopped at Wilson's Department Store on east first avenue for school supplies.
1. **Saturday**
East First Avenue

1. Eric Graves thoroughly enjoys playing practical jokes on friends; he works at the delwood post office, which is next door to the greyhound bus lines.   2. Last wednesday morning at two o'clock, when eric got off the night shift, he went to the bus station and dialed our telephone number.

**20
d-e**

3. When I heard the telephone ring, I was sure that it was an emergency long-distance call, perhaps from my sick uncle who lives in sevier county in arkansas or from my cousin who was vacationing in the capitan mountains near roswell, new mexico.   4. Since our telephone never rings at that hour of the morning, i imagined all kinds of horrible things — maybe my honeymooning sister had fallen into niagara falls, or possibly my brother, who is attending yale university, had been rushed to a hospital for an emergency operation.

5. After he had stumbled in the darkness over our siamese cat and had knocked over Mom's morris chair, Dad finally reached the telephone.   6. later he told us that he was so worried about the possibility of an explosion at nuclear laboratories, inc., where he works, that it never occurred to him to turn on the lights.   7. his only thought was to answer that telephone.

8. "hello!" Dad boomed into the receiver at last. 9. "yes, this is the home of george cates; this address is 4602 brockton lane.   10. of course, i did!"   11. That was all i heard Dad say before he slammed down the receiver.

12. The next morning was thursday, thanksgiving day. 13. At nine o'clock, the family all piled into our buick station wagon for a holiday trip.   14. No one mentioned the telephone call of the night before as we drove along apache drive, crossed the pecos river, and headed for the davis mountains.

15. When we stopped at the norwood hotel for our thanksgiving dinner, however, Dad finally told us about the telephone call.   16. when he had answered, a man's voice (which, of course, was that of eric graves at the bus station) asked several questions as if trying to be sure he had the right number.   17. After this, the voice asked innocently, "did you have to get up out of bed to answer the phone?"

18. "of course, i did!"   19. Dad sounded like a cherokee indian on the warpath.

20. "o, i'm so sorry," apologized the practical joker in mock sympathy. "you go right on back to bed."

● REVIEW EXERCISE B.   Copy the following sentences, using capitals wherever needed.

1. after i had gone to the grocery store at the corner of thirty-first street and stonewall avenue, i stopped by the twin oaks lumber company, which is two blocks south of the main street in that area, cooper boulevard.

2. vacationing in the west, we saw electric peak, which is on the northern boundary of yellowstone national park; we also saw devils tower, which is in northwestern wyoming, before we returned home by way of sylvan lake in custer state park in south dakota.

3. mr. proctor lives in ardmore, carter county, oklahoma; north of the city is one of america's most interesting parks, platt national park, in murray county.

4. since i plan to study medicine at northwestern university, i'm taking courses like latin and biology in high school.

5. leaving ecuador in south america on a banana boat named *bonanza*, they went through the panama canal and sailed through the caribbean sea to nassau in the bahama islands.

6. my brother, a roman catholic, belongs to the newman club; he is a freshman in college, attending st. edward's university, which is a hundred miles south of here.

7. in the spring, usually the first saturday after easter, the ladies' missionary society, a baptist organization, gives a picnic for teen-agers.

8. at bethany high school, every freshman is required to take american history I in the fall and geography I in the spring.

9. while in washington, D.C., we saw the ford theater, where lincoln was shot.

10. later we drove along riverside drive and saw the lincoln memorial, which is on the banks of the potomac river in potomac park.

20f. Capitalize titles.

(1) Capitalize titles of persons.

EXAMPLES   Captain Taylor, President Matthews, Superintendent Davis

Do not capitalize titles used alone or after the person's name unless they are titles of important government figures or titles of other persons in very high
positions.

EXAMPLES   **S**enator **W**atson conferred with the **P**resident.
Bill Simons is **p**resident of the Science Club.
Mr. **Y**ates, the **p**rincipal of our school, knows
Professor Owens.

Names of official positions, such as *senator* or *mayor*,
are not capitalized unless used with a name or to refer
to a particular person.

EXAMPLES   **T**he race for **m**ayor was close.
Governor Raines offered the **M**ayor his support.

Titles that come before a name are always capitalized: *Dr. Jones, Mr. Black, Miss America.*

Words of family relationship (like *father, uncle, sister,
cousin*) are capitalized when used with a person's name.

EXAMPLES   **A**unt Jane, **C**ousin Harriet

Words of family relationship may be capitalized
or not when used in place of a person's name.

EXAMPLES   "Yes, **M**other." [*Mother* is used in place of the
woman's name.]
"Yes, **m**other."

When preceded by a possessive noun or pronoun,
words of family relationship are not capitalized.

EXAMPLES   "Yes, *my* mother will go."
Harry's father has been promoted.

EXCEPTION   When family-relationship words like *aunt* and *grandfather* are *customarily* used before a name, capitalize them even after a possessive noun or pronoun.

EXAMPLES   My Uncle Homer lives in Iowa.
You will like Mary's Grandmother Murray. [You customarily call these people *Uncle Homer* and *Grandmother Murray.*]

(2) Capitalize the first word and all important words in the titles of books, magazines, newspapers, articles, historical documents, works of art.

EXAMPLES   *Reader's Digest, Home Book of Quotations, Portrait of My Mother,* Bill of Rights, *Treasure Island.*

The words *a, an,* and *the* written before a title are capitalized only when they are part of a title: the *Saturday Review, The Education of Henry Adams.* Before the names of magazines and newspapers, *a, an,* and *the* are usually not capitalized in a composition: I was reading the Denver *Post.*

Unimportant words in a title are *a, an, the,* and short prepositions and conjunctions.

EXAMPLES   *A Connecticut Yankee in King Arthur's Court*
The Decline and Fall of the Roman Empire

(3) Capitalize words referring to the Deity.

EXAMPLES   God, Father in heaven, His will

▶ NOTE: The word *god,* when used to refer to the pagan deities of the ancients, is not capitalized.

   EXAMPLE   The poets of ancient Greece paid tribute to the gods.

20f

● EXERCISE 9. Number on your paper from 1 to 10. If the capitalization among the following phrases and sentences is correct, write a plus sign (+) after the appropriate number on your paper. If the capitalization is wrong, write the correct form.

1. mr. Arnett
2. *A Tale Of Two Cities*
3. my mother's aunt
4. elected president of her class
5. the president of the United States
6. among the pagan gods
7. My Aunt Clara taught me to respect god.
8. *battle of the centaurs*
9. my father and Senator Hall
10. *the Mystery of Edwin Drood*

● EXERCISE 10. Write 4 sentences of your own to illustrate each of the 3 rules for capitalizing titles (You will have 12 sentences in all.)

● REVIEW EXERCISE C. Copy the following sentences, and use capitals wherever needed. In this exercise apply all the rules you have learned in this chapter. Be prepared to give a reason for each capital that you use.

1. dr. reeves, speaking to the student body of lamar high school, advised all freshmen to read *how to win friends and influence people.*
2. on the sunday before labor day, we drove as far as the murphy motel, a mile west of salem, virginia; the manager, a mr. jones, told us he was a member of the virginia tourist court association.
3. waiting for a city bus at the corner of twenty-first street and hemphill drive, we admired the westlake shirts in henson's window display.
4. father and his brother, my uncle edward, told me about rockefeller center and about the shops on fifth avenue in new york city.
5. professor smith studied at the library of congress and the folger shakespeare library during july and august.

6. in *the world around us*, a textbook published by harcourt, brace and company, are many full-page colored illustrations.

7. i especially like the photograph — made by pan american world airways — of mt. mckinley, in alaska.

8. in his junior year at jonesville high school, uncle tom studied latin, french, english, geometry, and art.

9. "the gods of the pagans did not offer the hope that christianity does," rev. smith concluded. "our god promises immortality."

10. after the texans so bravely fought against the forces of general santa anna in 1836, the alamo became famous as the "shrine of texas liberty"; like the statue of liberty on bedloe's island, the alamo is a symbol of american freedom.

SUMMARY STYLE SHEET

GEOGRAPHICAL NAMES

New York *City*	a *city* in New York
Abilene *State Park*	a *state park*
Smoky *Mountains*	climbing *mountains*
Atlantic *Ocean*	in the *ocean*
Sixth *Street*	a narrow *street*
Mississippi *River*	a deep *river*
business in the *East*	the *east* wind
Eastern fashions	an *eastern* suburb
Lake Superior	near a *lake*

ORGANIZATIONS, INSTITUTIONS, BUSINESS PRODUCTS, SPECIAL EVENTS, CALENDAR ITEMS, RACES, AND RELIGIOUS GROUPS

Oakdale Garden *Club*	a *club* for gardeners
Reed *Moving Company*	a *moving company*
Chief *Theater*	a drive-in *theater*
Rosedale *High School*	a small *high school*
Biltmore *Hotel*	a good *hotel*
World War II	a *world war*
the *Colonial Period*	in *colonial times*

Memorial *Day*	Christmas *day*
English, French, Latin	*language, history, science*
History I, Algebra II	*history, algebra*
the *Senior Prom*	a *senior* in high school
August, December	*summer, winter, fall, spring*
Negro, Caucasian	
Roman Catholic, Presbyterian	

TITLES

Principal Wiley	Mr. Wiley, the *principal*
the *President* [*Senator, Congressman* — any high government official]	the *president* of the club, a *senator's* duties, a *governor's* signature
The Last of the Mohicans, Black Beauty, Alice in Wonderland	
New York *World*	
God and *His* universe	the *gods* of the ancients
Uncle Fred	my *uncle*
I miss *Father.*	Joe's *father*

CHAPTER 21

End Marks
and Commas

PERIODS, QUESTION MARKS,
EXCLAMATION POINTS, COMMAS

You can learn good usage by listening to acceptable grammar and by speaking correct English in your daily conversations. Spoken English, however, will not help you learn punctuation, which is used only in written language. In a conversation, for instance, you would never say, "How are you question mark" or "Oh boy exclamation point" or "I am on my way to the Smiths apostrophe period." Only *by mastering the rules* in this and the following chapter and *by applying these rules to everything you write* can you learn to punctuate properly.

End Marks

21a. A statement is followed by a period.[1]

EXAMPLES   Henry seldom reads his assignments.
             We did not think that it was going to rain.

[1] For an explanation of the kinds of sentences, see Chapter 2, pages 41-42. For the position of end marks with quotation marks, see Chapter 22, page 485.

441

21b. A question is followed by a question mark.

EXAMPLE   When did you arrive?

▶ NOTE: Distinguish between a declarative sentence containing an indirect question and an interrogative sentence which asks a question directly.

EXAMPLES   He asked me how I worked the problem. [declarative]
How did you work the problem? [interrogative]

21c. An exclamation is followed by an exclamation point.

EXAMPLES   Hurray! We won!
How it poured!

21d. An imperative sentence may be followed by either a period or an exclamation point, depending upon the purpose of the sentence.

EXAMPLES   Please close the door when you leave.
Close that door!

If you fail to use end marks of punctuation correctly, you do not know what a sentence is or where it ends. If you do not know these things, review Chapter 4 of this book, and do the exercises on pages 87–97.

● EXERCISE 1.   Copy the following sentences, inserting the proper end marks — periods, question marks, exclamation points. Begin each sentence with a capital letter. Whenever an end mark and quotation marks come together *in this exercise*, place the end mark *inside* the quotation marks.

When did I learn to swim well, I was only ten years old what a day sit down and make yourself comfortable I'll tell you all about it

It began the night Red Hopkins gave a party there were

four of us — Bob, Mac, Red, and I after playing baseball until it was dark and then wrestling with one another for almost an hour, we were really tired Red, of course, won at wrestling he always does steal the limelight from everybody else

That night was no exception when we were resting by quietly watching television, Red got up and barked, "Hey, you fellows" we wondered what he wanted to do next "Do you want lessons on how to swim get off the piano stool I'll lie on top of it and show you the way to do the breast stroke and the crawl"

While he was showing off, I thought to myself, "Creepers who does he think he is anybody can do that"

Arising, I approached Red and said, "Do you know how to do the trudgeon crawl or the six-beat stroke" he shook his head "well," I continued, "stand aside, please I'll show *you* how to swim" everyone enjoyed my performance — everyone except Red

The next day, however, Red enjoyed it when he found out from my sister that I couldn't swim a lick with loud laughter he asked Bob, Mac, and me to join him for a swim at Magnolia Lake that afternoon after school "Oh, no" I exclaimed "I can't possibly go haven't you heard about that arithmetic test tomorrow"

"Since when," he asked, "do you study after school we'll be back before dark, in plenty of time for you to study" I had no answer I had to go

As soon as we got to the lake, Red started in "all right, *now* you can *really* show us that trudgeon crawl what's the matter are you scared there's the pier go on and show us"

What could I do when I started to admit that I couldn't swim, Red yelled, "What's stopping you go on" my whole ten-year-old frame shook with anger I had no choice

While they watched, I raced down the pier and dived into water that was more than twenty feet deep imagine my joy when I found that I *could* swim I shouted, "Hey, I'm swimming" then everybody, even Red, laughingly praised my unusual "dog crawl" as I happily splashed about in the deep water

21 b-d

● EXERCISE 2. Write a paragraph of about 150 words telling of an interesting incident that took place in one of your classes recently — the time Helen was caught writing a note, the morning you worked a problem on the board and explained your solution to the class, the day you knew all the answers, or the first time you cooked bacon and eggs in home economics class. Use *all three* end marks several times in your paragraph. As you proofread, be sure that all end marks of punctuation are correct.

● EXERCISE 3. For further practice in using end marks, turn to Exercises 5–9, pages 91–97.

21e. An abbreviation is followed by a period.

EXAMPLES
N.J.	New Jersey
U.S.A.	United States of America
B.C.	before Christ
C.P.A.	Certified Public Accountant
E.S.T.	Eastern Standard Time
gals.	gallons
oz.	ounce

▶ EXCEPTION: Some abbreviations are written without periods. When in doubt, consult your dictionary.

EXAMPLES
ATS	Army Transport Service
CSC	Civil Service Commission
rpm	revolutions per minute

Commas

Like other marks of punctuation, commas are necessary for clear expression of written ideas. Notice how the comma affects meaning in this pair of sentences.

Did she finally marry Tom?
Did she finally marry, Tom?

If you fail to use needed commas, you may confuse your reader.

CONFUSING   My favorite cousins are Mary Jane Paul Jean Elizabeth Ann and Ted. [How many cousins?]

CLEAR   My favorite cousins are Mary Jane, Paul, Jean, Elizabeth Ann, and Ted.

Too much punctuation is just as confusing as not enough punctuation. Especially is this true with commas.

WRONG   Bill, is the best speller, in the freshman class, and will beat, Joe, In the contest, tomorrow.

RIGHT   Bill is the best speller in the freshman class and will beat Joe in the contest tomorrow.

Have a *reason* (either a definite rule or a matter of meaning) for every comma or other mark of punctuation that you use. When there is no rule requiring punctuation and when the meaning of the sentence is clear, do not insert any punctuation mark.

21f.   Use commas to separate words, phrases, and subordinate clauses written in series.

WORDS IN SERIES   **Sandwiches, fruit, candy,** and **cookies** filled the picnic box. [nouns]
Can you **act, sing,** or **dance?** [verbs]
It was a **rough, narrow, dangerous** road. [adjectives]

PHRASES IN SERIES   Those puppies play **on the back steps, in the flower beds,** and **under the house.**

SUBORDINATE CLAUSES IN SERIES   My parents are interested in **what I do, where I go,** and **how I behave.**

(1) When the last two items in a series are joined by *and*, you may omit the comma before the *and* if the comma is not necessary to make the meaning clear.

**21
e-f**

Some writers always prefer to use this comma, whether or not it is necessary. Follow your teacher's instructions on this point.

CLEAR WITH COMMA OMITTED   Sugar, coffee and celery were on sale last Saturday.

NOT CLEAR WITH COMMA OMITTED   We elected our class officers: president, vice-president, secretary and treasurer. [How many officers were elected, three or four? Does one person serve as secretary and treasurer, or are two people needed for separate jobs?]

CLEAR WITH COMMA INCLUDED   We elected our class officers: president, vice-president, secretary, and treasurer.

▶ NOTE: Some words — such as *shoes and socks, rod and reel, shampoo and set* — are used in pairs and may be set off as one item in a series.

     EXAMPLE   For supper we had ham and eggs, lettuce and tomatoes, and peas and carrots.

(2) If all items in a series are joined by *and* or *or*, do not use commas to separate them.

EXAMPLES   I bought him a tie and a shirt and a hat.

              Harry or Ralph or Walter can make the poster.

(3) When the last adjective in a series is thought of as part of the noun, the comma before the adjective is omitted.

EXAMPLES   He is a talkative, popular disc jockey.

              He is a popular disc jockey.

Like *movie star* and *orchestra leader*, *disc jockey* should be considered as one word. Since *popular* modifies the unit *disc jockey*, the comma is omitted before *disc*. (It would be as wrong to put a comma after *popular* as it would be to write *a jolly, Santa Claus.*)

(4) Main clauses in series are usually separated by semi-colons. Short main clauses, however, may be separated by commas.

EXAMPLE   **Firecrackers exploded, horns honked, whistles blew.**

● EXERCISE 4. Copy on your paper each series in the following sentences. Insert commas wherever needed. Before each series, write the number of the sentence in which it appears.

1. We caught catfish bass and perch.
2. Robert Browning says that youth is good that middle age is better and that old age is best.
3. She fluttered her long curled dark eyelashes.
4. It was an unusual attractive floor lamp.
5. Today's menu has pork and beans liver and onions and peaches and cream.
6. My little brother can read write add subtract multiply and divide.
7. Who won — Bill or Joe or Jim?
8. A wise monkey sees no evil speaks no evil and hears no evil.
9. Do you want French dressing mayonnaise or vinegar on your salad?
10. What is it that has eyes and can't see legs and can't walk and teeth and can't eat?

● EXERCISE 5. Number on your paper from 1 to 10. Think of an appropriate series of words, phrases, or clauses for each blank below; then write each series, properly punctuated, after the corresponding number on your paper.

1. —— are among my classmates.
2. We noticed —— all along the highway.
3. The —— movie star enjoyed the extravagant publicity.
4. Our teacher said that ——.
5. I want —— for my birthday.
6. The —— autumn leaves are beautiful indeed.
7. You can make high grades by ——.
8. I am taking three courses: ——,

9. At the party we —— for hours.
10. Young people enjoy television because ——.

● EXERCISE 6. Copy the following sentences, inserting commas wherever needed.

1. The stems roots and leaves of plants require nitrogen iron phosphorus and other minerals in order to grow to maturity to manufacture chlorophyll and to produce seeds.
2. I was especially proud of the beautiful polished wings of my glider model airplane; I made them out of soft light balsa wood.
3. Do you know that sulfur is used for manufacturing matches plastics paper and insect sprays?
4. On the surface of the moon are round deep craters and steep rugged mountains.
5. Meteorites that once struck the earth made similar craters in Arizona Russia and Canada.
6. A person living in the United States could expect to live 35 years in 1800 40 years in 1850 47 years in 1900 and 68 years in 1950.
7. New wonder drugs like penicillin aureomycin and terramycin have practically conquered pneumonia.
8. Mosquitoes sang crickets chirped and frogs croaked.
9. Our teacher told us that a normal person has many fears that he sometimes feels insecure and that he is often unhappy.
10. Whether he is dribbling a basketball swatting a home run or playing tiddlywinks, George has the marks of a real sportsman because he tries hard plays fair and smiles good-naturedly — win lose or draw.

● EXERCISE 7. Write 10 sentences, each one containing a correctly punctuated series, as follows:

2 sentences with a series of nouns
2 sentences with a series of verbs
3 sentences with adjectives in a series
1 sentence with a series of subordinate clauses
2 sentences with a series of phrases

21g. Use commas to set off expressions which interrupt the sentence.

To "set off" means to use two commas — one before an interrupting expression and one after it. If an interrupter comes at the beginning or at the end of a sentence, only one comma is needed.

EXAMPLES   Joe, of course, didn't answer her question.
Of course, Joe didn't answer her question.
Joe didn't answer her question, of course.

(1) Appositives with their modifiers are set off by commas.

An appositive is a word or group of words following a noun or pronoun and meaning the same thing. An appositive usually gives information about the noun or pronoun which precedes it.

EXAMPLES   We asked Mr. Johnson, our **teacher,** to solve the problem.
Homer, the **villain,** threatens to kidnap Nell.
May I introduce you to Mrs. Mills, my **neighbor?**

In these sentences, *teacher, villain,* and *neighbor* are appositives set off by commas.

When you set off an appositive, be sure to include with it all words which modify it.

EXAMPLES   I saw Mr. Sadler, *the* **principal** *of our school,* at the band concert.
Dora Watts, *the* **girl** *I told you about,* will be here tomorrow.

Sometimes an appositive is so closely related to the word preceding it that it should not be set off by commas. Such an appositive is usually a single word.

EXAMPLES   my sister Sarah
Alexander the Great
my cousin Al

21g

● EXERCISE 8. Your job is to punctuate the appositives in the following sentences correctly. Copy on your paper the word preceding each appositive, the appositive itself, and the word (if any) following it. Supply the necessary punctuation. Most of the appositives you list will need to be set off by commas; a few of them, however, will not need any commas.

EXAMPLE 1. My brother Bill discussed the brakes with Mr. Mays the owner of the garage and with Joe the car dealer.

1. **brother Bill discussed**
   Mays, the owner of the garage, and
   Joe, the car dealer

1. As I was telling Mr. Reed my neighbor the more I know relatives, the better I like friends. 2. Yesterday at dawn my family was startled out of bed by a loud explosion the dying gasp of my Uncle Jasper's car. 3. A few seconds later, we heard Uncle Jasper announce, "This is my brother Ed's address 1601 Jeffers Avenue. 4. Won't they be surprised to see us their loving kinsmen?"

5. Snorky my little cocker spaniel expressed our unhappy surprise by barking noisily at the intruders our uninvited and unexpected relatives. 6. Then High Voltage their Saint Bernard lumbered forward and tried to make breakfast out of Snorky. 7. Dad untangled the snarling animals and tied both of them Snorky and High Voltage in the back yard. 8. The dogs mortal enemies spent the rest of the day growling and yapping at each other.

9. That fight a minor incident was only the beginning of the turmoil at our house. 10. Wilbur Uncle Jasper's youngest boy took an immediate fancy to a hand-painted vase a treasured heirloom and dashed it to smithereens against the kitchen cabinet. 11. While Aunt Mamie was apologizing for Wilbur, Uncle Jasper was chasing Sylvester his oldest boy. 12. Sylvester, in turn, was chasing my sister Beulah in order to cut her hair with Mother's best sewing scissors.

13. Just before I left the house a building that we used to call home Uncle Jasper said, "We're going to spend our vacation a full two weeks with you."   14. To be polite to these wild parasites, we have to stay home all day and play boring games especially canasta and checkers.   15. Even our bedtime formerly ten o'clock has changed to midnight.   16. Since Aunt Mamie has insomnia a disease prohibiting sleep after 4 A.M. everybody gets up for an early breakfast.   17. My head aches when I think about the length of their visit a whole week and five long days.

18. A while ago, however, Mother a wonderful person smiled at my complaints.   19. "Take heart, Elmer my son" she said playfully "Remember that every relative has his day.   20. Our day will come on a Thursday in November Thanksgiving when we'll drop in on *them*!"

(2) Words used in direct address are set off by commas.

EXAMPLES   **Answer the doorbell, Ted.**
That program, James, goes off during the summer.
Miss Nelson, may I leave class early?

● EXERCISE 9.   Copy and correctly punctuate the following sentences.

1. Do you remember Helen what Romeo's last name is?
2. Mr. Chairman I move that we adjourn.
3. Please let me go to the show Dad.
4. Yes Miss Lawrence I will help you.
5. What is the answer to the riddle my wise friend?

(3) Parenthetical expressions are set off by commas.

Parenthetical derives from the word *parenthesis*. A parenthetical expression can be set off by parentheses (rarely used) or by commas. Expressions commonly used parenthetically are: *I believe* (*know, suppose, hope, think*), *of course, however, on the contrary, on the other hand, in my opinion, for example, to tell the truth, nevertheless, in fact, generally speaking*.

EXAMPLES   He did not**, however,** arrive on time.
            For example, tomatoes are classified as a
            fruit.

▶ NOTE: These expressions are not *always* used as inter-
           rupters.

    NOT USED AS AN INTERRUPTER   **I believe** that Mother
    is the best cook in town.
    USED AS AN INTERRUPTER   Mother**, I believe,** is the
    best cook in town.

    NOT USED AS AN INTERRUPTER   She was not interested
    in my opinion.
    USED AS AN INTERRUPTER   That story**, in my opinion,**
    has too much dull description.

▶ NOTE: A contrasting expression introduced by *not* is
           parenthetical and must be set off by commas.

    EXAMPLE   It is the spirit of the giver**, not the gift,**
    that counts.

**(4) Words such as *well, yes, no, why* are followed by a
comma when they are used at the beginning of a
sentence or remark.**

EXAMPLES   **No,** I have not answered her letter.
            Why, surely you haven't forgotten already!
            Well, have it your way.

● EXERCISE 10.   Find the interrupters in the following sentences. List each one, properly punctuated, on
your paper. Number your answers to accord with the
numbers of the sentences.

EXAMPLE   1. **For instance Jack Rogers in my opinion is con-
               siderate of others.**
           1. **For instance,**
              , in my opinion,

1. To tell the truth I have never seen a flying fish.
2. I do know however that some birds can swim.

3. No person of course can see everything in existence; everybody has to depend upon the word of authorities.
4. Well my father is I believe an authority about fish that can fly.
5. In fact he has seen a Catalina fish fly as high as twenty feet in the air.
6. Having large fins not wings this fish skips along the top of the water and then suddenly leaps skyward.
7. These fish generally speaking are about a foot or a foot and a half long.
8. Yes there are other animals that fly without wings.
9. Some squirrels for example can glide from one tree to another; they fly about at night not in the daytime.
10. On the contrary I am sticking to the truth; these squirrels use their tails as rudders and their skins as built-in parachutes.

(5) In dates and addresses every item after the first is enclosed by commas.

Enclosed means having a comma before and after.

EXAMPLES   **On January 2, 1958, I changed my address to 645 Commerce Street, Columbus 12, Ohio.**
On Monday, December 3, we drove to Kansas City, Kansas, to see the parade.

● EXERCISE 11.   Copy and correctly punctuate any of the following sentences that need commas. If a sentence is correct as it stands, write *C* (for *correct*) after the proper number on your paper.

1. In August 1957 I spent a week with Martha, who lives at 234 Oakdale Drive Birmingham 20 Alabama.
2. Were you in St. Louis during May or June in 1956?
3. This letter is addressed to Mr. M. K. Cranberry 4608 Cherry Blossom Lane Appleton Wisconsin.
4. Horace Mann was born in Franklin Massachusetts which is not very far from Providence Rhode Island.

5. The Constitution of the United States was signed on September 17 1787 eleven years after the Declaration of Independence was adopted on July 4 1776.

● EXERCISE 12.   Answer the following questions with sentences using correctly punctuated dates and addresses.

1. What is your mailing address?
2. How old will you be in January, 1978?
3. Where is your school located?
4. On what day and in what year did Columbus sight land in the New World?

● EXERCISE 13.   Below is a list of parenthetical expressions or interrupting elements. Use each one, correctly punctuated, in sentences of your own.

EXAMPLE   1. our new coach
                1. **The main speaker was Mr. White, our new coach.**

1. the umpire	6. Michigan
2. for instance	7. 1958
3. well	8. no
4. not a full glass	9. I think
5. however	10. on the contrary

(6) A nonrestrictive clause is set off by commas.

A *nonrestrictive* clause is a subordinate clause used parenthetically; it merely adds information not necessary to the main idea in the sentence.

EXAMPLE   Ted Davis, **who is a senior,** won first place.

In this sentence, *who is a senior* is a nonrestrictive clause set off by commas. The main idea is *Ted Davis won first place*. The subordinate clause is not necessary to identify Ted Davis and can be left out without affecting the meaning of the sentence. *Most adjective clauses which modify proper names are nonrestrictive and require commas.*

Carefully study the nonrestrictive clauses in heavy print below:

1. **The Empire State Building, which has 102 stories,** is the world's tallest building.
2. **I was very proud of my mother, whose talent and charm impressed everyone.**
3. **Tony Hodges, who is a professional athlete,** has won four trophies.

▶ NOTE: Not all subordinate clauses, of course, are non-restrictive. In fact, an adjective clause beginning with *that* is seldom nonrestrictive because it is necessary to the meaning of the sentence; therefore, it is not set off by commas. Notice how the meaning of a sentence changes when you leave out a necessary adjective clause:

I'd like to throw every hat that she buys into the garbage can. [I'd like to throw every hat into the garbage can.]

Freshmen who play hooky should be expelled. [Freshmen should be expelled.]

All buildings which were firetraps were torn down. [All buildings were torn down.]

If an adjective clause tells *which one*, then it is *not* set off by commas. Notice in the sentences above that *which were firetraps* tells which buildings, *who play hooky* tells which freshmen, and *that she buys* tells which hat.

● EXERCISE 14.   Seven of the following sentences contain nonrestrictive clauses; copy and properly punctuate these sentences. Three, however, are correct as they are written; for these, write *C* (for *correct*) after the proper number on your paper.

1. Bertha Jean Snodgrass who is my second cousin will visit me next week.
2. We take the Shreveport *Times* which has especially good comics.
3. Highways that have eight lanes are built for speed and safety.

4. You should know my father who likes to tinker with anything mechanical.
5. All girls who cut their hair short look gawky.
6. Theophilus Snead who has a short haircut looks gawky.
7. I attend Cottonwood High School which has an enrollment of 368.
8. All contestants who answer this very difficult question will win $64,000.
9. The hog-nosed snake which some people fear is not poisonous.
10. In *The Man of Feeling* which is a very sentimental story Harley who is overcome by his great devotion to the heroine falls dead upon hearing that his love is returned.

(7) A nonrestrictive participial phrase is set off by commas.

A participial phrase (see page 67) is a group of words containing a participle.

Nonrestrictive participial phrases, which are not necessary to the sentence, are set off by commas.

If you know how to punctuate nonrestrictive adjective clauses, you will find it easy to punctuate participles that are parenthetical. Both are used as adjectives, and both are set off by commas. The only real difference, as the following sentences show, is that the nonrestrictive clause has a subject and verb; the phrase, of course, does not.

NONRESTRICTIVE CLAUSE   Senator Stewart**, who was hoping for a compromise,** tried a filibuster.

NONRESTRICTIVE PHRASE   Senator Stewart**, hoping for a compromise,** tried a filibuster.

NONRESTRICTIVE CLAUSE   *Alice's Adventures in Wonderland,* **which was written by Lewis Carroll,** has become a classic.

NONRESTRICTIVE PHRASE   *Alice's Adventures in Wonderland,* **written by Lewis Carroll,** has become a classic.

▶ NOTE: Like the adjective clause, the participial phrase
is *not* parenthetical when it is necessary to the meaning of a sentence, or when it tells *which one*. Therefore,
commas are *not* used.

EXAMPLES   Senators **hoping for a compromise** tried
filibustering. [not all senators, only the
ones hoping for a compromise]
A book **written by Lewis Carroll** has become a classic. [not just any book, but one
written by Lewis Carroll]

● EXERCISE 15.   Copy and correctly punctuate the
following sentences.

1. Louis Pasteur working hard in his laboratory took time
out to treat people for rabies.
2. The "House of Tiles" built in Mexico City during the
sixteenth century is now famous as the "House of San-
born."
3. Their youngest child loved by everyone is not at all
spoiled.
4. My left big toe badly bruised by the blow began to swell.
5. Miss Danby trying not to smile offered to help us put
on the stage make-up.

● EXERCISE 16.   Many of the following sentences
contain nonrestrictive clauses or participial phrases
and therefore require commas. Some sentences, however, are correct. If a sentence is correctly punctuated,
write *C* (for *correct*) after the proper number on your
paper. If it is incorrect, copy on your paper the word
preceding each comma and place the comma after it.
Number your answers to accord with the numbers of
the sentences.

EXAMPLES   1. **The man who wrote the book is John Evans.**
         1. **C**
         2. **John Evans who wrote the book gave a talk.**
         2. **Evans,**
            book,

1. An adolescent likes to single out a hero who can dazzle the nation with his novel "brand" of crooning or acting.
2. This hero worship which adults sometimes say is a common "affliction" of teen-agers takes many forms.
3. For example, when Chester Crooner moans through a catchy ditty, his young audience reacting suitably to his sentimental singing swoons or gasps or faints.
4. During his reign which seldom lasts more than a year or two followers imitate his haircut or echo his coined expressions.
5. Soon, however, Two-Gun Gus from Gremlin Gulch blasting his way into the hearts of Saturday-night movie-goers steals the limelight from Chester who doesn't fake melodies on a broken-down banjo or wear a blue and red bandanna.
6. Within a few weeks, companies which specialize in "G.G.G. Bandannas" suddenly have a tremendous business.
7. Every young person who respects the latest fads wears a bandanna with the label "G.G.G." meaning "Gus, Gremlin Gulch."
8. Before long, Peery Musical Company performs a similar feat by manufacturing "Mi-Mi-Fa" banjos which have strings adjusted to the only notes Gus can play.
9. In time, though, even Gus must leave the stage to make room for someone who has patented a new brand of music that "sends" teen-agers.
10. In my opinion, the attention that young people pay to singing idols is more beneficial than harmful.
11. A youngster interested in novelty bandannas and banjos is not likely to be a statistic on the list of juvenile delinquents.
12. Dudley Pierce who lives next door to me is learning music so that he can play the piano as his favorite movie star plays it.

13. When the movie star that he admires fades into a has-been, the boy will not lose interest in music.
14. My final point which seems very sane to me is that hero worship is a necessary part of growing up.
15. A person who hurriedly tries to bridge the gap between childhood and adulthood nearly always feels left out and unsuccessful.
16. The main reason which is a very simple one is that it takes several years to bridge this gap.
17. A typical adolescent being entirely too old to play hopscotch and far too young to vote or join the army thinks he is just marking time until he finally does grow up.
18. Looking around, this adolescent filled with restless ambition sees successful actors and crooners.
19. He finds himself an idol that becomes a symbol for *Success* spelled with a capital letter.
20. "Someday," the youngster thinks to himself, "I may become the brightest star of all shining even more brilliantly than the one I now admire."

● EXERCISE 17. Copy the following sentences, inserting commas where needed. This exercise covers the use of commas with expressions which interrupt the sentence (Rule 21g).

1. When Mr. Key my geography teacher visited Barrow Alaska in January 1957 he found the temperature seventeen degrees below zero.
2. Well I do know that Ottawa not Montreal is the capital of Canada.
3. Joe will you write to me at 237 Candona Drive Athens Colorado?
4. That plant is I think an Indian fig which is commonly called a prickly pear.
5. On August 6 1945 the United States dropped an atomic bomb on Hiroshima Japan.
6. Yes I have seen the granite mountains of Acadia National Park which is on Mount Desert Island located east of Bangor Maine.

7. Please do not on the other hand overdo the decorations Henry.

8. I felt sorry for Silas Lapham a businessman who had suddenly become rich when he attended the party of the socialites in Boston Massachusetts; Silas confused by both gloves and wine makes many blunders that dismay the other guests.

9. There are many copper and iron mines in Borneo the third biggest island in the world.

10. Why in March 1957 my family left Hartsville North Carolina and moved to Highland Park a suburb of Chicago Illinois.

21h. Use commas before *and, but, or, nor, for* when they join main clauses.

A comma goes before a co-ordinating conjunction when a completed thought is on *both sides* of the conjunction. Do not be misled by compound verbs which often make a sentence look as though it contains two main clauses.

COMPOUND SENTENCE   **Nell is never afraid of the stage, and she always impresses an audience with her witty comments.**

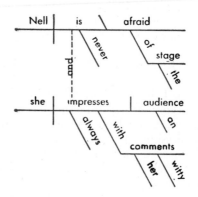

COMPOUND VERB   Nell is never afraid of the stage **and** always impresses an audience with her witty comments.

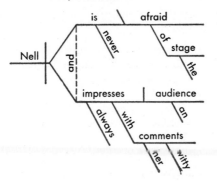

Study the following correctly punctuated compound sentences, noticing that main clauses (with a subject *and* a verb) are on both sides of *and, but, or, nor, for.*

Either the gift was lost in the mail**, or** he has forgotten to thank me.

Mr. Cooper will not buy another dog**, for** the eighty-year-old man does not wish to die and leave a brokenhearted pet behind.

Everyone was at the game**, but** Joe arrived an hour late.

He did not come to my birthday party**, nor** did he even bother to answer the invitation.

Into the garbage pail she flung the burned cake**, and** her mother helped her start another.

▶ NOTE: When the main clauses are very short, a comma is not required.

EXAMPLE   The lights were off **and** the door was locked.

● EXERCISE 18.   Many sentences in this exercise contain main clauses joined by the conjunctions *and, but, or, nor, for.* Do not copy the sentences. Number on your paper from 1 to 20. Decide where the commas should come, and write on your paper after the proper

21h

number the word preceding each comma; add the comma and the conjunction following it. If a sentence (perhaps containing compound verbs) is correct as it is written, write *C* (for *correct*) after the proper number on your paper.

EXAMPLES   1. Beaumont won the first inning by two runs but Houston was leading in the third inning by a score of 6 to 2.
   1. **runs, but**
   2. Fred whispered something to George and quickly left the stadium.
   2. **C**

1. The long drought that had crippled the farmers and ranchers finally ended for day after day the rain came down in sheets.
2. The beds of streams that had long been dry came to life and the caked soil became green with grass.
3. For a time the ranchers rejoiced for their cattle began to grow fat.
4. The smiles, however, soon faded into anxious frowns for the rains did not stop.
5. Small streams turned into raging rivers and the rivers became large lakes greedily engulfing the countryside.
6. Frightened sheep huddled on the hilltops and the carcasses of many fat cows floated down the rivers.
7. After more than three weeks of flash floods and torrential downpours, levees began to break and towns were demolished by the waters.
8. During one flash flood more than six inches of rain fell in my home town and left six feet of water in the city square.
9. Not only were places of business ruined as merchandise floated out broken doors and windows but several persons were drowned when their houses were washed away.
10. Soon the American Red Cross set up first-aid stations near the town and provided food and clothes for the homeless.

11. Neighboring cities began to chip in with their relief dollars and merchants pledged twenty per cent of their sales receipts for the Flood Fund.
12. The state legislature passed an appropriation bill of $30,000 to help the flood victims and the national government came forward with assistance for the disaster area.
13. Americans are always quick to help an unfortunate neighbor for they believe in the old motto, "All for one and one for all."
14. The people in my town courageously began the clean-up job and soon opened their stores for business.
15. At last the weather became more merciful and settled down to normal and the bright sun and dry winds came forth to challenge the angry streams and rivers.
16. Squads of rescue workers helped each rancher clear debris away or they helped farmers replant crops.
17. Civic organizations did not fail to anticipate a possible typhoid epidemic nor did they forget to combat the hordes of mosquitoes infesting the once-flooded area.
18. In spite of the tragic consequences of too much water too fast, the flood had good psychological effects for both farmers and ranchers could now hope for a big production for the first time in seven years.
19. They laughed as they gave credit to the new governor for breaking the drought or as they feigned dismay upon hearing someone mention the incoming "flood" of mail.
20. During adversity Americans face and conquer their problems and after calamity they can laugh their troubles into oblivion.

21i. **Use a comma after an introductory adverb clause, an introductory participial phrase, or a succession of introductory prepositional phrases.**

An introductory clause or phrase comes first in a sentence and precedes a main clause.

21i

INTRODUCTORY ADVERB CLAUSE   **After Alex had batted the ball over the fence,** the crowd screamed with delight and cheered him on to a home run.

INTRODUCTORY PARTICIPIAL PHRASE   **Pausing for a moment in the doorway,** the teacher smiled at the class.

SUCCESSION OF INTRODUCTORY PREPOSITIONAL PHRASES   **Near the gate at the end of the lane,** I watched the wild stallion race across the prairie.

A short introductory phrase does not require a comma unless a comma is necessary to make the meaning clear.

EXAMPLES   **In this state** we have a sales tax.

In this state, taxes are low.   [The comma is necessary to avoid reading *state taxes*.]

● EXERCISE 19.   The sentences in this exercise contain introductory clauses and phrases. Decide where commas should be used. Copy on your paper the word preceding each comma and place a comma after it. Number your answers to accord with the numbers of the sentences. Since 3 of the sentences do not require commas, you should write *C* (for *correct*) after these numbers on your paper.

EXAMPLE   1. **Hurrying down the aisle of the theater I stumbled into a little girl.**

1. **theater,**

1. Riding a plane bound for Kansas City last summer I met a very unusual author.   2. After we had introduced ourselves to each other he began to tell me about his writing.   3. Convinced that tension is the root of all personality disorders he made it his business to teach Americans how to relax.   4. After I had asked him several questions he said that our attitudes toward everyday problems affect our health.   5. "Living in the hurried atmosphere of a big city a man gets so tense that he barks at everybody and becomes a nuisance to himself," the author explained.

6. "After work he ought to take a nap; before work he should take prescribed exercises for relaxation; during the day he can eat crackers and whistle to get his mind off his troubles; at bedtime he should take a warm bath."

7. When I later told my father how to conquer tension he just sat silently and glared at me.   8. Watching his strange reaction to my newly acquired knowledge I suggested that he needed to sit in a tub of warm water and whistle as he ate crackers.   9. At last he spoke.   10. "If you say another word about relaxing I'll boil you in oil!" he stormed at me.   11. Undaunted by this outburst of temper I advised Dad to scratch between his shoulders for fifteen minutes.   12. In seconds his muscles would start tingling and thus relieve his nervous jitters.   13. Encouraged by his silence I told him that wiggling his toes could also reduce tension.   14. Just as I started to tell him about another exercise he started screaming for Mother.

15. Dashing into the room Mother seemed to know what was wrong with Dad.   16. In the next room for the last twenty minutes of our discussion she had overheard our conversation.   17. Smiling gently at both of us she ushered Dad out of the room and calmed him down.

18. Seeing that he was a nervous wreck, I later advised Mother to call a doctor.   19. Instead of becoming alarmed over Dad's condition she quietly told me why he was so upset.   20. Shortly after he had arrived home from the office he found that my sister Janie had been using his best pipe for blowing soap bubbles; when he had recovered from this surprise he learned that Mother had not only given away his favorite overcoat to a charity drive but had also paid $450 for a new squirrel cape for herself.

SUMMARY OF USES OF THE COMMA

21f. Use commas to separate words, phrases, and subordinate clauses written in series.

21g. Use commas to set off expressions which interrupt the sentence.

(1) **Appositives**
(2) **Words in direct address**
(3) **Parenthetical expressions**
(4) **Words such as** *well, yes, no, why* **when used at the beginning of a sentence**
(5) **Items in dates and addresses**
(6) **Nonrestrictive clauses**
(7) **Nonrestrictive participial phrases**

21h. Use commas to separate main clauses joined by *and, but, or, nor, for* **unless the clauses are very short.**

21i. Use a comma after an introductory adverb clause, an introductory participial phrase, or a succession of introductory prepositional phrases.

● REVIEW EXERCISE A. Write sentences of your own to illustrate the rules for commas listed above, as follows:

> 3 sentences illustrating Rule 21f
> 7 sentences having the 7 kinds of interrupters listed in Rule 21g
> 5 sentences with main clauses joined by *and, but, or, nor, for* (Rule 21h)
> 5 sentences illustrating Rule 21i

● REVIEW EXERCISE B. *Comma Rules* 21f–21i. Select from the following sentences all words which should be followed by a comma. List these words on your paper, placing a comma after each one. Number your answers to accord with the numbers of the sentences.

EXAMPLE   1. No Kate I did not talk to Mr. Huey the manager of the bookstore.
            1. **No, Kate, Huey,**

1. Well I like dates not prunes.
2. Some of the synonyms for *wit* are *humor sarcasm irony* and *repartee*.
3. I sold three tickets Bill sold four Martha sold ten and Hank sold twelve.
4. We looked everywhere for the keys — under the car in the house on the porch around the garage and among the weeds.
5. When we looked for them in the ignition switch however we found them.
6. This letter which is dated July 1947 is addressed to Mr. John Commander R. F. D. 3 Culver City California.
7. About ten o'clock on the morning of Saturday February 23 we entered the city limits of Hartford Connecticut.
8. Steve you know of course that Bill hates teas receptions and formal dinners.
9. We left Moravia which is a resort town in New York and we drove on to Owasco Lake which is near Syracuse.
10. Wanting to be noticed the baby jumped up and down in his crib and shook the railings and then he started whimpering piteously.
11. After I had broken the beautiful cup Mrs. Smith gracious hostess that she is assured me that she didn't mind but I am going to buy her another one just like it.
12. No Mother I did not do the dishes nor did I make the beds; I did however bake you a coconut cake for your birthday which is tomorrow May 25.

● REVIEW EXERCISE C. *End Marks and Commas.* Copy the following sentences, inserting end marks and commas as needed. (Whenever an end mark or a comma and quotation marks come together in this exercise, place the end mark or comma inside the quotation marks.)

1. Dennis do you know Alphonso Looney who has been a freshman for two years now
2. Well what a character

3. Although he practically never makes a passing grade his teachers like him and they are amused by his antics

4. In fact Alphonso has plenty of sense for he can find all kinds of short cuts on the rocky road to learning

5. Mr Poteet our conscientious hard-working English teacher tries to help Alphonso learn to punctuate but Alphonso dreaming about retiring from school at the age of forty hears only one sentence in a hundred

6. For example one day Mr Poteet trying to explain dialogue to the class said, "When you are quoting someone it is all right to use *ain't* and other grammatical errors Be sure however to use quotation marks"

7. "Yippee" yelled Alphonso "Chalk me up an *A*"

8. Can you guess what Alphonso did

9. Yes he started his composition with quotation marks and he ended it of course with quotation marks

10. After getting his paper back with an *F* on it Alphonso asked Mr Poteet a question

11. "Mr Poteet would you fail a composition if it had only one little tiny minor single error on it"

12. "Why no Alphonso you know better than that"

13. Smiling from ear to ear Alphonso responded, "Get ready to give me an *A* tomorrow"

14. "What next" exclaimed the teacher

15. Well believe it or not Alphonso handed in an attractive long impressive composition the next day

16. Before Mr Poteet returned the papers however he asked Alphonso to stay for a few minutes after class

17. After the bell had rung Joe and I being curious waited in the hall and we heard every word that they said

18. "Alphonso" the teacher droned, "you are an intelligent likable boy but you can't win by being lazy"

19. "Oh no" protested Alphonso vigorously "You know Mr Poteet I try hard to make good grades You surely didn't fail me again"

20. "Yes I did and you made only one error a very serious one You omitted all end marks of punctuation One thing more Alphonso before you leave" snapped Mr Poteet "You should work to learn not to make a grade"

CHAPTER 22

Other Marks
of Punctuation

Semicolons

A semicolon is part period and part comma. It says to the reader, "Stop here a little longer than you stop for a comma but not so long as you stop for a period." A stronger mark of punctuation than the comma, the semicolon can take the place of a period when it comes between two complete thoughts (main clauses) that are closely related.

EXAMPLE   Fred listened attentively to the joke. His half smile gradually changed into an ear-to-ear grin.
[two simple sentences]

Fred listened attentively to the joke; his half smile gradually changed into an ear-to-ear grin.
[one compound sentence with two main clauses]

22a. Use a semicolon between main clauses not joined by *and*, *but*, *for*, *nor*, *or*.

22a

469

Study the sentences below, noticing that each semi-colon has a complete thought on *both* sides of it and that the two main clauses are *not* joined by a co-ordinating conjunction like *and* or *but*.

> **The swimming pool looked cool and inviting; the boys raced toward the water like little pigs dashing toward a full trough.**
>
> **Yesterday morning I washed the dishes and swept the kitchen; then I went to the grocery store.**

When the thoughts of the main clauses are *very closely connected*, as in the sentences above, a semicolon is better than a period.

● EXERCISE 1. Read the following and decide where semicolons may be used. Copy on your paper the word before each semicolon, and write the semicolon after it. In some instances, you may prefer to use a period. If so, write the word before the period, the period itself, and the word (capitalized) following the period. In class be prepared to explain your preference for a period and to point out the subjects and the verbs of the main clauses.

EXAMPLES 1. **I'll never forget those bathing beauties by chance, Charles and I happened to be at Horton City Park last July 4, the day of the contest.**
      1. **beauties. By**
      2. **The girls walked gracefully along the platform the crowd clapped, whistled, and sighed its approval.**
      2. **platform;**

1. A woman suffers most when she is silent a man is most miserable when she isn't silent.
2. Anatole France's play, called *The Man Who Married a Dumb Wife*, illustrates this truth the story of the play is based upon an anecdote from the works of Rabelais.

3. If I remember correctly, the hero married a girl who could not speak she had something wrong with her tongue and was physically unable to utter a word.

4. For a time all was peaceful in the household of the newlyweds however, before long the husband grew lonely.

5. He longed to hear his wife's voice one day he decided to take her to a doctor to find out whether or not something could be done to get her to speak.

6. The doctor examined the young wife's mouth then he announced, "An operation may successfully free her tongue."

7 Overcome with joyful hope, the husband agreed to an immediate operation within a few days his wife had recovered and could speak as clearly as anyone else.

8. She could also speak longer and louder than her husband moreover, she soon learned to scold and to nag and to gossip.

9. Morning, noon, and night she talked and talked and talked her poor husband, growing frantic, went back to see the doctor.

10. "Please, doctor," he pleaded, "perform another operation to shut her up I want her back as she used to be — a silent woman."

11. The doctor had only this to say: "I'm very sorry I can't help her I can only recommend deafness for you."

12. There is, of course, a moral to this story no power known to man can stop a woman's tongue once it has started wagging.

22b. Use a semicolon between main clauses if there are commas within the clauses.

This use of the semicolon often helps to make the sentence clear.

CONFUSING	She will invite Mary, Betty, and Sue, and Tom will ask Eric and Steve.
CLEAR	She will invite Mary, Betty, and Sue; and Tom will ask Eric and Steve.

22b

CONFUSING   After the fire we found Mike standing in the middle of the lot, now covered with charred debris, and, looking tired and discouraged, he began to scrape through the ashes as if he were trying to uncover something of value.

CLEAR   After the fire we found Mike standing in the middle of the lot, now covered with charred debris; and, looking tired and discouraged, he began to scrape through the ashes as if he were trying to uncover something of value.

● EXERCISE 2.   Follow the directions for Exercise 1 as you decide where to use semicolons in the following sentences.

1. The quiet road, many miles from the main highway, went through the hills very hesitantly, and, at times, it seemed to disappear altogether under the bushes growing along it.
2. There were no houses nearby, but, seeing the remains of a few old rock chimneys, we knew that someone must have lived here many years ago.
3. After traveling about ten miles along this road, we noticed a small square area, which was fenced around with iron rails, and inside the fence, all overgrown with grass and wildflowers, were old graves.
4. A few of the graves, dating back to the early 1800's, had crude stone mounds on top, with traces of names that the elements had not yet scratched out, but others, having only two stones marking the site, had no names.
5. As we stood silently at this gentle place, we wondered what stories these people could tell about early settlements, about the hardships of pioneers, or about the terrors of the wilderness, for perhaps they once had trouble with the Indians.
6. The Comanches, according to our history books, once roamed this lonely area, and, quite possibly, some of these people died during hostile skirmishes.
7. We could not, however, get any answers from the stones, the grass, or the wildflowers, and, on our way back, the crumbled chimneys were silent, too.

PATTERNS OF PUNCTUATION

PATTERN   Main clause; main clause.

EXAMPLE   Hank made a touchdown during the last quarter; we won by a score of 6 to 0.

PATTERN   Main clause, { and / but / for / or / nor } main clause.

EXAMPLE   Hank made a touchdown during the last quarter, and we won by a score of 6 to 0.

PATTERN   Introductory clause, main clause.

EXAMPLE   Since Hank made a touchdown during the last quarter, we won by a score of 6 to 0.

● REVIEW EXERCISE A. *Semicolons, commas, periods.* Keeping in mind the patterns above, decide how to punctuate the following sentences. Do not copy the sentences. Instead, copy the word preceding your mark of punctuation, and then write the needed semi-colon, comma, or period. Number the groups of words by sentences.

EXAMPLE   1. If you will write to the company you can get a free sample of the toothpaste however, this offer lasts only until next Tuesday

    1. **company,**
       toothpaste;
       Tuesday.

1. Many of our customs have their roots in old superstitions for example, when you cover your yawns with your hand you are not only being polite but also paying respect to superstition

2. Men used to take devils very seriously these demons were very real and terribly vicious

3. Horned devils supposedly sat in trees or on high buildings and there they passed the time of day by shooting poisoned arrows into the hearts of the unfortunate men walking below

4. John Bunyan sometimes heard the voices of evil spirits and Martin Luther once threw an inkstand at one of them

5. Since the air seemed to be infested with hordes of devils many men believed that these imps would seize every opportunity to enter the body and corrupt the soul of a man

6. To yawn was to create the opening that the devils were seeking but if a person would cover the yawn with his hand he could stop the invisible invaders from entering his body

7. When someone sneezes in our presence we often say "God bless you" very quickly this custom is also based upon ancient lore about devils

8. Although a sneeze is no more than a noisy spray of moisture it seems to call for a special and an immediate blessing

9. Long ago men believed that demons were continually trying to put spells on people however, when a person sneezed he shook off the curse and thus deserved a blessing

10. Since it has to do with the expression "knock on wood" a third example of the relationship of customs to old beliefs is perhaps the most widespread practice of all

11. When my friend Lucy is very confident she often brags about something like never missing a word on a spelling test then suddenly she freezes with fearful anticipation of failure and adds quickly, "Knock on wood"

12. In order to be sure that she will make a perfect score on the next test Lucy finds a piece of wood and knocks on it vigorously to help her out I do the same thing

13. This custom hinges on an old idea that demons lived in trees now these devils would occasionally help a person by bringing him good luck

14. As Shakespeare's Iago tells us in plain language a devil has to *appear* good at times for otherwise he could not lure men away from right doing

15. These tree-dwelling devils were not fools they knew how to use "good luck" for their own evil purposes

16. They also expected men to perform certain rituals one of these was a kind of thanksgiving ceremony

17. When a man was enjoying a run of good fortune he was obligated to show his gratitude by knocking on a tree and the devils living inside the tree not only heard the thank-you knocks but also extended the period of good luck

18. After men had moved from the country to large cities no tree was convenient therefore, wood became an appropriate substitute

19. I imagine that our grandchildren will go on knocking on wood, blessing a person who sneezes, and covering their yawning mouths but these customs are rather foolish actions for men living in an enlightened age

20. They are far more illogical than the superstition about the ladder and bad luck when you walk under a ladder it could fall on you and break your bones and this is a power which is not within the reach of ordinary devils

Colons

The colon calls the reader's attention to what comes next. A colon means, "Notice the following."

22c. Use a colon after the salutation of a business letter.

EXAMPLES   **Dear Mr. Randolph:**
Gentlemen:
Dear Sir:

▶ NOTE: Do not use a colon after the salutation of a *friendly* letter. The salutation of a friendly letter is followed by a comma.

22d. Use a colon before a list of appositives or a list of items, especially when the list comes after expressions like *as follows* and *the following.*

**22
c-d**

EXAMPLES   The principal's desk was cluttered with all kinds of papers: **unopened letters, absence reports, telephone messages,** and **unpaid bills.** [appositives]

I have three hobbies: **sewing, cooking,** and **painting.** [appositives]

That summer we traveled through the following states: **Arkansas, Kentucky, Tennessee, Virginia,** and **North Carolina.** [list of items]

The equipment that you will need is as follows: **a light jacket, heavy boots, a rifle, several cartons of shells,** and **a sharp hunting knife.** [list of items]

▶ NOTE: Do not use a colon in a sentence like the following one, in which there is no pause before the series.

EXAMPLE   I bought bananas, avocados, and lemons.

22e. Use a colon between the hour and the minutes when you are writing the time.

EXAMPLES   7:45 P.M.
10:14 A.M.

▶ NOTE: A colon is also used to divide the numbers of Biblical chapters and verses:

EXAMPLES   Isaiah 25:1
John 3:16

● EXERCISE 3. Number from 1 to 10 on your paper. Decide where colons should be in these sentences. If a sentence does not need a colon, write *C* (for *correct*) after the proper number. If a colon is required, write the word preceding the colon, and then write the colon.

EXAMPLE   1. The crops grown in sunny semitropical lands are as follows vegetables, grains, grapes, citrus fruits.
     1. **follows:**

1. In science class we have to learn the meaning of the following words *amphibian*, *chromosome*, *neutron*, *oxidation*, and *vertebrate*.
2. Miss Thompson invited George, Harry, and Sammy.
3. The farmer explained the uses of the various parts of the plow landside, clevis, jointer, and beam.
4. Experts can identify a fingerprint by observing the nature of the following marks arches, whorls, loops, and composites.
5. At 10 45 the Sunday school teacher closed the lesson by reading Romans 14 12.
6. At 8 20 the agent told us that the 6 10 train would not arrive before 9 15 P.M.
7. Along the midway were several kinds of rides a roller coaster, a whip, two merry-go-rounds, and a Ferris wheel.
8. There were sandwiches, cold drinks, and candy on our television tables.
9. The results of the contest are as follows Joan wins the first prize; Everett, second prize; and William, third prize.
10. At an airport I like to listen to the many noises motors roaring before take-off, loud-speakers announcing departures and arrivals, passengers dropping quarters into insurance machines, telephones ringing at every counter, and skycaps greeting incoming passengers with "Take your baggage, lady?" or "Taxi, sir?"

Italics or Underlining

Italics are printed letters that lean to the right, *like this*.

When you are writing or typing, indicate italics by underlining the words you want italicized. If your composition were to be printed, the typesetter would set the underlined words in italics. For example, if you should type

Daniel Defoe wrote <u>Robinson Crusoe</u>.

the sentence would be printed like this:

Daniel Defoe wrote *Robinson Crusoe*.

22e

22f. **Use italics (underlining) for titles of books, works of art (pictures, musical compositions, statues), names of newspapers, magazines, and ships.**

EXAMPLES   <u>Romeo and Juliet</u>
<u>The Story of David Crockett</u>
the <u>Saturday Evening Post</u>
the <u>New York Times</u>
<u>Old Ironsides</u>

▶ NOTE: When written in a composition, the words *a*, *an*, *the* before a magazine or newspaper title are not italicized.

EXAMPLES   Our class reads the educational issues of the <u>Reader's Digest</u>.

Do you like the comics in the <u>Evening Post</u>?

ITALICS AND QUOTATION MARKS

Magazine articles, chapter headings, and titles of poems, when referred to in a composition, should be placed in quotation marks. Titles of book-length poems, of course, are italicized (underlined).

EXAMPLES   He assigned Chapter VIII, **"**The Food You Need,**"** beginning on page 125 of <u>Your Health and Safety</u>.

Have you read the short story called **"**The Ambitious Guest**"** in Nathaniel Hawthorne's book <u>Twice-Told Tales</u>?

"Figures — Freckles — Foresight,**"** an article in <u>Good Housekeeping</u>, is interesting.

22g. **Use italics (underlining) for foreign words, words referred to as words, and letters referred to as letters.**

EXAMPLES   <u>R.S.V.P.</u> means <u>répondez, s'il vous plaît</u>.
The word <u>existence</u> has three <u>e</u>'s.

● EXERCISE 4. List on your paper all words and word groups in the following which should be italicized. Underline each. List also those titles which should be enclosed in quotation marks. Place quotation marks around them. Number the word groups by sentences.

1. Christopher Columbus and his crew sailed on three ships: the Santa María, the Niña, and the Pinta.

2. Some foreign phrases, like faux pas and qui vive, can often express ideas more clearly than English words can.

3. I just got back my report on Wade's book The Boy Who Dared. 4. The margin is full of red ink saying that William Penn's last name has two n's, that the word hunky-dory does not adequately describe the author's style, and that I should cross my t's and dot my i's when I write my report on The Life of Andrew Jackson.

5. After her long lecture, Miss Reece asked me to comment upon the popularity of Beethoven's Moonlight Sonata and of Mozart's opera The Marriage of Figaro. 6. Since I had been studying It Pays to Increase Your Word Power in the Reader's Digest, I had not heard her lecture on musicians. 7. I had, however, just learned two new words, reverberate and venerable; therefore, I solemnly answered, "Their venerable melodies have reverberated through the centuries." 8. Upon hearing my learned comment, George, who had been reading the comic strip Peanuts in the Tribune, dropped his newspaper in amazement. 9. Stunned by my reply, Miss Reece began to mumble something about Michelangelo and the beauties of his Kneeling Angel and Youth Crouching. 10. After the bell had rung, she told us to become familiar with such books as Lives of the Composers and Artists and Their Art.

Hyphens

22h. Use a hyphen to divide a word at the end of a line.

If you will notice the right margins of the pages of this book, you can see that hyphens are often used to divide words at the ends of lines. *These words are always divided between syllables.* If you need to divide a word and are not sure about its syllables, look it up in your dictionary.

WRONG   He spoke, but it was obvious that he didn't reco-
        gnize me.
RIGHT   He spoke, but it was obvious that he didn't recog-
        nize me.

When you are typing a business letter or writing a formal composition, avoid dividing capitalized words. If a word (like *happy-go-lucky*) is already hyphenated, then divide it *only* at the hyphen. You should also be sure to carry forward to the next line at least three letters of a divided word.

AWKWARD   Today I had a long conference with Mr. Tem-
          ple, who mentioned Teddy, your new broth-
          er-in-law. Mr. Temple said that he was very in-
          terested in hiring Teddy as foreman.
BETTER   Today I had a long conference with Mr. Temple,
          who mentioned Teddy, your new brother-in-
          law. Mr. Temple said that he was very inter-
          ested in hiring Teddy as foreman.

● EXERCISE 5.   Suppose that you are considering dividing the following words at the ends of lines. Check your dictionary to find out about syllabication; then copy each word and use a hyphen to indicate where you would make the division. If a word should *not* be divided, write "carry forward" after the proper number on your paper.

EXAMPLES   1. monument
           1. **monu–ment (or mon–ument)**
           2. month
           2. **carry forward**

1. swimming	5. impartial	8. whose
2. method	6. French	9. questionnaire
3. panorama	7. Indo-Chinese	10. spectacular
4. special		

22i. Use a hyphen with all prefixes before a proper noun and with the prefixes *self-*, *ex-*, and *all-* before any noun.

EXAMPLES   un-American   self-denial
                     pre-Christmas   ex-president
                     ante-Victorian   all-American

22j. Hyphenate compound numbers from *twenty-one* to *ninety-nine*. Hyphenate fractions when used as adjectives.

EXAMPLES   **twenty-three** students
                    a **two-thirds** vote, but **two thirds** of the votes

● EXERCISE 6. In the following sentences 10 hyphens are needed. Find the words that should be hyphenated and list them, correctly punctuated, on your paper.

1. The exstudents hoped that the proposal would pass by a two thirds majority.
2. About three fourths of the club members are under twenty one years of age.
3. The expresident told us about events that took place during the preChristian era.
4. Elected as an all American quarterback last year, he now brags about being a self made star.
5. December and January have thirty one days, but February has only twenty eight days, except during leap year, when it has twenty nine.

● REVIEW EXERCISE B. *Commas, semicolons, colons, italics, hyphens.* After you have decided how each sen-

22 i-j

tence below should be punctuated, write each word preceding a mark of punctuation and its punctuation, and each word requiring italics and hyphens. Number the word groups by sentences.

1. An ounce of study according to my father is worth a pound of excuses.
2. Seed plants which differ from both mosses and ferns produce not only seeds but also flowers a list of common seed plants would include trees and grain oaks maples pines wheat oats and corn.
3. After I had finished reading a chapter called Acids and Bases in my textbook You and Science I used litmus paper to detect acids in juices and soaps.
4. Later in the morning at the library I looked through the Readers' Guide and found many short readable illustrated articles about acids.
5. The time for Easter varies each year for it is determined by the full moon that comes on or after March 21 the earliest possible date for Easter is March 22 and the latest day is April 25.
6. Although gas and water have weight they tend to have no definite shape for they are liquid not solid matter.
7. Paul does your Uncle Joe still live at 4206 Lynn Drive Tacoma Washington?
8. Miss Parker read us a story about Narcissus a handsome vain young man who fell in love with his own reflection.
9. Miss Hall our English teacher said that we were to read one of the following books by May 15 A Lantern in Her Hand by Aldrich The Wisdom of Father Brown by Chesterton Parnassus on Wheels by Morley or The Trail of the White Mule by Sinclair.
10. When it is 10 30 P.M. in Calcutta India what time is it in Honolulu Hawaii and in Chicago Illinois?
11. Mirages do appear in the desert but you can also see them when you look at a hot dry highway.
12. Since hot air often wiggles and grows dense as it rises it sometimes looks like water on the pavement.

13. Heat travels three ways by radiation by convection and by conduction.

14. Near Cairo Egypt are three large Pyramids at Giza is the Pyramid of Cheops one of the Seven Wonders of the World.

15. In the Pyramid of Cheops which covers thirteen acres are air passages chambers for the king and queen and an underground chamber.

16. Standing as monuments of the ancients these sturdy gigantic Pyramids have weathered the elements for more than forty eight hundred years.

17. No I did not know that Mrs. Crawford your grandmother was vacationing at Palm Beach Florida on January 2 1958.

18. If you are interested in the origins of words you might look up atom enthusiasm or jostle in Webster's New International Dictionary if on the other hand you wish to build your vocabulary you should learn the meaning of words like neophyte candor intrinsic and intrepid.

19. I think that a mermaid is half fish and half woman and I have heard that a sea horse is part fish and part horse to tell the truth I haven't had direct experience with either animal.

20. Although in the days of Queen Victoria men of good taste chose drab dark blacks and grays a man living in the twentieth century likes flashy bright gay colors he talks over yellow telephones rides on green automobile tires sleeps on red pillowcases and uses a set of dishes having every color of the rainbow.

Quotation Marks

22k. Use quotation marks to enclose a direct quotation — a person's exact words.

Do *not* use quotation marks to enclose an *indirect* quotation, which does *not* give a person's exact words.

22k

DIRECT QUOTATION Margaret said, "I am going to Trenton Saturday." [the speaker's exact words]

INDIRECT QUOTATION Margaret said that she was going to Trenton Saturday. [not the speaker's exact words]

▶ NOTE: Place quotation marks at both the beginning and the end of the direct quotation; omission of the quotation marks at the end is a common error.

(1) A direct quotation begins with a capital letter.

EXAMPLES Pat said, "The doors will open at 6:30."
Neil asked, "Should we go early?"
"The first feature starts at 7:45," she replied.

▶ EXCEPTION: If the quotation is only a fragment of a sentence, do not begin it with a capital letter.

EXAMPLE Known as the "advocate of brotherly love and low taxes," the candidate belligerently attacked every one of his opponents.

(2) When a quoted sentence is divided into two parts by such interrupting expressions as *he said, she replied,* or *Jerry added,* the second part begins with a small letter.

EXAMPLES "I believe," Nell said, "that you can save the dress."
"If you have a good idea," Joan replied, "tell me what to do about this bad scorch."
"Well, a hot iron nearly ruined the sleeve of my brown dress," Nell continued; "however, buttermilk and sunshine restored the original color."

If the second part of a broken quotation is a new sentence, it begins with a capital.

EXAMPLE "I'm sorry that I can't go with you," Mary apologized. "Thank you, though, for inviting me."

(3) A direct quotation is set off from the rest of the sentence by commas.

EXAMPLE "I believe," said our teacher, "that we can arrange to watch the state legislature in action next Friday afternoon."

(4) Other marks of punctuation when used with quotation marks are placed according to the following rules:

Closing quotation marks are always placed outside commas and periods.

EXAMPLE "The apple pie was good," she said, "but the strawberry ice cream was better."

Closing quotation marks are always placed inside colons and semicolons.

EXAMPLES Socrates once said, "As for me, all I know is that I know nothing"; I wonder why everyone thinks he was such a wise man.

The following aviators received medals of honor for "service beyond the call of duty": Wilfred Grant, Jacob Glasgow, and Hugh Dumas.

Closing quotation marks are placed outside question marks and exclamation points if the quotation is a question or an exclamation; otherwise, they are placed inside.

EXAMPLES Phil asked, "What time do you have?"

Is his motto still "Stay in the game and pitch"?

"Out of my way!" John yelled.

Don't tell me to "just be calm now"!

(5) Use single quotation marks to enclose a quotation within a quotation.

EXAMPLES Nancy said, "Then he remarked innocently, 'I was only trying to help.'"

Mr. Hughes answered, "The phrase 'world enough, and time' is from one of Andrew Marvell's poems."

22l. **When you write dialogue (two or more persons carrying on a conversation), begin a new paragraph every time the speaker changes.**

EXAMPLE   "My!" exclaimed Hildegarde in amazement when Mary joined her in the cafeteria line. "You really got yourself a haircut!"

"Yes, I thought I'd let it rest a while from permanents," Mary explained.

"It surely is stubby! Every hair is resting in a different direction."

"I can't do a thing with it. My hair looks the same before and after I comb it," Mary commented as she reached for a tray and silverware. "What would you do with it if it were yours?"

After a long silence, Hildegarde answered, "Well, if it were mine, I'd stay at home in the daytime and come out only after dark."

22m. **Use quotation marks to enclose titles of chapters, articles, poems, and other parts of books or magazines.[1]**

EXAMPLES   I need to review Chapter XIV, "Your Inborn Behavior."

His report summarized "The Road to Zerka" from *Time*, the news magazine.

● EXERCISE 7.   Write 5 sentences of your own to illustrate Rules 22k, 22k(2), (4), and (5).

● EXERCISE 8.   These two dialogues are designed to test your ability to use quotation marks and the other marks of punctuation used with quotation

[1] For the correct way of indicating titles of books and magazines, see page 478.

marks. As you copy each dialogue on your paper and insert quotation marks and other necessary punctuation, be sure to start a new paragraph with each change of speaker. If you should have difficulty working out this exercise, reread the dialogue under Rule 22l, page 486, noticing the end punctuation and the position of other marks of punctuation with quotation marks.

1

Those are odd sounds coming from Junior's room observed Dad, laying aside the evening paper. One! we heard Junior say firmly. Yeow squalled Hey Bag, our cat. Two snapped Junior. Yeow! Yeow squawked the cat. What on earth could be going on in there Mother asked as she and Dad eased toward the door of Junior's room. That's fine, Hey Bag. Now count to three, demanded Junior, simultaneously pinching the tail of the sputtering cat three times. Son! Stop that this instant exclaimed Dad, his every other word punctuated by the meows of the counting cat. Junior leaped to his feet and stroked the cat gently. School's out, Hey Bag! Come on, and I'll rob my piggy bank to get you some liver. Of all things! Dad continued to scold. Later that night, after hearing Dad's lecture, which Mother entitled Be Kind to Animals Every Day in Every Way, Junior promised, I'll never do it again, Pop. Never! Then, as a kind of afterthought, he added, Do you suppose Hey Bag and I can get a job with the circus when I grow up?

2

I don't know what I'm going to do with Junior, complained Mom. Dad raised his eyebrows. You don't? Well, what has that four-year-old been up to now? You know, Henry, Mom continued, that he believes everything we tell him. Yes, answered Dad impatiently. This morning, explained Mom, he asked me Who made us? I answered simply, God did. Dad breathed a sigh of relief. So that's all you're worried about! But that's not all, Mom hurried on; then Junior asked, Where is God? I answered, Everywhere. In the air? he asked. Yes, yes, I replied. Then I told him that he should go outside and play in the yard. That's nothing Dad assured her to fret about. Sit down and relax. Have another cup of coffee. Suddenly Junior's angry voice drifted into the kitchen. Stop! I said to stop! Going to the door, Dad observed, Why, he's only reading his picture dictionary quietly under the tree. Stop it, God, Junior said more firmly. How do You expect me to keep my place when You keep turning the pages? Looking very serious, Dad motioned Mother to the door, saying The wind was flipping the pages of his book; now the breeze has stopped. Thank you, Sir, Junior reverently addressed the still air.

● EXERCISE 9.   Write a page of dialogue that will show your ability to use quotation marks correctly. Perhaps you would like to retell a favorite joke in your own words and let the dialogue of the speakers (Mutt and Jeff, Pat and Mike, or Bonehead and Deadhead) carry the action forward. Better still, report the exact words of a real conversation that will entertain your classmates. You can get ideas for interesting dialogues if you will remember definite situations — for example, arguing about a play on the baseball diamond, apologizing for a social blunder, trying to make an escape from a chattering salesman, or mistaking a stranger for an old friend.

Apostrophes

If you are forgetting to use apostrophes in your compositions, start being more careful, because apostrophes are necessary for expressing your ideas clearly. For instance, there is a big difference in the meaning of *shell* and *she'll*, *its* and *it's*, or *shed* and *she'd*. To prevent mistakes in using apostrophes, study and apply the following rules.

THE POSSESSIVE CASE

The possessive case of a noun or a pronoun shows ownership or relationship.

OWNERSHIP   Bill's hat

                 my scrapbook

RELATIONSHIP   the man's sister

                 a day's work

                 his writing

Personal pronouns in the possessive case do not require an apostrophe:

my, mine	our, ours
your, yours	their, theirs
his, hers, its	whose

To show possessive case for other pronouns (like *one*, *everyone*, *somebody*, etc.) and for nouns, however, you need to use an apostrophe and an *s*, or in some words merely an apostrophe.

everyone's ideas	a man's job
somebody's pencil	David's cousin
nobody's fault	ladies' hats

22n. To form the possessive case of a singular noun, add an apostrophe and an *s*.[2]

EXAMPLES   Dad's car
the man's speech
Gladys's mother

[2] Many writers prefer to use only the apostrophe with words ending in *s*, but you will find the use of apostrophes easier if you always use the 's (apostrophe and *s*) with singular words in the possessive case, whether the word ends in *s* or not. Either way is correct.

22n

● EXERCISE 10.   Form the possessive case of each of the following words. After each word, write a related or possessed noun.

EXAMPLE   1. **Joe**
          1. **Joe's bicycle**

1. Ruth	3. Louis	5. anyone	7. Ed	9. child
2. boy	4. cousin	6. somebody	8. one	10. friend

(1) The words *minute, hour, day, week, month, year,* etc., when used as possessive adjectives, require an apostrophe.

EXAMPLES   a year's subscription
           a hard day's work
           this morning's paper

(2) Words indicating amount in *cents* or *dollars,* when used as possessive adjectives, require apostrophes.

EXAMPLES   a dollar's value
           a cent's worth

22o. To form the possessive case of a plural noun not ending in *s,* add an apostrophe and an *s*.

EXAMPLES   sheep's wool
           policemen's badges

● EXERCISE 11.   Correctly use the possessive case of these words in sentences.

          1. men   4. deer
          2. children   5. people
          3. women

22p. To form the possessive case of a plural noun ending in *s,* add the apostrophe only.

EXAMPLES   boys' club
           babies' toys

▶ NOTE: Do not use an apostrophe to form the *plural* of a noun. Remember that the apostrophe shows ownership or relationship; it is nearly always followed by a noun.

WRONG **Two girls' forgot their coats.**
RIGHT **Two girls forgot their coats.** [simple plural]

RIGHT **Two girls' coats are hanging in the hall.** [The apostrophe shows that the coats belong to the two girls.]

● EXERCISE 12. Revise the following phrases by using the possessive case.

EXAMPLE 1. the meetings of the athletes
         1. **the athletes' meetings**

1. a lunch for girls
2. absences of students
3. the shoes for boys
4. salaries of teachers
5. textbook for sophomores
6. duty of the voters
7. food for invalids
8. the work of actors
9. uniforms for nurses
10. spirit of the players

SUMMARY

Study the following examples of Rules 22n, 22o, 22p:

Singular	Singular Possessive	Plural	Plural Possessive
friend	friend's home	friends	friends' home
woman	woman's purse	women	women's purses
dog	dog's teeth	dogs	dogs' teeth
enemy	enemy's attack	enemies	enemies' attacks

● EXERCISE 13. On your paper make a four-column chart like that given above, using the words listed below. If you do not know how to spell the plural form of any of these words, use your dictionary. Add suitable nouns to follow the possessive case.

1. cousin
2. lady
3. girl
4. doctor
5. guard
6. milkman
7. jockey
8. umpire
9. child
10. actress

22
o-p

● EXERCISE 14.   List on your paper the words requiring apostrophes in the following sentences. After each word with an apostrophe, write the noun following it. Before each word group, write the number of the sentence in which it appears. Remember that only plural words ending in *s* require just an apostrophe.

EXAMPLE   1. The principals criticism of several boys behavior was justified.
   1. **principal's criticism**
      boys' behavior

1. A womans love for souvenirs is often the topic of mens conversations.   2. Last night the main topic of our crowds conversation was Margaret Smiths strange assortment of keepsakes.

3. The other day after class, disregarding her history teachers amazement, Margaret lined up four souvenirs across the top of Mr. Hortons desk.

4. "Although all of my friends billfolds are often empty," she told Mr. Horton, "I'll always have this dollar with me, the one with Mortimers name written across George Washingtons forehead.   5. At his sisters birthday party two years ago, Mortimer promised to buy me a chicken dinner at Harrys Café.   6. Because of a great-aunts death in Idaho, however, Mortimer, obeying his familys wishes, had to go spend the summer with his great-uncle."

7. "Did he, with a gentlemans respect for a promise, give you the dollar for the dinner?" Mr. Hortons question was answered by Margarets quiet smile and by several classmates loud laughter.

8. Pointing to another treasured souvenir, Margaret went on, "Now this is a bottle of perfume, which Patsys cousin gave me last December."   9. She sighed dreamily and continued, "That chunk of rock, lying by Henrys elbow, is a piece of 'fools gold,' which my two brothers hogs rooted out of the mud near our cow pond."

10. When Margaret started relating the history of a piece of garlic, Mr. Hortons interest lagged; he told her to pack up her souvenirs and to be on time for her next class.

22q. **In compound words, names of business firms, and words showing joint possession, only the last word is possessive in form.**

COMPOUND WORDS   mother-in-law's house
nobody else's business

BUSINESS FIRMS   Davis and Smith's Hardware Store
Wizard Freight Company's trucks

JOINT POSSESSION   Bill and Tom's motorboat
Ann and Sue's room

22r. **When two or more persons possess things individually, each of their names is possessive in form.**

EXAMPLE   Ann's and Sue's blouses

● EXERCISE 15. Copy and correctly punctuate the following phrases. If a phrase does not need an apostrophe, write *C* (for *correct*) after the appropriate number on your paper.

1. Hals car keys
2. the keys to the car
3. a freshmans ideas
4. the firemens dance
5. an hours drive
6. forty cents worth
7. worth forty cents
8. letters from friends
9. several friends advice
10. Al and Bills bicycle
11. a months salary
12. last weeks *Post*
13. a six weeks vacation
14. Jims and Eds posters
15. Randolph Companys sale
16. the boys at school
17. childrens wisdom
18. from the mouths of babes
19. in two years time
20. two girls suggestions

● EXERCISE 16. List in order on your paper all words requiring apostrophes. After each word with an apostrophe, write the thing possessed or related. Number your list by sentences.

**22
q-r**

1. One Saturday night, while I was waiting for a bus in front of Millers Shoe Store, I watched two little boys selling the next mornings paper. 2. One boys name was Leonard, and the others name was Cleve.

3. "Read tomorrows news tonight!" yelled Leonard. 4. "Read all about Colorados blizzard, the mayors operation, and the Charity Funds progress!" 5. All the while, Cleve was silently watching the suns disappearance behind dark clouds overhead; he made no effort to catch a customers attention. 6. Leonards yelling, however, was not getting much better results than Cleves silence; neither boy had sold one of the Cloverville Publishing Companys newspapers. 7. In fact, every passer-by rushed past the two boys newsstand as though he were both deaf and blind.

8. Angry because of his partners attitude, Leonard scolded, "Cleve, are you going back to Mr. Longs office without selling any of the companys papers? 9. A mans job out here is to advertise each days news and to sell at least three dollars worth in an hours time." 10. Cleves face was still turned upward; he seemed as indifferent as a jalopys spark plugs when the battery groans dead.

11. Walking back and forth at the traffic light, Leonard waved his papers under cab drivers noses and pedestrians chins. 12. Trying to get the peoples interest, he bellowed, "Read about your citys new crime wave! 13. Buy your childrens favorite comics — Happy Homers adventures and Supermans victories!" 14. The boys words sold only thirty cents worth of news; no one cared about "tomorrows news tonight."

15. After a few minutes, when it began to rain, Leonards hopes for good sales completely vanished. 16. But Cleves hopes were high! 17. Dashing forward, he had in an instant the full attention of every passer-bys eyes and ears. 18. "Step right this way, folks," he barked. "Umbrellas for sale! Buy yourselves fifteen cents worth of umbrella. 19. These eight sections of Sundays paper can cover your heads!" 20. In ten minutes time, Leonard and Cleves newsstand had sold out, and two very wet little boys were happily racing toward Mr. Longs office.

CONTRACTIONS

22s. Use an apostrophe to indicate where letters have been left out in a contraction.

A contraction is a word made up of two words combined into one by omitting one or more letters. Notice how words can be contracted (shortened) by the use of the apostrophe to show where letters are left out.

EXAMPLES   **He is not** here.   **He isn't** here.
                 They will miss the bus.   **They'll** miss the bus.
                 I had won the game.   **I'd** won the game.

Ordinarily, the word *not* is shortened to *n't* and added to a verb without any change in the spelling of the verb:

is not	isn't	were not	weren't
are not	aren't	has not	hasn't
does not	doesn't	have not	haven't
do not	don't	had not	hadn't
did not	didn't	would not	wouldn't
was not	wasn't	should not	shouldn't

When the *n't* is added to *shall, will,* or *can,* however, there is a change in spelling:

        will not   won't [*o* replaces the *ill*]
        shall not   shan't [the *ll* is dropped]
        cannot   can't [one *n* is left out]

A second kind of commonly used contraction joins shortened verbs or verb helpers to nouns or pronouns, as follows:

they are	they're	Joe will	Joe'll
I am	I'm	we shall	we'll
it is	it's	you have	you've
who is	who's	they had	they'd
that is	that's	she would	she'd

Other useful contractions are:

        let us   let's
        of the clock o'clock

22s

● EXERCISE 17. Study the contractions on page 495 so that you will be able to write any 25 of them correctly when your teacher dictates to you. Each time you write a contraction, be sure to use the apostrophe exactly where the letters are left out.

● EXERCISE 18. Copy the following sentences, using apostrophes wherever needed.

1. After schools out, shell mow Mr. Smiths yard.
2. Shed already mended Pauls shirt.
3. Mr. Cook hadnt met all of the girls mothers.
4. I didnt know that he doesnt like ice cream.
5. Lets drive by Tommys Drugstore to see whether or not theyre there.
6. This holidays death count is a result of drivers high speed and carelessness.
7. Dadll be home by four oclock.
8. Cant you understand Poes poems?
9. Ellen wont listen to those boys advice.
10. Dont buy two dollars worth of that cheese.

ITS AND IT'S

The word *its* (meaning "belonging to or related to *it*") is the possessive form of the personal pronoun *it*. As you know, personal pronouns — like *its*, *his*, *yours* — never have apostrophes in their possessive forms.

EXAMPLE **The canary does not know its name.**

The word *it's* is a contraction of *it is*. The apostrophe takes the place of an omitted letter.

EXAMPLE **It's time to go.**

● EXERCISE 19. Write 10 original sentences with *its* and *it's*, using each word correctly at least 5 times.

WHOSE AND WHO'S

Like *its,* the pronoun *whose* is in the possessive case and does not have an apostrophe.

EXAMPLE   **Whose** name did you draw?

The word *who's* is a contraction of *who is* or *who has.* The apostrophe shows where the omission occurs.

EXAMPLES   **Who's** going to the party?
I do not know **who's** been here.

● EXERCISE 20. Try to make a perfect score on this exercise, which gives you practice in the use of *its* and *it's* as well as *whose* and *who's.* Number on your paper from 1 to 20. Choose the correct word in parentheses, and write it after the corresponding number on your paper. Be able to explain why your answers are right.

1. (*It's, Its*) is a contraction of *it is.*
2. (It's, Its) beginning to snow.
3. (*Who's, Whose*) is a contraction of *who is* or *who has.*
4. (Who's, Whose) that attractive girl?
5. (Who's, Whose) girl is she?
6. (It's, Its) blade is very dull.
7. The kitten started washing (it's, its) face.
8. I don't know (who's, whose) pencil this is.
9. I'm sure that the organization will solve (it's, its) problems.
10. Did he say that (it's, its) the right answer?
11. Our class should make (it's, its) wishes known.
12. Why, (it's, its) not ten o'clock yet!
13. I kept watching the acrobat, (who's, whose) stunts delighted the crowd.
14. The hostess will introduce Betty Owens, (who's, whose) won national recognition as a swimmer.
15. (Who's, Whose) responsible for this equipment?
16. (Who's, Whose) been tampering with my chemistry set?
17. I'm glad that (its, it's) all over now.

18. The team was proud of (its, it's) four runs.
19 Mr. York, (whose, who's) just returned from France, is an interesting speaker.
20. Mrs. Parker, (whose, who's) husband is a senator, takes part in many community activities.

22t. Use the apostrophe and *s* to form the plural of letters, numbers, and signs, and of words referred to as words.

EXAMPLES   The word *grammar* has two *r*'s, two *a*'s, and two *m*'s.

Grades on this test ran from the lower 70's to the upper 90's.

Circling the &'s in my composition, the teacher said to spell out all *and*'s.

● EXERCISE 21. Number from 1 to 10 on your paper. Correctly form the plural of each of the following italicized items:

1. learning his *ABC*
2. cross your *t*
3. no *if* about it
4. + and −
5. *p* and *q*

6. making *F*
7. to pronounce the *r*
8. the early *1950*
9. no *6* or *7* in the answer
10. his *oh* and *ah*

● REVIEW EXERCISE C. *All uses of the apostrophe.* List in order the words requiring apostrophes below. Be sure that you insert the apostrophes exactly where omissions occur in contractions and after the *s* in plural words. Number your list by sentences.

EXAMPLE   1. A cars performance depends largely upon the owners attention to needed repairs; some manufacturers guarantees cover the cost of replacing defective parts.

1. **car's
owner's
manufacturers'**

1. Ive just finished todays assignment. 2. After two hours hard work, Im not through revising it, although I have taken time to dot my *i*s and cross my *t*s. 3. Now Ill need to go back and strike out some *and*s and *so*s. 4. If Id follow my English teachers instruction, Id also add action verbs to replace too many weak *were*s. 5. Its a job to write a composition on "My Familys Most Remarkable Character."

6. My papers purpose is to describe my mothers main characteristics. 7. To begin with, shes remarkably unselfish as she looks after her two boys needs and helps solve her husbands problems. 8. Its not easy at our home to keep everything going along smoothly, but shes always on the job. 9. If the boys fireworks on July 4 or their ball games in the back yard bring in dozens of complaints, shell manage somehow to restore the neighborhoods peace.

10. One day a neighbor, whose blatant voice on the telephone would have frightened anybody elses parent, didnt ruffle my mothers feathers a bit. 11. He stormed, "Those boys voices wont let a mans wife get even a few minutes rest!"

12. "Oh, Mr. Pugh," Mother answered sweetly, "I hope you havent finished your lunch. Why, its barely twelve oclock. 13. Id just started over to take you a piece of coconut cake that Ive made according to your mother-in-laws favorite recipe." 14. Naturally, this neighbors objections to the boys voices were quickly squelched by Mothers kindness. 15. "Ill be over in half an hours time." 16. To make her promise good, Mother dashed over to Graves and Lacys bakery to buy a coconut cake.

17. My mother, whos known for her one-track mind, has had many narrow escapes. 18. For example, one night without a moments notice, she had to drive to St. Louiss main terminal within forty-five minutes. 19. Driving over loose gravel on the dark highway, Mother didnt think about anything except, "Its almost time for my only nephews train to arrive." 20. When the cars wheel hit a pile of gravel and swerved into the ditch, narrowly missing a telephone pole, Mothers only thought was this: "I didnt remember

221

to put the steak out to thaw, and Im wondering whether or not my sisters boy will eat last nights meat loaf."

● REVIEW EXERCISE D. *All marks of punctuation and capitals.* Copy and correctly punctuate the following sentences, using capital letters wherever needed.

1. After Chapter XXI is a section entitled living things as a hobby in this chapter is a discussion of *invertebrate* (spelled with three *e*s) animals which means those animals that have no backbones the sponge and jellyfish which live in the ocean are classified as invertebrate

2. While swimming off padre Island in the gulf of mexico last summer were you ever stung by a jellyfish beneath their bloated bodies are many tentacles these waving dangerous arms have stinging cells that corner strike and paralyze tiny unsuspecting animals which are then sucked up into the jellyfishs mouth and eaten

3. Have you ever examined the inside of a camera one that takes ordinary snapshots well you should lets take a look right now at mine its unloaded when I click the shutter watch this circular hole that lets in light notice that it changes its shape after ive opened the time exposure you see george that little hole governs the light that reaches the film inside the camera if you let in too much sunlight your snapshot will be too dark if you dont let in enough light your picture will be entirely too dim you should learn more about photography its not only an interesting hobby but also a real art

4. According to Mr. Hall my science teacher the invention of the steam engine started a world-wide revolution now known as the industrial revolution recognizing the power of expanding steam james watt a british scientist used the steams energy to move a piston this moving piston forced a flywheel into action because sliding valves kept fresh steam rushing toward the piston watt was able to keep the flywheel spinning other scientists soon began to look to steam not to horses for power and they started inventing different types of engines these inventions led to a major revolution of industries everywhere

● REVIEW EXERCISE E. *All marks of punctuation.*
Copy and correctly punctuate the following sentences.

1. Believing in the virtues of self government our fore-
   fathers fought for these rights life liberty and the pursuit of happiness

2. Bob Evans sailing over the last hurdle easily won the
   race Fred Evans his brother came in a slow second

3. Hurrah shouted David I knew youd make it Bob When
   are you heading for the Olympics

4. Ellen is knitting her first jacket a pink light wool one
   with no sleeves whatever

5. Well he does I believe still live at 268 Fairway Lane
   Des Moines Iowa

6. Fathers Day comes on the third Sunday in June and
   Mothers Day comes on the second Sunday in May

7. Chester dreams of working at the Brookhaven National
   Laboratory at Upton Long Island New York

8. Ive carefully studied Chapter 21 End Marks and
   Commas and Chapter 22 Other Marks of Punctuation
   therefore I use commas for appositives and for series
   quotation marks to enclose titles of chapters and semicolons to separate main clauses not joined by but and
   or for nor

9. Jimson weed was named after Jamestown Virginia
   and wistaria vines were named after Caspar Wistar an
   anatomist

10. A devilfish doesnt have a forked tail and a sand dollar
    wont buy a chocolate soda but an electric eel can
    shock you

CHAPTER 23

Spelling

WAYS TO LEARN TO SPELL

Are you the kind of student who shrugs his shoulders and dismisses the subject of spelling with "I just can't spell — never could"? Do you believe (as you misspell one word six different ways) that a good speller is mysteriously blessed with some divine talent? Do you look upon your own inability to spell as a "natural" deficiency, and then resign yourself to living with it as best you can? If your answer to these questions is *yes*, you obviously don't *want* to learn to spell — at least not enough to do something about it.

The truth is that work is the key to becoming a good speller, and everyone has to work at spelling words correctly. If you are willing to make the effort, you can become a good speller. No one else can be of much help to you. Learning to spell is your own personal responsibility.

1. *Keep a "spelling page" in your notebook.*

Whenever you misspell a word on a paper *in any course*, find out immediately how to spell that word correctly. Then list it on your "spelling page" in your notebook. Although this method of learning to spell does take time, it will not in the long run take as much time as you will use later trying to learn the same word after you have misspelled it for years. Getting rid of the error then would be as hard as getting rid of a bad habit. If, on the other hand, you will pick up a word as soon as you stumble on it, it will never become a big boulder in your path to good spelling.

One way to record your words is to prepare a spelling page with four columns. In the first column, correctly spell the word you missed. (Never enter a misspelled word on your spelling page.) In the second column, write the word again, this time divided into syllables. In the third column, write the word once more, circling the spot that gives you trouble. In the fourth column, give the reason for your mistake, or set down any comment that will help you to learn the word. (Do not clutter up your spelling page by listing the same word over and over. List each word only once, and then concentrate on learning it.)

EXAMPLE

probably	prob′a·bly	pr⊘bab⊘ly	**Pronounce correctly.**
usually	u′su·al·ly	usu⊘lly	*usual* + *ly* **(Study Rule 23c.)**
tragedy	trag′e·dy	tra⊘ged⊘y	**Keep** *g* **and** *d* **straight;** *tragedy* **has** *rage* **in it.**

2. *Get the dictionary habit.*

If you keep an accurate spelling page (the only kind that is of any value), you will need to look up your misspelled words in the dictionary. Don't guess about the right spelling. After all, you have already used your best guess and have missed the word; and a second stab in the dark can lead only to a further distortion of the word. Play safe by using your dictionary. The very experience of looking up the word helps you to fix the word in your mind so that you will remember it longer.

As you no doubt know, however, looking a word up in the dictionary is sometimes not so easy as it sounds. For instance, if you have no idea about how to begin a word (like *pneumonia*, *chihuahua*, or *physique*), you may wear out yourself and your dictionary before you can find it. Whenever you have to spend more than three minutes searching for such a word, ask your teacher how it begins. Then, with your open dictionary before you, learning to spell the rest of the word will be easy, downhill work.

3. *Proofread your papers before handing them in.*

Proofreading is the process of rereading carefully in order to catch any errors that you have written. Although it takes only a few minutes, it makes a great difference in the correctness of your work.

As you proofread and look for spelling errors, be sure to eliminate all botchy handwriting. When, for example, you carelessly dot closed *e*'s, make your *o*'s look like *a*'s and your *g*'s like *q*'s, or hurriedly write over letters to make your teacher guess how you meant to spell the word, you will make twice as many spelling errors as you would if you were more careful about your handwriting.

4. *Learn to spell by syllables.*

A syllable is a word part which can be pronounced by itself. For instance, the word *thor′ough* has two syllables; the word *sep′a·rate* has three syllables; the word *par·tic′u·lar* has four syllables.

When you divide a long word into its syllables, you are really making a number of shorter words out of it (these shorter words may have no meaning by themselves), and since short words are easy to spell, you make spelling easier. The word *characteristic*, for example, is a long word that may prove hard to spell unless you can divide it into syllables. Then it becomes much easier: *char'ac·ter·is'tic.*

Look up the following words in your dictionary, and divide each one into syllables. Pronounce each syllable correctly, and learn to spell the word by syllables.

1. quiet	5. apparent	9. acquaintance
2. fascinate	6. similar	10. awkward
3. candidate	7. benefit	11. existence
4. temperature	8. definition	12. beautiful

5. *Learn to pronounce words correctly.*

Since you often spell words according to the way you pronounce them, mispronunciation causes misspelling. For instance, if you say *mis·chie'vi·ous* instead of *mis'chie·vous,* you will spell the word incorrectly by adding an extra syllable. Again, if you say *gov'er·ment* instead of the correct *gov'ern·ment,* you will leave out an important letter.

Below is a list of words commonly misspelled because of mispronunciation. (For a list of other words often mispronounced, see pages 352–53.) Carefully study the correct pronunciation. In class, practice saying these words under the guidance of your teacher.

athlete ăth'lēt	library lī'brĕr'ĭ
boundary boun'dȧ·rĭ	mathematics măth'ē·măt'ĭks
everybody ĕv'ĕr·ĭ·bŏd'ĭ	prepare prē·pâr'
environment ĕn·vī'rŭn·mĕnt	recognize rĕk'ŏg·nīz
identity ī·dĕn'tĭ·tĭ	than ~~th~~ăn
introduce ĭn'trō·dūs'	then ~~th~~ĕn
just jŭst	umbrella ŭm·brĕl'ȧ

6. *Use your ears, eyes, and pencil when learning to spell a word.*

When you try to master the correct spelling of a word, there are three steps you should take.

First, *pronounce the word*, noting its syllables. As you know, thinking of a word syllable by syllable makes the spelling easier.

Second, *study the word*, noticing especially any letters which might make the spelling hard. Notice, for example, that *doctor* has two *o*'s, that *where* has *here* in it, and that *across* has only one *c*, being composed of two little words: *a + cross*.

Third, *write the word*. Spelling is of use only in writing. The movement of your hand in making the letters will help to fix the spelling in your mind.

To gain practice in looking at and in writing commonly misspelled words, copy each of the following words; carefully observe the silent letters in heavy print as you write. Then have a friend (your teacher may wish to do this in class) dictate the words to you.

answer	often	before	hour
awkward	mortgage	instead	seems
whole	condemn	read	surely
toward	column	meant	though
know, knew	rhythm	aisle	through
knowledge	subtle	tonight	trouble
written	used to	discipline	ninety

7. *Learn lists of commonly misspelled words.*

The majority of the spelling errors made by students are made on a relatively few, frequently written words. Many of these words, listed below, should look very easy to you. But you should study the list until you know how to spell *all* of these words. If you miss any of these little words, you will make a *serious* error in spelling. (If you *must* misspell a word, don't choose a second-grade word like *doesn't;* misspell a whopper like *Mephistophelean* that everyone else can't spell.)

Study the following list, and don't turn the page until you can spell every word here.

across	color	hoping	speak
again	coming	laid	speech
all right	country	later	straight
almost	dear	likely	surely
always	doesn't	making	tear
among	eager	many	they
any	early	minute	thing
began	easy	none	think
belief	February	off	through
bigger	forty	once	tired
blue	friend	paid	together
built	grammar	raise	truly
business	guess	really	Tuesday
busy	half	safety	very
buy	having	shoes	wear
can't	heard	some	Wednesday

A list of other commonly misspelled words will be found on pages 524–27.

8. *Learn to spell by making associations.*

Make any kind of association that will help you to remember a difficult word. For example, the word *earnest* has two words in it, *ear* and *nest; delivery* has *liver*. You can link rhyming words, putting an easy word with a hard one: *ear, hear; truly, unruly; loose, noose.* You may think of absurd but useful sentences such as the following:

1. Take the *g* off *grammar* and the *b* from *banana*, and the words left would read the same both backward and forward: *rammar, anana.*
2. I do *cough enough, though.*
3. Since O.K. has two letters, *all right* should *always* be spelled as two words.
4. *O! O!* Those *sophomores* are *monotonous!*

5. On that very *quiet* day I was *quite* bored and decided to *quit* working.

Find the words within the words as you learn to spell the following:

EXAMPLE   **Laboratory** has both **labor** and **rat.**

bulletin	opportunity	attacked	handkerchief
ninety	courteous	attention	apologize
meant	explanation	excellent	permanent
copies	immediately	apparent	conscience

Spelling Rules

Although most spelling is learned by memorizing words, you can "figure out" the correct spelling of many words after you have mastered the rules given on the following pages.

23a. Write *ie* when the sound is ēē, except after c.

EXAMPLES   **yield, niece, brief, receive, deceit**
EXCEPTIONS   **seize, either, weird, leisure, neither**

Write *ei* when the sound is not ēē, especially when the sound is ā.

EXAMPLES   **neighbor, weigh, foreign, heir; height**
EXCEPTIONS   **friend, science, fiery**

● EXERCISE 1.   Write the following words, supplying the missing letters (*e* and *i*) in the correct order. In class be prepared to explain how the rule applies to each word.

1. f...ld	6. bel...ve	11. w...ght	16. ...ther
2. p...ce	7. rec...ve	12. rel...f	17. n...ther
3. cash...r	8. f...rce	13. p...r	18. w...rd
4. ch...f	9. fr...ght	14. ach...ve	19. s...ze
5. c...ling	10. h...ght	15. pr...st	20. r...gn

23b. When the prefixes *il–, in–, im–, un–, dis–, mis–, re–,* and *over–* are added to a word, the spelling of the word itself remains the same.

A prefix is a letter or group of letters added to the *beginning* of a word to change its meaning. Take, for example, the word *do;* by adding the prefixes *un–* or *over–,* you have the words *undo* and *overdo.* The spelling of the word *do* does not change. Study the following examples:

il + literate = **il**literate   dis + approve = **dis**approve
in + numerable = **in**numerable   mis + step = **mis**step
im + mortal = **im**mortal   re + organize = **re**organize
un + certain = **un**certain   over + rule = **over**rule

● EXERCISE 2. Number from 1 to 10 on your paper. Correctly spell each word below as you add the prefix on the left to the word on the right.

1. un	necessary	6. mis	spell
2. re	commend	7. in	adequate
3. il	legal	8. over	run
4. im	mature	9. dis	ease
5. dis	appear	10. dis	solve

23c. When the suffixes *–ness* and *–ly* are added to a word, the spelling of the word itself remains the same.

A suffix is a letter or group of letters added to the *end* of the word to change its meaning: *kindness, kindly.* Notice below that the spelling of a word does not change when *–ness* or *–ly* is added:

sure + ly = sure**ly**   attractive + ness = attractive**ness**
usual + ly = usual**ly**   faithful + ness = faithful**ness**

▶ NOTE: There are a few exceptions to this rule, as follows:

1. true + ly = **tru**ly   due + ly = **du**ly

23
a-c

2. Words ending in *y* change the *y* to *i* before a suffix:

happy + ness = happiness   easy + ly = easily
friendly + ness = friendliness   hearty + ly = heartily

● EXERCISE 3. Correctly add each suffix on the right to the word on the left.

1. occasional ly
2. real ly
3. serious ness
4. absolute ly
5. dark ness
6. actual ly
7. clean ness
8. bare ly
9. plain ness
10. especial ly

● EXERCISE 4. Number from 1 to 10 on your paper. First, correctly add the suffix *–ly* to these words: *hungry, true, necessary, noisy, sleep*. Then add the suffix *–ness* to *tardy, happy, saucy, flighty, heavy*.

● EXERCISE 5. Correctly spell the words indicated.

1. *movable* with the prefix *im*
2. *lonely* with the suffix *ness*
3. *possess* with the prefix *re*
4. *personal* with the suffix *ly*
5. *sincere* with the suffix *ly*
6. *mean* with the suffix *ness*
7. *satisfied* with the prefix *dis*
8. *weird* with the suffix *ness*
9. *natural* with the prefix *un*
10. *run* with the prefix *over*

23d. Drop the final e before a suffix beginning with a vowel.

EXAMPLES   hope + ing = hoping
fame + ous = famous
love + able = lovable
admire + ation = admiration

EXCEPTIONS   dye + ing = dyeing [to prevent confusion with the word *dying*]
Keep the final *e* before *a* or *o* if necessary to retain the soft sound of *c* or *g* preceding the *e*:

outrage + ous = outrageous
notice + able = noticeable

● EXERCISE 6. Write correctly the words formed as indicated.

1. become + ing
2. guide + ance
3. continue + ous
4. surprise + ed
5. shine + ing
6. ridicule + ous
7. please + ant
8. believe + ing
9. courage + ous
10. determine + ation

23e. Keep the final e before a suffix beginning with a consonant.

EXAMPLES

hope + **ful** = hop**eful**
care + **less** = car**eless**
love + **ly** = love**ly**
amuse + **ment** = amuse**ment**

EXCEPTIONS

argue + **ment** = argu**ment**
awe + **ful** = aw**ful**
true + **ly** = tru**ly**
due + **ly** = du**ly**

● EXERCISE 7. Correctly write the words formed as indicated.

1. safe + ty
2. rude + ness
3. true + ly
4. state + ment
5. sincere + ly
6. require + ment
7. hate + ful
8. forgive + ness
9. argue + ment

● EXERCISE 8. Apply Rules 23d and 23e as you add each designated suffix and decide whether or not to keep or drop the final *e*. (In this exercise there are no exceptions to the rules.)

1. announce + ment
2. use + age
3. treasure + er
4. imagine + ary
5. definite + ly
6. care + ful
7. sincere + ly
8. write + ing
9. virtue + ous
10. desire + able
11. sensitive + ness
12. revere + ent
13. sure + ly
14. hope + less
15. arrange + ment
16. have + ing
17. complete + ly
18. safe + ty
19. lose + ing
20. nine + ty

**23
d-e**

THE PLURAL OF NOUNS

23f. Observe the rules for spelling the plural of nouns.

(1) The regular way to form the plural of a noun is to add an s.

SINGULAR	boat	nickel	teacher	house
PLURAL	boats	nickels	teachers	houses

(2) The plural of some nouns is formed by adding es.

The *e* is necessary to make the plural form pronounceable in words ending in *s*, *sh*, *ch*, and *x*.

SINGULAR	bus	bush	match	box
PLURAL	buses	bushes	matches	boxes

● EXERCISE 9.   Correctly write the plural of each of the following words:

1. guess	5. dollar	8. branch
2. ax	6. cafeteria	9. speech
3. tongue	7. watch	10. amateur
4. wall		

(3) The plural of nouns ending in y *following a consonant* is formed by changing the y to *i* and adding es.

SINGULAR	sky	army	story	baby
PLURAL	skies	armies	stories	babies

(4) The plural of nouns ending in y *following a vowel* is formed in the usual way.

SINGULAR	delay	key	boy	guy
PLURAL	delays	keys	boys	guys

● EXERCISE 10.   Write the plural of the following words:

1. lady
2. relay
3. donkey
4. copy

5. butterfly
6. ally
7. lullaby

8. quantity
9. jalopy
10. day

(5) The plural of most nouns ending in *f* or *fe* is formed by adding *s*. The plural of some nouns ending in *f* or *fe* is formed by changing the *f* to *v* and adding *s* or *es*.

As you study the formation of the plurals in the following words, notice the way the words are pronounced.

SINGULAR	roof	belief	leaf	wife	calf
PLURAL	roofs	beliefs	leaves	wives	calves

● EXERCISE 11.   Write the plural of each of these words:

1. thief
2. chef
3. life

4. knife
5. giraffe

(6) The plural of nouns ending in *o following a vowel* is formed by adding *s*. Nouns ending in *o* and referring to music also take the *s* in the plural.

SINGULAR	radio	rodeo	alto	solo	piano
PLURAL	radios	rodeos	altos	solos	pianos

(7) The plural of most nouns ending in *o following a consonant* is formed by adding *es*.

SINGULAR	buffalo	hero	tomato	domino
PLURAL	buffaloes	heroes	tomatoes	dominoes

● EXERCISE 12.   Write the plurals of these nouns:

1. shampoo
2. soprano
3. mosquito

4. hobo
5. veto

23f

(8) The plural of a few nouns is formed by irregular methods.

SINGULAR	man	louse	tooth	child
PLURAL	men	lice	teeth	child**ren**

(9) The plural of compound nouns (more than one word) is formed by making the principal word plural.

The "principal" word is the word modified. For instance, in *brother-in-law*, *brother* is the word modified by the phrase *in-law*.

SINGULAR	brother-in-law	editor in chief
PLURAL	brothers-in-law	editors in chief

(10) The plural of compound nouns ending in *-ful* is formed by adding s to the end of the word.

SINGULAR	spoonful	handful	cupful
PLURAL	spoonfuls	handfuls	cupfuls

(11) Some nouns are the same in the singular and the plural.

SINGULAR AND PLURAL   deer, trout, Japanese, sheep

● EXERCISE 13.   Write the plural form of the following words:

1. woman
2. ox
3. foot
4. son-in-law
5. maid of honor
6. armful
7. mouse
8. man-of-war
9. deer
10. Chinese

(12) The plural of foreign words is sometimes formed as in the foreign language.

SINGULAR	crisis	datum
PLURAL	crises	data

(13) The plural of other foreign words may be formed as in the foreign language or by adding s or es.

SINGULAR   appendix
PLURAL   appendices *or* appendixes

(14) The plural of numbers and letters is formed by adding an apostrophe and s.

SINGULAR   Place a *g* after the 6.
PLURAL   Put the *g*'s and *6*'s in the second column.

● EXERCISE 14. Try to make a perfect score on this exercise, which covers all parts of Rule 23f. After you have numbered from 1 to 20 on your paper, write the plural form of each of the following nouns. After each one, write the number of the division of Rule 23f that applies (1–14).

1. shelf
2. paper
3. gas
4. joy
5. echo
6. radio
7. cuff
8. yourself
9. solo
10. woman
11. trout
12. zero
13. library
14. church
15. *A*
16. lieutenant colonel
17. handful
18. handkerchief
19. Negro
20. index

WORDS FREQUENTLY CONFUSED

If you will master both the meaning and the spelling of the words in the lists on the following pages, you can eliminate many errors in your compositions. Study only a few at a time, and really master them.

all ready	[pronoun plus adjective] When he arrived, we were *all ready* to go.
already	*previously* Henry has *already* gone.

all right	[This is the only acceptable spelling. Although it is in the dictionary, the spelling *alright* has not yet come into good usage. The dictionary says "not proper usage."]
all together	*everyone in the same place* When we were *all together*, we opened the gifts.
altogether	*entirely* He was *altogether* wrong.
an	[used before a vowel sound] *one* I ate *an* apple.
and	*plus, in addition* I ate oranges *and* bananas.
brakes	*stopping devices* The *brakes* on Dad's car are good.
breaks	*shatters, severs* A last straw *breaks* a camel's back.
buy	[verb] *purchase* She will *buy* new shoes.
by	[preposition] *near* She sat *by* me.
choose	[used for present and future tense] *select* You may *choose* your own partner.
chose	[past tense — rhymes with *hose*] Yesterday she voluntarily *chose* to take a nap after lunch.
clothes	*what you wear* My *clothes* need pressing.
cloths	*pieces of material* We need fresh *cloths* for the tables. My dusting *cloths* are very dirty.
coarse	*rough, crude* The *coarse* material is very durable. He never uses *coarse* language.

course
path of action or progress; unit of study; track or way; also used with of to mean as was to be expected.

I am taking a *course* in algebra.
The airplane lost its *course* in the storm.
He is at the golf *course*.
Of *course*, you have met Elmer.

● EXERCISE 15. Number on your paper from 1 to 20. Write after the proper number the correct one of the words given in parentheses in the sentences below.

1. Betty has (all ready, already) handed in her paper.
2. (Alright, All right), I'll mow the lawn now.
3. Pack (clothes, cloths) suitable for formal wear.
4. Are you taking a (course, coarse) in sewing?
5. He did not, of (coarse, course), remember me.
6. His (coarse, course) manners offended everyone.
7. Last night we (chose, choose) our leader.
8. Did you sit (by, buy) him?
9. The mechanic adjusted the (breaks, brakes).
10. Joe (an, and) Jean are twins.
11. You can (choose, chose) your own music.
12. Down (by, buy) the barn is a swimming hole.
13. You will need soft (clothes, cloths) for polishing the car.
14. I'm sure that the baby will be (all right, alright).
15. A fragile piece of china (breaks, brakes) easily.
16. She talked to Joe (an, and) him.
17. They were (altogether, all together) at Thanksgiving.
18. May we (choose, chose) between a dance and a picnic?
19. He was not (altogether, all together) satisfied.
20. Are they (already, all ready) to go now?

● EXERCISE 16. Write original sentences correctly using the words you have just studied. Use each word at least once.

hear
to receive sounds through the ears
Did you *hear* the President's speech?

here   *this place*
Come *here*, Rover.

---

its   possessive of *it*
The bird stopped *its* singing.

it's   *it is*
It's an easy problem.

---

lead   [present tense, pronounced lēd] *to go first*
Lead the way.

---

led   [past tense of *lead*]
Last week he *led* us to victory.

lead   [pronounced lĕd] *a heavy metal;* also *graphite* in a
              pencil
The *lead* on my line was too heavy for the cork.

---

loose   [rhymes with *noose*] *free, not close together*
The string on the package is too *loose*.
The car swerved out of the *loose* gravel.

lose   [pronounced lōōz] *to suffer loss*
Do not *lose* our lunch money.

---

moral   *good;* also *a lesson of conduct*
He is a *moral* man.
These fables all have a *moral*.

morale   *mental condition, spirit*
The *morale* of the citizens is low.

---

passed   [verb, past tense of *pass*]
He *passed* us in the corridor.

past   [noun or adjective or preposition]
I didn't inquire about his *past*.
Her *past* experience got her the job.
I went *past* the house.

---

peace   opposite of *strife*
After the long war, *peace* was welcome.

piece   *a part of something*
Do you care for a *piece* of pie?

● EXERCISE 17. Number on your paper from 1 to 20. Write after the proper number the correct one of the words given in parentheses in the sentences below.

1. Sitting in the back row, we could hardly (here, hear) the speaker.
2. The class is proud of (its, it's) progress.
3. The commander praised the division's high (morale, moral).
4. It is already (passed, past) nine o'clock.
5. Facing defeat, he did not (lose, loose) courage.
6. Then Fuzzy (lead, led) us to his injured master.
7. Mother told us to stay (here, hear).
8. Yesterday he (led, lead) us to victory.
9. The strings came (lose, loose).
10. I have (passed, past) those examinations.
11. Her daily conduct shows that she is a (moral, morale) person.
12. Trying to get (lose, loose), the monkey tugged at the chain.
13. Can you (here, hear) me now?
14. (It's, Its) too late to catch the early train.
15. There he found true (peace, piece) of mind.
16. She shouted, "I'll give her a (peace, piece) of my mind!"
17. When my shoelace came (lose, loose), I tripped and fell.
18. She just (past, passed) me in the hall.
19. This (peace, piece) of chicken is bony.
20. Clara never seems to (lose, loose) her temper.

plain	*not fancy;* also *a flat area of land;* also *clear*
	Nancy wears very *plain* clothes.
	The storm lashed the western *plains.*
	He made his point of view *plain.*
plane	*a flat surface, a level;* also *a tool;* also *an airplane*
	The debate was conducted on a high *plane.*
	Are you taking *plane* geometry?
	He made the wood smooth by using a *plane.*
	The *plane* arrived at the airport on time.

principal	*head of a school;* also as an adjective, *main* or *most important* I had a long talk with the *principal.* Winning is not our *principal* goal.
principle	*a rule of conduct;* also *a law* or *a main fact* He lives by certain *principles.* I don't know the first *principles* of physics.
shone	[past tense of *shine*] The sun *shone* this morning.
shown	*revealed* He has not *shown* me his scrapbook.
stationary	*in a fixed position* The chairs were not *stationary.*
stationery	*writing paper* Use white *stationery* for business letters.
than	[a conjunction, used for comparisons] He enjoys swimming more *than* golfing.
then	[an adverb or conjunction indicating *at that time* or *next*] I polished my shoes; *then* I combed my hair. Did you know her *then?*
their	[possessive of *they*] The boys gave *their* opinions.
there	*a place* [also to begin a sentence (see page 35)] I'll be *there* on time. *There* aren't any cookies left.
they're	*they are* *They're* at the station now.

● EXERCISE 18. Write 20 sentences correctly using the words you have just studied; be sure to include every word at least once.

● EXERCISE 19. Number from 1 to 20 on your paper. Write after the proper number the correct one of the words given in parentheses in the sentences below.

1. Say what you mean in (plane, plain) English.
2. Mr. Carver is the (principal, principle) of our school.
3. The last reel of the movie was not (shone, shown).
4. The bleachers didn't seem very (stationary, stationery).
5. He said that not paying debts is against his (principals, principles).
6. She is two inches taller (than, then) Mary.
7. That night the big moon (shone, shown) brightly.
8. Did you buy a box of blue (stationary, stationery)?
9. (Than, Then) he erased the board and started over.
10. He knows how to use a (plain, plane) in his shop.
11. Your (principal, principle) problem is learning to spell.
12. What did you do (than, then)?
13. A lone cowboy was crossing the (plain, plane).
14. Do you still live (their, they're, there)?
15. She has mastered the basic (principals, principles) of grammar.
16. Do you drink your coffee (plain, plane) or with cream and sugar?
17. I can work much faster (than, then) he can.
18. All of the freshmen invited (their, there, they're) parents to the party.
19. (Their, There, They're) coming here tomorrow.
20. (Their, There) are two *s*'s in *omission* and in *possible*.

threw	*hurled*
	Freddy *threw* three balls.
through	*in at one side and out at the opposite side*
	The fire truck raced *through* the heavy traffic.
to	[a preposition; also part of the infinitive form of a verb]
	She told us *to clean* the windows. [infinitive]
	She has gone *to the store*. [prepositional phrase]
too	[adverb] *also, more than enough*
	I like polo, and Ted does, *too*.
	He was *too* tired to think clearly.

two	*one + one*
	I noticed *two* packages on the sofa.

---

weak	*feeble; lacking force;* opposite of *strong*
	Grandmother is too *weak* to walk yet.
	We could not hear his *weak* voice.

week	*seven days*
	Dad has been gone a *week*.

---

weather	*conditions outdoors* [no *h* sound]
	The *weather* suddenly changed.

whether	indicates alternative or doubt [pronounce the *h*]
	She didn't know *whether* or not to enter the contest.

---

who's	*who is, who has*
	I can't imagine *who's* at the door now.
	Who's been marking in my book?

whose	[possessive of *who*]
	Whose bicycle is this?

---

your	[possessive of *you*]
	What is *your* idea?

you're	*you are*
	Joe, *you're* the best friend I have.

● EXERCISE 20. Number on your paper from 1 to 20. Write after the proper number the correct one of the words given in parentheses in the sentences below.

1. The (whether, weather) in Mexico City was pleasant.
2. Dad (threw, through) the skates into my closet.
3. Sally is going to the concert. Are you going, (to, too, two)?
4. Next (weak, week) the Senators will play Tulsa.
5. We were in Boston a (weak, week).
6. The ball crashed (threw, through) the window.
7. We were (to, too, two) tired to study.
8. (Your, You're) trying too hard, Tommy.
9. (To, Too, Two) of the puppies are brown.

10. I don't remember (whether, weather) I signed that letter or not.
11. I got (weak, week) in the knees when she announced my entrance.
12. (Your, You're) sleeve is torn.
13. I have forgotten her name, (to, too, two).
14. (Whose, Who's) bat is it?
15. Well, tell me (whether, weather) or not you won.
16. The water seeped (through, threw) the basement window.
17. (Whose, Who's) going to be first?
18. Did you stop by the drugstore, (to, two, too)?
19. I'm going to buy (to, two, too) presents.
20. Is hot (whether, weather) hard on leather goods?

● REVIEW EXERCISE A. Write 20 sentences correctly using in order the following words.

1. your	6. its	11. moral	16. their
2. whose	7. there	12. plain	17. breaks
3. to	8. then	13. shown	18. and
4. buy	9. stationary	14. loose	19. lead
5. week	10. principle	15. chose	20. piece

● REVIEW EXERCISE B. Number on your paper from 1 to 20. Write after the proper number the correct one of the words in parentheses in the sentences below. List the words in correct order.

1. Patrick Henry once said that his (past, passed) experiences made (plain, plane) the pathway of the future.
2. Dissolving salt spreads (threw, through) water evenly; this process is called "diffusion."
3. To protect (they're, their, there) crops, farmers near (here, hear) have declared war on destructive rabbits.
4. (Alright, All right), I'll admit that I'm (already, all ready) discouraged.
5. After he had (shone, shown) us the movie, he (then, than) (lead, led) us back into the classroom for a discussion.

6. (Its, It's) interesting that we (hear, here) better in this room than in (their, there).

7. When (they're, there, their) is no furniture in a room, sound waves are louder (than, then) in a room filled with chairs and people.

8. The model (plain, plane), uncontrolled by a person on the ground, needs perfect balance to sail (threw, through) the air smoothly.

9. For (weaks, weeks) now, I've been reading (peaces, pieces) of information about spaceships and gravity.

10. Three things have (led, lead) scientists to hesitate about space travel: cosmic rays, atmospheric pressure, and coming home.

300 WORDS FREQUENTLY MISSPELLED [1]

absence	apologize	bargain
abundance	apparent	basketball
accidentally	appearance	beautiful
accommodate	appetite	beginning
accurate	appreciate	belief
achievement	approaching	believe
acknowledgment	appropriate	beneficial
acquaintance	approval	bicycle
acquire	argument	biscuit
across	arrange	bookkeeper
advice	assistant	brake
advise	association	break
aerial	athletics	breathe
aisle	attach	bruise
all right	attacked	bulletin
almost	attention	bureau
amateur	awful	buried
among	awfully	business
annual	bachelor	cafeteria
anonymous	banana	calendar

[1] This list includes some but not all of the spelling words taken up as individual problems elsewhere in this chapter.

campaign
candidate
captain
caricature
cellophane
cemetery
certain
character
college
column

coming
committee
comparatively
completely
complexion
conquer
conscience
conscious
convenience
copies

cordially
correspondence
courageous
courteous
courtesy
criticism
customer
cylinder
defense
definitely

delivery
descent
description
despair
desperate
develop

dictionary
dining
diphtheria
dirigible

disappear
disappointment
discipline
disease
dissatisfied
doesn't
dutiful
earnest
economical
ecstasy

efficient
eighth
embarrass
endeavor
equipment
equipped
especially
etiquette
exaggerate
excellent

exercise
exhausted
existence
explanation
extraordinary
familiar
fascinating
fatigue
faucet
February

fierce
fiery

finally
foreign
forty
fourth
fragile
gasoline
genius
government

governor
grammar
grateful
guarantee
guard
gymnasium
handkerchief
happened
height
heroes

hoping
horizon
hospital
humorous
imitation
immediately
indispensable
influence
initial
interest

irresistible
kerosene
knowledge
laboratory
license
lightning
likelihood

loneliness
losing
lying

marriage
martyr
matinee
meant
medicine
medieval
mentioned
minimum
mischievous
misspelled

monotonous
mortgage
movable
municipal
necessarily
necessary
necessity
nickel
ninety
ninth

nuisance
occasionally
occurred
o'clock
omitted
opinion
opportunity
optimistic
orchestra
original

parachute
parallel

particularly
pastime
perhaps
permanent
personally
perspiration
picnic
picnicking

planning
pleasant
pneumonia
possess
possibility
practice
prejudice
prisoner
privilege
probably

procedure
professor
pronunciation
propeller
purpose
pursue
quiet
quite
realize
really

receive
recognize
recommend
referred
rehearse
reign
relief
repetition

representative
restaurant

rhythm
sandwich
satisfactorily
schedule
scissors
seize
semester
separate
sergeant
shining

similar
sincerely
sophomore
souvenir
specimen
speech
speedometer
strategy
stretch
subtle

success
sufficient
suggestion
superintendent
superior
surgeon
surprised
syllable
sympathy
symphony

synonym
tariff
television

temperament
tendency
themselves
thoroughly
tomorrow
tournament
traffic
tragedy
transferred

truly
twelfth
tying
tyranny
umbrella
undoubtedly
unnecessary
until
using

vacuum
vengeance
vicinity
villain
waist
waste
Wednesday
weird
writing

Review Exercises

In this section are additional exercises on grammar, usage, sentence structure, and mechanics. Your teacher may assign these exercises as review drills or as tests. As you prepare for these assignments, (1) review all the rules in the chapter covered by the exercise, (2) reread explanations of those rules that you have forgotten, and (3) study those sections that you find difficult, giving special attention to examples.

Chapter 1: The Parts of Speech

● EXERCISE 1.   Number from 1 to 25 on your paper. Copy the italicized words below. After each one, give its part of speech (*n.*, *pro.*, *adj.*, *v.*, *adv.*, *prep.*, *conj.*, or *interj.*). Base your answer on the way the word is used in the sentence.

It was a cold, dark   (1) *night.* Cliff and I had been fishing (2) *for* catfish in the muddy   (3) *waters* of Henley's Creek. (4) *At* nine o'clock we   (5) *decided* to go home,   (6) *for* we knew our parents expected   (7) *us* by ten.

(8) *Soon* we   (9) *became* aware of the fact that we   (10) *were* lost. For hours we   (11) *steered* the boat   (12) *through* brushwood and rough waters as we looked for a familiar landmark. Because of thick clouds, our   (13) *search* for the North Star was   (14) *futile.*

Shortly after midnight, a flashing red light brought us boys   (15) *hope.* Thinking that my worried father was coming to our   (16) *rescue,* I yelled,   (17) *"That* light must be on Dad's boat!"

As the flashing light drew near us, a   (18) *friendly*

528

(19) *but* strange voice asked, (20) *"Hey,* are you guys lost?"

"And how!" shouted Cliff. (21) *"Where* are the docks?"

(22) *"That* I don't know," the man replied glumly. After a (23) *dismal* silence, he added, (24) *"I* am lost (25) *too!"*

Chapter 2: The Parts of a Sentence

● EXERCISE 2. Make two columns on your paper. Label the first *subject* and the second *verb.* After numbering from 1 to 10, write each subject and verb below in the appropriate column. Be sure to include all parts of a verb phrase or a compound subject or verb.

1. In 1962 an American safely orbited the earth.
2. Charles and I have discovered the cause of mirages.
3. Every knife in the kitchen was dull.
4. Finally the motor of the plane sputtered, coughed, and died.
5. Here are many tempting treats for the children.
6. Is there a key to this riddle?
7. In Puerto Rico there are several short rivers.
8. Can woodpeckers harm or possibly kill a young tree?
9. Exactly how does a cricket chirp?
10. Origins of words like *soap opera* and *monkey wrench* interest Mr. Davis.

● EXERCISE 3. Number from 1 to 15. Then make a list of the italicized words below. After each word, write its function in the sentence, using these abbreviations: subject, *s.;* verb, *v.;* predicate adjective, *p.a.;* predicate nominative, *p.n.;* direct object, *d.o.;* indirect object, *i.o.*

1. José Greco presented a spectacular Spanish *ballet.*
2. Mr. Smith showed the *class* an old map.
3. Stars on the map *symbolize* state capitals.
4. At first, geometry seemed both *useless* and *difficult.*

5. Soon Mr. Ames gave *me* many reasons for liking mathematics.
6. Lying on the table were several *boxes* of wet matches.
7. When the tennis coach does it, the stroke looks very *easy.*
8. Of course, there are several *types* of measles.
9. The mountain *towers* thousands of feet above the others in the range.
10. Old-fashioned spelling bees are becoming *popular* again.
11. How *unhappy* the winner was!
12. The thought of money was never *far* from the miser's mind.
13. When were *double eagles* last minted in the United States?
14. Mr. Watts has not yet offered *Paul* a Saturday job.
15. Unfortunately, the general's plan had a fatal *flaw.*

Chapter 3: Phrases and Clauses

● EXERCISE 4. Make three columns on your paper. Label the first column *phrase or clause*, the second *use*, and the third *kind*. Then number from 1 to 20. In the first column, write the first and last words of each italicized phrase or clause below. In the second column, write how each is used: *adjective, adverb, subject, direct object, predicate nominative,* or *object of the preposition*. In the third column, if the word group is a phrase, write *prepositional, participial, infinitive,* or *gerund;* if it is a subordinate clause, write *adjective clause, adverb clause,* or *noun clause.*

1. Riddles *with difficult solutions* fascinate me.
2. People usually like riddles *that are familiar or easy.*
3. They enjoy *giving quick, right answers.*
4. It is fun, however, *to provide an occasional challenge.*
5. I do this by *creating my own riddles.*
6. My purpose is *to baffle everyone.*
7. The game becomes more interesting *because it is competitive.*

8. The form *of the game* differs from the ordinary way of telling riddles.
9. To clarify the rules, I explain the idea *of "pyramid riddles."*
10. The main difference is *that I give a series of clues.*
11. *Guessing the answer* becomes easier with each new clue.
12. *Whoever gets the right answer first* wins the game.
13. *Whoever wins* tells the next riddle.
14. You may test your skill *with the following clues.*
15. The answer to this pyramid riddle is a short word *used frequently as a noun or an adjective.*
16. You may say *that you are in it, especially now.*
17. The word may be used *to describe a horse, a continent, a mood, or seven centuries.*
18. *Welcomed by thieves and feared by cowards,* this familiar visitor arrives and departs at regular intervals.
19. *Omitting the initial letter of the word,* you will spell the name of Noah's sailing vessel.
20. The answer would be "park" *if the first letter could put its heels over its head.*

Chapter 4: Writing Complete Sentences

● EXERCISE 5. The following paragraphs contain sentence fragments and run-on sentences. Rewrite the paragraphs, removing all fragments and run-ons by changing the punctuation and capitalization.

I enjoyed history class this morning. Although I sometimes think that dates and historical events are dull. Today I learned many interesting facts about the history of medicine. Especially about the work of Harvey, Jenner, Pasteur, and Florence Nightingale.

For many centuries men knew very little about the blood, in 1624 William Harvey's theory of blood circulation started a kind of revolution in medicine. Two hundred years later Edward Jenner found out that a person who had had cowpox was immune to smallpox, this discovery helped Jenner find a good way to fight smallpox, by vaccination. Thus preventing the disease rather than attempting to treat it. In the nineteenth century Louis Pasteur learned how to kill bacteria, later he explained Jenner's success. By pointing out how germs fight germs. Though Florence Nightingale was not a scientist, she was dedicated to the nursing profession, after studying the latest nursing techniques, she traveled to Crimea, there she helped wounded soldiers. Often working nineteen hours a day. Modern medicine is greatly indebted to these pioneers.

Chapter 5:   Agreement

● EXERCISE 6.   Number from 1 to 25 on your paper. If a sentence is correct, write *C* after the appropriate number. If a verb does not agree with its subject, or if a pronoun does not agree with its antecedent, write the correct form of the verb or the pronoun after the proper number.

1. Everybody at the polls seemed eager to cast their vote.
2. Each of the girls were hoping to win the portable radio.
3. Have Nancy or Jack cleaned the fish yet?
4. Neither of the dogs have enough sense to chase a rabbit.
5. Neither Ann nor Eloise have ever been water-skiing.
6. Anybody in their right mind would agree with me.
7. As Mark Twain points out, some of the situations in Cooper's novel are ridiculous.
8. A large stock of articles damaged in the recent fire are for sale in the bargain basement.
9. The assembly was arguing among themselves about the vote.
10. The mark of a good leader is their ability to serve others well.
11. Here are several comic valentines.
12. All along the highway was signs warning motorists about icy bridges.
13. Do either of you know what Job's friends were like?
14. Down goes the red flags of the referees!
15. There is several ways to tell time without a watch.

16. Mrs. Jones, along with her husband and two daughters, go to Colorado every summer.
17. Strangely enough, one characteristic of an only child is that they seldom suffer from loneliness.
18. Racing to the scene of the accident were a police car and an ambulance.
19. All of the scouts knows how to give first aid.
20. Each of these ballpoint pens is good but expensive.
21. Where has Ralph and Bruce gone?
22. Either Nell or her brothers run errands for Grandma Ford.
23. It don't really make much difference to me.
24. Coffee, tea, or a coke keeps me awake.
25. The players sitting on the bench was cheering louder than the pep squad.

Chapter 6: The Correct Use of Verbs

● EXERCISE 7. Number from 1 to 25 on your paper. If a sentence is correct, write *C* after the appropriate number. If the form of the verb is wrong, write the correct form after the proper number.

1. When we arrived, the second feature had began.
2. I saw enthusiasm in her eyes.
3. No one has spoke a word to me about your surprise.
4. Have you already wrote the address on the envelope?
5. As the referee counted, Hairy Joe gradually comes to his senses.
6. Have you ever saw an onion skin under a microscope?
7. Before the tornado struck, our lights had went out.
8. Yesterday, Coach Stinson gave a talk about sportsmanship.
9. I laid down, but I did not sleep.
10. I sat on the steps for a while and talked to Dad.
11. After the storm live wires were lying in the streets.
12. Have those socks shrank?
13. Two fox terriers lay in front of the fire.
14. These books have lay on my desk for two days.

15. George raised up and started to answer the doorbell.
16. I have never swum in Lake Whitney.
17. Grandpa shouldn't have drank strong coffee.
18. The bell ending the fifth round had just rang.
19. One boy says that Lucille done it.
20. During the hurricane several fishermen drowned.
21. I use to play marbles for keeps, until I lost all I had.
22. A bone in my left wrist was broke.
23. Is the janitor suppose to close and lock windows?
24. Our team was inches from the goal line when time run out.
25. Miss Yeats learns us good grammar.

Chapter 7: The Correct Use of Pronouns

● EXERCISE 8. Number from 1 to 15 on your paper. If a sentence is correct, write *C* after the proper number. If a pronoun is wrong, write the correct form of the pronoun after the appropriate number.

1. Keep this a secret between you and I.
2. Us boys will carry the baggage.
3. At camp Sam and me were tentmates.
4. If it is she who is supposed to be in charge, let me know.
5. Were you calling Jerry or me?
6. If you and her go, I'll go.
7. He kept Howard and I after school.
8. Please don't tell anyone but Mrs. Carter or her about our plan.
9. He thought it was us.
10. Please wait for Sid and him.
11. Are you and him related?
12. Frank and he are absent.
13. We girls were pretty angry.
14. Have you seen Helen or she?
15. It couldn't have been them.

Chapter 8: The Correct Use of Modifiers

● EXERCISE 9. Number from 1 to 15 on your paper. If a sentence is correct, write *C* after the appropriate number. If a sentence has an incorrect, dangling, or misplaced modifier, rewrite the sentence after the proper number, giving the correct form of the modifier or making the meaning clear.

1. Two ounces are more heavier than twenty drams.
2. To avoid cramming for a test, keep up with daily assignments.
3. My brother Joel is more intelligent than any boy in his class.
4. Those storm clouds look even worser than they did an hour ago.
5. Which would be the best New Year's resolution — to be more patient with others or to stop telling little lies?
6. Robert is the wittiest of the two.
7. Stained with grease and full of holes, I gave the old shirts to the Thanksgiving Clothing Drive.
8. I couldn't make a good report on the importance of recruiting football players with the hiccups.
9. After going into a spin, a strange type of fit, the veterinarian said that my dog had distemper.
10. After burning the grass under the wire fence, Sam doused the charred ground with water.
11. Having been sprayed last week, the yardman noticed the dead crab grass.
12. When thoroughly baked, take the ham out and let it cool slowly.
13. When you are angry, count to ten twice and then remain silent.
14. The man looked awkward holding the sleeping infant who was threading his way through the crowds at intermission.
15. Otis was talking about the low salaries of the men who work sixty hours a week emptying garbage in Principal Ramsay's office this morning.

Chapter 9:   Varying Sentences

● EXERCISE 10.   The following groups of sentences are unnecessarily short or monotonous. Combine the ideas in each passage into varied, smooth, effective sentences. Use any means you wish — compound verbs, introductory phrases, appositives, subordinate clauses, and so on.

1. My hobby is photography. I have here an unusual picture. It is a picture of the stars. In this picture the stars are long white streaks.
2. I worked hours to get this effect. I propped up the camera in my back yard. Then I set the time exposure. Hours later I closed the shutter.
3. The picture shows the movement of the earth. The movement of stars is very slow. We cannot see it happen. This picture made me curious about the stars.
4. Stars do not really rise and set, but they apparently do so in my picture, for the earth is turning, but we cannot see the real motion of the stars, for they are too far off.
5. We have, of course, seen streaks of light. We call these streaks shooting stars. They are not stars at all. They are meteors.

Chapter 20:   Capital Letters

● EXERCISE 11.   Copy the following sentences, using capitals wherever needed.

1. in 312 a roman emperor named constantine accepted christianity.
2. not only the english but also the french were pioneers in north america.
3. by sailing west, columbus hoped to find a new route to the east.
4. on mother's day my mother ate at the el matador in the atlas building.
5. "we should pay god the respect due him," uncle john insisted.

6. on july 4, 1776, the declaration of independence was adopted.

7. by going around africa and across the indian ocean, a portuguese explorer found a new route to asia.

8. is staten island in new york bay?

9. the stedmans will move to the city if marie's father becomes president of the oil company.

10. the twenty-fifth president of the united states was theodore roosevelt.

11. wallace stevens was an american poet and an insurance executive.

12. on september 2, 1945, world war II ended.

13. our high school offers a course entitled press photography.

14. after graduating from horton high school, bruce entered carleton college at northfield, minnesota, to major in history.

15. beginning in the west, the industrial revolution soon affected the whole world.

16. we turned east, found a parking place on a side street, and finally registered at the astor hotel.

17. the indian river, a lagoon in florida, is 165 miles long.

18. at easter principal norton went to oklahoma.

19. the future farmers of america will meet on labor day.

20. at the library i finally found the *index to poetry and recitations*.

Chapter 21: End Marks and Commas

● EXERCISE 12. Copy the following sentences, inserting end marks and commas as needed.

1. Loam contains sand clay and humus

2. From the top of the Abbey of Mont-Saint-Michel one may look over the farms of Normandy

3. Mr Raines my science teacher asked the class where energy comes from

4. Interested and puzzled the students echoed his question: Where does energy come from

5. Charcoal is nearly all carbon and gasoline is a compound of carbon and hydrogen

6. Please explain Henry how spontaneous combustion occurs

7. What is the ideal humidity

8. What a surprise that was

9. A scrawny friendly stray dog strolled over to the catcher and the umpire stopped the game temporarily

10. Frances looked at jewelry then tried on shoes and finally bought a red sweater with her birthday money

11. Although they had only primitive tools to work with the Mayas built huge pyramids

12. Have you seen Mr Carter our new history teacher

13. Do you know that the *Nautilus* which was the first atomic-propelled submarine sailed under the icecap of the North Pole on August 3 1958

14. He will disqualify all players who cheat for the coach believes that integrity is more important than victory

15. How can you be so calm

Chapter 22:   Other Marks of Punctuation

● EXERCISE 13.   Number from 1 to 20 on your paper. From each of the following paired items, choose the correct one of the two forms. After the proper number on your paper, write the letter of the column (A or B) that contains the correct form.

A	B
1. Alfred struck out, then Bob hit a home run.	1. Alfred struck out; then Bob hit a home run.
2. I enjoyed playing: golf, tennis, and baseball.	2. I enjoyed playing golf, tennis, and baseball.
3. The minister based his sermon on John 6:51.	3. The minister based his sermon on John 6 51.
4. Dear Sir:	4. Dear Sir;
5. Is this tie yours?	5. Is this tie yours'?
6. I read "Lord Jim," a novel by Conrad.	6. I read *Lord Jim*, a novel by Conrad.

7. There are too many *if*'s about it.
8. a short poem entitled "Rags"
9. "Bounty" rhymes with "county."
10. forty-three cents
11. I lack self-confidence.
12. "It's my turn," yelled Joe!
13. I answered, "I'm not sure".
14. He asked, "Why not"?
15. It's raining now.
16. at seven oclock
17. The dog wagged it's tail.
18. three week's pay
19. Whose letter is this?
20. Charles replied, "My motto is "Silence is the best policy." "

7. There are too many *ifs* about it.
8. a short poem entitled *Rags*
9. *Bounty* rhymes with *county*.
10. forty three cents
11. I lack self confidence.
12. "It's my turn!" yelled Joe.
13. I answered, "I'm not sure."
14. He asked, "Why not?"
15. Its raining now.
16. at seven o'clock
17. The dog wagged its tail.
18. three weeks' pay
19. Who's letter is this?
20. Charles replied, "My motto is 'Silence is the best policy.' "

Capitalization Style Sheet

Mexico City — a city in Mexico
Ocala National Forest — our national forests
Twenty-ninth Street — across the street
Houghton Lake — a shallow lake
the South — a mile south
North America — northern Wisconsin
the Explorers' Club — a club for explorers
Ford Motor Company — an automobile company
Central High School — a new high school
Pomona College — four years in college
the American Revolution — a successful revolution
the Wrigley Building — a Chicago building
the Fourth of July — the fifth of July
the Senior Ball — a ball given by seniors
the Freshman Class — freshman classes
English, French, Latin — social studies, physics, art
History II — a course in world history
Winter's frosty breath — spring, summer, winter, fall
Principal Langley — Mr. Langley, the principal
the President (U.S.) — the president of our club
the Senator — a senator's duties
God made His will known — tribal gods of the Indians
Don't tell Mother (*or* mother) — Don't tell my mother
Uncle Bill — my uncle
Ivory soap
the Democratic party
a Negro, a Presbyterian, a Swede
The Last of the Mohicans
the Reader's Digest

The reference materials in the endpapers are reproduced here for the convenience of schools where book covers are used, or where ownership stamps or labels ordinarily are placed inside the front or back covers.

Correction Symbols

ms	error in manuscript form or neatness	**k**	awkward sentence
cap	error in use of capital letters	**nc**	not clear
p	error in punctuation	**ll**	run-on sentence, begin sentence here
sp	error in spelling	**gr**	error in grammar
frag	sentence fragment	**w**	error in word choice
ss	error in sentence structure	**¶**	Begin a new paragraph here.
ref	unclear reference of pronoun	**t**	error in tense
		∧	You have omitted something.

Index

Bread-and-butter note, 260–61: model of, 261

Break, principal parts of, 122

Breve, 349

Bring, principal parts of, 122

Britannica Atlas, 328

British Authors of the Nineteenth Century, 327

"Bunyan, Paul," article, 299

Burst, principal parts of, 122

Bursted, 123

Business letter, 262–73: adjustment letter, 272–73; appearance, 262; arrangement on page (*illustration*), 263; body, 265; complimentary close, 265; envelope, 267; folding, 268; form, 263–67; heading, 264; inside address, 264; model of, 266; order letter, 270–71; parts of, 263–67; punctuation in, 263–66; request letter, 269–70; salutation, 265; signature, 267; spacing, 263–64; stationery, 262

Business telephone calls, 418–20

But, in double negative, 139

Buy, *by*, 516

Call number, 316

Can't hardly, 139

Can't help but, 139

Capital letters, 426–40: beginning of quotation, 484; business firms, 430; business products, 430; calendar items, 430; Deity, words pertaining to, 437; dictionary authority for, 342; events, 430; *father*, *mother*, etc., 436–37; first word of sentence,

426; geographical names, 428; government bodies, 430; historical events and periods, 431; *I* and *O*, 426; in a divided quotation, 484; institutions, 430; languages, 433; organizations and clubs, 430; planes, 430; proper adjectives, 432; proper nouns, 427; quotations, 484; races and religions, 430; review exercises, 433–35, 438–39; school subjects, 433; seasons, 432; *senior*, *sophomore*, etc., 431; ships, 430; summary style sheet, 439–40; titles, 436–37

Card catalogue, 314–21: author card, 317; "see" and "see also" cards, 319; subject card, 318–19; title card, 318; use of, 316–21

Case: defined, 140; nominative, 142–44; objective, 144–49; of pronouns, 140–58; possessive, 140, 489–94; review exercises on pronouns, 146–48, 149–51, 153–58

Catch, principal parts of, 121

Characterization, in narrative writing, 279

Check list: for compositions, 236; for written reports, 307

Choose, *chose*, 516

Choose, principal parts of, 122

Class discussion, 392–94: etiquette in, 393; participating in, 392

Classified telephone directory, 412–13

Clause: adjective, defined, 75; adverb, defined, 76; dangling, 165; defined, 71; distinguished from phrase, 72;

KEY TO SUPPLEMENTARY DRILL

If additional drill is required, see Warriner and Blumenthal's ENGLISH WORKSHOP, New Series, Grade 9. The rule numbers in this text are keyed below to appropriate lessons in the Workshop.

Text Rule No.	Workshop Lesson No.	Text Rule No.	Workshop Lesson No.
1a	1	5m	68
1b	2	5n	70
1c	3		
1d	5,6	6a	74
1e	7,8	6b	74
1f	9	6c	74-9,81
1g	9	6d	80,81
1h	10		
1i	10	7a	84
1j	10	7b	85
		7c	86
2a	13,18,19	7d	86
2b	13	7e	87
2c	14	7g	89
2d	15		
2e	16	10a	95
2f	16	10b	95
2g	16	10c	96
2i	22	10d	97
2j	22		
2k	23	11e	98
2l	24		
		12a	99
3a	28	12c	99
3b	28	12d	99
3c	28	12e	100
3d	29	12h	101
3e	30	12i	102
3l	31	12j	102
3m	31	12k	102
3n	31	12n	103
3o	32	12o	103
3p	32		
3q	33	20c	46
3r	34	20d	46
		20e	47
4a	38	20f	48
4b	37		
4c	37	21a	41
4d	37	21b	41
4e	42	21c	41
		21d	41
5a	65	21f	53
5b	65	21g	54-6
5c	66	21h	57
5d	66	21i	58
5e	66		
5g	67	22k	59
5h	67	22l	59
5i	67	22n	60
5k	68	22o-p	60
		22s	61